THE PHILOSOPHY AND POLITICS
OF BRUNO BAUER

This is the first comprehensive study in English of Bruno Bauer, a leading Hegelian philosopher of the 1840s. Inspired by the philosophy of Hegel, Bauer led an intellectual revolution that influenced Marx and shaped modern secular humanism. In the process he offered a republican alternative to liberalism and socialism, criticised religious and political conservatism, and set out the terms for the development of modern mass and industrial society.

Based on in-depth archival research, this book traces the emergence of republican political thought in Germany before the revolutions of 1848. Professor Moggach examines Bauer's republicanism and his concept of infinite self-consciousness. He also explores the more disturbing aspects of Bauer's critique of modernity, such as his anti-Semitism.

As little else is available on Bauer, even in German, this book will be recognised as a very valuable contribution to the history of ideas and will be eagerly sought out by professionals in political philosophy, political science, and intellectual history.

Douglas Moggach is a professor of political science and philosophy at the University of Ottawa and a member of Clare Hall, University of Cambridge.

MODERN EUROPEAN PHILOSOPHY

General Editor

Robert B. Pippin, *University of Chicago*

Advisory Board

Gary Gutting, *University of Notre Dame*
Rolf-Peter Horstmann, *Humboldt University, Berlin*
Mark Sacks, *University of Essex*

Some Recent Titles

Daniel W. Conway: *Nietzsche's Dangerous Game*
John P. McCormick: *Carl Schmitt's Critique of Liberalism*
Frederick A. Olafson: *Heidegger and the Ground of Ethics*
Günter Zöller: *Fichte's Transcendental Philosophy*
Warren Breckman: *Marx, the Young Hegelians, and the Origins*
of Radical Social Theory
William Blattner: *Heidegger's Temporal Idealism*
Charles Griswold: *Adam Smith and the Virtues of the Enlightenment*
Gary Gutting: *Pragmatic Liberalism and the Critique of Modernity*
Allen Wood: *Kant's Ethical Thought*
Karl Ameriks: *Kant and the Fate of Autonomy*
Alfredo Ferrarin: *Hegel and Aristotle*
Cristina Lafont: *Heidegger, Language and World-Discourse*
Nicholas Wolterstorff: *Thomas Reid and the Story of Epistemology*
Daniel Dahlstrom: *Heidegger's Concept of Truth*
Michelle Grier: *Kant's Doctrine of Transcendental Illusion*
Henry Allison: *Kant's Theory of Taste*
Allen Speight: *Hegel, Literature and the Problem of Agency*
J. M. Bernstein: *Adorno: Disenchantment and Ethics*

THE PHILOSOPHY AND POLITICS
OF BRUNO BAUER

DOUGLAS MOGGACH

University of Ottawa

CAMBRIDGE
UNIVERSITY PRESS

PUBLISHED BY THE PRESS SYNDICATE OF THE UNIVERSITY OF CAMBRIDGE
The Pitt Building, Trumpington Street, Cambridge, United Kingdom

CAMBRIDGE UNIVERSITY PRESS
The Edinburgh Building, Cambridge CB2 2RU, UK
40 West 20th Street, New York, NY 10011-4211, USA
477 Williamstown Road, Port Melbourne, VIC 3207, Australia
Ruiz de Alarcón 13, 28014 Madrid, Spain
Dock House, The Waterfront, Cape Town 8001, South Africa

http://www.cambridge.org

First published 2003

Printed in the United Kingdom at the University Press, Cambridge

Typeface ITC New Baskerville 10/12 pt.   *System* LATEX 2ε   [TB]

A catalog record for this book is available from the British Library.

Library of Congress Cataloging in Publication Data
Moggach, Douglas.
The philosophy and politics of Bruno Bauer/Douglas Moggach.
p.   cm. – (Modern European philosophy)
Includes bibliographical references and index.
ISBN 0-521-81977-6
1. Bauer, Bruno, 1809–1882 – Views on republicanism.   2. Republicanism.
3. Republicanism – Germany – History.   I. Title.   II. Series.
JC423 .M644   2002
321.8′6–dc21   2002024455

ISBN 0 521 81977 6 hardback

CONTENTS

Preface   *page* ix

Introduction: "The Friend of Freedom"   1

I. FOUNDATIONS: AESTHETICS, ETHICS, AND REPUBLICANISM

1 "The Idea Is Life": Bauer's Aesthetics and Political Thought   21
2 "Free Means Ethical": Idealism, History, and Critical Theory   40

II. JUDGING THE OLD ORDER

3 "The Other of Itself": The Critique of the Religious
   Consciousness   59
4 "Revolution and the Republic": The State and
   Self-Consciousness   80

III. THE EMANCIPATORY PROJECT

5 "Only the Ought Is True": Hegel, Self-Consciousness,
   and Revolution   99
6 "To the People Belongs the Future": Universal
   Right and History   119

IV. JUDGING THE REVOLUTIONARY MOVEMENT

7 "The Fire of Criticism": Revolutionary Dynamics, 1843–1848   139
8 "The Republic of Self-Consciousness": Revolutionary
   Politics in 1848   157

Epilogue: After the Revolution: The Conclusion of the
Christian-Germanic Age   180

Appendix: Bruno Bauer, "On the Principles of the
Beautiful" (1829)   188

Notes   213
Bibliography   264
Index   285

PREFACE

This book has been long in the making. My first article on Bauer, in 1989, depicted him as a radical subjectivist. I returned to the subject in 1992, when I located Bauer's prize manuscript on Kant in the archives of the Humboldt-Universität, Berlin. This text convinced me to revise my thinking on Bauer completely. I began a draft of the present manuscript during a sabbatical in 1995, at the Scuola Normale Superiore in Pisa, where I benefited greatly from discussions with Claudio Cesa. A colloquium on the150th anniversary of the Revolutions of 1848 sponsored by the University of Ottawa, then celebrating its own sesquicentennial, was an occasion to reflect on the heritage of Left-Hegelian thought and to clarify the issues that divided republicans and socialists. My Visiting Fellowship at Clare Hall, Cambridge, provided me with a hospitable and stimulating environment in which, finally, to complete the work.

To the President and Fellows of Clare Hall, to Claudio Cesa, H. S. Harris, Gareth Stedman Jones, and Lawrence Stepelevich, who offered advice and encouragement, to Andrew Chitty and Joseph McCarney, for their insightful criticisms, I extend my sincere thanks. Quentin Skinner's work convinced me that Bauer's critique of the Restoration state and religion, of liberalism, and of socialism could best be integrated in a republican frame; I am grateful to him for our conversations in Cambridge on republicanism and aesthetics. Robert Pippin and two anonymous reviewers for Cambridge University Press provided valuable comments on the manuscript. Peter Foley ably assisted in translating Bauer's Latin manuscript and saved me from some egregious mistakes. All remaining errors in the text are entirely my own.

I acknowledge the assistance of the International Institute for Social History, Amsterdam, where I undertook most of my research, and of the archives of the Humboldt-Universität. The IISH also kindly granted permission to reproduce the cover illustration, contained in the Barnikol archive and originally published in Ernst Barnikol, *Bruno Bauer, Studien und Materialien, aus dem Nachlass ausgewählt und zusammengestellt von*

P. Reimer und H.-M. Sass (Assen van Gorcum, 1972). The Social Sciences
and Humanities Research Council of Canada generously funded this
project as part of an ongoing study of Hegel, while the Research Services
and the Faculty of Social Sciences of the University of Ottawa provided
additional support and leave time. *The Bulletin of the Hegel Society of Great
Britain, The Owl of Minerva,* and *Dialogue: The Canadian Philosophical Review*
granted permission to publish revised versions of articles that have been
incorporated into Chapters 1, 2, 4, and 5 of the present work. Some
passages on the French Revolution and socialism and some of my translations of Bauer have previously appeared in *History of European Ideas* and
in a collection under my editorship published by the University of Ottawa
Press. I am grateful to Akademie Verlag for permission to publish as an
appendix the English version of Bauer's *Prinzipien des Schönen.*

I owe special thanks to my wife and children for their love and forbear-
ance. Alison, Iain, and Catriona have patiently endured extended periods
of preoccupation and unavailability. My parents and family have always
been models of courage, generosity, and dedication. They embody the
virtues of self-transcendence in the most admirable sense. To the memory
of my mother and father, I dedicate this book.

THE PHILOSOPHY AND POLITICS
OF BRUNO BAUER

INTRODUCTION:
"THE FRIEND OF FREEDOM"

To understand Bauer, one must understand our time.
What is our time? It is revolutionary.[1]
Edgar Bauer, October 1842

Bruno Bauer has provoked intense controversies since the 1830s, yet his work remains inaccessible, his meaning elusive.[2] He is most familiar as the object of Marx's sharp polemical attacks in *The Holy Family* and *The German Ideology*,[3] though Albert Schweitzer, in his widely noted *Quest of the Historical Jesus*, gives him a receptive and sensitive reading.[4] He is far more complex a figure than the caricature that Marx's denunciations make of him. In the decisive political circumstances of the German *Vormärz*, the prelude to the revolutions of March 1848, Bauer's is the voice of an original republicanism, inspired by Hegel. He is a theorist of revolution, of its causes and its failures. Analysing the emergent tendencies of modern society, he criticises both the old order and new ideological currents in the interests of a profound, republican liberation.

The literature on the Hegelian Left has depicted in diverse ways the revolution that Bauer theorises: as abstract-utopian posturing,[5] as a religious crisis,[6] or as a cultural degradation or mutation.[7] Recent commentators stress the political dimensions of the crisis and the interest of the Left Hegelians, Bauer foremost among them, in developing a theory of popular sovereignty and citizenship.[8] Important studies have linked them to the literary and political currents of their time[9] and traced the changing patterns of their relationships with early French socialism.[10] Others have demonstrated the affinity of their thought with Hellenistic theories of self-consciousness,[11] opening comparative perspectives on modern republican appropriations of Roman or neo-Roman themes.[12] These readings broaden the Left-Hegelian attack on religious estrangement to encompass the institutional and ideological expressions of the old regime.

1

Bauer himself sees the revolution that he theorizes as bearing epochal significance. It is a fundamental political, social, and cultural transformation, the completion of the unfinished tasks of the French Revolution, but also the pursuit of unprecedented challenges posed by the emergence of modern civil society. Its aim is the creation of a republican league of equal right, eliminating irrational privileges, refashioning social relations, and eradicating religious and political alienation. As the culmination of the emancipatory strivings of modernity, it fulfils the promise of the transcendental project, initiated by Kant and perfected, almost, by Hegel. It is this post-Kantian philosophical context that shapes Bauer's understanding of the political struggle.

In conditions of the Restoration and political reaction, Bauer defends the necessity of a political and social revolution based on a new conception of freedom. His republicanism is a theory of positive liberty or self-transcendence that combines ethical and aesthetic motifs derived from Hegel and particularly from the critique of Kant. Though rooted in political action, this transformation is to have consequences far beyond the political sphere. Bauer's work is a campaign waged on three fronts[13]: first, against the old order, the Restoration state, its social and juridical base, and its orthodox religious justification; then against liberalism as a defence of private interest, and as a warrant for subordinating the state to economic power; and, finally, against socialism, as another variant of particularity and heteronomy. The originality of Bauer's republicanism in the *Vormärz* is the Hegelian argumentation he deploys against both Restoration conservatism and liberalism. The longstanding antagonism of republicanism to these adversaries receives an innovative theoretical grounding in Bauer's work. A new opposition also appears, in the rupture between the republican and socialist camps, whose theoretical differences now attain sharpened formulation.

Before we examine these forms of critique, some preliminary problems of sources and interpretation require our attention. These are especially acute in the present case. Bauer was an enormously prolific writer. Approximately eighty published texts, totalling several thousands of pages, have been attributed to him in the decade after 1838 alone. Of these, more than a dozen are lengthy and significant books, covering interpretations and critiques of Hegel, the Old Testament, the gospels, modern theological currents, the Enlightenment, the French Revolution, and the contemporary German and European situation. Unlike the Feuerbachian corpus, for example, no critical edition of these works exists.[14] Marx alleges that Bauer could spin out a weighty tome from the thinnest spindle of a thought, but his writing is always provocative, often profound, and sometimes strikingly witty. One memorable image describes Hegel's berserk rage against all existing statutes[15]; this is Bauer assuming and relishing a pietistic pose, the better to celebrate his own revolutionary doctrine under the strictures of censorship. The writing is powerful, and vast in its sweep.

Beyond difficulties of range and extent, the interpretation of Bauer's work is fraught with additional problems of textual analysis. A daunting array of these uncertainties is described by Ernst Barnikol, the major contributor to the field.[16] In two cases, the anonymous *Posaune des jüngsten Gerichts* (*Trumpet of the Last Judgement*, 1841) and *Hegels Lehre von der Religion und Kunst* (*Hegel's Doctrine of Religion and Art*, 1842), which figure among Bauer's most important texts, the author adopts the ironic posture of a conservative critic of Hegel in order to defend the progressive character of the Hegelian system, but in doing so he also attributes to Hegel his own revolutionary views. Other sources show that he does not believe that Hegel actually held these positions, but he thinks that they are necessary consequences of Hegel's fundamental doctrines. In two other important books, *Kritik der evangelischen Geschichte des Johannes* (*Critique of the Gospel of John*, 1840) and *Die evangelische Landeskirche Preussens und die Wissenschaft* (*The Evangelical State Church of Prussia and Science*, 1840), Bauer expresses in the text central theses that are at odds with his statements in other contemporary communications. In these cases, the published texts are more cautious or more conservative than the private utterances, as recorded in his subsequently published correspondence, or in his unpublished letters to his fellow Left Hegelian Arnold Ruge.[17] A further complication arises from anonymous publications and the use of pseudonyms, largely too under the pressure of censorship.[18] It is not certain that all of Bauer's texts (at least the journalistic articles) are catalogued for the *Vormärz* period, and some attributions are disputed.[19] Because of the anonymity of important pieces published in Bauer's journals, the reconstruction of certain of his views on social and economic problems must remain tentative. Bauer's sometimes sketchy or ambiguous expositions of key topics are responsible for other intractable problems in deciphering his meaning. Even in the central category of mass society, for example, it is not always clear which adversaries specifically fall under this rubric.[20]

The critical literature on Bauer offers additional difficulties. In many instances, no secondary sources could be discovered. We are exploring virgin territory. This is the case for many of Bauer's articles from the period 1842–43, and for his studies of the French Revolution, the social question, and the German oppositional movement in 1843–49.[21] On other issues, such as Bauer's political critique in 1840–41, much of the literature represents views that appear indefensible in light of the evidence presented here. Finally, Bauer's career has frequently been broken into various, often incompatible phases.[22] The perception of radical changes of position during the *Vormärz* has led to widely divergent explanations of his aims and significance.

We can identify two schools of interpretation of Bauer's writings. The first maintains that Bauer's thinking sacrifices the relational polarities, mediations, and dialectical transitions of the Hegelian system, in favour of sharp antithetical oppositions. The Dutch theologian G. A. van den Bergh van Eysinga represents this view. He contends that "Bauer's error is not, as Marx thinks, that he was dependent on Hegel – so too was Marx! – but rather that he substituted self-consciousness for the Idea."[23] By this claim, van den Bergh van Eysinga means that Bauer surrenders the terrain of Hegelian objective and absolute spirit to the arrogation of subjective spirit, as if the latter could be self-grounding in the absence of the higher determinations of the system. From this standpoint, the abstract understanding, with its unmediated oppositions, takes the place of Hegelian reason in Bauer's thinking. He concludes of Bauer that "His rationalism was of Enlightenment, not of Hegelian origin."[24] Hans-Martin Sass, too, maintains that Bauer abandons dialectical transitions in favour of antithetical ruptures; but Sass locates the sources of this attitude in the Christian apocalyptic tradition rather than in the Enlightenment.[25] The antithetical character of Bauer's work has also been stressed by Daniel Brudney, who argues that the invocation of history by Bauer is a merely contingent feature of his thought. Brudney finds that Bauer's texts offer no consistent or satisfactory explanation of how the knowledge of history contributes to attaining the standpoint of universal self-consciousness; nor is it clear whether such knowledge is necessary to the critical perspective.[26] The dominant model of antithetics that Bauer employs in the 1840s implies, in Brudney's reading, that the past is simply to be repudiated and not dialectically assimilated: Devoid of positive content, history cannot orient consciousness or action in the present, which represents a radically new beginning.

As an example of a second line of interpretation, Ingrid Pepperle identifies a complex dialectic of history as self-production in Bauer's work, at least in the early 1840s. She follows an interpretative tradition initiated by Max Stirner and other contemporaries, however, which claims that a fundamental break in continuity occurs in Bauer's writing after 1843, when a vacuous social critique supervenes upon a highly acclaimed and rigorous criticism of religion.[27] Pepperle adopts her periodisation under the influence of Marx's critiques, concluding that Bauer's 1843–49 texts are of diminished theoretical value.[28] A similar judgement is expressed by Mario Rossi, who documents polemics and conceptual oppositions within the Hegelian school, and with various rival currents, and who offers careful analyses of specific Bauerian texts; but he too restricts his attention to the pre-1843 writings. Echoing Marx in the *Holy Family*, he sees Bauer's political position, even in this critical period, as largely theologically conditioned.[29] Pepperle differs in her recognition of the clearly political motivations of Bauer's early work but shares the discontinuity thesis.

Neither of these two types of interpretation is without merit. Each will find a partial vindication in the present account. But each reading, pressed too insistently, is inadequate to grasp the complexity of Bauer's understanding of history and freedom, and each distorts his genuine accomplishments. There are markedly antithetical elements in Bauer's thinking, and these become increasingly evident in his characterisation of the revolutionary situation in Germany after 1843. To this extent the critics are correct. The first approach, however, overlooks a centrally important dimension of Bauer's thinking in the 1840s, a specific model of judgement or of immanent critique that, in its approach to history, differs from the antinomic Enlightenment formulations to which Bauer's have often been compared. It differs, as well, from Kantian morality and equally from the more deterministic variant of critique developed in parallel by the young Marx. The second approach misses the continuity of Bauer's thought, especially his republican commitment, which he continues to defend in important texts long after 1843. It is certain that the focus of Bauer's thinking changes as he confronts different adversaries. We can, however, identify a consistent core in his work throughout the 1840s, in the Hegelian idea of the unity of thought and being. This idea is the basis of his republicanism.

As Bauer already states in his first writing, the prize manuscript of 1829, the unity of concept and objectivity is the central idea of Hegel's idealism.[30] This unity is not static but represents a process of change, development, and progress, as objective reality is remodelled through the experience of rational freedom. Hegel expresses this dynamism through his concept of *Wirklichkeit*, the actuality of reason.[31] This concept translates Aristotle's idea of *energeia*, the presence or activity of form and end in matter.[32] In passages that Bauer draws upon to sustain a revolutionary reading of his meaning, Hegel describes the dynamism of reason as its ability to transform given objectivity into the vehicle of spirit, and to surpass the limits of its previous achievements.

> [S]pirit likewise has the property of dissolving every determinate content it encounters. For it is the universal, unlimited, innermost and infinite form itself, and it overcomes all that is limited. Even if the objective content does not appear finite and limited in content, it does at least appear as something given, immediate and authoritative in nature, so that it is not in a position to impose restrictions on thought or to set itself up as a permanent obstacle to the thinking subject and to infinite internal reflection.[33]

> History has to do with reality, in which the universal must in any case assume a determinate form. And no limited form can establish itself permanently in the face of thought or the concept. If there were something which the concept could not digest or resolve, it would certainly represent the highest degree of fragmentation (*Zerrissenheit*) and unhappiness (*Unseligkeit*). But

if something of this kind did exist it could be nothing other than thought itself in its function of self-comprehension. For thought alone is inherently unlimited, and all reality is determined within it. In consequence, the fragmentation would cease to exist, and thought would be satisfied with itself. This, then, would be the ultimate purpose of the world.... [P]rogress, therefore, is not an indeterminate advance *ad infinitum*, for it has a definite aim, namely that of returning upon itself.[34]

The process of realisation of reason is not for Hegel a movement without closure, or what he calls a spurious infinite,[35] constantly reproducing the rift between concept and objectivity. The history of spirit possesses in comprehending reason a point of repose, or of reflection back into unity. Hegel describes the movement of reason as a system of syllogisms, based on the mutual relations and changing functions of universality, particularity, and singularity.[36] The universal stands in different ways for the rational concept; the particular is the medium in which the concept is to be embodied; the singular is the achieved embodiment of the concept, though subject to revision and reformulation. In the unfolding of the syllogisms, the universal acquires objectivity and concreteness by incorporating the particular as an aspect of itself, while the particular elevates itself to universality, stripping off its contingent nature to become the expression of a higher principle. The conclusion of the syllogism contains these two intersecting movements and also a further movement that crystallises the result as a new determinate principle.[37] Following up this argumentation, Bauer contends that the historic process is doubled, as an open-ended objective striving, and as a subjective completion or return to unity within the rational self. His concept of infinite self-consciousness maintains these two sides. Hegel himself takes the dynamism or *Wirklichkeit* of reason to be a hallmark of freedom. In this respect, too, Bauer's thought follows his lead.

> Spirit endures contradiction because it knows that it contains no determination that it has not posited itself, and consequently that it cannot in turn get rid of. This power over every content present in it forms the basis of the freedom of spirit.... [A]ctual freedom does not therefore belong to spirit in its immediacy but has to be brought into being by spirit's own activity. It is thus as the creator of its freedom that we have to consider spirit in philosophy. The entire development of the concept of spirit represents only spirit's freeing of itself from all existential forms which do not accord with its concept; a liberation which is brought about by the transformation of these forms into an actuality perfectly adequate to the concept of spirit.[38]

The realisation of reason can be traced in a sequence of stages, wherein the mediation of universal and particular is achieved in different forms. For Hegel, the philosophy of antiquity depicts a moral substance of which particular members are manifestations, properties, or accidents, not fully individuated by the possession of an autonomous moral conscience. The classical Greek doctrine of virtue aims to produce what Hegel calls the beautiful individual, an exemplar of a predetermined set of values that integrate the person into the substance of the community.[39] The dissolution of this consciousness, in Stoicism and Epicureanism, represents a withdrawal from the engulfing moral substance of the *polis* into subjective interiority or self-limitation. Despite the seeming radicality of the Epicurean programme, its principal ethical injunction not to exceed limits – to seek to minimise pain and not to maximise pleasure – is consistent with the requirements of classical thought, and antagonistic to unbounded modern self-assertion.

In Hegel's account, to which Bauer remains faithful, the modern emphasis on freedom overthrows the classical fixity of limits and the naturalness or givenness of values and relations. In the modern conception, autonomous subjects, possessing instrumental reason, confront and dominate the objective world, extracting new forms from the operation of discoverable causal patterns but also being subject to these patterns in the shaping of their own teleological projects.[40] The liberalism typical of modernity renders community not as the moral substance of individuals but as the instrumental context for the pursuit of private ends. Its positive achievement is to emancipate the individual from previous collective bonds, but it has simultaneously obscured the creation of new forms of community, distinct from the substantial communities of the past. Liberalism is thus one-sided and does not offer an adequate account of the forms of modern solidarity. The ancients, in contrast, neglected the essential moment of personal independence. Hegel's theory of objective spirit proposes to overcome the defects of both schools, while retaining their positive achievements. Following Fichte,[41] Hegel maintains that other subjects are not to be treated merely as obstacles or instruments to individual purposes but can act as conditions of an enlarged personal freedom.[42] The legitimacy of social institutions can be determined according to this criterion. Though mutual limitation remains a permissible figure, occupying a specific place within a larger continuum (one that Hegel designates as abstract right), it is not the exclusive form of reciprocity[43] but must be completed and transcended in political relations. Community no longer depends on given substantial ends or determinations, as in antiquity, but is engendered and sustained in freedom. Modernity allows particular subjects to emerge from a universe of abstract possibilities through their choice of determinate projects. Their particularity is not merely given but evolves within reciprocal relations, sanctioned by shared normative schemes that are robust enough to accommodate diversity and opposition, and do not demand uniformity, conformism, or thoughtless acquiescence. Unlike classical substantiality, modern particularity requires recognition of the free choice that it exerts within its range of possible options. Particulars thus crystallise, in distinction from all others, yet connected to them in manifold relations. Logically, Hegel analyses this process in the dialectic of the one and the many[44] and traces out its elaborations through the levels of objective spirit. To anticipate the argument of later chapters, the point of Bauer's critique of the masses can best be appreciated in respect to Hegel's characterisation of modern freedom. Mass society suppresses the emancipatory prospects of modernity in favour of a rigid conformity, and rests on particular, private interests that militate against rational and conscious adherence to a universal end, the promoting of freedom in all aspects of social life. Bauer will propose republicanism as a doctrine of transcendence of restrictive private interest.

Hegel's *Philosophy of Right* is the theory of the free and infinite personality as the highest political accomplishment of modernity.[45] Modern subjects live with and integrate a diversity of roles and demands, and they generate a high degree of social differentiation, and yet they can formulate and participate in a general interest and practise autonomy in its most robust sense. The substance of what subjects will is made rational and intersubjectively valid in modernity through participation in ethical institutions, the family, civil society, and the state. For Hegel, the state is an institution of ethical life, charged with realising the fundamental values of the community and concretising its understanding of freedom. The principle of political autonomy complements and perfects the more elementary form of freedom as the capacity of choice – that is, the inability of any cause to determine the will without the will's own compliance. It is that basic form which is worked out in abstract right; but it must be supplemented by the more conscious forms of freedom lying beyond this sphere. Abstract right, the right of property or of giving oneself an objective presence in the world, is the beginning of the intersubjective process through which particularity is elevated to universality. In carrying out their projects, subjects produce a new universal, a complex society that is inwardly differentiated and that is sustained through mutual recognition. The universal becomes concrete by containing and giving voice within itself to the particular, the principle of distinction; likewise, the particular is integrated into a new and more articulated universality that does not suppress its freedom, as classical societies did, nor exist as a mere instrumental context for private purposes, as liberals typically believe. Hegel follows this intersubjective process through the spheres of inner morality, receiving its confession of its own inadequacy: it needs to draw the criteria of its judgements not from an abstract interiority but from the network of existing social ties.[46] Only in *Sittlichkeit* or objective ethical life can the contradictions in social relations be dissolved and the unity of concept and objectivity be secured. The unity of universal and particular attains initial concrete reality through the activity of appropriation, production, and exchange in civil society. This entails reciprocal social relations, rather than isolated acts of will, as originally appears to be the case in abstract right. Finally, in the state the synthesis of particular and universal acquires conscious expression as a real, rather than merely formal, unity.

After Hegel's death, the increasingly conservative political climate of the Restoration proved inimical to the hopes of his school for further progress in rational freedom. For his republican disciples, important elements of his original project required rethinking. In light of political and social developments, Hegel's defence of constitutional monarchy[47] was unwarranted, and his pessimism about the solution of the social question unfounded.[48] To address these deficiencies in Hegel, their conceptual sources within his theory must be identified. The system of objective spirit was to be thoroughly recast, though, for Bauer at least, this can be done consistently with Hegel's own principles.[49] Elaborating upon a suggestion made in print by Arnold Ruge, though it may not originate with him, Bauer envisages a public morality to complement the private morality that Hegel describes in the *Philosophy of Right*. It is the absence of such a public account, his republican followers claim, that is responsible for Hegel's hypostasis of the universal as a separate sphere, as a state that does not explicitly acknowledge its foundation in popular sovereignty. Hegel has thus not succeeded in synthesising universality and particularity. The former is divorced from its basis in subjective action; the latter is too narrowly conceived to open to genuine self-transcendence or autonomy. The figure of the republican citizen is underdeveloped. Bauer's own republicanism, the basis of his political reflections in the *Vormärz*, emerges on this terrain.

For Bauer, the unity of thought and being, the true and central idea of all philosophy, attains its most adequate expression in Hegel, despite the limits of his institutional descriptions. But Hegel's formulation is not yet perfected; there remain in the synthesis of concept and objectivity other theoretical deficiencies beyond the political and institutional, which also stand in need of revision. From this assessment follows Bauer's conviction that Hegel's account of the present can be rectified by an inner engagement and conceptual development, a correction and not an abandonment of the Hegelian system. In this he differs from the Feuerbach of 1839, or the Marx of 1843.[50] Hegel maintains that we can grasp the rationality of history only retrospectively, but we cannot anticipate it. Bauer transforms this claim into a prospective, ethical idealism, though one that takes its bearings from reflection on the historical process. We determine our maxims by reference to history, analysing its current configuration and its inner contradictions, and thus knowing how to act in accord with its objective requirements. It is a Hegelian theory of history as the becoming of freedom that gives access to universality, that allows subjects to judge what is demanded by the universal end, concretely promoting emancipation from irrational institutions and practices. The invocation of history provides Bauer with a solution to the abstract subjectivism he finds in Kant, and to the mere negativity he finds in Enlightenment criticism, which breaks with history. A further problem that Bauer identifies in Hegel's account of Absolute Spirit is the retention of apparently transcendent elements, with inadequate reference to their subjective origin; consistently with Hegel's fundamental principles, these must now be purged away.

In addressing these problems, Bauer uses his central concept of infinite self-consciousness, a term taken from Hegel's theory of subjective spirit, to reconfigure the Hegelian absolute. One effect of the change that Bauer effects is to bring art and philosophy into close proximity, and to exclude religion henceforth as a form of alienated reason, while recognising its historical necessity. Bauer's divorce of religion and philosophy within Absolute Spirit has been frequently investigated in the literature, though his political motivations have not been clear, and his republicanism obscured. The defining trait of Bauer's project is his insistence on the immanence of the universal in history. History is the becoming of freedom and self-awareness, the record of our struggles for liberation, but also the saga of failed attempts, of alienation, which are necessary if we are to discover the meaning of our rational autonomy. Bauer's account entails the repudiation of all doctrines of freedom based on the assertion of particularism, whether religious, economic, or political. It is simultaneously the critique of hypostatised or false universals, transcending the power of individuals. These include the absolutist state and the fetishistic objects of religious belief. Bauer contends that all attempts to assert freedom on the basis of particular interest are doomed to failure by virtue of their irrationality; and all abasement of human powers before transcendent forces is to be overcome. These are the objects of his republicanism.

Objectively, the unity of thought and being as a process is never complete; it is an infinite striving to secure the always elusive accord between relations, institutions, and understandings of freedom. Subjectively, however, the movement is perfected in individual self-consciousness, through self-transcendence and internalising of the lessons of history. The process thus contains two dimensions, an objective exertion extending into infinity, and a subjective consummation or conscious return to self from otherness. It is the unity of the sublime struggle for freedom and the beautiful self, a self that differs from the beautiful individuality of the classics because it is achieved through surmounting contradictions, and not because its contradictions are yet undeveloped. Here Bauer's resolute modernism is apparent. The process of history is not chaotic or anarchic, but is governed by reason and its dialectical unfolding. Freedom entails a permanent process of transformation. "All that is solid melts into air,"[51] but the results of our actions do not disappear. The fluidity of reason leaves behind a result that can be rationally apprehended, and that continues to orient our activity. Theory is the identification of contradictions in reality that require resolution; it is accompanied by an ethical commitment to act to overcome them. In the absence of such actions, historical solutions are postponed or distorted. The revolutionary transformation of the present is directed by insight into the past, as the history of alienation and its overcoming. Bauer's ethical idealism differs from the Kantian form by admitting history into a defining role. The new concept of autonomy does not depend on an atemporal sense of duty, but is closer to what Kant calls perfectionism, where action is validated by its contribution to historical progress. Bauer takes this to mean an uncompromising commitment to remodel political and social relations and institutions. The knowledge of our freedom is not simply a moral postulate, as in Kant. Its conditions are theoretical: the understanding of history as a rational process, and of the present as marked by specific obstacles that must be overcome for progress to continue. In free self-determination, subjects transcend their previous self-understandings and renew the opposition between themselves and their products, whose finitude stands an inadequate embodiment of evolving subjective creativity. Freedom is the endless reshaping of the particular in light of the universal, itself in constant motion. Existing relations have no permanent validity, but constitute matter to be transformed. They are a not simply a given object, however, external and indifferent to us, but are the product of anterior subjective activity. Hegel had characterised such a stance as practical Jacobinism. This is exactly the political sense it assumes in Bauer's work.

Bauer's historical idealism and his republicanism are mutually reinforcing. Each with its subjective and objective dimensions, his idealism contains two components, one deriving from aesthetic concepts, the other from an ethical reading of history. Objectively, the ethics of historical perfectionism coalesce with an aesthetic image of the sublime, the infinite struggle for freedom that Bauer invites his contemporaries to share. Only the rational and autonomous subject can participate in this labour, as a freely self-determined task. Here, subjectively, the reflexively integrated, beautiful self, acting from motives of disinterestedness and universality, sustains the republican attitude. This revolutionary subject applies an ethical, critical judgement against the old order and against all claims to emancipation, in order to assess their validity and their right. This critique, differing from the moral adjudication of Kant and from Enlightenment forms, is clarified within Hegel's logic as the apodeictic judgement.[52] Its necessity lies in its claim to follow the real movement of history, but this necessity is one that rational subjects freely embrace. There is no predefined subject of the revolutionary act. All must inscribe themselves as actors in the drama of transformation. If we are to orient ourselves in the expression of autonomy, there must be universals, but these universals must not be treated as transcendent. They arise instead from the historical process itself as a process of emancipation, and the free self-identification of the particular with this universal. Subjective understandings of freedom, based on critical historical judgements, must pass into objectivity, and not remain in self-enclosed inner certainty. They must furnish maxims of practical activity, directive of political and social engagement. But in giving voice to what they perceive as universal interests, political actors must also confront their own limited subjectivity. They must not simply bracket their particular interests and identities, or refrain from expressing them, or reformulate them in politically acceptable discourse as public reasons. They must instead radically transform them. This is what Bauer means by the self-transcendence of particularity. This requirement emerges for him from the duality of the historical process, the unity of concept and objectivity secured through permanent struggle and conscious return to self. The reflexive remodelling of the subject as a vehicle of infinite self-consciousness is a central claim of his ethical and aesthetic idealism. For freedom to be real, for reason to be effective, heteronomous impulses and characteristics may not be simply concealed from public inspection, but thoroughly eradicated. Bauer's republican rigorism fuses claims of right with those of morality. He cannot admit that the criteria of legitimate external action may be less stringent than those governing inner ethical motivation, or that the juridical sphere can rightly have only the former in its purview. His radical doctrine of antonomy, and his republicanism, require the harmonisation of inner and outer aspects of subjective behaviour.

The first front on which Bauer opens his critical campaign is against the *ancien régime*, and its Restoration surrogates. Bauer denounces feudalism as a system of tutelage and of irrational privilege, monopoly, and exemptions. The universal is dispersed into multiple points, at which predatory private interests, both individual and corporate, cluster and oppose each other in order to secure additional advantages. Arrogating universality to itself, the authoritarian state that arises over these rigidly exclusive particulars thwarts and denies the self-activity of its people, and conceals the source of its authority behind a veil of religious sanctification. The state makes use of religion to bolster its authority, and, struggling against the emergent principles of freedom, seeks to halt its own development in historically retrograde forms. Private interest and progress are diametrically opposed.

Bauer maintains that it is the state, and not religion, that is the principal adversary of freedom, but his critique of religion itself is also far-reaching. It is integral to his account of the historical process as alienation and self-overcoming. He insists that his position differs fundamentally from

Enlightenment criticism, which, though offering superficial similarities, is based on a shallowly rationalistic explanation of religious manipulation, and on a restrictive idea of the subject and of freedom.[53] Bauer's critique in the *Vormärz* derives from the theoretical antagonism of faith and intellect, and from considerations of practical reason, the incompatibility of religious orthodoxy with the ethics of the republic. Religion posits a false or transcendent universal, which results in and sustains a narrow practical particularism. He excoriates the privatism and egoism of the religious attitude, and the sectarianism of the cult, seeking corporate privilege for itself. Even within the religious consciousness as alienated spirit, however, Bauer finds creativity at work in the original shaping of the material of sentiment and representation to the new form and determinateness of doctrine, while beneath this aesthetic activity lurks a mass of indeterminate feeling or unthinking acquiescence. The question of the genesis of religious doctrines takes up the problematic of artistic creativity that Bauer addresses in his first text of 1829. Against this order of alienated spirit, Bauer insists that the decisive political question is the source of the state's authority, whether in tradition and religious sanction, or in the popular will. This issue, the true meaning of 1848, is to be posed and fought out in utmost clarity, without mediation or compromise. Here is a genuine and unavoidable historical antinomy, to which only republicanism provides the solution. Though it might appear to be an ally in the republican revolution, liberalism is incapable of such a sustained combat against the old order.

Thus Bauer opens his campaign on its second front, as a critique of liberal possessive individualism and the constitutionalist state. Previous revolutions, the English and especially the French, must also be critically assessed. Their failings are instructive, both in their theoretical bases and in their tactical implications. The break between liberalism and republicanism is not an original feature of 1848, but Bauer imparts a new turn to the debate, criticising civil society, the dominance of economic interest, and the mass tendencies of modern society, a process accelerated by the French Revolution, and unconsciously reflected in the liberalism (as well as the socialisms) of 1848. He revives the classical republican themes of the opposition of commerce and virtue, but gives them a new shape, consistent with his Hegelianism. He develops a critique of constitutionalism as the political translation of private interest, and as a vacillating, compromising opposition to the feudal regime. Even in its most advanced form, that endorsed by Hegel, constitutionalism merely juxtaposes two diametrically opposed principles of sovereignty, popular and princely, and is unable to resolve the essential contention between them.

On its third front, Bauer wages a campaign against a new adversary, the emergent schools of socialism. The revolutions of 1848 fracture the Jacobin tradition, as each group in the popular alliance attains a clearer consciousness of its own specificity, and defines itself, in part, against its former ally. Bauer's work contributes to this process, and reflects the emergence of new forms of poverty and social organisation. He asserts that the objective of his new republicanism is not merely political, but social emancipation. The social question can be resolved, and the proletariat liberated, not by direct appeals to the particular interests of one class, but by a common struggle against privilege in all its forms, a struggle animated by republican convictions. The result of this combat, waged unremittingly, will be the attainment of equality and its inexorable generalisation throughout the spheres of social life.

As the revolutionary outbreak approaches and collisions intensify, Bauer's thought shows signs of strain. It is not yet that his aesthetic and ethical models separate and come into opposition with each other, as they do after 1848, but rather that the subjective and objective dimensions within each model reveal their potential incompatibility. The importance of the subjective moment, both of motivation and of inward fulfilment, is highlighted to the detriment of the objective process. A narrowness and sectarianism in Bauer's own outlook on questions of the purity of the revolutionary commitment can be understood from this perspective; we can thus offer an alternative explanation of Bauer's polemics against liberals and socialists, distinct from charges of renegadism or theoretical discontinuities. His account of liberation conflates right and morality, spheres that Kant, Fichte, and Hegel had succeeded in keeping distinct. The consequences are apparent in Bauer's texts on the Jewish question, for example. For Bauer, the possibility of full mutual recognition among citizens depends upon the subjective adoption of a republican attitude. Such recognition, and with it access to the sphere of right, therefore reposes upon a certain bearing in the sphere of morality. Bauer is not prepared to admit as legitimate any claim for the elimination of juridical inequality, wherein the potential beneficiaries of this equality act from particular religious interests, or are not imbued with fully republican sentiments. Only with difficulty can he admit a common front against mutual adversaries, and his adamance helps to foreclose the possibility of progress. This is a major weakness, and leads to his faulty diagnosis of the current situation, as well as to the diminution of his public status within the opposition movement after 1844. These problems beset many of his criticisms of the insufficiencies of the progressive forces in general. His theory requires that revolutionary subjects act freely, undetermined by particular interest, but few subjects in 1848 prove capable of the stringent demands that Bauer's critical judgement imposes. That there must be a point of rest or return to self from externalisation is necessary to avoid or mitigate the false universal or the passage to infinity, from which Bauer wishes to distinguish both his ethics of perfectionism and his aesthetics of the sublime. But this point of rest, the subjective side of the ethical and aesthetic programme, sometimes appears as an alternative rather than a complement to the objective process, a retreat, secured against the forces of historic decay, rather than a bridgehead from which new advances can be made. The subjective and objective dimensions remain harmonised in 1839–44, but increasingly they are under tension. Bauer criticises Hegel for his incomplete synthesis of concept and objectivity, but he does not himself resolve the problem.

The book is divided into four parts. The first establishes the foundations of Bauer's political thought, tracing the emergence of his model of aesthetic and ethical criticism, and discussing his reading of Hegel and Kant, wherein he formulates an idealism rooted in a Hegelian concept of history. The second part examines the critique of religion and the Restoration state. The third explores more fully the republican programme and the understanding of history in Bauer's texts of 1841–42. The fourth deals with the unfolding revolutionary situation and the emergence of the social question, addressing the critique of the liberal political movement, the repudiation of socialist alternatives, and the limits of Bauer's republicanism. A brief epilogue outlines his post-revolutionary thought. The 1829 Latin prize manuscript on Kant's aesthetics, published here in English translation for the first time, appears as an appendix to the work.

In interpreting Bauer, I have attempted, wherever possible, to take his own programmatic pronouncements to guide the initial approach to his texts. His sympathetic rendering of the thought of forgotten Enlightenment figures like Edelmann[54] provides a model for such interpretation. His insistence on the unity of thought and being and his invocation of social struggle are examples of these guiding ideas. The first supplies the general interpretative framework for this study; the second reveals the directive intention for Bauer's specific criticisms both of the old order in *Vormärz* Germany and of the oppositional currents emerging from liberalism and socialism. The exposition of Bauer's ethical and aesthetic idealism, of his republicanism, and of his recognition of the social question are, I hope, the major contributions of this text.

In approaching these issues, the heterogeneity and volume of Bauer's literary output during the pre-revolutionary period impose distinct methods of analysis. Some texts are fundamental theoretical statements. These include his 1829 manuscript on Kant, and, as I believe, the *Posaune*, despite its peculiar form.[55] The theoretical content of these texts is here discussed at length. In other cases, the philosophical import is relatively slight, but the text makes a significant political point. These texts are typically grouped thematically, except where it is necessary to distinguish shifts in emphasis among them. After establishing the general contours of Bauer's thinking in part one, the treatment is both chronological and thematic, tracing his development and his engagement with different adversaries, though frequently his encounters with various opponents merge, and it is impossible to unravel completely the three strands of his critique.

Some restrictions of scope must also be noted. This account is not a comprehensive intellectual biography of Bauer, but an examination of republican themes in his work before 1848. This limitation is imposed by the very diffuseness of his writing. Thus I have retained what I take to be strictly necessary to my subject, the relation between Bauer's republican politics and his aesthetic and ethical idealism, derived from a specific reading of Hegel. While I do not offer an extensive reconstruction of Bauer's religious theory in the mid-1830s, I suggest that the key to these texts is the fundamental idea of the unity of thought and being, and that they can be understood as experiments that Bauer undertakes to display this accord. In Bauer's critique of religion after 1839, I address the themes that are pertinent to his republicanism, especially the links among religion, possessive individualism, and the absolutist state. Further, I stress the central distinction between Bauer's critique of religion and that of the Enlightenment, to support my claim that there is a distinctive (Hegelian) kind of judgement at work in Bauer's texts. A subsequent detailed exploration of Bauer's theory of religion and its evolution would be most welcome, but I do not venture it here.

Except for the epilogue, the present account limits itself to Bauer's work prior to 1850. In the vast corpus of Bauer's writings, these texts form a relatively cohesive whole, dedicated to republicanism, the ethics and aesthetics of self-determination, and the forms of concrete political struggle. They are inspired by a particular and relatively consistent reading of Hegel, and they bear directly on the revolutionary experience of 1848–49. Even his later work is still conditioned by the contradictions of the revolutionary movement, which Bauer now assesses as a failure, but the political landscape has changed decisively. It is only after 1848 that the ethical and aesthetic models decisively diverge in Bauer's thought, and the aesthetic is reconfigured at the expense of the sublime. He abandons his historical perfectionism and the sublimity of the struggle for liberation. The correct practical stance is now, Bauer thinks, a disinterested aesthetic withdrawal from active ethical engagement while new social forces prepare themselves, under disciplinary duress if not by insightful personal exertion.[56] After 1848, Bauer looks particularly to Russia as a revivifying force for an exhausted and impotent Europe. Russia's is a cohesive society, not yet prey to the diremptions of modern egoistic individualism, but characterised by an all-encompassing unity of church and state. The unity of thought and being is now taken to be an attribute of a premodern social formation. Some of the roots of his later position can be identified in his *Vormärz* writings, but Bauer's later thought falls outside the scope of the Hegelian, ethical, and aesthetic republicanism that is our object.

Any rehabilitation of Bauer's work in the *Vormärz* must, however, be undertaken in full consciousness and acknowledgement of the baleful influence of his later writings. After the failures of 1848, he promoted a virulent anti-Semitism in the anti-liberal circles he came to frequent.[57] The recognition of Bauer's late, *sui generis* conservatism should not obscure the diametrically opposed position he held, and defended ably and publicly, prior to and during the revolutionary events. While many of Bauer's adversaries and critics admit that he held this progressive orientation before 1843, here we identify the same republican spirit infusing his work until after the defeats of 1848–49. Bauer's texts on the French Revolution and the social question (mostly subsequent to 1842) thus assume a renewed interest, and his multifaceted critique of modernity appears in a different light, more faithful, I feel, to its original intent.[58]

It would be remiss not to acknowledge here an abiding debt to Ernst Barnikol. Upon his death in 1968, he left uncompleted a voluminous manuscript on Bauer, representing more than forty years of research. Of this manuscript, conserved at the International Institute for Social History, Amsterdam, only a fraction has been published,[59] but even this fraction, in its almost six hundred pages, continues to set standards in the study of the Hegelian school for meticulous scholarship, rigorous analysis, and balanced criticism. Barnikol's interests were primarily theological, though he recognised clearly that Bauer's religious critique was politically motivated. It is this political inspiration that is at the centre of the present text. Independently of each other, Barnikol and van den Bergh van Eysinga compiled most of the original materials used here, and in the absence of a critical edition of Bauer's works, they are the best possible sources. The books, articles, and correspondence they amassed are deposited among the extensive archival holdings and rich bibliographic resources of the IISH. The interpretative context I provide, linking Bauer's Hegelianism with his republicanism, is not found in these sources, however. For van den Bergh van Eysinga, Bauer reverts to a pre-Hegelian, Enlightenment rationalism. Barnikol, anticipating Löwith, sees him as a precursor of Nietzsche. Here, instead, I stress Bauer's fidelity to the central Hegelian insight, the unity of thought and being, interpreted according to aesthetic and ethical criteria. This application of Hegel produces a specific account of republicanism, not identical to that of the Enlightenment or of French Jacobinism, but a critical development from them, following Hegel's logical pattern of advance from the infinite to the apodeictic judgement. Bauer devises an original model of critical theory, assessing the claims to emancipation and legitimacy raised by the myriad actors of the German *Vormärz* and Restoration Europe. In his vigorous defence of his work against the censors in 1844, he describes himself as the friend of freedom.[60] How he understands this freedom is the theme we here pursue.

I

FOUNDATIONS: AESTHETICS, ETHICS, AND REPUBLICANISM

"THE IDEA IS LIFE": BAUER'S AESTHETICS AND POLITICAL THOUGHT

Bruno Bauer's first critical foray, in 1829, is an assessment of Kantian aesthetics from the perspective of Hegelian logic. His depiction of art as a manifestation of spirit and the already problematical relation of art and religion anticipate the development of his thought on infinite self-consciousness in the 1840s. The central idea of the early manuscript, a Hegelian conception of the unity of thought and being, is the key to deciphering the complex and elusive meaning of Bauer's critical theory in the *Vormärz*.[1] This text, adjudicated by Hegel and awarded the Prussian Royal Prize in Philosophy, had been deposited among Hegel's correspondence in the archives of the Humboldt-Universität, Berlin. Presumed lost,[2] it was first published in 1996, in the original Latin, with German translation and commentary.[3] It provides an important new perspective on Bauer's thinking.

On August 3, 1828, the University of Berlin announced its annual Royal Prize competition.[4] The question, set by Hegel, was this:

> Whether the principles of the doctrine of the beautiful are adequately expounded by Kant in that part of philosophy which he took to be the critique of judgement, and whether they are consistent with the bases upon which the entire philosophy of this author depends.[5]

The prize, awarded on August 3, 1829, was won by Bruno Bauer, who had submitted a ninety-five-page Latin manuscript, *Dissertatio de pulchri principiis.*[6] Bauer was then a theology student at the University of Berlin, having enrolled in spring 1828; he was graduated in spring 1832.[7] He had attended H. G. Hotho's lectures on Hegel's *Encyclopaedia* in his first term and was enrolled in Hegel's course on aesthetics from October 1828 until April 1829. These sources are easily recognisable in the prize manuscript. The adjudication committee that recommended Bauer's text included Hegel and the classicist and art historian Ernst Heinrich Tölken (1785–1869). Comments by the historian Friedrich von Raumer (1781–1873) on the text, and on others submitted in the competition, are also extant,

as is the report of the faculty meeting of July 11, 1829, which designated
the winner of the prize. Hegel concurred with the philosophical content
of the piece. His criticism stressed the inadequate command of Latin
manifested by the anonymous author. The comments by other evaluators
agree that the linguistic form was the major deficiency of the text. One
reader remarked that the time had perhaps come to abandon Latin as a
language of scholarly communication.[8]

The significance of this early text is that it lays out the aesthetic concepts and the directive ideas that figure in Bauer's later reflections on infinite self-consciousness. From his earliest writing, Bauer follows Hegel in
stressing the unity of concept and objectivity. Bauer argues that art allows
us to intuit the results, and to conceptualise the process, by which thought
becomes manifest or objective. Hegel's system alone gives a proper ap-
preciation of the role of art in the realisation of reason. Kant anticipates
this result but is unable to sustain it. Bauer's manuscript examines the
account of intuition, concept, and idea in the *Critique of Judgement*, com-
paring their usage to Kant's previous writings, and to the reformulation
of these terms by Hegel. Bauer argues that the categories of cognition,
applied in the *Critique of Pure Reason*, underlie the doctrine of the beautiful in the *Critique of Judgement*; but he also contends that the antinomies
that characterise the First Critique are not finally eluded in the Third,
even though Kant himself tries to circumvent them or to offer a less
sharply dualistic explanation. In defending this position, Bauer's early
manuscript also supplies the major categories of a critical theory that,
though undeveloped in 1829, characterises his writings on politics and
society in the *Vormärz* period. His later work makes explicit the results
of his early reflections on the unity of thought and being and on art, re-
configuring absolute spirit, and bringing art and philosophy into closer
proximity. The structure of the aesthetic judgement, in its universality
and freedom from particular interest, is replicated in the critical judgements that Bauer articulates in the 1840s on the existing order and the
claims of contending political parties.

The prize manuscript develops the unity of thought and being, or
the self-actualising power of reason or the idea. The central claim of
Hegelian idealism is the *Wirklichkeit* or efficacy of reason, its ability to
realise itself historically in shaping objective reality. Bauer presents this
perennial theme of philosophy[9] in the forms in which it is conceived by
the Greeks, in the mediaeval period, and by Kant, who, according to the
manuscript, achieves the synthesis of Locke's empiricism with Cartesian-
Leibnizian idealism. Kant's synthesis involves the primacy neither of being
nor of abstract thought but is the attempt to think them together. The
initial result is an inadequate notion of their unity as merely subjective
and thus as unable to secure the desired unity with the object. Bauer
proposes to reexamine this process in light of Hegel's logic.

According to Bauer's presentation, reason or the idea is inadequately grasped in the first two historical moments: for the Greeks because of its givenness and immediacy, so that the rich internal articulations of the idea are not yet worked out; in the mediaeval period because faith suppresses doubt or the moment of subjective probing and reasoned assent. Faith upholds a fixed structure to which reason must conform as to an external object, one that is simply given and not produced out of rational effort. Both periods have a deficient understanding of freedom as self-determination. The third great historical moment, the philosophy of Kant, also imperfectly depicts the self-actualising power of reason. In his prize manuscript, Bauer criticises Kant for intimating, but failing to think through, this unity. Bauer elaborates the criticisms that Hegel makes of Kant in his Berlin *Aesthetics* lectures, supplementing these remarks with the logical analysis of categories provided by the *Encyclopaedia of the Philosophical Sciences*, in its 1827 edition.[10] In this interpretation, the particularly innovative feature of the *Critique of Judgement*[11] is its attempt to bridge the dualisms of thought and being, subject and object, freedom and nature, which Kant's philosophy generates in the domains of pure and practical reason. While Kant's analysis of beauty provides the outlines of a solution to the divorce of thinking and objectivity, it is unable to develop this insight systematically. The critical philosophy constitutes a unity, but a defective unity, that precludes simultaneous knowledge of the subjective and of the objective. Bauer's argument is that the *Critique of Judgement* offers not a solution to but a reproduction of the difficulties of Kant's basic schema, as elaborated in the two prior critiques.[12] The philosophy of Kant is the summit of previous philosophical development and prepares the way for the new philosophy, *philosophia neoterica*, which offers a definitive resolution of the diremptions of spirit.[13]

In relating the *Critique of Pure Reason* to the *Critique of Judgement*, Bauer argues that both are characterised by similar defects. While the idea of beauty and Kant's renewed sense of teleological reason partly restore the classical conception of the objective embodiment of reason, this embodiment is no longer immediate but must be worked out through the oppositions generated by free subjectivity. Bauer recognises that this is a great advance on the classical view of reason, but he contends that Kant does not understand the new attitude to objectivity that he introduced as guaranteeing the greater richness and concreteness of the rational idea, nor as effecting a genuine unity of concept and objectivity. In Kant, beauty remains only a subjective principle of reflection. Kant retreats from his own new principle by continuing to emphasise the incompatibility of thought and being, as he had stressed in the first two critiques.

The results of this deficiency are two-fold. The first is the merely subjective character of the Kantian idea, as regulative, not constitutive.[14] Thus, reason cannot gain access to the objective realm. Kant denies the actuality of reason, its causally formative character, or its power to realise itself in the world. The impotence of reason is replicated by that of the understanding, which is imprisoned in its own subjectivity through the distinction of phenomenon and noumenon. Kant depicts the determinations of the understanding as external and indifferent to the thing in itself. Against this conception, Bauer invokes Hegel, who stresses the dignity of the rational idea, issuing forth into objectivity. The idea unites objectivity and concept. In the syllogism of the idea, objectivity is endowed with rational form, while the concept acquires an explicit, distinct, and material existence. Beauty, life, and idea are moments in the process that constitutes the actuality of reason.

> The concept and objectivity are not two different things, but essentially a single totality, the idea itself. . . . The beautiful is a concept in which objectivity inheres, so that objectivity appears only in the concept, and the entire concept is contained in objectivity. Thus the idea is, through itself, life; or, life in its truth, in its substance, is precisely the beautiful.[15]

The harmony of beauty is not simply a subjectively gauged accord but is the immediate form of reason's objective manifestation. This conception recalls the world of Plato's *Symposium*, where beauty is the mode in which reason and the love of reason emerge; but the rational idea is no longer a rigid Platonic form. It is now, as modernity demands, mediated by subjective activity. Bauer's analysis concludes that Kant recognised the importance of this subjective principle but that he was unable to bring it into harmony with the objective. Kantian idealism remains one-sided.

In Bauer's reading, the converse of this limitation also besets Kant's description of beauty. While, in the First Critique, cognition is *merely* subjective in its divorce from objectivity, it is also *inadequately* subjective, in that it cannot give an account of the transcendental subject and of self-consciousness. These problems recur in the *Critique of Judgement*. Bauer describes as the pinnacle of his critique Kant's admission that philosophy is unable to know or represent the supersensible[16]; while the genuine knowledge of subjectivity is one of the goals to which philosophy aspires, and to which it attains in Hegel's system. Hegel shows that the transcendental subject is not unknowable; but this knowledge is of a special kind. It is not the cognition of the self as though it were a particular object, nor does it invoke the abstractly universal self to which Kantian practical reason offers access. Hegel agrees with Kant that self-consciousness is distinct from a cognitive subject-object relation[17]; the categories of objective knowledge can only partially apply to the subject. Knowledge of subjectivity is not attainable through the model of reflection, wherein subjects introspectively examine their psychic contents. An objectifying attitude would reveal only the particular characteristics of subjectivity in its inertness, but not the essential determinations of subjectivity as potentiality or activity, the capacity to transform or negate the given. From this conception, however, Hegel draws distinctly different consequences from Kant's: Rather than denying our ability to theorise subjectivity, Hegel contends that new cognitive categories must be evolved to reveal the specific character of active subjectivity.[18] By failing to develop these categories, Kant renders the subject unknowable. Kant's position that subjectivity is accessible only to practical reason and not to knowledge appears to Hegel to surrender the claims of reason. Self-consciousness refers to an interactive and syllogistic process, the creation of singularity as a dialectical unity of particular and universal.[19] The self is knowable through its activities, through the relations that it posits towards objects and towards other subjects.

Bauer's text offers only a very formal and fragmentary account of this process. It is extremely allusive about what is involved positively in a doctrine of self-consciousness as an active synthesis of subject and object. Bauer has not yet worked out his own position on the question, and he does no more than intimate the arguments that sustain Hegel's identification of the deficient subjectivity in Kant's own account. The manuscript does, however, introduce a distinction that will be of great consequence in Bauer's subsequent thinking. He distinguishes between genuine, creative subjectivity, the agency by which reason establishes its dominion in the world, and *mere* subjectivity, unable to engage with and transform its object. Bauer takes Kantian practical reason to be a variant of the latter. Consistent with his theme of the unity of thought and being, he stresses the inadmissibility of Kant's claim that reason and reality ought to conform, but cannot. The rejection of this Kantian "ought," and the attempt to reformulate it as an immanent critique of existing institutions and ideas of freedom, remain characteristic of Bauer's republicanism throughout the 1840s.

Even though it fails to reproduce the Hegelian arguments in their full range and depth, Bauer's conclusions on both the overly and the insufficiently subjective character of Kantian aesthetics reflect Hegel's own repeated criticisms of Kant's idealism.[20] In his *Lectures on the History of Philosophy*, for example, Hegel argues that in its cognitive dimension, Kantian philosophy understands itself purely as the consciousness of objects, but not of its own subjectivity, which remains an impenetrable beyond. Even as objective knowledge, however, it is intrinsically limited, because Kant's distinction of noumenon and phenomenon prevents him from demonstrating how, in appropriating the outer world, consciousness reconstructs the rational essence of the object.[21] Hegel's examination of practical reason adds an important dimension that, though absent from Bauer's text, reappears, at least in part, in his later ethical idealism. Kant generalises this subjective thinking only in a formal, abstract universal law, not in concrete intersubjectivity. Each subjectivity is a replication of

an identical structure of rationality, but Kant does not theorize the relationships among the subjects themselves. Just as Kantian cognition does
not penetrate the object, so Kantian morality does not advance to the
level of objective spirit but remains mired in inwardness. While Bauer
fails to address this aspect of Hegel's critique in the manuscript, he will
treat it in his later accounts of the universality implicit in the historical
process.

   In its basic argumentative structure, Bauer's manuscript thus does not
depart from the canonical Hegelian criticisms of Kant and frequently, as
in the explanation of self-consciousness, does not rise to their heights. It
does, however, amplify the brief remarks on the Kantian account of beauty
that were published posthumously in the introduction to Hegel's *Aesthetics*
lectures. Bauer applies the logical apparatus of the 1827 *Encyclopaedia* to
Kant's account of the four moments of aesthetic judgement, while di-
verging in some respects from Hegel's explicit account of Kant in that
text. In this second edition of the *Encyclopaedia*, Hegel treats Kantian philosophy as a variant of empiricism, thus relating it to what he calls the
second attitude towards objectivity.[22] While not assimilating these two
positions, he identifies a deep affinity between them. In the lectures on
the history of philosophy, which assume a similar vantage point to that of
the *Encyclopaedia*, Hegel highlights Kant's proximity to the empiricists, in
contrast to eighteenth-century rationalist metaphysics. The proponents
of this latter tradition, such as Wolff, take thought to be positive self-
identity, or being for self, whereas the Enlightenment displaces implicit
being in favour of relationship, or being for another. The Enlightenment
discovers that everything exists for the subject, but the subject may be con-
strued in different ways. Being may be related to consciousness either in
the form of utility, with the empiricists, or, as in Kant, as being for self-
consciousness.[23] In contrast, Bauer's text depicts Kant and the empiricists
as embarked upon distinct philosophical enterprises. Unlike the immediate identity of thought and being in Greek philosophy, modernity is the
striving for the mediated unity of objectivity and subjectivity, intuition and
concept, under the aegis of the realised Idea. Bauer's text distinguishes, as
aspects of modernity, rationalism (the first attitude towards objectivity of
the *Encyclopaedia* text)[24] from empiricism. The former seeks to derive this
unity unilaterally from abstract thought; the latter subordinates thought
in favour of the object. Bauer then depicts Kant more straightforwardly as
a synthesis of these two modern tendencies, ignoring Hegel's more complex typology. Kant's synthesis is an imperfect one, in that he sees the
concept or the understanding as subjective only, and the object itself as
that which transcends the cognitive power in the form of the unknowable
thing-in-itself. Self-consciousness, the name here given to the transcendental unity of apperception, is likewise immune from penetration by the
categories of cognition. Kant attempts to unify being and thought and

thus opens the way to the new philosophy, but the attempt remains sterile in his hands.

In the 1829 manuscript, Bauer's criticism of Kant's aesthetics begins with the Kantian relation of concept and intuition, then takes up the relation of concept and idea, or understanding and reason. It next examines the Kantian formulation of teleology in the relation of objectivity, concept, and idea; finally, it raises the problem of necessity, linking aesthetic and teleological judgements. It cannot be our purpose here to examine the validity of these particular criticisms of the Kantian project,[25] but to illustrate the thesis of the unity of thought and being as Bauer understood it in 1829. This understanding conditions his subsequent work.

Reconstructing the first moment, of quality, Bauer defines the disinterestedness of the aesthetic judgement to mean its separation from the appetitive faculty, as the published version of Hegel's aesthetics puts it.[26] Bauer now argues that Kant interprets this separation in light of his habitual dualism, which pervaded the critiques of pure and practical reason.[27] According to the Third Critique, the quality of aesthetic experience is constituted by the freedom of feeling. In the contemplation of beauty, the aesthetic judgement is liberated from every extrinsic determination. Here freedom means that the aesthetic feelings are not determined by empirical desire or the moral will, but nonetheless the sentiments evoked by beauty are subjectively necessary, as the fourth moment, of modality, will demonstrate. Kant's mistake, for Bauer, is to understand this freedom as implying the divorce of the subject from the object. Kant thus restricts the account of the aesthetic experience to a report of subjective states evoked in the presence of an object that subjects deem beautiful. As Bauer puts it, in their aesthetic apprehension, Kantian subjects do not refer to the object, nor penetrate it by thinking, but remain enclosed in their own subjectivity. Bauer contends that the essence of beauty is rather the harmony of being and subjectivity, and the overcoming of alienation as thought rediscovers itself in the element of otherness, in the aesthetic object that bears the character of purposiveness.[28] Aesthetic feeling points beyond itself to the infinite freedom of thought, which reconstructs the form, or the universal, rational essence of the object. What remains beyond this reconstruction is not the ineffable thing in itself, but mere "vain, weak, fleeting appearance,"[29] devoid of theoretical interest. Thus we "find the object in ourselves."[30] The cognitive act itself unites thought and being within one discrete experience, through the rational determination of form. Though distinct from cognition because it is effected without a definite concept, aesthetic experience provides the intuition of the unity of subject and object. The element in which it moves, that of feeling unconditioned by need, interest, or will, is a tangible expression or prefiguration of the freedom of thought – not in the divorce from objectivity, as Kant thinks, but in the transmutation of any given material. Kant's dualism prevents him from attaining this vantage point.

In respect to the second moment of aesthetic judgements, or quantity, Kant takes the universality they contain to be merely subjective – unlike logical judgements, which are determined by concepts. The universality of aesthetic judgements lies in the free play of the powers of cognition, which are set in motion by the contemplation of the beautiful object. In Hegel's logic, this position corresponds to a universal judgement,[31] bearing on the totality of subjects, all of whom are deemed to have the same reaction to beauty in virtue of their identical rationality. In his criticism, Bauer concludes that Kant's restriction of universality to its subjective side implies the negation of the intelligible dimension of beauty. Kant lays out the possibility of a concrete identity of idea and concept, of the understanding and reason, but then limits reason to a merely indefinite idea, whereby the supersensible cannot be known.[32] Just as the first moment erects an insuperable barrier between concept and intuition, now the concept and the idea are equally sundered and opposed.

Bauer's critique of the third moment assimilates, as does Hegel's own account, the Kantian categories of teleological and pure aesthetic judgements.[33] The idea of intrinsic finality that Kant develops in *The Critique of Judgement* is taken as an approximation of the Hegelian Idea, the synthesis of nature and freedom, of intuition and concept. But Kant defines the infinity of reason by opposing it to the realm of finitude. The idea proper to reason is unrepresentable, in that no object can correspond to it. Thus Kant takes reason to transcend cognition, or to exclude knowledge from itself; it is impervious to the concept or the understanding whose realm is objects in the phenomenal world. Objectivity is equally inaccessible to reason, Kant having defined the two realms precisely by their opposition; they merely *ought* to correspond. Bauer sums up the Hegelian critique:

> Thus the infinite or the absolute itself becomes relative, since it does not refer to objectivity, which has been posited through itself. Instead, [objectivity] remains outside it, and stands indifferently over against it. The idea, however, . . . is absolute, because it does not refer to something which, as alien, stands in opposition to it; but from its very self it emits objectivity and bears itself along in this [element]. As this totality of objectivity and concept, it is the truly rational.[34]

In respect to the fourth moment, of modality,[35] Bauer opposes the subjective necessity of the Kantian "ought" or *Sollen*, which rests on the opposition of being and concept. Kant's vindication of the universality of aesthetic judgements through the "ought" of the common sense is, for Bauer, a derisory alternative to Hegel's characterisation of necessity in the *Encyclopaedia Logic*. Like the implicit finality of the third moment, necessity is defined as the internal unity of being and reflection-into-self. Hegel understands this as the principle of internal organisation, or the consonance of the parts in an articulated whole. Living organisms are such totalities. The harmony of their parts is necessity, insofar as it sustains the unity of their form; but it is also the condition for the expression of their life, of their activities. To this extent, this inner accord is likewise an anticipation of freedom, a freedom realised fully only in the human species, which Kant rightly takes to be the ideal of beauty. Beautiful objects, too, partake of this necessary ordering of their parts; there is nothing extraneous or superfluous to the display of their meaning. But they express freedom in manifesting the power of reason or the idea to propel itself into objectivity, and, in thinking, to appropriate and reproduce the rational core of being.

Besides amplifying the critique of Kantian aesthetic judgement, a further contribution of the 1829 manuscript is to illustrate tensions in Hegel's late system, which are significant for the evolution of the Hegelian school, and of Bauer's own thinking in particular. The published version of Hegel's *Aesthetics* differs in its historical account from the perspective assumed in Bauer's text. The former situates Kant within the modern ethos of reflection, a culture of oppositions emerging from the abstract understanding. Kant's thought is symptomatic of this culture, because his philosophy re-creates the diremptions of thought and being, understanding and reason, which are characteristic of modernity; but at the same time, sensing a higher unity, he struggles to overcome these oppositions.[36] Bauer's interpretation partly follows this account, inasmuch as the oppositions of rationalism and empiricism are partly constitutive of this culture of diremption. What is distinctive in Bauer's presentation, however, is that he roots the development of this contradiction in the mediaeval opposition of faith and reason, as much as in the specific traits of modernity. This opposition is different in kind from the modern form. It presupposes an understanding not yet emancipated to lose, and to recover, its own way. It is not chronologically restricted to the mediaeval world, however; some of its elements persist into the modern period. This shift, unchallenged by Hegel's comments on the manuscript, will allow Bauer later in his text to realign art and philosophy as moments of absolute spirit. It is thus of greater theoretical consequence than the discrepancy noted previously, regarding Kant's relation to the rationalists and the empiricists.

While it is clear that Hegel did not change his systematic vantage point on the structure of absolute spirit, or the mutual relations of art, religion, and philosophy, a possible conclusion from Bauer's manuscript is that Hegel's aesthetics lectures of 1828 involved a polemic against contemporary versions of the subservience of art to religion. This point is further illustrated by recent interpretations of Hegel's controversial thesis of the end of art, which does not appear in Bauer's manuscript, but which is attested from other sources.[37] The published *Aesthetics* derives modern art's inability to illuminate truth from the unrepresentability of the absolute, in the complex configuration that it assumes in Christianity.[38] Though it does not envisage the end of art, Bauer's text offers indirect support for recent research on Hegel's elaboration of this thesis, namely its critical and polemical character. The critical bearing of the thesis consists in two claims, raised by the study of other unpublished manuscripts of Hegel's aesthetics lectures. First, art cannot, as it could in classical antiquity, elevate the individual consciousness to universality, because, in liberating subjectivity, the modern period generates sharply opposed interests that were hemmed in by the substantiality of the Greek *polis*. To overlook this crucial difference is to risk making art the vehicle of particularistic interests, merely disguised as universal. This is a distinctively modern danger. Secondly, Hegel's thesis of the end of art represents a rejection of the Romantic attempt to revivify the mediaeval past and to reconstitute modern art on the basis of such particular religious conceptions, in the service of the Restoration state.[39] Recent research contends that some of Hegel's students, notably Hotho, succumbed to this tendency and incorporated into Hegelianism elements that Hegel himself had repudiated.[40] Bauer's text indirectly sustains this reading, cautioning against a too ready assimilation of the late Hegel to orthodox and accommodationist positions in religious and political matters. But in stressing the ongoing productivity of art in relation to philosophy, it also contests the closure of the Hegelian system, a position it shares with much recent research on the *Aesthetics*. Art is validated neither by enshrining it in the past, nor by making it the handmaiden of theology, but by illustrating through it the inexhaustible fecundity of the philosophical Idea. The unity of thought and being implies a continuous process of creation.

Far from seeing art as exhausted, then, Bauer repeatedly lays emphasis on the affinity of art and philosophy, and on the effectiveness of their mutual relationship. He asserts that art is the highest object of philosophical contemplation.[41] As the immediate unity of thought and objectivity, art is a symbol of what philosophy achieves through an arduous conceptual evolution. Its grounding intuition is the very starting point from which philosophy proceeds. Bauer will develop this conception in his *Posaune des jüngsten Gerichts* of 1841, and in other texts of his critical period. His 1829 manuscript elevates art above its customary subordination in the Hegelian triad, to the detriment of religion. The latter here appears in the guise of faith, taken to be inimical to free inquiry as the element of reason. The manuscript underlines the opposition of faith and reason in its critique of the religious conceptions of the unity of thought and being. In view of Hegel's sharpened polemics against the party of pietist orthodoxy in 1827, as evidenced in the Preface to the second edition of the *Encyclopaedia*, as well as in his correspondence,[42] we may conclude with Bauer that it is not only the mediaeval period which is characterised by this contradiction. The modern proponents of pietism are not exempt from the deficiencies that Bauer attributes to the fideistic attitude. The intellectual battle against this tendency remains an important factor in the evolution of the Hegelian school.[43] It is decisive for Bauer's own fate.

The 1829 text offers a particular illumination of Bauer's intellectual development. His position as late as 1838, notably his defence of theological doctrines, reinterpreted in a Hegelian, speculative manner, can now be seen to be rooted in his conception of the unity of thought and being, and in his critique of the subjectivism of the Kantian *Sollen* or "ought": the abstract opposition of an idea and a reality unattuned to it and impenetrable by it.[44] These are the themes of the 1829 manuscript. His subsequent adoption of a Left-Hegelian perspective in 1839 involves a reconfiguration of this unity of thought and being in the doctrine of universal self-consciousness, which also contains other aesthetic motifs. Throughout the 1830s, he experiments with different ways of grasping this unity. During this period of theological speculation, Bauer distinguishes a type of religious representation that is open to speculative reinterpretation, and thus compatible with philosophy, from a dogmatic form that is repugnant to reason.[45] After 1839, the critique of the religious consciousness reveals the absorption or effacement of the former elements by the latter, so that the opposition of reason and religion becomes acute. The result is the opposition of all forms of religious representation to the emancipated philosophical self-consciousness. This is one of the many facets of the contemporary opposition between heteronomy and autonomy, but only one. Many interpretations have overstressed the religious dimension at the expense of Left-Hegelian politics.[46]

One important product of his early speculative period is Bauer's *Die Religion des Alten Testaments* (*Religion of the Old Testament*) of 1838. This is no straightforwardly Right-Hegelian or accommodationist work. It explores the extent to which a religious framework offers adequate resources for harmonising being with the demands of thought. It stresses the incompatibility of religious revelation and self-consciousness, and the self-determination of the latter. While the scope of this opposition is not yet as wide nor the contradiction as hostile as it appears in later texts, many of the elements that Bauer will combine in his texts of the 1840s are already present. In the name of the unity of thought and being, the 1838 book develops a Hegelian critique of both abstract universality and unmediated particularity, though the forms of these are not yet fully traced out. Bauer depicts religious experience as a product of self-consciousness, of which he proposes both a transcendental account (the subjective conditions that make possible a certain type of religious experience) and a historical, phenomenological account, tracing the objective, developmental stages in this consciousness. The text expressly invokes Hegel's *Philosophy of Right* for its theory of the state and community, providing evidence for Bauer's early interest in this work, which culminates in the conception of the historical process and the necessary transformation of the state in the *Landeskirche* and "Der christliche Staat."[47] The opposition between the religious consciousness and forms of ethical life is not grasped in all its consequence in 1838, but its extension is less a radical break than a process of continuous development in Bauer's thinking. What remains constant is the attempt to equate thinking and being, and to explore different channels by which this unity may be effected.

The unity of thought and being, the central theme of the 1829 manuscript, is a decisive feature of Bauer's political critique in the *Vormärz*. After he establishes his own specific Left-Hegelian stance in 1839–40, he retains the idea of the unity of thought and being in the dynamism and openness of infinite self-consciousness. The latter is not a static structure, but a process of becoming, the historical realisation of freedom. Bauer's theory of self-consciousness is not a retreat to an abstract antithetics of the understanding,[48] nor a mere subjectivism, but has as its basis the identity of self-consciousness and history. Antithetical oppositions are frequent in Bauer's texts. In the *Posaune*, he even calls for revolution against the past.[49] But these antitheses, between the new and the old order, autonomy and heteronomy, are integrated as elements in a larger, dialectical pattern. Bauer emphasises the antithetical features of the existing state and society, but he maintains that their effective overcoming depends on recognising the dialectical course of history. Reflection on history, as the product of self-consciousness, reveals an immanent universal process, whereby individuals can orient their activity and elevate themselves above their particular interests. The consistency of Bauer's project, and his resolute modernism, lies in his defence of an immanent universality. It is the universality of thought, uncompromised by any particular interest, and surveying the whole of its historical accomplishment.

Bauer criticises hypostatised or false universals, causal forces that transcend the power of individuals or impose themselves imperatively on individual activity. This is the basis of his rejection of religion and political absolutism in the 1840s. The transformative energy of thought must be distinguished from immediate, particular consciousness, because particularity is not self-determining. It reflects the values of the existing order and its egoistic material interests, and is therefore heteronomous. To avoid this determination by immediate interests, there must be universals, but these must remain immanent in the creative power of individual self-consciousness. Effective universality is located in history as the record of our own deeds. By this understanding of the historical process, we orient ourselves in the present, and from it we draw the practical maxims of action, especially of transformative political action. Bauer repudiates ideas of freedom based on the assertion of particular interests, whether religious, economic, or political; he identifies liberalism with such particularistic self-assertion. Even when it appears to resist and oppose existing institutions, Bauer claims that particular consciousness remains indeterminate, and it must elevate itself to universality before it can undertake a principled critique. Infinite self-consciousness demands that individuals acquire the discipline of universality, repudiating their attachments to alienated, merely given forms of life and achieving clarity about the intellectual bases of their opposition. Access to universality is not an immediate fact of consciousness or psychological datum but the result of intellectual labour that moulds the self according to universal purposes or a general will, as disclosed by critical reflection upon history. Under these conditions, the finite consciousness becomes the existence-form of the rational idea.

The aesthetic concepts of 1829 are the forms through which important aspects of this unity of particular and universal can be thought. They remain fundamental in Bauer's later critical theory. The disinterestedness of self-consciousness is manifest in its opposition to immediate subjectivity, and in its repudiation of private interest, the source of heteronomy. Its finality is that of self-determination, the subordination of the realm of spiritual production and of nature to the rule of freedom, together with the recognition that no product can encompass the richness of the creative subjectivity that is its source. Its universality and necessity are exhibited in the dialectic of universal, particular, and singular, through which the purging by the self of private engrossments occurs.[50] Here the aesthetic model converges with the demands of ethical idealism, another facet of the unity of thought and being as Bauer works it out in the *Vormärz*. True singularity is autonomous. It has reflected on, internalised, and made concrete the universal interests of emancipation; it has liberated itself from the fixity and rigidity of particular interests. For Bauer, autonomy is not action in accord with pure, timeless duty, but a historicised version of Kantian perfectionism, or *Vollkommenheit*,[51] taken as an uncompromising commitment to transform political relations and institutions. Duties are not fixed in an atemporal categorical imperative, but evolve in relation to the variable forms of ethical life in which subjects participate. Yet these duties originate in what can still be called pure, rather than empirical, practical reason, as their aim is freedom rather than happiness. The attainment of autonomy is the act of the individual subject, the agent of the dialectic of universal and particular, whose struggles bring about a new reality more closely, though never definitively, in accord with its concept. Subjects raise themselves to genuine universality by freeing themselves of determination by heteronomous impulses, and by repudiating transcendent universals, those religious and political institutions that claim to be underivable from self-consciousness, and exempt from history. The rational freedom of subjects begins with the rejection of all forms of heteronomy; its substance is found in the demands of the historical moment, interpreted by the critical judgement.

In an important respect, Bauer's theory of self-consciousness in the *Vormärz* is not anticipated in his 1829 critique of aesthetics, and yet this aspect too derives from an engagement with Kant and with the aesthetic judgement. Bauer's later theory manifests a close proximity to Kant's analytic of the sublime, particularly the dynamically sublime, as the supremacy of the moral consciousness over nature.[52] The experience of the sublime does not immobilise its subjects in the mode of contemplation, nor incline them to reflect on the paltriness of their efforts faced with the overpowering majesty of nature. It rather incites them to exert their powers. It is the ethical subjects who manifest grandeur in the valour of their struggles for freedom.[53] In his account of universal self-consciousness in the *Posaune* and elsewhere, Bauer celebrates the elevation of the infinite creative power of consciousness over its products, the inexhaustible productivity of freedom, but also its repugnance to any closed, circumscribed totality.

In this sublime objective process, the unity of subject and object, thought and being, is achieved in the historical process as a whole; reason does not imply a static structure, but transformational activity. It is the entirety of the process, and not its momentary incarnation in institutions or relationships, that effects the synthesis of concept and objectivity. Even if no particular object can be fully adequate to the rational idea, this position does not amount to the devaluation of objectivity in general, nor is it inimical to realisation of reason in the world. In Bauer's *Vormärz* texts, the unity of thought and being must be seen in two dimensions, a permanently incomplete objective task, and the reflection, distillation, and harmonisation of the process within the rational self-consciousness of individual subjects. This is the domain of universal self-consciousness, a reflection into self of dynamic objective processes originated by the subjects' deeds; it remains distinct from the passivity and introspection of the epistemic self-reflection, which treats inner psychic contents as objects, and which both Hegel and Kant criticise. But this dynamism of self-consciousness raises other potential problems. Bauer wishes to avoid the implication of the spurious infinite that the task of constant transformation readily evokes, and of which Hegel is forever critical.[54] He does so by reverting to the aesthetic judgement. As Bauer explains in the 1829 manuscript, an object is beautiful if its concept corresponds with its reality[55]; this definition applies *a fortiori* to the subject. It is the subject who stands as a point of relative repose, a recurrent figure of the realised unity of thinking and being. The beautiful unity and harmony of the autonomous self is the subjective culmination of the historical process, in distinction to the unfinished objective side, though both sides contain their own dynamics. The sublimity of the struggle for freedom, the endless objective movement, reposes upon a beautiful foundation, the unity of thought and being forged within the subjective consciousness itself. This unity is achieved by the subject's own efforts; it is not a permanent, immediate foundation, but is itself an ever-renewed result. Here the unity of beauty and the disharmony of the sublime are thought together in an active synthesis. This duality is the directive idea of infinite self-consciousness, as Bauer develops it in the 1840s.

Bauer does not regard this new formulation as a reversion to a Kantian *Sollen* or abstract ought, against which he had polemicised in 1829. He sees it rather as the self-actualising power of reason, enriched by its necessary educative process of alienation, withdrawing into itself from the inadequate forms of its realisation, and externalising itself anew in higher forms of ethical life. This theme is prefigured in the schema of reason in the 1829 manuscript, describing three moments of historical becoming: the constricted unity of the Greeks, the mediaeval opposition of faith and reason, and the diremptions of modernity, which also holds the power to reunite its extremes in a more comprehensive synthesis of subject and object. Of particular relevance to Bauer's later ethical thought is the distinction the manuscript proposes between two types of subjectivity. Mere subjectivity (*nuda*, or *abstracta subjectivitas*)[56] is impotent to effect its object, and so stands opposed and unreconciled to objectivity. It cannot bring about the unity of thought and being, which is the *telos* of philosophy. In contrast, Bauer describes rational subjectivity in its genuine element, as a moment of the universal, issuing forth into new forms of objectivity. The universal self-consciousness that he theorizes in the 1840s is likewise taken to be such a creative, transformative power, remaking objectivity in the image of rational thinking.

This complex of aesthetic and ethical ideas is fundamental to Bauer's later work, and his republicanism. His texts of late 1841 to mid-1842 analyse the political and ideological conjuncture in which self-consciousness asserts its rights. In *Die Posaune des jüngsten Gerichts* (1841),[57] to be analysed more fully in Chapter 5 of the present work, Bauer assumes a position that, for all its provocative radicality, is anticipated by the 1829 text: he reverses the theoretical priority of religion to art within the system of absolute spirit. He is now much more explicit about the significance of this reversal. In religion, self-consciousness is alienated, and appears to be passive, though it is never truly so. Rather, thought deceives itself about its own activities, attributing them to another, transcendent source, which it has unknowingly generated. This is a dialectical illusion, arising from the defects of positivity, the historically given limits of civil and political life. It is not simply a projection of ontologically fixed categories, as in Feuerbach's account of species attributes.[58] Art, in contrast to religion, reveals and affirms the activity of spirit, though still in a material element. It is thus more closely akin to philosophy. This conclusion accords perfectly with the 1829 manuscript, now drawing out the conclusions that were still implicit there.

In his anonymous continuation of the *Posaune* of 1842, entitled *Hegels Lehre von der Religion und Kunst*,[59] Bauer asserts, again provocatively, that Hegel's hatred of positivity leads inexorably to the overthrow of the state.[60] The critique of religion is the means to initiate political revolution.[61] As he had done in the *Posaune*, he stresses Hegel's affinity for the French Revolution and his contempt for petty German conditions. Bauer's account also draws heavily on his 1829 criticism of Kant's aesthetics. Elaborating his critique of religious alienation, he contends that the categories of religion "invert the laws of the real, rational world, alienate the universality of self-consciousness, rend it violently away or bring it back to representation as an alien, limited, sacral history."[62] He stresses that theology is determined by material interests, the survival of the sect and of the cult immobile against the forces of progress. It stands in opposition to the aesthetic disinterestedness of universal self-consciousness, which is both pure (untainted by the forms of positivity) and free (open to change and self-renewal).[63] While not burdened with the defects of the positive order, self-consciousness is nonetheless objective, in that it responds to the specific contradictions of the times, and finds their immanent solution. He characterises the freedom of self-consciousness in terms he had used in 1829 to describe the aesthetic judgement, in its qualitative liberation from any particular interest. This aesthetic self-consciousness is not merely contemplative. To find it so is to deny the power of spirit to change the world, as Bauer had argued against Kant in 1829. It is rather the active power of self-realisation in ever renewed forms, the infinite confidence of creativity that it need never bid the present moment stay. Objectively, the unity of thought and being is achieved in a process of permanent transformation.

Hegels Lehre develops the theme of the historical productivity of spirit as purely immanent action, requiring no forces transcendent of individuality.

> Reason is the true, creative power, for it produces itself as infinite self-consciousness, and its ongoing creation is the "rich production which is world-history." [Hegel, *Philosophy of History*, 18.] As the only power which exists, spirit can therefore be determined by nothing other than itself, or its essence is freedom. This is not to be understood as if freedom were simply one of the properties which men possess among others. On the contrary, "all properties of spirit exist only through freedom, all are only means for freedom, all seek and bring forth only freedom." "Freedom is the only truth [*Wahrhafte*] of spirit." Freedom is the infinite power of spirit, whereby I am dependent on nothing other [than myself], that is, that I am always only

self-relating [*bei mir selbst*] even in all oppositions and contradictions, and in all relations and determinations, since all of them are posited only by myself and in my self-determination. "Spirit is the self-relation, which is self-consciousness." Freedom, the only purpose [*Zweck*] of spirit, is also the only purpose of history, and history is nothing other than spirit's becoming conscious of its freedom, or the becoming of real [*wirklichen*], free, infinite self-consciousness. [Ibid., 20–23.][64]

The means whereby this general idea of freedom assumes determinacy are the will and activity of individuals, who act not as unconscious bearers of a transcendent purpose but as responsible, creative, autonomous subjects.[65] These individual subjects are designated as both *telos* and *energeia* of the historical process. In their elevation of themselves to a universal perspective, free subjects prove themselves to be the effective unity of thought and being. While the objective unfolding of reason is a constantly renewed task, it is the reality of such free self-consciousness that is the subjectively rational.

Hegels Lehre also completes the restructuring of absolute spirit that had already been adumbrated in Bauer's early critique of Kant's aesthetics. "Faith excludes all doubt,"[66] he had there written, and thus it eliminates the questioning and the seeking of proof that are proper to reason. Art, in contrast, is more closely aligned with philosophy, because both portray the active penetration of being by thought. In 1829, Bauer had not yet fully realised the implications of this position. In *Hegels Lehre*, the radical opposition of religion to art and philosophy is thematic. Against religion as indeterminate feeling, art and philosophy share determinacy and clarity, and a common ethical root.

> The content of art according to Hegel is the individual self-consciousness. In it the ethical powers are not merely a fortuitous, God-given supplement or gift, nor a superficial covering over the merely natural. Rather, self-consciousness is an inner, personal drive [*Leidenschaft*], whose character is a particular, determinate ethical power.[67]

Religion is always thought alienated, while art is a moment in the overcoming of alienation and in the unity of thought and being. Even if the artistic standpoint is limited in its ability to manifest truth by the materiality of its expressive forms, it stands infinitely closer to philosophy than does the abject religious spirit. It is art that reveals the secret of religion, its alienated human origin. In his conclusion, Bauer evokes an image he had employed at the end of his 1829 text, but he infuses it with an optimistic content. In the earlier text, the cold and lifeless forms of abstract reflection had secured, in Kant's system, a victory over the forces of reason and concreteness. The triumph is now that of liberated reason, exulting in the defeat of subjection and alienation.

Hegel thinks that if we repudiate the objectivity of art [i.e., if we now occupy a higher theoretical standpoint than that represented by art. DM], we repudiate in this free production of the human spirit also that objectivity which we honour in religion as an alien, revealed [truth]. But art has revealed this [truth] as our own creation, as our own thought, or, if you will, as our heart. If then we repudiate the objectivity and external appearance of art, we want to recognise no other object or no other objectivity than thought, than self-consciousness, than the thinking of thinking, that is, the ultimate unity of thinking and object. Art has taught us that religion is our own thought. If now we transcend the outer objectivity of art, what can that mean but that we want to grasp thought in the form of thought? After the labour of art, shall we again treat our thought as something alien, granted to us as a gift? The objectivity of art is the humanising of religion. Now that art stands astride the ruins of the fortress which held us imprisoned, and shouts "Victory!", should we then return to the prison, to barbarism, to inhumanity? No! No![68]

This image of exultant victory recurs in an article published in the *Rheinische Zeitung* of 1842, reviewing a performance of Beethoven string quartets. Here Bauer attributes a politically transformative role to art. He stresses the identical object of art and philosophy, awakening the powers of spirit to their untrammelled employment. Art, in this case music, is the intuition of freedom, rendering concrete and accessible the content of philosophy; but now the unity of thought and being, as depicted in art, is even more directly evocative of practical activity than is theoretical speculation. In his unpublished Jena manuscripts, Hegel had contrasted the musical/restless and the plastic/restful.[69] For Bauer, too, music is *stürmerisch*, sublime. It is a symbol of his theory of self-consciousness.

But what are the struggles, sufferings, and contradictions for which this quartet awakens our sympathies and whose resolution it hails? It is one and the same struggle, which mankind knows and must undergo: the sufferings and resolution which every art depicts in its fashion. It is the struggle of mankind with itself, which only assumes different forms. It is the struggle which expresses itself in our own breast as the conflict of feelings or as the struggle of thoughts which impugn each other. It is the struggle of persons, who belong together according to the idea, but who are cut off from each other in this world of deception. They seek each other, approach each other, lose each other again or are torn apart, seek each other all the more eagerly, because the spiritual powers, which are pent up in their breast, belong together; and at last, after a thousand wanderings, they find each other for ever. It is, finally, the struggle with the eternal powers, which have their origin only in the human breast, but which again appear in the world of deception as alien, other-worldly, violent powers, which want to repress or imprison man, who alone has given birth to them. But the man who lives and struggles in art is the true, free man, who is conscious of his omnipotence. He will not allow himself to be captured, he struggles against the apparently other-worldly pressure. If he succumbs for a moment, it is only in appearance. He does not rest from his exertions until he has summoned and finally compelled the rancorous and threatening voice of the tyrant – for it is after all only the voice of his own breast – to accompany in perfect harmony his last celebratory song. The prison is shattered, the fortress is stormed, and on its ruins man sings the song of his freedom.

Criticism and philosophy have to reason long, before they can convince man of his humanity. Beethoven plucks him rejoicing from his prison, and in his symphonies, with a drum roll, he thunders out to him that he is free. The philosopher must follow many by-ways; Beethoven storms the fortress head on, and already in his initial advance he lets the prisoners know that the hour of their liberation is at hand.[70]

In the same passage, Bauer describes the orchestra itself as a symbol of emancipated society, in that the exertion and perfection of each individual is requisite for the realisation of the whole. The strivings of each performer for excellence in no way impair the development of other individuals, but are their very condition. The artistic harmony thus attained is the result of the fullest deployment by all members of society of their specific qualities. In rational social forms, individuals are not limits to each other's perfection, but, to anticipate Marx in the *Manifesto*,[71] the free development of each is the condition for the free development of all. The unity of thought and being requires not one exemplar, but many.[72]

Bauer's critical theory in the 1840s is an attempt to identify such liberated subjects, and to unmask the pretensions of particular interests disguised as universals. The vicissitudes of that quest, and of its failure, are those of the revolutionary movement itself. The bastions of positivity resisted the onslaught, and the oppositional forces proved unprepared for the assault, as Bauer had, after 1842, increasingly predicted. Bauer's view of history, his criticism of the old order, and his revolutionary ethics are all rooted in the unity of thought and being, the central insight that, for all the differences in interpretation and application, he derives unequivocally from Hegel, and voices already in 1829. The themes of the early manuscript recur in many forms in Bauer's later writings. Most important, the text alerts us to a directive idea in his work, a concern for the objective realisation of reason, and the consequent critique of subjectivism. We should be careful not to read his critical theory as a type of such subjectivism. His view of history and the ethics of republican transformation must be examined with this injunction in mind.

2

"FREE MEANS ETHICAL": IDEALISM, HISTORY, AND CRITICAL THEORY

Bauer's critical theory attains its mature form after 1839, with the complex interweaving of aesthetic and ethical motifs in an original, Hegelian republicanism. The diffuseness of Bauer's writings requires us first to examine the model synthetically, reconstructing it from its many fragmentary expositions, and exploring its general outlines, as it applies to the subjective and the objective dimensions of history. We can then trace its detailed elaboration through the writings of the *Vormärz*. The Hegelian idea of the unity of thought and being, expressed in the language of infinite self-consciousness, is fundamental to Bauer's conception of the historical process, the necessity it contains, and the critical judgements it elicits. In the 1840s, Bauer employs the concept of infinite self-consciousness to describe this unity. This concept replicates features of Hegelian objective spirit and develops the relation between self-consciousness and its historical manifestations. Bauer proposes to derive legitimate and determinate content for this consciousness through a specific form of ethical idealism, to which the previous literature on the Left Hegelians has been insufficiently attentive: a conception of an evolving *Sittlichkeit* infuses his model of immanent critique, his doctrine of autonomy, and his repudiation of heteronomy. The thought of the historical process as a whole permits a universal perspective from which to make judgements on the existing order. These judgements articulate Bauer's republicanism in the 1840s, though the limits of his political critique will also appear in a sharpened dichotomy between universal and particular interests, especially apparent after 1843. We must first restrict our attention to the formal aspects of the critical theory. The substance of Bauer's conception of history, and of his republicanism, will be treated subsequently, as these ideas unfold more concretely in his texts of 1839 to 1849.

Bauer's central concept, infinite self-consciousness, is clearly of Hegelian origin. Hegel describes personality as the ability to give oneself one's own determinations, to transform given particularity into conscious individuality by investing it with reflective choice. In the beautiful individuality of classical Greece, individuals, exemplifying predetermined values, *aretai* or excellences,[1] stand in the relation of accidents to the substance of their community, in that their autonomous moral conscience is not yet fully developed. Against this constricted unity, Hegel credits modernity with the perfection of the free and infinite personality, which is capable of enduring and reconciling contradictions in a higher, more differentiated totality.[2] The *Philosophy of Right* gives a complex account of autonomy as willing and participating in the modern institutions that determine us, that endow our particular aims and actions with content and with intersubjective recognition. In Hegel's own concept of universal self-consciousness, this recognition of the self in other subjects is purely formal, occurring, as a facet of subjective spirit, in abstraction from a definite institutional context; this latter is established through the higher determinations to which Hegel gives the name of objective spirit.[3] Bauer's infinite self-consciousness is a variant of these ideas, but for him, no set of institutional forms can adequately express or permanently orient the creative fullness of the self. This shift towards the subject does not entail for Bauer a retreat to a merely subjective idealism or to an antithetics of consciousness, but refers us rather to the historical process as a whole.

> Our time has the distinction of being that in which the historical spirit turns back into itself out of its previous evolution and extension, gathers itself together, collects in memory all the moments of its development, and works them up into a spiritual unity.... In our time, therefore, there occurs the process in which the self-consciousness of absolute spirit will complete and close off the recollection of its historical revelation. For this recollection, no essential historical moment will be lost, least of all the real totality of historical appearance [*Erscheinung*]; on the other hand, nothing of the limits and deficiencies of the former conception remains behind, and the first step in its completion consists in the reflection on those limits, as they transcend themselves [*wie sie sich an ihnen selbst aufheben*]. This task of chastening, purification, and transfiguration modern criticism has taken over.[4]

While emphasising the antithetical features of the existing order, Bauer maintains that their overcoming depends on recognising the dialectical pattern of history. Reflection on history, as the product of self-consciousness, opens the possibility of an immanent universal, whereby individuals can elevate themselves above their particular interests. This process has two sides: It comprises subjective self-transformation, and objective judgements about the correspondence between existing institutions and the universal concepts they embody. These judgements are of a special type. Bauer's version, upon which his political criticism is based, corresponds in principle to what Hegel's *Logic* describes as the apodeictic judgement.[5] Its underlying necessity is rooted in the unity of the historical process, which has now been divulged to critical awareness, and depicted in its essential features, largely as the achievement of the Hegelian system. Hegel's supreme merit is to permit for the first time a comprehensive grasp of history, from which vantage point the present can be assessed and changed.

Consistent with Hegel, Bauer insists that self-consciousness is not an immediate, particular awareness, but results from a highly mediated, syllogistic process, the creation of singularity as a dialectical unity of particular and universal. Self-consciousness is a historicised version of the transcendental unity of apperception. The self is the formal principle of unity that maintains itself against the multiplicity of content; it appropriates this content by critical reflection, transforming given properties into conscious acquisitions. Beyond this formal unity, the self possesses a rich historical content. The theory of self-consciousness depicts subjects' activities in unifying experiences under concepts, encountering contradictions that these concepts entail in relations towards objects and other subjects, and acting practically to give reality, or a changed reality, to the concepts. From his earliest writing to his critiques of the failures of 1848, Bauer regularly differentiates two types of self-consciousness: the *merely* subjective, which cannot transpose itself into actuality, and which remains a mere *Sollen* or an impotent "ought" above it; and the subjective-infinite as the vehicle for the actualisation of reason, as a moment in a syllogism whereby the universal is mediated with the particular. The universal becomes concrete by the assimilation of particular contents, while the particular elevates itself to universality by becoming the self-conscious bearer of reason. In this singularity, the mutual fusion of unity and diversity, of universal and particular, the abstract opposition of the extremes is overcome. Bauer's central theoretical concept rejects the antithetical posing of elements in fixed oppositions, in favour of their dialectical mediation. It is through this synthetic process that self-consciousness becomes the organ of reason and of spirit. The language of self-consciousness stresses the formal side of this process, its roots in the subjective actions of individuals. It avoids the implications of transcendence that Bauer finds in some of Hegel's own formulations.

Yet for all its stress on the mediating activity of individual consciousness, Bauer's programme is not a radical subjectivism.[6] While van den Bergh van Eysinga, for example, is correct to state that Bauer replaces the Hegelian Idea with self-consciousness, this substitution does not occur entirely at the expense of the universality of reason. Bauer does not renounce the universal attributes of Hegelian spirit; rather, it is their (sometimes) deceptive appearance as a power independent of rational subjects that he seeks to annul. These aspects must now be shown to be predicates of self-consciousness itself. Already in the mid-1830s, Bauer characterises critique as the power that self-consciousness exerts over objectivity, leaving no object untransparent, but negating the rigid positivity of things, and recognising its own work in the element of externality.[7] The bearers of critical self-consciousness are concrete empirical subjects, but in their universal, not particular characters.

> When we employ the category of self-consciousness, we do not mean the empirical ego, as if this had constructed its conceptions [Anschauungen] out of pure accident or arbitrary combinations.... Unlike the immediate ego, ... the developed self-consciousness ... relates to reality with a wholly different consciousness, a critical consciousness.[8]

Bauer depicts the self as mediating the extremes of universality and particularity, each of which both seeks and repels the other. Citing Hegel's *Philosophy of Religion* lectures, he elaborates,

> In thinking, I elevate myself to the Absolute over everything finite and am infinite consciousness, and at the same time I am finite self-consciousness, indeed I am this according to my whole empirical determination.... I am determined in myself as infinite against myself as finite, and in my finite consciousness against my thought as infinite. I am the feeling, the perception, the representation of this unity and this mutual struggle, I am that which holds together the competing elements, the effort of this preservation and the labour of mind [Gemüt] to become master of this contradiction. I am not one of those caught up in the struggle, but I am both opponents and the struggle itself.[9]

While the struggle is internal to self-consciousness, its contents or substantial aims originate from a universality inscribed in history and shared by rational subjects. From his interpretation of Hegelian objective spirit, Bauer derives the claim that the particular consciousness in opposition to existing institutions is indeterminate, and it must elevate itself to universality before it can undertake the principled critique of the positive. Genuine self-consciousness requires that individuals free themselves of determination by alienated, merely given forms of life. The pure, productive self-activity behind all concrete and limited forms of embodiment is the true element of freedom, and the essence of history. The product of activity is never an adequate embodiment of the infinite creativity of subjects; but the process of negation is controlled by their insight into the rational course of history. This provides an immanent concept of universality, whereby subjects can extricate themselves from the grip of particularity and of the existing order, and judge the historical situation in light of its objective contradictions and possibilities. It also yields a substantive content for the formal process of self-transformation. Subjects commit themselves to specific tasks, set by their historical context, which itself is a moment in the unfolding of the potentialities of self-conscious freedom.

These motifs are developed in a text that anticipates by more than a year Marx's "Theses on Feuerbach."[10] Here Bauer identifies the insufficiencies of previous philosophical traditions, both materialist and idealist, stressing the differing conceptions of freedom that arise from each of these traditions. He censures previous idealism, including Hegel's, for retaining seemingly transcendent entities and forces; in the *Philosophy of History*, for example, Hegel occasionally appears to hypostatise Absolute Spirit, to treat it as a subject, distinct from concrete individuals, that heteronomously determines or sanctions historical outcomes, though this reading is inconsistent with Hegel's logical and phenomenological accounts.[11] Hegel's apparent failure to clear away the vestiges of earlier religious metaphysics leaves individuals under the control of powers beyond their grasp, and of mysterious and irrational origin. Likewise, in Bauer's analysis of the unhappy religious consciousness, the production of a transcendent universal, in the mode of representation or *Vorstellung*, corresponds to the freezing of particularity in forms of egoism, whether of the cult or of the self, and the devaluation and dissolution of the bonds of ethical life. Bauer also points to a second version of heteronomy, which appears in eighteenth-century materialism. This position took sensuousness, and not rational self-determination, to be the defining characteristic of humanity.[12] Ultimately because of its inadequate, passive, and particularistic understanding of liberty, the republicanism of the French Revolution had failed to achieve a fundamental emancipation from the presuppositions and institutions of the old order; other proximate causes were at work, to which Bauer is attentive in his detailed histories. He repudiates the particularism of the immediate consciousness, which is the common basis of Enlightenment individualism, nineteenth-century liberalism, and the egoistic anarchism of his contemporary Max Stirner.[13] Particularity in its various guises is heteronomously shaped by the impress of the existing order, and by the narrow and egoistic material interests that correspond to it. All these forms represent spirit sunk in substantiality, thus erecting a transcendent power over itself.

The immanent presence of the universal in history, as recorded by the theory of self-consciousness, must also be distinguished from another form of immanence, the pantheistic substance metaphysic of Spinoza, which is reproduced in D. F. Strauss's reading of Hegel, and in his interpretation of the gospels as a product of the mythological consciousness of the early Christian community; and, relatedly, in Feuerbach's materialism.[14] Bauer describes this approach also as mysterious, because it invokes a universal which is immediately effective, without showing how it operates, how it is taken up and internalised by individual self-consciousness. Lacking the decisive moment of individuality, of form, which self-consciousness alone can provide, it dissolves individuals into

an amorphous whole, an undifferentiated and thus premodern universal.
Bauer will later offer a similar characterisation of socialism.[15]

> Spinoza's substance, although the dissolution of the religious representa-
> tion, is still the absolute in the form of a *thing*. Only in self-consciousness do
> the separated relations, all oppositions and contradictions, come into their
> unity, that is, they know themselves as one, since each one knows the other
> as itself. Self-consciousness does not proclaim itself as the absolute, but as
> infinite movement through all forms and oppositions of its creations, [it
> is] only the development of itself.[16]

Bauer's recurrent attacks on Spinoza, and on the implicit Spinozism of
Strauss and Feuerbach, offer further insight into his critical procedure.
As Bauer already noted in his 1829 manuscript, Hegel defines necessity
as the unity of being and reflection. This concept reformulates Spinoza's
problem of the correspondence between the two attributes of extension
and thought, grasping this as a relation between substance and subject in
the category of modality. Bauer follows Hegel in defining substance, as extension, not just as a spreading out in space, but as a succession in time.
The contribution of Bauer's ethical idealism is the emphatic rejection
of one possible interpretation of Spinoza, according to which extension
or substance is primary in respect to thought, or directly causes reflection. Any correspondence of thought and being thus secured would be
heteronomous. Bauer insists that the accord must be brought about by
subjective activity, both on the self and on substance. The formal characteristics of substance must be seen as the product of self-consciousness.
The Spinozism of Feuerbach and Strauss consists in this, that they do not
achieve an understanding of spontaneous formative action.

While Bauer acknowledges that Hegel's own philosophy retains a
Spinozistic dimension, he insists (in his pre-1848 writings) that this is
in principle offset by Hegel's Fichteanism, the recognition that self-
consciousness must appropriate and shape its world, and not simply be
immersed in it. In his texts of 1841 and 1842, Bauer defines *substance*
in Aristotelian language as the material cause, ascribing to self-
consciousness the power of formal causality. The substantial is not syn-
onymous with the objectivity towards which rational subjectivity aspires
but represents an undifferentiated unity, an amorphous universal, from
which the particulars have not yet emerged. Hence the term may be used
to describe early forms of community like the *polis*, whose members are
imperfectly individuated with respect to modern subjectivity. But, as the
Posaune will argue, the substantial is also an essential moment in the emergence of that modern subjectivity itself; it is a moment, however, that must
be assimilated and overcome.[17]

The solution to the antinomies of modern thought and experience
is to be found in a new form of judgement, which avoids the defects of

false or transcendent universality, and of rigid particularity. Universality is to be retained, but as an immanent history of self-consciousness; and particularity is to renounce its own limitations by reflecting on and internalising this process. In this sense, the objective course of history and the philosophy of self-consciousness are one. For Bauer, the unity of concept and objectivity in history is not the recognition of a given institutional structure, as might be concluded from the *Philosophy of Right*. It cannot be attained without a radical transformation of the objective order; but this transformation is prescribed by the historical process itself, understood as a whole. This idea may appear similar to a Kantian regulative principle or *Sollen*, rather than a Hegelian unity of thought and being. Indeed, Bauer seems to assert as much:

> Knowledge is free, frees the spirit, and its determinations transform the previous content into a new form, therefore also into a new content, into the laws of freedom and self-consciousness. Philosophy is therefore the critique of the existing: through knowledge, the spirit posits a distinction between knowledge and what is. What is and what should be are distinguished. The *ought*, however, is alone the true, the legitimate, and must be brought to recognition, mastery, and power.[18]

Despite this explicit affirmation, Bauer does not regard his formulation of self-consciousness as a reversion to a Kantian "ought," the abstract opposition of an idea and a reality unattuned to it, and impenetrable by it. Kant's atemporal moral subjectivity is an expression of what Bauer calls the *merely* subjective; it is impotent to effect its object, to engage with the real tendencies of the present, and so stands opposed and unreconciled to objectivity. It cannot bring about the unity of thought and being. Bauer's own *Sollen* is, in contrast, taken to be a constitutive power, and not a subjective regulative principle. The "ought" can be described as objective, insofar as its content is derived from analysis of the historical project of freedom, and of its specific configuration in the present. It brings to light an existing negative; it thus functions as a determinate negation, an identification of vital oppositions in the consciousness and institutions of the present, which make possible a transition to a higher and freer form of ethical life. What ought to be done is what the present requires, as the resolution of its essential contradictions, as the verdict that the present executes upon itself. This "ought" expresses the self-actualising force of reason, returning to itself from its alienation and from the inadequate forms of its realisation, and remaking objectivity in the image of thought. Formally, from the perspective of individuality or agency, the task of transformation can be accepted only as a free and rational commitment, an ethical decision. It is not allotted to any particular set of subjects by virtue of their social or political function. Like Fichte's concept of *Aufforderung* or elicitation, self-consciousness summons us to recognise and act upon our knowledge of freedom[19]; but this Fichtean juridical notion acquires an objective, material content through the historical phenomenology of consciousness. It invites, but does not enjoin, practical participation in the historical movement, helping to propel it forward by identifying and exacerbating, so resolving, immanent contradictions.[20] Self-consciousness is subjectivity in its genuine element, as a moment of the immanent universal, both as theoretical critique and as practical action. Bauer thus continues to insist on the objectivity of his principle. Though differing in important ways, Bauer, like Marx in *The German Ideology*, claims that his theory encapsulates the real historical movement, rather than juxtaposing to it an extraneous subjective ideal. In its essential features, Bauer's approach represents the apodeictic form of judgement. As Hegel defines it,

> Subject and predicate correspond to each other and have the same content, and this *content* is itself the posited *concrete universality*; it contains, namely, the two moments, the objective universal or the *genus*, and the *individualized universal*. Here, therefore, we have the universal which is *itself* and continues itself through its *opposite* and is a universal only as *unity* with this opposite. A universal of this kind, such as the predicate *good*, *suitable*, *correct*, etc., is based on an ought-to-be and at the same time contains the *correspondence* of existence to that ought-to-be; it is not this ought-to-be or the genus by itself, but this *correspondence* that is the *universality* which constitutes the predicate of the apodeictic judgement.[21]

In Bauer's theory of infinite self-consciousness, history is the objective universal, and autonomous, judging subjects are the individualised universal. Being and thought are identical in that the former is the content, the latter the form wherein this content comes to self-cognition. The subject of the apodeictic judgement also contains two moments, the opposition of being and the "ought," but this is recognised as an inner relation of the subject to itself. Bauer's distinction of particular and universal moments of self-consciousness meets this requirement in principle; we shall see how it acquires its specific content.

Bauer takes self-consciousness to encompass these two moments. It refers both to the movement of reality, and to its reflection in knowledge. It appears objectively, as the movement of history brought about by the emancipatory strivings of individuals, but it assumes a subjective shape when the process is grasped as a unity by individual subjects, who theoretically appropriate the results of the movement. In the process whereby self-consciousness vindicates its rights, the first moment

> is history, as spirit lives immediately in it and is present there as inner soul. As in this determination history is still immediately external and pure extension, so because of this pure externality it is also pure inwardness and subjectivity. . . . Both this elementary outwardness and inwardness are

here one and the same. The next stage is the real, conscious, voluntary separation of this interiority and outwardness, when history in its entire range becomes an object of consideration and of literary representation as a coherent whole. This progress stems from the power of objectivity itself, which gathers itself together out of its rarefaction in inwardness and seeks to condense, or it is the act of inner spirit in the object, which it animates as universal soul and now works up into self-consciousness.[22]

The content of infinite self-consciousness is the progression of external historical reality, which subjects recognise as their own accomplishment. In this lies its objective universality, and its immanence. These subjects likewise contrast with the more particularised subjects favoured by Enlightenment thought. In 1842, quoting approvingly the first edition of Hegel's posthumous *Lectures on the Philosophy of History*, Bauer maintains that only freedom, and not any given or particular determination, is the truth of spirit. History is not heteronomous determination by an alien force. Now, on the basis of Hegel's philosophical achievements and the experiences of modernity, history can be seen to be the record of our own self-production, as spirit struggles to grasp its own concept and to endow this concept with fluid forms. When subjects attain this insight, their consciousness unites the thought of history with its material process, concept with objectivity.[23]

The primacy of freedom means that, unlike the classics, no substantive goods can be recognised as permanently valid; there are no *tele* or purposes prescribed by nature. Unlike the Enlightenment, the end is autonomy, not the satisfaction of the claims of empirical practical reason for happiness. If Bauer's *Sollen* is distinct from the Kantian version, it also differs from the critical thinking of the Enlightenment, which effects upon the existing order a process that Hegel defines as the infinite judgement. This is characterised by a purely negative bearing towards actuality, and an overly particularised subject. The infinite is presented as disjointed, falling into two antagonistic sides, or combining contradictory assertions.[24] Here the term *infinite* bears a different sense from Bauer's concept of infinite self-consciousness. In the infinite judgement of the Enlightenment, the universal is dirempted, but in infinite self-consciousness, it reflects back into itself from its extension, and attains unity and explicit self-knowledge. The recognition that reason is all reality is Hegel's great principle of idealism,[25] and it is this truth that enables the transition from the infinite judgement, with its conflicting sides, to the apodeictic judgement. The contrast becomes apparent if we compare Holbach's *Le christianisme dévoilé* with Bauer's *Entdeckte Christenthum*.[26] While defending it against its pietist and romantic critics, Bauer sees the Enlightenment as an expression of a shallow rationalism that takes deceit and manipulation to be the sources of religion, thus failing to engage with the profound issues of alienation and the activity of self-consciousness that religion presupposes. For Bauer, the ground of religion is less duplicity than the self-abasement of reason before the lower capacity of representation or *Vorstellung*, or the alienation of human attributes in a transcendent domain. In religion, self-consciousness is seemingly passive, though it is never truly so. Rather, thought deceives itself about its own activities, attributing them to an alien source. That this is a dialectical illusion, and not simply a projection, differentiates Bauer's interpretation from the contemporary position of Feuerbach.

> The religious spirit is that splitting of self-consciousness in which its essential determinateness appears over and against it as a separate power. Before this power, self-consciousness must necessarily lose itself, for it has ejected into it its own content, and as far as it can still maintain itself for itself as ego, it feels itself as nothing before that power, just as it must consider it in turn the nothingness of itself.[27]

Still, Bauer reverts to antinomic depictions of religion and self-consciousness that can obscure the differences between his own thought and that of the Enlightenment. His approach to this question partly vindicates the charge of antithetical thinking frequently levelled against him, in opposition to the Hegelian sense of sublation[28]; but even this antinomy is ultimately dialectical. Once it has attained its fullness, self-consciousness overthrows the religious principle, but retains it in recollection as a necessary stage of its development, a necessary process of estrangement in which alone freedom is discovered. No essential content can be lost. As Bauer had argued in *Religion des Alten Testaments*, the Enlightenment could comprehend religion only as error and deception, thus as pure contingency[29]; it could not yet write the history of the alienation and redemption of spirit as an immanent and necessary process. Bauer sees his own thought as completing and transcending the Enlightenment standpoint. The critical judgement of the Enlightenment itself helps to effect the transition to a higher form. Unlike the perspective attained by infinite self-consciousness, which recognises only rational freedom as its essence, the Enlightenment clung to particular, sensuous attributes of the self, and mistook material extension and material satisfaction as the essential, common determinations of subjects.

> The French have generally conceived the movement of self-consciousness at the same time as the movement of a common essence, of matter, but could not yet see that the movement of the universe first becomes genuinely for-itself and is brought together into unity with itself only as the movement of self-consciousness.[30]

This limitation had important political consequences. Asserting the primacy of matter over spirit, the republicanism of the eighteenth century identified freedom with the rearrangement of existing positive elements, not with the exercise of autonomous creative activity. Its doctrine of virtue recurred to the past for particular examples, but did not grasp the historical process as a whole, as the history of the alienation and recovery of reason. In Bauer's conception, virtue is not the replication of the past, but the anticipation of the new through the comprehension and criticism of history, unlocking essential possibilities of the present. Now appears the great conjuncture in which the rational rights of subjectivity can definitively assert themselves. The opponents of freedom are the foes confronted by Enlightenment liberalism. Absolutism and a politicised, authoritarian religion still prevail, but the revolutionaries of the *Vormärz* forge new weapons to combat them. Self-consciousness has progressed since its eighteenth-century manifestations: Enriched by their struggles and fortified in their opposition, the progressive forces are able to appropriate the results of previous revolutions, and propel the political and social movement forward. The criterion is no longer immediate subjectivity and the rigid forms of its utility, but rational subjects who comprehend and transcend themselves in the flux of historical becoming.

> This transition consists in nothing other than the freeing of the atoms which up till now have been fixed in their own right, but which from now on can only win their equal justification by giving up the immediate rigidity with which they had held fast to their presupposed rights, and by setting themselves in unity with each other through the conquest of themselves. Self-denial is the first law, and freedom the necessary consequence.[31]

The work of the infinite judgement, in its negative bearing towards the objective order of ethical life, is to suspend particularity in that domain, especially religious conceptions and interests, and to purify the universal of irrational content. The supreme principle of the Enlightenment is that everything exists for the subject, but it did not yet possess an adequate understanding of that subject, continuing to represent it in the mode of immediacy, as the particular. When the infinite judgement comes to englobe even this particular, to expose it to a thorough critical scrutiny, the rigid immediacy of the subject itself is undermined. Through its irresistible movement and extension, the infinite judgement turns dialectically into a higher, apodeictic mode. In place of the mutilated human essence arising from particularity, which is also its own starting point, the Enlightenment discovers the universal concept of humankind, but in a general, abstract form. It thus effects the transformation into self-consciousness, regaining subjectivity for itself, permitting it to grasp its own universality concretely and to posit it in the world, and opening up the theoretical perspective from which the totality of the historical process may be assessed. That perspective is Hegel's. The principle of freedom, enunciated in the Enlightenment and the French Revolution, now needs to be practically elaborated in order to sweep away the vestiges of positivity and alienation, and irrational forms of ethical life.

Bauer's model of immanent critique is further differentiated from Marx's historical determinism. Although *The German Ideology*, which gives the fullest account of Marx's position on this question in the 1840s, remained unpublished for almost a century, the mutual polemics between the two camps make the issues clear.[32] Both theories claim apodeictic status, and both eschew as utopian any detailed description of future states; but the fundamental difference arises in the subjective underpinnings of revolutionary action. Marx sees a subjective necessity at work in the emergence of a universal class: The revolutionary subject itself is generated under necessity. For Marx, the bonds of collective labour and common interest are forged under the constraint of the capitalist accumulation process, creating the proletariat as the universal agent. Through its revolutionary act, the proletariat is to transform this social necessity into a free universality; but the coalescing of the many into one, with a single class interest, is a historically determined process. This class is objectively motivated to defend its common material interests, which demand, through the emancipation of labour, the complete restructuring of the productive apparatus, of civil society, and of the state. In Bauer's view, such an account remains heteronomous. He denies that the particularity of the proletariat can transform itself into a genuine universal.[33] As in the case of Jewish emancipation, he rejects the assertion of particular interest as a basis for liberation. He holds, finally, that revolutionary action is not necessitated by social position, nor can it be ascribed to any particular group. While the apodeictic judgement claims an objective necessity, identifying specific contradictions that require resolution, Bauer maintains that its subjective dimension is left free. There is a definite task to be performed, but no predetermined actors to effect it. The shape of this resolution, and the commitment to undertake it, entail acts of creative liberty by individual subjects.

While the theory of history reveals what contradictions objectively must be overcome, the rational commitment to fulfil this task arises in Bauer from an expressly ethical sense of freedom. Essential features of Bauer's republicanism derive from his doctrine of autonomy, which repudiates ideas of freedom based on the assertion of particular interests, whether religious, economic, or political. Equally, Bauer rejects hypostatised or false universals, which impose themselves imperatively on individual activity. He defines autonomy as a process of self-relating:

> As the free personality establishes itself inwardly through the act in which the self disregards everything by which it could be externally determined, relates itself to itself and determines itself in its inner infinity only by itself, so by this very act the person opposes himself, as the essential, to what is

external, removing from it the right to independent validity, and making it into the appearance and immediate existence of his will.[34]

The accord of the external with the rational will is the essence of ethical life or *Sittlichkeit*, as Bauer interprets it. His thought consistently opposes what Kant calls empirical heteronomy, and the transcendent versions of rational heteronomy. Kant defines heteronomous principles as those that denote an external object to which the will must conform. He distinguishes two forms – empirical heteronomous principles designate objects of sensibility, while rational heteronomous principles refer to intelligible goods that are independent of and prior to the moral will.[35] The latter form can be further distinguished into two types, consistent with Kant's text: first, the determination of the will with reference to universals that claim (or to which are attributed) a transcendent status; and second, perfectionism or *Vollkommenheit*,[36] doctrines of perfection for the sake of which an action is performed. Kant cites Leibniz as an example of the latter kind, Plato of the former. Unlike utilitarianism, which is an application of empirical practical reason aiming at happiness or need-satisfaction, perfectionism is a type of pure practical reason, aiming at freedom. Its defect for Kant is to misconstrue the basis of moral actions in terms of their effects, rather than their maxims, or else to build anticipated effects of an action illicitly into the maxim itself.

Bauer's historicisation of autonomy imparts to infinite self-consciousness its subjective commitment to transformative action. Rejecting Kant's separation of maxim and effect, and taking the historical process as the operation of an immanent universal, Bauer understands autonomy not to mean action in accord with pure, timeless duty, but to imply perfectionism, defined as an uncompromising commitment to the transformation of political relations and institutions. For Bauer, subjects attain their rational freedom by liberating themselves from determination by empirically heteronomous impulses, and from the illusions of transcendent rational-heteronomous principles. Their struggles bring about a new reality more closely, though never definitively, in accord with its concept; they are the *dynamis* and *energeia* of history.[37] "Free means: ethical!"[38] – but the ethical in Bauer must be understood in its perfectionist sense, even though Kant himself repudiates this form. It is an ethical, and not merely moral, stance, because it is rooted in the historical record of the forms of *Sittlichkeit*. Thus Koigen, in his history of philosophical socialism, is incorrect to claim that there is no trace of ethical idealism in Bauer.[39] Bauer's ethic prescribes that the self is to be shaped into a rational, aesthetic whole, proving its own autonomy in the world, and so participating in the struggle for historical progress. The partisans in this struggle are "citizens in the republic of self-consciousness,"[40] whose task it is to prove in activity the human face of universality. The vision of a new form of ethical life, open to constant transformation, is inspired by a comprehension of the dialectical unity of history. This idea also takes up the motifs of the aesthetic model, deriving from Bauer's earliest work. The objective dimension is that of the linear infinite, the unfinished, sublime struggle against all limitations of freedom. The subjective dimension is that of the reflexive infinite, the beautiful consummation achieved by the self-conscious individual, or the return of reason from its externality, enriched by its passage. That there may be an unresolved tension between and within these two forms becomes apparent as the revolutionary situation unfolds.

The application of Bauer's model of apodeictic judgement to the *Vormärz* political order will be traced subsequently. Its main features are our present concern. Two types of republicanism are typically distinguished: an instrumental account of political involvement to defend freedom in the private sphere, and a transformative type in which political participation makes possible an otherwise inaccessible freedom.[41] Bauer's republicanism is of the latter kind. It involves a critique of the existing state, as well as of rival conceptions of emancipation, notably liberal possessive individualism and socialism. In both absolutist and liberal-constitutionalist forms, the state arrogates universality to itself, denying the claims of the self to rise to universality by its own efforts. Like the religious consciousness that it sustains and nourishes,[42] the nonrepublican state is always a "beyond," a spurious infinite rising over a mass of particulars without achieving a genuine integration of its moments. Against this static configuration, Bauer asserts the power of free self-consciousness. "The movement surges ahead precisely because it serves the general interest."[43] The unity of the empirical self with universality is a concrete historical possibility; the task of the present is to bring this possibility to fruition.[44]

Bauer stresses the inability of the Restoration state to undertake this necessary work. He summons to the task the genuine revolutionary forces, those who seek the overthrow of the existing state, because it is incapable of completing its historically necessary emancipatory mission. Bauer's affirmation of a republican revolution links the triumph of free self-consciousness with the victory of a previously excluded class, understood not as a social category but as the partisans of the emancipatory principle. As Marx and Lenin will later do in reflecting on the Paris Commune, Bauer advocates not mere participation in the existing state but the creation of a new form of state to accommodate the principle of universal rational freedom. The existing tutelary state cannot simply be taken over and used for progressive purposes, but its instruments and structures must be completely refashioned in the name of freedom and autonomy.[45]

Bauer's republicanism also contests the liberal defence of immediate economic interests. Based in materialist utilitarianism, liberalism constricts the universality of spirit through the domination of the object, as particular goal of satisfaction, or material appropriation. Bauer argues that this equation of freedom with accumulation is a form of heteronomy, a determination of the individual by the external force of property. For Bauer, freedom is not simply the freedom to enjoy, to amass property, or to validate one's immediate, contingent personality. The republicanism he envisages is distinct from appeals to the virtue of the past but is rooted in the specific character of modern development. He offers a new articulation of the eighteenth-century republican theme of the opposition of virtue and commerce.[46] He does not (yet) envision the triumph of substantiality, a return to agrarian simplicity – this will follow in the 1850's – but recognises new features of the nascent industrial order, while polemicising against its unprecedented dangers. The liberal view of freedom as the assertion of private right contributes to the dissolution of society into a mass, an aggregate of competing individuals heteronomously determined by its relation to property. Bauer argues that the tradition-bound pre-revolutionary order and liberal atomistic individualism mirror each other as expressions of particular interests, religious in the one case, economic in the other. Both militate against the rational self-determination of the subject, the elevation of consciousness from particular to general interest.

The distinction of heteronomy and autonomy underlies Bauer's description of the mass tendencies of modern society. Opposed to the forces of progress, the masses represent inertia and stagnation. Their inarticulate consciousness constitutes the real bulwark of the status quo. It is inaccurate to equate the masses here exclusively with the emergent industrial working class.[47] Despite his pessimism about the capacity of the proletariat for autonomous action,[48] Bauer describes as a principal component of the masses the vacillating liberal bourgeoisie, whose attachment to private economic interest makes concerted opposition to the existing state impossible. Historically, this egoistic orientation has caused the failure of previous revolutions; Jacobin political struggle had been unable to extirpate this attitude.[49] Criticising the abstract individualism and egoism of civil society, Bauer calls for a new, liberated individuality that subordinates accumulation in favour of a freely chosen identification with the progressive and revolutionary thrust of the historical process. Such a transformation, he contends, is not limited to politics, but suffuses all social relations with dynamism and justice.[50]

The league of equal right, created through heroic exertion and uncompromising struggle both against the old order and against the encroaching forms of modern civil society, is the essence of Bauer's republicanism. In 1843, he confidently affirms, "To the people belongs the future."[51] At the same time, the principle of particularism constantly lurks as a menace to freedom and self-determination, threatening the all-encompassing triumph of civil society over the emerging republican community. The serenity he invokes as an aphorism in his earliest text, of 1829, gives way in his writing to a profound sense of crisis.[52]

After 1843, a sense of impending failure underlies the judgements that Bauer formulates on the revolutionary movement itself. His criticisms of the defective self-consciousness of the opposition parties are wide ranging.[53] In them, he proposes not a juridical theory of politics, but an ethical one, asking what theoretical bearing one must have to count as a genuine member of the progressive forces. Bauer's recognition of the self-determining character of the judging subject means that no prescribed revolutionary agent can be invoked, but also raises the possibility that no concrete subjects may prove equal to the task. He imposes extremely stringent conditions on candidates for revolutionary consciousness, requiring the repudiation of particular interest. The precondition for political emancipation is the renunciation of all particularistic ties with the past. To defend a traditional identity or traditionally sanctioned rights is systematically to exclude oneself from participation in the progressive struggle, whose aim is to overcome and not to ratify all such inherited status. This is the root of Bauer's critical position on Jewish emancipation in 1843–44, whereby, for many of his contemporaries, he forfeited his leading role in the republican movement.[54] Here the relation of particularity and universality is clearly an antithetical opposition; and here the criticisms noted by van den Bergh van Eysinga and others are most directly relevant.[55] A similar process can be detected in Bauer's writings on mass society, in the antithesis between the self-activity and self-definition of critical thought, and the passive, merely sentient, heteronomous existence of the masses, even though he stresses that this category is not ahistorical. The French, for example, had succeeded in transforming themselves temporarily into a people by their heroic revolutionary exertions[56]; but Bauer's criticisms of the inadequacies of the current revolutionary movement become increasingly shrill as the crisis atmosphere deepens. The people to whom he appeals constitute an ever constricting circle. Despite his fiery proclamations of radicalism, Bauer's republicanism can find no adequate revolutionary subject. Its central claim, to unify thought and objectivity, erodes.

Repudiating the monarchical constitution and actively defending popular sovereignty,[57] Bauer retains his republican orientation until after the defeat of the Revolutions of 1848. Even in 1852, in a text that is highly problematic in other respects, he continues to describe his own work as completing the emancipatory transcendental project formulated by Kant.[58] That the revolutions failed to shake the existing order led to his subsequent repudiation of the architectonic power of reason.[59] In the 1850s, he opted for *Zusammenhang*, for coherence, for an objectivity impervious to subjective intervention, against the demands for political and social reform. These came to represent for him mere, and impotent, sub-jectivity. Bauer then disclaims perfectionism for the sake of a different figure, a beautiful unity or coherence: not the aesthetic unity of the self as artefact, nor the substantiality of the *polis*, but the solidity of premodern agrarian society. When he abandons the idea of creative subjectivity, the unity of thought and being assumes for Bauer the form of reconciliation with the positivity of the existing order. In its sacrifice of the becoming of reason to mere being, it is a reconciliation – or surrender – more com-plete than any dreamed of in Hegel's philosophy. Our concern, however, is not to investigate Bauer's subsequent transitions, but to delineate his republican stance in the *Vormärz*.

II

JUDGING THE OLD ORDER

"THE OTHER OF ITSELF": THE CRITIQUE OF THE RELIGIOUS CONSCIOUSNESS

Bauer's 1829 manuscript asserts that faith excludes all doubt, and thus it raises a doubt about the compatibility of religion and philosophy as moments of absolute spirit. The question that preoccupied Bauer throughout the 1830s was the possibility of a rational faith. His intellectual experiments initially seek to establish the unity of thought and being through a speculative account of the doctrines of Christianity (such as the incarnation and the immaculate conception), whose sole justification is to exemplify logical categories. He attempts these reconstructions in the articles he published in *Zeitschrift für spekulative Theologie*, edited by him between 1836 and 1838, as well as in earlier submissions to *Jahrbücher für wissenschaftliche Kritik*.[1] The importance of these articles is that they constitute a failed attempt to identify thought and being on the basis of religious representation. Bauer's response to his question of the 1830s is a resounding negative. As Zvi Rosen rightly maintains, "Only lack of knowledge of the source material can explain why certain scholars claim that Bauer suddenly became an atheist after holding orthodox views on religion for years."[2] In the 1838 *Religion of the Old Testament*, Bauer's account stresses the subjective basis of religious experience. Unlike the theology of contemporary pietists and of Schleiermacher, this experience is not located in ineffable feelings of dependence on a transcendent absolute, but represents stages in the acquisition of self-consciousness. Religious experiences are differentiated by the subjective conditions of their genesis: A legalistic subordination to an authoritarian deity underlies what Hegel's *Phenomenology* had defined as the first relationship, a relation of exteriority between God and man.[3] The messianic consciousness of the later books of the Old Testament heralds a new and higher form, perhaps anticipating Hegel's third relationship, the immanence of the universal in the concrete community; but at this stage of development, consciousness can only point up the inadequacy of the law, not yet propose its effective overcoming. The objective conditions are not yet at hand for a genuine transcendence of estrangement, which is the very foundation of the religious law. Bauer will take up this argument again in his *Herr Dr. Hengstenberg*, of 1839.

Bauer's historical account of the stages of the religious consciousness also differentiates his approach from that of the early Fichte, in its emphatic claim that knowledge of the supersensible or of subjectivity itself is possible. He thus offers an elaboration of the argument that, in 1829, he had described as the summit of his critique of Kantian philosophy. Fichte's *Versuch einer Kritik aller Offenbarung* remains tied to the Kantian problematic,[4] stressing the inaccessibility of the supersensible to theoretical cognition. Distinguishing, as in his later writings, causes from freedom and causes from nature, Fichte stresses the insufficiency of practical reason alone to raise individuals to respect for the moral law, without the concurrence of sensibility. This is the rationally justified role of religion. Fichte contrasts rational, natural, and revealed religion, depending on the relation of sensibility to practical reason in each case. Natural religion implies that sensibility is already consistently subordinate to the promptings of reason; rational religion presupposes that sensibility has been vanquished (as would be the case only for perfectly rational beings, but not for humans, who combine sensuousness and reason). Revealed religion has its authority in conditions where sensibility is not yet disciplined, and is thus necessary and appropriate to the present and past states of culture. Anticipating a question that will greatly exercise Feuerbach and Strauss, Fichte also maintains that certain attributes of God must hold as implications of practical reason alone: Divine omniscience and omnipotence are required to distribute happiness according to virtue. In this text, at least, Fichte's conception of the subject, based on the matrix of reason and sensibility, is neither social nor historical.[5] Bauer's account differs in these respects. Developing themes from Hegel's *Philosophy of Religion*,[6] he links forms of religious experience and forms of ethical life, and depicts these as an evolving theoretical self-apprehension.

The more specific achievement of the texts of the 1830s is to locate the logical structure that, for Bauer, defines the religious consciousness: It is the immediate identity between a particular subject, or a particular community, and the universal, achieved without self-transcendence, but in virtue of some given attribute. This identity is asserted by the religious consciousness as a monopolistic claim, excluding other particulars from equivalent status. The essence of religion for Bauer is thus a hubristic particularism, which also confers a transcendent status on the universal, as a separate realm, divorced from concrete social life, and inaccessible to genuine individual efforts. It is not an acquisition, but a gift, arbitrary and irrational. The immediate identity of universality with particularity makes a rational synthesis incomprehensible or impossible. As Bauer recognises the structural identity of the privatised religious consciousness with the political basis of the Restoration order, his political radicalism is cemented. In its particularism and monopolistic self-assertion, the religious sect is the antithesis of the republican community. Bauer makes the transition to republicanism by early 1840.

To recognise that Bauer's critique of religion is intertwined with political motifs is not to reduce religion to a merely instrumental role as an ideological support of the old order. This is the error that, according to Bauer, Enlightenment critics of religion had made, but its effect was to diminish the analytical power of their theory, and it led to incorrect assessments of subjectivity and of history. In Bauer's thinking, religion is fundamental to the understanding of the historical process, and thus is a necessary object of his critical theory. Critique explains why alienation occurs, giving both a general statement of its character, as a rigid particularism combined with a hypostatised universal, and a description of its evolutionary sequence. The immediate unity of particular and universal first occurs in the form of the substantial community of antiquity, especially the *polis*. As the claims of emergent subjectivity burst these confines, the constricted, naturally determined community of the Greeks dissolves into the spiritless world of Hellenistic and Roman imperial authority. In this figure, the One, the emperor, arrogates the authoritative voice of the community to himself, leaving others bereft of rational self-determination. The political realm thus appears as a transcendent universal, immediately one with the person of the emperor. The only solution available to the ancients was Stoic withdrawal into private self-reflection. The flight of the creative intellect left those incapable of this demanding inner discipline as a mass, determined by heteronomous impulses, but without political weight. This is the terrain on which Christianity emerges, as the unhappy consciousness that knows itself to be free, but cannot assert this freedom concretely, and so transposes it into a celestial domain. Nor does it comprehend the real meaning of its freedom as rational self-determination. Rather, freedom appears as caprice and mere particular self-assertion, which, repressed as sinful, constantly rears up again. In this relation of abjection, various movements of particularistic sectarianism occur, but these represent no real progress, or only further sacrifice the bonds of genuine ethical life to the authoritarian demands of the doctrinal system. The extremities of religious alienation in modern Protestantism betoken a dialectical transition to a new form of consciousness.

The views recapitulated here emerge in various texts written between 1839 and 1844. They are not yet fully formulated in Bauer's first explicitly critical texts. In its relation to his nascent republicanism, the development of Bauer's criticism of religion unfolds in three stages, represented by the publication of *Herr Dr. Hengstenberg*, the critique of the gospel of John, and the three-volume critique of the *Synoptics*. We will examine each of these stages in turn.

Bauer's first direct critical intervention into the political issues of the day is his text *Herr Dr. Hengstenberg. A Contribution to the Critique of the Religious Consciousness.*[7] Written as a series of letters to his brother Edgar, to serve as a propaedeutic to the latter's theological studies, it was composed in November and December 1838 and published by Ferdinand Dümmler in early 1839.[8] The context of the work is the heightening opposition to the Hegelian system mounted by conservative and pietist forces in the state. This is attested by Ernst Wilhelm Hengstenberg's triple attack, under the title "Der Verfall der Hegelschen Schule" ("The Decline of the Hegelian School"), appearing in Friedrich Tholuck's *Literarische Anzeiger* in August, September, and October, 1838, and Heinrich Leo's book, *Die Hegelingen*, of the same year.[9] Both works stress the social consequences of the open attack on religion then being waged by the Left Hegelians. While Hengstenberg traces this position back to Hegel himself, Leo distinguishes Hegel's lack of clarity on the central question of religion and philosophy from the impudence of his followers, who publicly proclaim the mythological character of the Gospels, the falsehood of Christianity, and ultimately atheism. Hengstenberg exerted powerful influence on the declining Friedrich Wilhelm III through his connection with the Kamarilla, a circle of court advisers that has been described as an ultra-conservative alliance of pietist clergy and landed proprietors. He called on the state to suppress the teaching of Hegelianism in the schools as disruptive of social tranquillity.[10]

What had particularly incensed conservative proponents of the Restoration was the publication, in early June 1835, of the *Life of Jesus* by D. F. Strauss,[11] of Tübingen. Immediately, on June 11, the state of Württemberg instituted proceedings to expel the author from the *Tübinger Stift*. In his book, which rapidly went through four editions, Strauss depicts the Hegelian distinction between philosophy and religion, concept and representation, as an antinomy. The contents of religion are not identical to those of philosophy but reflect a lower, pre-rational awareness. Religion is thus displaced within the system of absolute spirit. In describing God as pure subject devoid of predicates, or whose predicates are posited only by limited human representation, Strauss anticipates Feuerbach's argument in the 1841 *Essence of Christianity*.[12] He contends, further, that the gospel reports are mythological accounts of the early experiences of the Christian community, rather than revealed truth. In his subsequent text, *Streitschriften zur Vertheidigung meiner Schrift über das Leben Jesu (Polemics in Defense of My Life of Jesus)*,[13] Strauss defends a constitutional monarchist position, similar to Hegel's, and criticises the obscurantist politics of the Restoration, linking pietist theology and political oppression. The second volume of the *Streitschriften* attacks Schelling's philosophy of identity and the conservative theological current it inspired.[14] Strauss stresses Hegel's political liberalism, his consistent distinction of the rationally real from the positive or merely existing,[15] echoing Hegel's own defence, in 1827, of his procedure in the *Philosophy of Right*.[16] Though he never adopts a republican political stance, Strauss plays a central role in defining the political oppositions of the German Restoration. He insists that the contradictions between general and particular interests cannot be resolved in a separate religious sphere but only in the concrete community, the vehicle of conscious liberty. Strauss's analyses challenge orthodox claims that divine infinity and human finitude are reconciled in the person of Christ alone. It is rather the human species in its historical becoming, or its generic being, that realises this synthesis. The consequence of the religious arrogation of universality is to abandon the concrete community to a narrow and stifling egoism. The common elements of religious and political criticism are evident here: Universality must be reintegrated into the relations of social life. The dangers to the Restoration order are manifest. The conservative forces are quick to react.

In these circumstances of growing reaction, Bauer emerges to defend the progressive character of Hegel's system. He names Hengstenberg as a worthy adversary. While many spokesmen for the religious interest merely give voice to the shapeless and indeterminate conceptions of mass society [*die Masse*], and thus offer no point of attack, Hengstenberg develops a clear if erroneous position, against which criticism can take aim.[17] Bauer recognises the danger he runs in launching his attack. Recalling the horrors of mediaeval and early modern religious persecution, he depicts Hengstenberg as invoking the terrestrial authority to extirpate heresy, or any deviation from his own interpretation of religious doctrine. To Bauer's attack on Hengstenberg should also be compared the sharpened polemical tone of the fourth edition of Strauss's *Leben Jesu* (1839).[18] It has been suggested that Bauer's attack on Hengstenberg may have been prompted by the progressive figures in the ministry of education and religious affairs, including Johannes Schulze and the minister Karl von Altenstein, a close friend of Hegel's who had been responsible for his appointment to a professorship at the University of Berlin in 1817.[19] Both opposed Hengstenberg's growing political influence arising from his central position in the Kamarilla. Schulze and Altenstein later collaborated in securing Bauer a position in theology at the University of Bonn, where he gave his *Habilitationsrede* on October 23, 1839.[20] Bauer's support for Hegel's conception of religion was coldly received by his Bonn colleagues, who were designated the Schleiermacher faculty of Prussia. The text of his *Habilitationsrede* has not been discovered. In *Die gute Sache der Freiheit*[21] of 1842, Bauer characterises his Bonn address as developing two basic convictions: the need for the dissolution of the religious consciousness in the higher determinations of thought, and the claim that this dissolution is in accord with the ultimate truth of Christianity (meant here, presumably, is the unity of God and man, or of infinite and finite, which Christianity proclaims). Bauer says he worked out the implications of these two claims in the winter of 1839–40. The republican community is the genuine resolution of the aspirations voiced in Christianity.

In *Herr Dr. Hengstenberg*, Bauer does not yet identify himself with the extreme views that Leo ascribes to the Left Hegelians. He wishes simply to distinguish the positivity of apologetics (equated with the spirit of the Old Testament, on the one hand, and the fixity of the understanding, on the other) from what he calls the living pulsations of spirit, incarnate in Christianity correctly understood – that is, as Hegel understands it. Bauer thus derives an opposition between law and gospel, and denies an immediate historical continuity between Judaism and Christianity, a theme he had already developed in his book *The Religion of the Old Testament* (1838). Hengstenberg, in contrast, construes the relation of the Mosaic law and Christian revelation as noncontradictory.[22] Bauer illustrates the difference with respect to the concept of love. If in the Old Testament the love of God and neighbour is a mere command beside others, not grasped in its generality,[23] Christianity offers a genuine dialectical synthesis, freeing this attitude from its particularity and limitation, and recognising it as the expression of the human essence. Here this synthesis is still seen to have a transcendent ground. The universality to which humankind aspires is acquired in a properly conceived relation, not yet to itself, but to divinity. Such an aspiration would be vain, however, were human beings not already in essential oneness with the deity. In subsequent texts, Bauer will very soon identify the universality of self-consciousness in purely immanent terms.

> Only that is a rational ground, in which both what founds and what is founded interpenetrate [*sich zusammenschließen*] through the unity of their essential content. This ground would therefore only be internal, that is owing to the nature of both sides, if a determinateness were revealed in God which corresponded to the essential nature of man. This unity would then bring together both sides from within, and would found the religious observance. It does so at least in Christianity, in the measure that God proves in his revelation that His essence is love, and that it belongs to His essence to receive into unity with Himself man, who stands in distinction and opposition [*Gegensatz*] to Him. Thus it is also clear that it is the essence of man to transcend in unity his opposition to God. This love in Christ is effectively an inner principle [*Grund*] which man can follow in freedom, since he consciously follows his true concept when he follows that which is necessary in the concept of divinity.[24]

In its properly theological content, the text separates the spirit of Christianity from its dogmatic form, thus undermining the religious ideology of the Restoration state.[25] It is also of interest in formulating a version of the religious alienation of self-consciousness. Here the reference is to the externality of the law as the Old Testament describes it, as the command of an Other. "In its historical existence, the religious spirit has not yet worked out its concept in itself and still stands in contradiction to it, so that its will appears as the Other of itself, and not yet as its own will, but as the will of God, as a will essentially different from its own."[26] Within the span of two years, as we will soon see, Bauer will describe the Christian principle itself as burdened with such an externality. He will then draw out the implications of his own position regarding a genuinely immanent universal, now located in history. The acknowledgement of a transcendent ground is merely a stage in the maturation of consciousness, to the knowledge of its own truth and scope.

In contrast to the modern notion, Bauer here depicts the limitation of the subjective principle in classical as well as biblical antiquity. It is still engulfed in substance.

> All of antiquity lacked the thought of the infinity of personality. In the time of its dissolution, the particular moments of the notion were extruded, but even in Greece and Rome, when they were still unweakened, the person, however freely he moved in the substance of the social whole [*Volksganzen*], still had not yet cut himself off from it and grasped himself freely for himself as infinite.[27]

This position will be elaborated as a stage in the dialectic of self-consciousness in *Die Posaune* of 1841. Bauer already contrasts the determinate moral substance of the *Volk* with the oppressive indeterminacy of the mass, but he depicts the people in their premodern guise of substantiality. The concept he develops in 1840 attempts to synthesise the free universality implicit in the modern conception of personality with the possibility of new communal, republican forms.

After this public break with apologetics in the Hengstenberg text, Bauer's rapid political and theoretical radicalisation can be traced through an analysis of his Gospel critiques, whose composition spans two years from the spring of 1840. Bauer sees this series as a single project, in continuity with his 1838 *Religion of the Old Testament*; together they constitute a critique of the stages of revealed religion, but simultaneously a critique of the forms of self-alienated spirit in history. These texts are also personally crucial for Bauer, because the publication of the first volume of the *Synoptics* initiates the academic inquiry leading to his dismissal from the University of Bonn in March 1842.[28] The series comprises *Kritik des evangelischen Geschichte des Johannes (Critique of the Gospel of John)*, completed May 8, 1840,[29] with a dedication to Edgar Bauer dated August 21 of that year; *Kritik der evangelischen Geschichte der Synoptiker. Erster Band (Critique of the Synoptic Gospels, Vol. 1)*, written between August 1840 and February 1841,[30] and *Zweiter Band (Vol. 2)*, begun in May 1841,[31] with a conclusion dated July 1841; and *Kritik der evangelischen Geschichte der Synoptiker und des Johannes. Dritter und letzter Band (Critique of the Synoptic Gospels and John, Vol. 3)*, begun at the end of January 1842, completed at the end of March, and published in May of that year.[32] The critique of John has a distinct theoretical status from the *Synoptic* series. Because of their thematic unity, it will be convenient to treat the latter as a group, and to trace the evolution of Bauer's theoretical position in them, though their composition overlaps with texts discussed in chapters 4 and 5. It should be noted that Bauer begins the *Landeskirche* immediately after the critique of John's gospel. The first volume of the Synoptics is contemporary with the "Der christliche Staat." The composition of the second volume of the *Synoptics* immediately precedes that of the *Posaune des jüngsten Gerichts*, and the third volume immediately succeeds the writing of *Hegels Lehre*.

The *Johannes* text is composed against the background of Bauer's definitive repudiation of religion. His correspondence of December 1839 develops a sharp opposition between philosophy and theology. On January 5, 1840, he writes: "But as religious interest I understand that theoretical interest in religion which has its ground in the movement of philosophical science, that is, in the inner diremption and limitation [*Mangelhaftigkeit*] of philosophy."[33] The task of criticism is thus to free philosophy of its limitation, to develop the opposition of the two forms, whereby the religious interest is eliminated. The interplay of political and theoretical motifs in this development is clearly illustrated in Bauer's letter to Marx of April 5, 1840:

> Here [in Bonn] it also became clear to me what I did not yet want to admit in Berlin, or admitted to myself only with difficulty, that everything must fall. The catastrophe will be fearsome and must be a great one, and I might even say that it will be greater and more immense than the one in which Christianity entered the world. What is coming is too certain for us to be unsure about it even for a moment. . . . If the opposition triumphed in France, even after such a great reaction, this triumph will be even more certain and will occur sooner in an area where there is only a mute apologetics to fight against. . . . The hostile powers are now arrayed so closely together that a single blow will decide. The people who wanted to look out for themselves when they drew the state ever more into their interest have thus prepared their own final overthrow, and so they deserve thanks.[34]

In the context of a crisis that will thus engulf the existing religious and political order, Bauer's critique of John's gospel demonstrates in detail the opposition between the free self-consciousness and the religious spirit. Ostensibly, he wishes to restore the Christian principle to its true terrain, to grasp it as a product of creative self-consciousness, by annulling the positivity of Christianity, and what he calls the rigid reflection-character of its concepts. These concepts derive from the abstract understanding, rather than from speculative reason, that leads them back to their subjective source. He thus develops further the argument he had directed against Hengstenberg. Although he does not yet overtly draw this conclusion in the text, the restoration of the Christian principle is at the same time its overthrow, the exposure of its subjective source. This, according to Bauer's report, is the thesis he had already defended in his Bonn *Habilitation*. His critique is the demonstration of the necessity of Christianity as a stage in the development of human spirit, but a stage now transcended. Dissolving the Christian religion into its essence against its dogmatic forms, Bauer can then depict the movement of this essence to still higher and more universal determinations of free and autonomous self-consciousness. In this text, the relation of thought and being is at the forefront, and when Bauer speaks here of absolute spirit, the fundamental direction of his transformation of the categories is already in evidence.

To account for the positivity of Christian dogma, Bauer develops a critique of evangelical pragmatism, an alienated formative or literary activity that invents dramatic incidents, valueless in themselves, simply as a stimulus for a dogmatic pronouncement or act. In a succeeding stage of elaboration of the unhappy consciousness, a further display of its ensnarement in its own products, an apologetic theology then seizes on the incidents as well as on the immediate abstract reflection to which they give rise, and attempts to preserve the form against the true content. The original pragmatism and the subsequent apologetics are incapable of engendering true unity of thought and being, but only

> gospel harmonies, not a unity in which the defective shapes of the moments, alien to each other, were taken up and reconciled, but only the mechanical and violent forcing together of the elements. The moments were taken up just as they lay at hand, they remained in the shapes in which they were found, and they counted as absolute truth because the movement in which they transcend themselves was hemmed in by deceptive art and by violence.[35]

The characteristic of this consciousness is thus its inability to distinguish the contingent from the necessary. It is the affirmation of particularity, the irrational defence of the particular as the necessary manifestation of a universal that, uncomprehended, remains estranged from it. In this sense, John the evangelist is already the first apologistic theologian. While Bauer overtly concedes in this text that the Synoptics have preserved Christ's discourse in its authenticity (though not without some elements of subsequent reflection),[36] he describes John as the archetype of ecclesiastical speculative theory, transforming the synoptic material into elaborate abstractions. Thus Christ's immediate consciousness and pronouncements are confused with the later consciousness of a member of the religious community. From this point of view, the ground of positivity is the preservation of the limitations of subjectivity against the universal: an important observation whose consequences appear in the account of freedom in *Die Posaune*, as the transcendence of particular interest. In the *Johannes*, Bauer argues:

> The more subjectivity still has particular aspects in it which are not yet overcome by universal culture [*Bildung*], so much the more will the process of historical recollection and representation still have particularities in it which are not yet reconciled with the universality of the object, and so stand in contradiction with it.[37]

The text differs in a number of respects from the *Synoptiker* series. In his treatment of the sources of gospel material, the distinction between Bauer's conception and that of Strauss is less apparent than in *I. Synoptiker*[38]; this is a surprising reticence on Bauer's part, as he had already published a number of criticisms of Strauss's procedure.[39] While distinguishing Christ's own consciousness from that of the early church, the *Johannes* does not so clearly differentiate the later reflecting spirit of the individual evangelist from the community itself, nor has Bauer so explicitly derived his theory of the literary origin of the gospels. For example, he denies a direct dependence of John's gospel upon Philo's logos-theory, but posits instead a diffuse cultural influence operating over a broad area.[40] He thus, like Strauss, stresses the beliefs that the author of this gospel shares with his contemporaries. This is not inconsistent with his later account, but does not distinguish as sharply the raw material from the finished work of art. Moreover, it is not yet the Christian principle itself that he explicitly attacks, but only its positivity. However, in a brief assessment of the philosophy of Philo, Bauer does clearly depict the consequences of positing the absolute as substance. Here he anticipates his later position on subjectivity, as well as his later criticisms of Strauss.

> In this unity of the divine all distinction and inner determinateness disappear. Simple Being remains the ultimate and the highest, and nothing can be said of it, except that it is. Theory and conception represent here the sinking of spirit into pure being, that is, spirit loses itself with all the riches of determinateness in pure Nothingness.[41]

Similarly, he later contends in *I. Synoptiker* that "the conception of substance is critical – see Spinoza – but even so falls back again into immediate recognition of the positive – see Spinoza."[42] Developing his notion of subjectivity in the *Johannes*, Bauer describes the historical process as the progressive evolution of self-consciousness. The true meaning of a form of life is never fully transparent to its authors and agents, who live this life in its immediacy. Its significance is grasped only from a subsequent and more mature perspective, where the diverse manifestations of a previous culture can be demonstrated as a totality.[43] This retrospective conception of judgement appears to contrast sharply with Bauer's ethical idealism of the 1840s, which requires us to make such an assessment of our own present; but Bauer goes on in the text to argue that it is precisely the achievement of the present to secure the theoretical vantage point from which contemporary subjects can evaluate its potentialities. In contrast to the evolutionary view of the past as he describes it in the *Johannes*, he contends that current forms of religious apologetics (in both Lutheran, and reformed or Calvinist versions)[44] seek to subordinate reason to one earlier moment of its development, with all the incompleteness and particularity that still clothe the principle. Criticism, on the contrary, can reveal both the meaning and limitations of previous forms. The method of religious apologetics is that of the understanding, which, instead of rational unity, sees only particular shapes externally conjoined. The method of criticism is that already described in *Religion of the Old Testament*, to reflect on this external reflection – not, as in apologetics, in order to consolidate it in its positivity, but rather to lead it back to unity in self-consciousness.[45]

Elaborating his concept of subjectivity, Bauer holds that the theory of divine inspiration of the gospels is an unworthy conception of spirit. It reduces the human subject who authors the biblical text to the status of pure instrumentality, while it either derogates the absolute spirit (which Bauer does not yet repudiate) to an external memory aid, or else causes it to violate the freedom of the subject by imposing itself immediately. The passage in which he criticises this conception is of great interest, because Bauer, echoing Hegel,[46] here provides an abstract description of teleology, the dialectical fusion of purpose, means, and execution, as the process that vindicates the rights of subjectivity. The freedom of self-consciousness and the labour of teleology are equated.

> Spirit ... can never be a means standing between purpose and its execution, but as spirit it always reaches beyond the position where it appears as a means, and encloses together in itself both the other extremes, purpose and execution. As this inner movement, spirit is not only a mechanical means which stands between history, the direct experience of it, and its reproduction in the memory; so if spirit nonetheless takes on for a moment the position of means [*Mittel*], still it is at the same time the inner of both extremes. It is already active in historical appearance, is its soul, and as such is effective on those in whose lives this history occurs. As it now already lives implicitly as soul in the witnesses and in those who hear from witnesses, so is it also active in them as their own inner soul, so that as self-consciousness and as memory of itself it can reproduce itself.
>
> In the movement of these three determinations the first is history, as spirit lives immediately in it and is present there as inner soul. As in this determination history is still immediately external and pure extension, so because of this pure externality it is also the pure inwardness and subjectivity.... Both this elementary outwardness and inwardness are here one and the

same. The next stage is the real, conscious, voluntary separation of this interiority and outwardness, when history in its entire range becomes an object of consideration and of literary representation as a coherent whole. This progress stems from the power of objectivity itself, which gathers itself together out of its rarefaction in inwardness and seeks to condense, or it is the act of inner spirit in the object, which it animates as universal soul and now works up into self-consciousness.[47]

Here Bauer describes the process whereby the immediate awareness elevates itself to self-consciousness by passing through the universality of substance, a theory central to *Die Posaune.* He proceeds to argue that his own time is precisely this moment of condensation of spirit, a great historical turning point that lays bare the essence of the past and opens up the realm of the future. The processual unity of thought and being as grasped in Hegel's philosophy is the key to this comprehension. It is noteworthy that Bauer designates criticism here as the self-consciousness of the Christian spirit – that is, Christianity comprehended as the work of spirit and therefore transcended. In 1840 he can still depict this process as the reclamation of the Christian principle for self-consciousness, stripped of its positivity. In this sense his position recalls that of the young Hegel himself.[48] But while Hegel seeks reconciliation, Bauer will soon explicitly repudiate religion in the interest of historical transformation of consciousness and society. The *Johannes* does not yet take this step.

If the procedure of criticism seems uniform, as the repetition of one and the same act, this comes from its ideal simplicity and does not constitute an objection to it. For, to express it abstractly, it is the pure self-subsistence of the Christian self-consciousness [*das reine Beisichseyn des christlichen Selbstbewußtseins*] which wants to be finally by itself even in the given, the positive, and in the particular gospel data. If, as the activity of this self-consciousness, criticism is always merely the one [*das Eine*], it is the one which is necessary after millennial striving, or if it appears uniform, it is not the fault of criticism, but rather stems from the nature of the object, that it always simply lets particularities which want to count immediately as universals suffer their fate.

It is only in the beginning that criticism seems destructive, dissolving, or to be empty, unfilled implicitude. In itself that pure self-consciousness of the Christian spirit is not empty, nor it is arbitrarily posited as if it were an accident, but in its simplicity it bears the result produced by the entire previous historical development. When this pure implicitude fills and mediates itself through the process of criticism, it takes up into itself the entire content of the gospels which correspond to it, but it thereby takes up this content on the one spiritual ground, and here in this concrete universality it reproduces the contents in a form which overcomes the limits of the previous conception.[49]

In the *Johannes*, Bauer is still willing to depict the historical process as the phenomenological unfolding of Absolute Spirit, even though he has already privately reached atheist conclusions that will soon require the reformulation of this concept. Even now, however, Bauer insists on the immanence of the absolute. History is the fusion of universal and particular, in which the infinite is anchored in individual consciousness and the individual is elevated to infinitude. Bauer stresses this element of synthesis, which is a recurrent theme in his texts and which is the theoretical basis of his concept of universal self-consciousness; but he does not yet accentuate the element of diremption that will become increasingly apparent as finite substance and finite consciousness are equated with positivity in opposition to the historical dynamic.

> If we always consider the Whole as the historical appearance of the self-consciousness of absolute spirit, it could be objected that we have now displaced the limit of the particular [*die Schranke des Besonderen*] or the finite in general, into the divine spirit. But absolute spirit is not beyond the finite and its limits, because then it would itself be limited, indeed even more limited, because it would then have these limits indomitably outside itself and could not penetrate and sublate them. Rather, it is itself the movement of experiencing its own nature in the finite and traversing it. But because it is a transition, because it is movement and history, it does not remain fixed within these limits, but passes through them to attain complete historical awareness of itself.[50]

With the exacerbation of political oppositions in 1841–42, the repressive policy of Friedrich Wilhelm IV, and the heightened constitutionalist and democratic demands of the progressives,[51] Bauer launches an open assault on the ideological basis of the romantic-legitimist position. The opening salvo is volume I of *Kritik der evangelischen Geschichte der Synoptiker*, completed in March 1841. This attack is simultaneous with his direct engagement with F. J. Stahl's politico-religious orthodoxy, in "Der christliche Staat."[52] Bauer's object in his critique of the *Synoptics* is to undermine the pretensions of dogmatic Christianity, mobilised in defence of the absolutist order. He wishes to demonstrate the contradictions that arise from the immediate transposition of the religious conception into actuality. The incidents described in the gospels are the product of the religious consciousness rather than objective factual reports, and as such they necessarily stand in contradiction with nature and history. Bauer says that the critique of John has convinced him of the possibility of a purely literary origin of the gospel narrative, and he now formulates the hypothesis that the *Synoptics* too may contain no given, positive content. The literary form might thus itself generate its own corresponding material.[53] This conclusion, an extension of the results of the *Johanneskritik*, forms the basic proposition of the *Synoptiker* trilogy. Bauer attempts to establish the historical priority of Mark, and then the specific task of elaboration and reconciliation confronted sequentially by Luke and Matthew.[54]

At the same time, Bauer argues for a dialectical discontinuity between his earlier text on John and his critical treatment of the *Synoptics*. Though he had already insisted on the presence of reflection elements in the first three gospels, he had also shown that their particular subjective element was less in evidence than in the case of John.[55] Thus he preserved the appearance that the *Synoptics* contained the words of Christ in their originality. He now suggests that at the earlier stage of the argument this presupposition was necessary in order to develop the specificity of John's text in its purity, but that this appearance can now be criticised. Both the *Synoptics* and John are now taken to represent stages of reflection on the same principle. The former are literary reflections on the original experiences and struggles of the Christian community, taken up in all their positivity, while John undertakes the reflection on this reflection, and thus produces the dogmatic form of the religious principle in opposition to its simple implicitude.[56] This reflection differs from that which gives rise to genuine self-consciousness, however, because the former must let the positive stand as immediately valid. Religious reflection cannot criticise its own presuppositions, but simply forces them into an external unification. In the first two volumes of the *Synoptiker* series, Bauer employs the dialectical method he has previously described: He preserves the appearance of the historical existence of Christ, which he then calls into question in volume 3. Here Bauer identifies himself as the critical Antichrist, [57] and shows that the very conception of the Messiah is itself a literary product.

Bauer's method illustrates a sharpening of the opposition between self-consciousness and the religious consciousness. For the reclamation of the latter by the former, it is no longer sufficient simply to denude it of positivity and thus restore it to its true terrain. The transition now entails the overcoming of a limit that is the very ground of that form. In Bauer's earlier critique of Hengstenberg, this limit had existed in the Old but not the New Testament. Now it is the religious spirit in all its manifestations that is held to fetter the freedom of consciousness.

> Thus, the religious spirit is that splitting of self-consciousness in which its essential determinateness appears over and against it as a separate power. Before this power, self-consciousness must necessarily lose itself, for it has ejected into it its own content, and as far as it can still maintain itself for itself as ego, it feels itself as nothing before that power, just as it must consider it in turn the negation of itself.[58]

The Christian form of religious alienation is now clearly distinguished from the folk religions of antiquity. "In the pagan religion the divine as a particular encountered the human as an equal, while in the Christian consciousness the divine as pure universality is sundered from the human as the empirical individual."[59] Here Bauer stresses the constriction of subjectivity into particularity when confronted by the pure universal constituted as a separate sphere. This stance defines the unhappy consciousness of the Christian community. At the same time he qualifies his earlier positive assessment, according to which Christian subjectivity is a unilateral advance over ancient substantiality, because this subjectivity is now taken to be radically vitiated, abstract, and abject. The characterisation of Christianity as the abstract religion is elaborated in *Die Posaune* and *Das entdeckte Christenthum*.[60] The notion of particularity developed here is also one of the bases of Bauer's characterisation of the masses in 1843–49.

Bauer's relatively favourable depiction of the classical folk religions does not, however, lead him to stress the idea of ancient substance over modern subjectivity. Rather, his polemic against substantiality is notably sharpened. In this respect, Bauer's critique of Strauss is significant. Strauss had depicted the gospels as the immediate mythical manifestation of the collective experience and struggles of the early Christian community, without demonstrating the mediation of this content into form through the labour of individual self-consciousnesses.[61] Bauer, more vigorously than in his *Johannes* text, takes issue with this approach. He stresses the literary origins of the texts and criticises Strauss's view of the prior existence of Messianic expectations.[62] He sees the difference in approach as a struggle within Hegelianism between incompatible principles, Spinozist determinism and heteronomy, or the immediate causal impact of substance on consciousness, as opposed to the autonomy of rational thinking. Bauer contends that Strauss here clings to the notion of the community as substance, which supposedly reveals itself in its pure generality; he is not yet internally free of his object, but merely reproduces the inspiration hypothesis at a different level. Strauss's achievement is thus a negative if important one, to demonstrate to criticism that it must strip itself of all orthodox preconceptions.[63]

> Tradition in this form of generality, which has not yet reached the true and rational determinateness of universality only attainable in the individuality [*Einzelheit*] and infinitude of self-consciousness, is nothing other than substance, which has departed from its logical simplicity and has taken on a definite form of existence as the power of the community. This view is mysterious, since in every instant in which it would explain and bring to awareness the process to which the gospel history owes its origin, it can only bring forth the appearance of a process, and it must betray the indeterminateness and defectiveness of the substantiality relation....[64]
>
> But it is always an individual who has formed this content, or they are individuals who have formed the particular stories, and it is again a single person who has united them artistically into a whole. The people, the community

as such, can create nothing immediately in their mysterious substantiality and out of this, but only the subject, the individual self-consciousness, can bring it to form, to content, and therefore also to the determinateness of content.[65]

As will be seen in *Die Posaune*, Bauer differentiates the creative universal self-consciousness from the immediate particular awareness, and attributes artistic and architectonic power only to the former, even within the limits of the religious relation. This difference introduces important nuances into his critique of substance. Bauer distinguishes autonomous and heteronomous consciousness, not according to the Kantian criterion of adherence to a timeless moral law, but according to a historical standard, the degree of freedom from reigning preconceptions, and the exercise of untrammelled creativity. Bauer defends a historical version of Hegelian *Sittlichkeit*, the evolving unity of thinking and being, against Kantian *Moralität*. But creativity responds to a need experienced by those who cannot themselves formulate a solution; it is not divorced from the conditions of its genesis. The limited creativity that the gospel authors manifest within the confines of the religious consciousness gives voice to a need experienced by the early Christian community for a comprehension of its own sources. It is not the case, as in Strauss, that the community itself creates an inchoate account and sanctifies it as tradition, upon which the gospel authors subsequently draw. Rather, the indeterminate and generalised need merely sets the precondition and the limits within which creativity can work (including the alienated creativity that is still burdened with the defence of positive and irrational dogmas). Thus, for example, the early stirrings of the Christian consciousness are satisfied by Mark's account of Christ's adult life.[66] The later community yearns for a fuller story, and this need is gratified by the history of Christ's ancestry, conception, birth, and childhood. This Luke and Matthew frame, while retaining as much as possible of Mark's literary creation.[67] It is the work of art that catalyses the transition from the lower to the higher form of consciousness, even within the confines of the religious relation.

At the same time, Bauer equates the Straussian critique with the religious principle itself, in that both seek to impose the universal immediately on the particular. For Strauss, this universal is the community, for the religious spirit it is God, but for both it is the power of substance as abstract universal that seeks to engulf individuals, who can, in reality, mediate the universal with themselves only through their labour. Evident in this passage too is Bauer's evolving critique of the forms of objective spirit, and of absolute spirit still admitted in the *Johannes*. The reformulation of both concepts Bauer will shortly accomplish in *Die Posaune*.

Bauer also offers a redefinition of his own standpoint that differs markedly from his self-characterisation in the *Johannes*. "Criticism is on the one hand the last act of a determinate philosophy which must thus free itself from a positive determinateness which still constricts its true universality, and on the other hand the very presupposition without which it cannot raise itself to the ultimate universality of self-consciousness."[68] Criticism thus no longer occupies a position of transcendence merely in respect to the religious consciousness, as in the *Johannes*, but it is also the elimination of positivity from Hegelian philosophy, whose categories Bauer will shortly redefine. This purification is the precondition for a new and higher form of manifestation of spirit. "The real positive can only be born if the negation has been serious and universal."[69]

Bauer further characterises his own theoretical development, explaining why criticism must also be directed against its own presuppositions. It must be purged of that positivity with which the conditions of its genesis have marred it. In its initial emergence, the new principle is still implicit, still burdened with some of the positivity of the old, which has itself become indeterminate. This lack of definition is necessarily shared by the new principle, which requires the labour of self-consciousness and the heightening of objective oppositions in order to be brought to full determinateness. Here Bauer enunciates a position that will be central to his conception of revolutionary transformation.

> In such moments when two opponents measure each other with all their powers, the negation has still formulated its language, its principle and the execution of this principle in dependence on its opponent. It is not yet internally free. It is the complete image of its foe, and both worlds are in themselves the same world, even if one is reversed or opposed to the other.... Criticism must therefore direct itself against itself, and dissolve the mysterious substantiality in which up till now it and its object have been contained. The development of substance itself drives it on to the universality and determinateness of the idea and to its real existence, to infinite self-consciousness.[70]

This entanglement with positivity is the limit that must be dissolved before philosophy can freely remake the world, and this limit still reigns over parts of the Hegelian system, the Straussian form of criticism, and Bauer's own previous development. The new principle has been implicated and ensnared in the old, and must now appear in its purity, as the complete negation of the existing order. The task of criticism is to furnish the theoretical weapons of the struggle and to lead the struggle itself. No compromise is to be entertained. Bauer's unflinching radicalism is already announced.

The second volume of the *Synoptiker* series, in publication as of August 16, 1841, is characterised by a further sharpening of the polemical tone. Building upon the results of "Der christliche Staat" as well as his preceding biblical critique, Bauer contends that the more clearly

criticism restores the original world of self-consciousness, the more slav-
ishly does apologetics defend the positivity of the religious principle. In
his discussion of Christ's miracles,[71] he maintains that he does not oppose an aprioristic rejection of their possibility to the gospel reports, as
a shallow rationalism would do, but rather dissolves the letter of the text
through its own determination, so that we no longer have any miraculous tales.[72] The stories remain, but not as positivity. They are rather a
history, a necessary history, of self-consciousness. The Christian idea that
God and humankind are of the same essence, that "spirit in its individuality is not too weak and worthless to be able to absorb universality into
itself or to elevate itself to it,"[73] appears to the religious consciousness to
mean that a single empirical person bears the universal power of spirit in
himself.[74] This idea in turn gives rise to that of miracles, the immediate
effectivity of the universal as such, which reveal the universal to be present
in the particular individual by his power to annul all natural and social
relations.[75] In contrast, Bauer again defines the freedom and universality
of self-consciousness through the notion of teleology and labour.

> Self-consciousness, on the other hand, the true universal, which genuinely
> contains the nature of the particular in itself, sublates nature in mediated
> fashion, in that it ennobles it in its spiritual existence and suffering and
> makes it the bearer of moral determinations; or it sets the law in motion
> so that nature is drawn out of the crudity of its immediate appearance; or
> finally in art it elevates the natural determinateness through form to an
> expression of spirit and its infinity. Compared with this struggle with the
> properties of nature, with industry and art – what can miracles signify? What
> comparison can there be? The expression of rash impatience, which wants
> to see immediately at hand what is only given to labour and exertion. . . .
>
> Self-consciousness is the death of nature, but in the sense that in this
> death itself it first brings about the immanent recognition of nature and its
> laws. Spirit ennobles, honours, and recognises even that which it negates.
> If it wanted to negate violently and externally a power whose ideality it
> is, it would ruin itself, for it would destroy an essential moment of itself.
> Spirit does not rant, rage, rave, and roar against nature, as it would do in
> miracles, in this denial of its immanent laws; but it works through the law
> and brings it to consciousness. Through this certainly difficult labour it
> attains a new representation, a form which it does not have in its natural
> immediacy. In short, the death of nature in self-consciousness is its trans-
> figured resurrection, but not the maltreatment, derision and slandering of
> nature which it must experience in miracles.[76]

Bauer now stresses that the religious relation is the immediate and
indeterminate imposition of the universal on the particular, so that
there can be no real dialectical fusion of the two terms, but each remains fixed and transcendent. Herein a whole is constituted, but a dirempted whole. In *Hegels Lehre* of early 1842, Bauer will describe thus the

conclusions he reaches in the second volume of the *Synoptiker*.

> Finally, the gospel reports [*Urberichte*] are [for Bauer] nothing other than free, literary products, whose soul is the simple categories of religion. What is specific to these categories, however, is that they reverse the laws of the real, rational world. They alienate the universality of self-consciousness from [the world], rend it violently away, and restore it in the form of representation only as an alien, heavenly, or as an alien, limited, sacred history.[77]

He also draws the political consequences of the fate of particulars when universality is similarly arrogated by the state. The critique is overtly directed against Roman imperialism, but can equally be interpreted as a generalised depiction of the Restoration absolutist state. Bauer can thus ground not only an ideological dependence of absolutism on religion, but also the identity of their formal structures.

> In the Roman world, the modern principle of individuality and personality was already announced, and already prevailed in the manner which was then possible, as immediacy. The lord of the world had mounted the throne in Rome to concentrate and represent all interests, all rights, and the mass of all in his own person, and now there disappeared ethical life [*Sittlichkeit*] and the substantial bonds which first make the individual into a whole. In the place of moral unity had entered the power of one person, who would count for all and in place of all. So the atomistic points reacted to each other and were compelled to win back support and solidity in their personalities, if they did not want to succumb utterly.[78]

Bauer reiterates the relation between religious consciousness, the atomistic dissolution of social connections, and the masses: "When the one is everything and alone represents the pure universality of self-consciousness, to the others remain only stupidity and, finally, evil."[79] As Bauer has already argued in "Der christliche Staat," religion and the tutelary state share this relation of universal and particular. The dialectical victory of the power of the self over absolute but restrictive universality is the uncompleted task of the modern world. Christianity and absolutism are yoked together against subjectivity, against the principles of freedom and equality.

In the third volume of the *Synoptics*, of early 1842, the fundamentally political inspiration of Bauer's critique of religion is ever more apparent. Christianity and feudalism are equated from a perspective whose highest values are the freedom and equality of self-consciousness. Bauer chooses Matthew's parable of the vineyard as the occasion for his most trenchant criticism.

> The parable does not want to teach equality in heaven, nor the inadmissibility of a distinction of rank, but rather the absolute opposition which the lord of heaven sets up absolutely arbitrarily. The parable is the pure realisation

[*Durchführung*] of the conception of absolute arbitrariness, which is proper to the religious principle in its completion, that is in its absolute diremption from natural relations and from the ethical fullness [*Sittlichkeit*] of the life of the people, from the state and the family. It is a striking expression of the revolution which must occur when the religious principle has extricated itself from all living, moral and determinate content of the human spirit. Then there rules indeterminateness, pure arbitrariness.

'Is it not permitted to me to do what I will to my own?' (Mat 20, 15).... Let it not be said that some egalitarian principle in Christianity has brought freedom into the world! In the hands of religion even the implicitly truest principles – here that of universal equality – are always inverted again and turn into their opposites: the thought of equality into that of arbitrary favour, the thought of spiritual equality into that of a naturally-determined privilege, the thought of spirit into an adventitious, so unnatural nature. The true principles are absolute error in their religious depictions, because they calumniate mediation and repel it from themselves. As long as Christianity reigned, only feudalism held sway. When nations began to educate themselves morally, – toward the end of the middle ages – Christianity received its first dangerous blow, and a free people, genuine freedom and equality and the destruction of feudal privileges first became a possibility when in the French Revolution the religious principle was rightly assessed.[80]

Again emphasising the liberating character of his religious critique, Bauer asserts that the only refutation of his work would be the proof that man has not the right to cast off his chains. As much as Fichte, he conceives his theory as a system of freedom. It is the liberation of subjectivity from all constraints, including its own immediacy, thus leading subjectivity back into unity with its own historical being. The self is to be shaped into a rational, aesthetic whole proving its own autonomy in the world, and thus leading the struggle for progress. The ideal is that of the Renaissance man giving form to the world by his deed, but now inspired with a vision of the dialectical unity of the historical process. The present is the great conjuncture in which the rational rights of subjectivity can be definitively asserted. The opponents of freedom are the same foes confronted by Enlightenment liberalism, political absolutism, and religion, but the revolutionaries of the Restoration era forge new weapons to combat them. The criterion is no longer immediate subjectivity and the rigid phenomenal forms of its utility, but rational subjects who comprehend and transcend themselves in the flux of becoming.

Objectivity too is recast as the historical record of self-consciousness. The Hegelian *telos* of history as the development of freedom is retained, but its completion and termination in the present are repudiated in favour of an open revolutionary future. Bauer describes religion and self-consciousness as antinomies, in that genuine liberation requires the eradication of the religious principle. The struggle against religious alienation has assumed a new and higher form than in the Enlightenment,[81] whose critique is that of the infinite judgement, not of self-consciousness as a universal power.

Religion and the absolute state, with which it shares the essential features of alienation and repression, are thus set in a historical problematic that differs fundamentally from the utilitarian calculus of the earlier modern revolutionaries. Though Christianity is particularly hostile to free subjectivity, it has been an essential moment of its unfolding, even if its theoretical and institutional forms now have a purely negative significance for self-consciousness. It represents the completion of the religious consciousness in pure abstraction, the dissolution of all genuine ethical bonds, and the shedding of all determinacy of thought.[82] Bauer contends that the presupposition of Judaism is the subordination of nature to the religious interest, but this religion maintains the importance of the natural bonds of kinship and ethnicity. Christianity eliminates this limited *Sittlichkeit* in favour of the purely abstract self.[83] Christianity thus drives alienation to a pitch where it must be overcome. This idea, expressed in the third volume of the *Synoptics*, becomes the theme of *Das entdeckte Christenthum* of 1843.

> Within the sphere of self-alienated spirit it was necessary, if liberation were to be fundamental and were to occur for all humanity, that the former limitations of collective life [*des allgemeinen Lebens*] be eliminated, that alienation become complete, and that it engulf all that is human.[84]

The relation between religion and the state, and their common opposition to free self-consciousness, Bauer treats more fully in a series of texts whose composition corresponds approximately with that of *I. Synoptiker.* Here he works out more explicitly the character of his republicanism, in its enmity to the Restoration state and its social supports. His critique of religion anticipates and complements these developments. It is entirely consistent with them, and springs from the same political motivations.

"REVOLUTION AND THE REPUBLIC": THE STATE AND SELF-CONSCIOUSNESS

Simultaneously with his biblical critiques, Bauer's political interventions occur in the context of the growing conservatism of the Prussian state. In the era of Frederick the Great, Prussia had posed as the model of reforming enlightened absolutism. These reforming tendencies continued in the wake of the French Revolution through the efforts of Stein and Hardenberg.[1] King Friedrich Wilhelm III, however, retracted or circumscribed the reforms that had been enacted under the duress of the Napoleonic occupation and refused to fulfil his promise of a constitution. Officially, Prussia considered itself a *Rechtsstaat* or constitutional state, to the extent that its activities were to be governed by a fundamental law, the *Allgemeines Landrecht* of 1794, but that document failed to delimit the power of the crown, or to provide a doctrine of the derivation of power from the consent of the governed.[2] Being compatible with both aristocratic privilege and serfdom, it did not establish juridical equality among subjects. It could not satisfy liberal or republican aspirations. An initial wave of protest and opposition, which assumed the ambiguous form of the *Burschenschaften* movement, was repressed with the enactment of the Karlsbad decrees of August–September, 1819. After 1830, agitation was revived.[3] The struggle centred on the representative character of the Prussian provincial assemblies and, increasingly, on the demand for a constitution and a single, unified parliament for Prussia.[4]

The accession of Friedrich Wilhelm IV on June 7, 1840, initially aroused great hopes of renewed reform. Edgar Bauer informed his brother Bruno on June 13, 1840: "Most people cherish the highest expectations of the new government, the King will hold himself above the parties."[5] As his correspondence of January and February 1840 indicates, Bruno Bauer was considerably less sanguine about the prospects of reform from above.[6]

The popular illusions were soon shattered. In the name of patriarchal monarchy, the new king unequivocally rejected reform and opposed concessions even to moderate constitutionalism. He instituted a policy of political and cultural reaction, calling to Berlin Schelling, Stahl, and other exponents of Romanticism and pietism.[7] The king was seen to encourage conservative demands for a religious restoration, breaking the subordination of the church to the state that had been effected by the union of Lutheran and reformed congregations in Prussia. The marshalling of religious orthodoxy in defence of the regime led to further radicalisation of the opposition movement.[8] Thus, with the accession of Friedrich Wilhelm IV, the Prussian state decisively severed its links with any remaining progressive, reformist tendencies of its past.[9]

Hostility towards the regime crystallised around the Left Hegelians and helped to focus this movement in turn. Bauer's intervention at a banquet in honour of Karl Theodor Welcker, held in Berlin on September 28, 1841,[10] to recognise the achievements of South German liberalism, demonstrates his opposition to the Prussian regime. It also illustrates his criticism of the constitutionalist, reformist position of the liberals as halting and vacuous, at the same time as he is developing a revolutionary alternative in *Die Posaune*. The banquet was organised by Bruno Bauer's brother-in-law Adolph Rutenberg, as a protest against the increasing dominance of conservatism in Prussia. In a letter to his brother Edgar, Bauer reports the explanation of his participation that he offered to a university inquest into the affair:

> My participation in the speeches and toasts given on this occasion was limited, aside from my general approval, to a toast which I made to Hegel, particularly to his conception of the state, about which many erroneous notions are widespread in southern Germany. I wanted to explain thereby how much Hegel's views surpass those prevalent in the south in brilliance, liberality and decisiveness.[11]

His participation at the Welcker event provoked the personal intervention of Friedrich Wilhelm IV.[12] According to instructions from the king, the participants in the Welcker event were to be denied access to Berlin and excluded from all official posts.[13] An investigation of Bauer's *I. Synoptiker* had already been initiated by J.A.F. Eichhorn, minister of education and religious affairs, on August 20, 1841[14]; the king's hostile attention sealed the fate of Bauer's academic career, however. The unorthodoxy of *I. Synoptiker* served as the pretext for his dismissal from the University of Bonn in March 1842, at Eichhorn's initiative.[15] His predecessor in office, the liberal minister Karl von Altenstein, friend and associate of Hegel and protector of Bauer, had died in early 1840, and was replaced by Eichhorn under Friedrich Wilhelm IV. In the 1830s, Eichhorn had been active in the *Zollverein*, a customs union promoting north German trade, but was now the major architect of the new king's conservative cultural policy, including the purge of Hegelians from the universities.[16]

These events have great theoretical significance for the Left-Hegelian movement, and for Bruno Bauer in particular. But this significance has often been misconstrued. Even texts that have recognised the political tenor of Left-Hegelian writings frequently place their radicalisation and their criticism of the existing German regimes only in the year 1842.[17] Zvi Rosen, for example, asserts that only after Bauer's discharge from the University of Bonn in March 1842 does he come to regard the state as standing in opposition to the demands of liberating self-consciousness. Rosen describes Bauer's political writings of 1840 as an emotional appeal to the state to introduce liberal reforms. He depicts Bauer's toast to Welcker in September 1841 as an endorsement of the view that the Prussian state is still advancing towards reform, even though Bauer's affirmation of Hegel here implies a critique both of the existing order and of the inadequate view of freedom as private interest that liberalism defended. Bauer had already by this time completed the *Posaune*, which reinterprets Hegel to emphasise the radical critique of existing institutions implicit in the doctrine. His oppositional stance is incompatible with the position that Rosen attributes to him. Likewise, Harold Mah stresses the emergence of a theory of ideology among the Prussian Left Hegelians as a response to the opposition of reason and reality, resulting from the ongoing transformations of the premodern social order; but, because, like Rosen, he misses their polemic character, Mah sees Bauer's political writings of 1840–41 as evidence of bad faith or obtuseness, in that Bauer fails to observe the state's conservative turn. According to Mah, this ambiguous relation to the Prussian state is clarified only in 1842.[18] A similar view is more recently represented by Robert Nola.[19] This is a chronological error, which misrepresents the evolution of German political thought and of the opposition movement. Attributing belated origins to the critique of the state implies, besides, some fundamental theoretical misapprehensions.

Just as Bauer's own career in the *Vormärz* is frequently broken up into incompatible phases, so the literature on the Left Hegelians in general tends to divide the movement into distinct periods: a phase of religious criticism lasting until 1842, then a brief period of political critique, which leads to the dissolution of the school by 1844. The predominant focus on the religious consciousness as a form of alienation, and on problems in the architectonic of absolute spirit, has obscured the centrality of political criticism, and particularly the role of Hegel's *Philosophy of Right* in setting the agenda for Left-Hegelian theory from its very beginnings.[20] Moreover, if political criticism is taken to dawn relatively late, it might seem reasonable to connect it not to the Hegelian system itself, but to the growing disavowal of Hegel that is evident in some Left-Hegelian circles after 1842; the case of Marx is a prime example. An analysis of Left-Hegelian texts and correspondence shows, rather, that between 1840 and 1842, the critique of the state is decisive, and that it derives from an inner engagement with Hegel's systematic arguments in the *Philosophy of Right*. The Hegelian Left develops a shared problematic (with many individual variations) in response to Hegel's theory of the state, and to specific problems in his account of right. While the results are far different from Hegel's own system, and resemble the negative freedom whose effects he had condemned in the French Revolution, they are nonetheless motivated by the inner tensions of that system.

According to Left-Hegelian readings, the *Philosophy of Right* is defective in two respects. Hegel's theory of action lacks an adequate principle of individual or collective political autonomy; and the Hegelian state is an illusory community. Even though Hegel defends a constitutionalist position far removed from the absolutist pretensions of the Prussian Restoration monarchy, he repudiates popular sovereignty. Hegel's equation of action and private appropriation in civil society results in the fixing of the universal in a separate sphere. The state must be insulated by its constitutional but undemocratic character from the corrosive influence of civil society, the sphere of ineradicable particularism. In a genuine dialectical synthesis, universality strips off its abstract character and is rendered dynamic by its assimilation with particularity, and the particular contents likewise shed their contingent and arbitrary character, to elevate themselves to universality.[21] Instead, in the *Philosophy of Right*, the rift between civil society and the state generates the form of spurious universality.[22] The state that Hegel describes is a universal suspended above, but not penetrating, the particulars it subsumes. It does not transform them in the wellsprings of their action. Instead, it posits, above the sphere of private interest, an abstract and passive identity: that of subjects of princely (if constitutionally circumscribed) power. It cannot establish their active identity as citizens of a republic.[23]

It has been argued since 1840 that the political system that Hegel describes in the *Philosophy of Right* is not an inevitable outcome of his premises, and that a broader, republican construal of a state grounded in the rational intersubjectivity of the sovereign people is possible. The intersubjective potential of objective spirit is thwarted by Hegel's institutional structure, itself arising from a restrictive view of action. This potential can be redeemed through the alternate institutional account available in the republican model.[24] Republicanism is distinguished from Hegel's constitutionalism by its express endorsement of popular sovereignty; it differs from liberal constitutionalism in its repudiation or marginalisation of possessive individualism as a conception of freedom. It may also be (but is not necessarily) distinguished from democracy, understood in its minimal sense as a commitment to universal suffrage.

Between 1840 and 1842, Arnold Ruge argues that Hegel's exposition of virtue in the *Philosophy of Right* is purely private and individual, and must be complemented with a discussion of public virtue, which could lay the foundation for popular sovereignty. This position requires active recognition of one's fellows not only in self-interested contractual relations, but in the wide-ranging functions of citizenship.[25] Like the current criticisms of Ludwig Siep or Michael Theunissen,[26] Ruge points out the assymetry of Hegel's account of the state, where the synthetic moment of unity prevails over the analytic moment of personal independence, initiative, and self-determining inner engagement with political structures and fellow citizens. Ruge's critique is a typical expression of the Hegelian republican left in *Vormärz* Germany. He contends that Hegel's account of the modern form of community and his doctrine of autonomy secured by political order fail to achieve their objectives. This failure results not only because the preferred institutional forms of the *Philosophy of Right* thwart individual participation, but because Hegel refuses to countenance republican virtue and voluntary self-transformation, whence his theory of political autonomy is insufficiently robust.[27] In harmony with Hegel's intention, Ruge and other republicans agree that the state should be the representative of the moral substance of individuals, the repository of the collective interest. It can attain the status of genuine community, however, only if its universality is the citizens' own conscious work.

On the basis of these shared concerns, diverse solutions emerge. Even though he never made the turn to republican politics, but endorsed Hegel's constitutionalism, D. F. Strauss argued that only the species or the community can resolve the contradictions between general and particular interests. Universality and freedom attain authentic expression in the forms of collective, generic being, and not in the work of isolated, world-historic individuals who appear to be outside the community's reach. The community must re-appropriate its essence from the separate religious realm in which it has been enshrined.[28] The common thematic of religious and political criticism is here apparent: Universality must be reintegrated within the community. Similarly, Feuerbach's writings of the 1840s develop the idea of the community's elevating itself to conscious universality through acknowledgement of a collective species-being, with mutual recognition and common concerns gradually supplanting egoism as a social bond. Feuerbach accepts Hegel's account of individual action as essentially egoistic, but he therefore seeks to limit its scope. The community is to be based upon a harmonious identity with nature, not its conquest and appropriation.[29] As Marx points out in 1844, however, Feuerbach is too little concerned about politics, and offers no reformulation of the state.[30] Slightly later, in 1843–44, Marx's own initial theoretical endeavours are also shaped by criticisms of action and community in the *Philosophy of Right*. Hegel's limiting of labour to individual appropriation forecloses the possibility of generating intersubjective relations in the process of production, and not only in circulation. Marx

comes to differentiate himself from the strictly political opposition movement by arguing that the state is *necessarily* alienated from the life of the
community and cannot, even if reformed, represent true universality. He
contends that community can be attained only through the transformation of civil society itself, by the absorption of universality into the sphere
of particularity, the sublation of both moments and the overcoming of
their diremption.[31] The nature of this proposed synthesis, whether it produces real or only formal unity, is at the heart of the polemics between
republicans and socialists in the later 1840s, but both positions originate
from a shared criticism of the Hegelian state.

Simultaneously with Ruge, Bruno Bauer seeks to supplement Hegel's
possessive individualist account of action, not with a concept of collective production, but with a form of civic humanism. Bauer reactivates
the distinction of *praxis* and *poiesis*, upholding the possibility for individuals to act autonomously in elevating themselves above their immediate
(heteronomous) interests and representing the universal as a condition
for their access to the political realm.[32] Bauer's ethical perfectionism
implies a sublime and unrelenting struggle to transform political and
social relations and institutions. Bauer describes Hegel's constitutionalist state as an inconsequent and untenable compromise between absolutist tutelage and the supremacy of the people.[33] Bauer's own position
may be described as a republican rigorism.[34] The prospect of citizenship is open to all individuals, but only insofar as they can demonstrate
the appropriate ethical commitment to the transcendence of particularity. They may not, for example, raise any claim to emancipation based
upon private interest, without disqualifying themselves as genuine republicans. Those whose consciousness, by nature of their work or their
acquisitive orientation, is sunk in matter are not absolutely incapable of
such self-determination, but have to undergo a more arduous process of
self-discipline before they can rise to free self-activity. This claim is central to Bauer's position on the Jewish question, which will be examined in
Chapter 7.

The development of the problematic of self-conscious freedom, which
culminates in the *Die Posaune des jüngsten Gerichts* (*The Trumpet of the Last
Judgement*) of August–October 1841,[35] can be traced through two texts
on the state that Bauer writes between May 1840 and April 1841. These
texts represent not only a deepening political radicalisation but also an
enrichment of the theory of self-consciousness. In response to the perceived inadequacies of Hegel's account in the *Philosophy of Right*, Bauer
develops a new dialectic of the will. First, in 1840, he makes the state
the locus of this dialectic, transforming the account with which Hegel
begins the *Philosophy of Right*. Bauer describes the universality of the will,
its capacity to abstract from any given content, as a dynamic process of
constant transformation and historical progress. The state is, initially, the

agency of this process. Next, the texts of 1840–41 also redefine particularity, the second term of the syllogism of the will. Bauer identifies religious particularism and possessive individualism as forms of egoism; as particularity, they must be purged in the name of a new republican political order. Third, in 1840–41, Bauer begins to develop a critique of the liberal and constitutionalist state, as well as of the Restoration monarchy: Neither form is adequate to the task of representing the universality of the will and consciousness. Bauer's theory of universal self-consciousness incorporates these motifs.[36]

According to the *Briefwechsel*,[37] Bauer planned to begin the *Die evangelische Landeskirche Preußens und die Wissenschaft* (*The Evangelical State Church of Prussia and Science*) at the end of May 1840, thus prior to the death of Friedrich Wilhelm III. It appeared in a first anonymous edition shortly after July 3, 1840.[38] Although it prefigures the exacerbation of the political struggles of the 1840s, the text, at least in its immediate inspiration, cannot be considered to figure directly in the literature announcing liberal intentions at the accession of the new monarch. An example of the latter type would be Friedrich Köppen's book on Frederick the Great, which revives memories of the reform era.[39] Again from the *Briefwechsel*, we learn that the direct stimulus which caused Bauer to articulate his views on the relation of Church and State was the recalcitrant position of the Catholic Church, predominant in the new Rhenish provinces of Prussia, on the question of mixed marriages. The second issue of immediate importance, the proposed dissolution of the union of the Lutheran and Calvinist Churches, which the Prussian state had effected in 1817, is more directly addressed in the text itself. In its ultimate form, however, the theoretical scope of the work far exceeds the modest compass of these questions.

The most obvious, and frequent, explanation of the text is that Bauer is still defending the Prussian state as an agency of historical progress and enlightenment against the historically regressive claims of the churches, which according to him have lost all spiritual content and have sunk to the status of pure positivity. The principle of modernity is that of constant transformation. The state is the vehicle of such development, to the extent that it has shed its former attachments to particularistic interests; these, by virtue of their fixity, would impede its forward impetus.

This interpretation of the text would not be at odds with its explicit argumentation. However, it would be a serious error in the assessment of Bauer's intellectual and political evolution to understand his relation to the state itself as still basically unproblematic by the summer of 1840. In the *Landeskirche*, he expresses only tentative reservations on the relation of the state with philosophy as the organ of progress,[40] but his private utterances on politics are already far more radical than the views overtly expressed under the pressure of censorship in the text itself.

Here the letter to his brother of February 4, 1840, is particularly significant in tracing Bauer's development to a radical political stance:

> People in Berlin will not admit that the collision between the state and the Roman Church has gone so far, or that the demands which the Archbishop makes are based on a principle whose recognition the state had praised when it took over these [the Rhenish] provinces. This cannot be admitted because the government still clings to the religious interest, whose consistent and extreme claims it fears in the Archbishop and his conduct. . . . The government is afraid to let things develop into an open struggle because it wants to use the religious interest for its own purposes. Hence the entirely theological form of the struggle up till now. . . .
>
> The real reason why the Catholic claims were not clearly perceived, why real struggle with them was not possible and could not be permitted, is now becoming ever more apparent. The State must preserve a religious interest in itself and limit the further development of philosophy. Philosophy formerly owed a duty [*consolidarisch verpflichtet*] to the state and was therefore restricted; it had set its own limits for itself, since it was seemingly left free but really privileged, i.e. it shared in the advantages of government. But precisely because it has been bound [*gefesselt*], it is driven beyond all bounds and limits. Prometheus in chains was freer than when he went about freely teaching men to sacrifice. The free Prometheus was admittedly a sophist in his doctrine of sacrifice, but in the agony of his chains he was elevated above all powers. Because science is expelled, it is left to itself. It is no longer wanted, good! So, it is emancipated, and I too am free, so far as I serve the outcast. I have never felt so fortunate, so free![41]

It is thus apparent that even before the installation of the regime of Friedrich Wilhelm IV, Bauer already sees the Prussian state in the grip of reaction, opposing further historical evolution that is promoted by the development of philosophy.[42] Bauer presents the opposition in an abstract form, but a form that envelops a progressive political content: liberation from absolutist and religious tutelage, the emancipation of self-consciousness, the advent of a society predicated on free individuality. It is noteworthy, too, that Bauer is already suggesting grounds for Hegel's apparent accommodation with existing institutions.[43] Here the implication is that of an external compromise arising from the privileged status of philosophy in the state; subsequently, in the reformulation of the categories of the dialectic of the will, he will propose an internal critique. However, even if for Bauer Hegel accommodates outwardly, the spirit of his philosophy is subversive of the existing order. Later, in "Bekenntnisse einer schwachen Seele," Bauer summarises the Hegelian legacy as "atheism, revolution, and the Republic."[44] His two texts on the state, of 1840 and 1841, illustrate the evolution of this new criticism, and contribute to its formulation.

In the *Landeskirche*, Bauer claims that the real essence of the state is free development. It is the dialectical agency of historical progress. While he expresses in the text an awareness of contrary tendencies that might pervert the state in its progressive function, he holds that its essence requires that the churches now be subordinate to it, specifically that the unity of Lutheran and Reformed churches in the Prussian state church or *Landeskirche* be preserved. The Union is an act of political transcendence of religious oppositions, in the face of those who would restore the independence of religion, the determinate basis of which, according to Bauer, has been completely eroded by the Enlightenment. The argument proceeds at two levels. On the one hand, Bauer seeks to depict the relation of the free self-consciousness to the religious consciousness. On the other, he traces a dialectic of church, state, and science as moments of the state's own development, as its own inner struggle. Thus the text traverses both the levels of subjective and objective spirit. The object is to produce an account of political evolution, and an assessment of present contradictions, on the basis of which the apodeictic judgement can be exercised. The necessary political task, as revealed by reflection on history, must be identified and defended.

Bauer argues that the historically progressive work of the Enlightenment has been to undermine the determinate representation (*Vorstellung*) and exclusivity of the particular churches and their dogmas, and to grasp the concept of man (though still abstractly) as a universal, against the deformations caused by religious particularity. The Enlightenment thus transforms the religious consciousness into self-consciousness. To restore the independence of the Churches would be counter to the process of historical evolution; as products of spirit they no longer effectively exist, but are purely positive institutions impotent even to perpetuate their own existence without the support of the state.

> When now the determinate representation [*bestimmte Vorstellung*], for which the Idea [*Idee*] is still limited [*beschränkt*] to this particular object, falls away – and it has fallen through the Enlightenment – so there still remains the Idea, indeed it is now first raised to its pure and universal form, and the particular dogma has become [instead] a system or a world view or a spiritual atmosphere, which penetrates and determines all activity and thought and literature. Out of the rubble of the single dogmas rises the philosophical thought [*Gedanke*] or, in its completion, the system of the Absolute Idea or art, which in its creation brings to perception the general reconciliation of oppositions . . . [the idea] in which immediate humanity, when it has overcome itself, rises again as the new man. In this suffering and conquering humanity – for it is genuinely universal and has elevated itself to the perfect form of universality – could the divided Churches finally be unified.[45]

The Enlightenment is thus the moment at which the subjective consciousness begins to rise to universality, overcoming the effects of the divisive understanding that opposes one limited positivity to another.[46] This is an argument that Bauer further elaborates in *Das entdeckte Christenthum* of 1842–43.[47] Thus Bauer retraces the movement of Hegelian subjective spirit. He also reproduces the argument at the level of objective spirit, delivering a panegyric to the state. He stresses its essential unity with science against religion, based on its free relation to the historical process. Both state and science are dynamic forces, cancelling all positivity.

> The Union is the unity of essential contradictions: but can the Church ever constitute itself as such a unity? Never! As a pure positive power, as an institution which must always have a visible unity . . . the Church cannot bear essential contradictions within itself. But the state can, it alone can, for it alone, as the reality of immanent, human purposes, as the free development of the rational, gives free play to everything that belongs to this development. It does not inveigh, is not spiteful, is not constrictive [*Er eifert, grollt, erwürgt nicht*], even in the liveliest development it does not lose patience and can calmly bear the contradictions which emerge in its evolution. The state even recognises essential contradictions as its real element when it binds the separated churches into one congregation. The state does not want to force history. But the historical powers against which force might have been exerted, the separate evangelical churches, were as such essentially no longer present, they had no more power which could have succumbed to force. Rather the Union as a condition [*Zustand*] existed already, and the State had nothing more to do than to recognise it, that is, to legitimate that which existed in the form of accident, to recognise the result of history, to elevate the existing fact to a free deed.[48]

In a striking passage, Bauer proceeds to identify the state with the pure negative power of determination, in opposition to all positivity. Its essence is the constant generation and annulment of its material products, the restless energy of endless negation. Here Bauer depicts the state as the form of existence of objective spirit, which is never self-satisfied but constantly creates new contents out of its infinitude. It is the moral limit [*sittliche Schranke*] as determinateness in struggle with the particularity of the ego, which, as indeterminate will, rages against all positive statutes.[49] In the process, both terms are sublated. Bauer here reformulates Hegel's account of the dialectic of the will, making the state the bearer of the negative moment of universality; this is a fundamental step towards his later theory of self-consciousness. Positivity is forever being dissolved and crystallised anew, not by the immediate, indeterminate, subjective ego, but by the State as locus of dynamic objective spirit. The State is

> the result of the struggle through which the purpose of morality, and its reality, are raised to a higher content, and the initially empty infinity has made itself into moral purpose and has attained legal recognition. The

State is then again the reaction against the result, since after the resolution of the struggle it lets its pure infinitude appear again against the particular form of the result. It is immortal, eternal.[50]

As we have confirmed from his correspondence, however, Bauer has already recognised that the Prussian state has sided firmly with religion against philosophy and historical progress. So the panegyric becomes a polemic: In the *Landeskirche* he describes the ideal state, not the existing Prussian state. He has done so through a subtle transformation of the Hegelian system, introducing three important modifications whose full consequence unfolds in subsequent texts. First, while for Hegel the concept (or philosophy) sublates representation (or religion) in its higher totality without eradicating it, Bauer treats the two terms as antinomies. Mediation gives place to profound, radical transformation. Here those critics who claim that Bauer thinks in antinomies are fully justified, though the meaning of the antinomy is perceived only when we understand the historical process dialectically. The politicisation of religion and its use as an agency of legitimation by the absolutist state has engendered profound opposition to both on the part of the opposition forces, and religion can no longer be admitted as an element of the totality, as a form of absolute spirit. Bauer thus repudiates his efforts of the 1830s to think the unity of thought and being through religious forms of representation. In alliance with philosophy, the state now occupies the terrain of free subjectivity, but it is a state whose content is the radical annulment of the present: a revolutionary state. While Bauer does not yet break overtly with his Hohenzollern allegiance in the text,[51] and while he situates the dynasty's activities in the context of Enlightenment reform, the nature of the state he describes is far different from the current political programme in Prussia as he understands it.

Second, Bauer revises the notion of Hegelian objective spirit itself. Its objectivity is infused with the restless fire of subjectivity. It is endowed with ceaseless energy that does not permit it to enclose the determinate in a totality in which infinity is reflected, but to negate the given immediately. Objective spirit is depicted as subjectivity transformed, in the sense that particular consciousness in opposition to existing institutions is simply indeterminate, and it must be elevated to universality before it can undertake the principled critique of the positive. Here it is still the state that effects this sublation of particularity to individuality; but with increasing radicalisation, a more profound opposition to the existing Prussian state, Bauer will soon modify this requirement, and insist on the formative capacity of the individual citizen. The Hegelian programme of political reconciliation will be subject to a still more fundamental reformulation, in the *Posaune des jüngsten Gerichts*.

This dynamic account of objective spirit is connected, finally, with a new conception of the dialectic of the will. The implication of Bauer's argument is that Hegel's dialectic of the will is doubly constricted. As Hegel depicts this syllogism in the *Philosophy of Right*, will must externalise itself in the medium of objective nature, but is indifferent to the form this externalisation assumes. Hegel presents the universality of the will as the negative, abstractive capacity of subjects to withdraw their will from any given object and reassert it in another; but in its application to individuals, Hegel describes it as merely the formal condition for the exchange relation. It founds the sphere of abstract right, in which recognition is first located.[52] Externalising themselves through appropriation, subjects demand recognition as particular, in the objectivity of their products as the transient incarnation of their will. They also demand recognition in their universality, in their capacity to abstract their will from any particular products. Intersubjectivity arises from recognition of others who act identically.[53] While Hegel clearly intends that more complex and adequate structures of mutual recognition complement this basic form, it is the particularistic and possessive-individualist account of action that Bauer and the Hegelian Left repudiate. In the *Landeskirche*, Bauer applies the dialectic of the will to the state, not only to individuals situated at the level of abstract right. The state's universality is its ability to concretise itself in the forms of *Sittlichkeit* or ethical life, but never to rest content with the realisation of freedom it has thus secured. It constantly rescinds its products, as mere particularity that cannot manifest the plenitude of its creative power, of its consciousness of freedom. Its task is to discipline the indeterminateness of the individual consciousness and to raise it to the knowledge of freedom and autonomy. When, subsequently, Bauer situates this universality in the political activity of individual citizens of a republic, rather than in the state itself, the individuals whom he invokes are those who are not constricted by a merely proprietary conception of freedom, but who can rise to the ethical demands of republicanism.

Far more than in his correspondence of the same date, Bauer is cautious in manifesting in the text his opposition to the growing political and religious reaction. He expresses awareness of conflicting tendencies that might pervert the state in its essential function.

> It is true that the state in its empirical form of existence, in its natural basis, still possesses a determinateness which limits it externally, and introduces into its development that contingency which makes it impossible for it to display the idea in all its purity and without contradiction.... Science, pure thought, goes beyond the state, thought with its law can – indeed, must – come into contradiction with the limited determinateness of the state; in its pure necessity thought can collide with the rational necessity which in the state is entangled with material relationships and still possesses accidental determinations in itself....

> If the state renounces us, and in us the principle of the Union, we do not renounce it, we hold fast to the supreme law of the state, and in the end it will be seen who has chosen the better part. We stand fast and will persevere.[54]

Of great significance for Bauer's further development is the notion of the mass, which is here depicted as the basis – still the necessary basis – for the reception of a new practical principle. Appearing initially in relatively few awarenesses, new determinations of consciousness then penetrate beneath into the masses of society.

> A new principle can never emerge in thin air, it must have a mass, which, even if idle and inert, nevertheless provides the necessary basis, and as far as we know the basis is always inert and cannot itself be as definitely and decisively formulated as is the principle which it bears. It is then a universal law, which we can lament but not change, that a new principle always comes to consciousness in relatively few minds, preserves and forms itself, and in descending beneath finally encounters a mass which it stirs only dully and which can scarcely be raised out of its indifference. In this nether world, which is still ruled by its immediate gravity and natural determinateness, the reformed dogma of predestination – properly understood – has its eternal truth, while the free spirit, which as such grasps the principle, is elevated above the immediate determinateness and indifference, and draws the impetus for its deeper formation from its tension with the mass and its inertness. Indifference has, however, not only that odious form of material idleness and dullness, but it can just as much be the form of an inner life which has indeed cut itself loose from the ruling statutes, but in its indecisiveness trembles to and fro and is receptive to the blow of the principle when it comes. Finally, in its highest – dialectical – significance, indifference is the final conclusion of the history of the old and the herald of the new; it is the sign that spirit has returned into itself out of its old forms, or conversely has put itself in order internally and has prepared a pure place for the new.[55]

The argument stresses the ideal character of the new principle, and the weight of inertia that opposes it; but the mass is still ultimately receptive to innovation, though dully. This formulation bifurcates society between those who announce the new principle, and those who remain imprisoned in positivity. By 1843, Bauer will generalise the notion of the masses to depict civil society as a whole.[56] Later still, Bauer comes to doubt the potential receptivity of the masses to change. The inertia and indifference of the masses in relation to principles will be explained through the notion of atomistic private interest, of egoism and particularism that freeze the subject in positivity and prevent the effective recognition of the universal. Bauer then subsumes into the masses important elements caught up in the revolutionary process, the proletariat as well as the vacillating bourgeoisie. While here *die Masse* appears as the necessary basis of change, it will come to be represented as its greatest foe.

When Bauer writes his second text on the state, from December 1840 to April 1841, it is not yet the contradictions within the revolutionary movement that absorb his attention, but rather the sharpening opposition between the demands of free self-consciousness and the state, which has by now firmly allied itself with the religious party. "Der christliche Staat und unsere Zeit" ("The Christian State and Our Time"), published in *Die Hallische Jahrbücher*, June 7–12, 1841, is an eloquent and elegant reply to the work of the conservative historian F. J. Stahl,[57] *Die Kirchenverfassung nach Lehre und Recht der Protestanten* (*The Church Constitution in Protestant Doctrine and Law*, Erlangen, 1840). Stahl argues there for a restoration of the independence, indeed the priority, of the Churches relative to the state. This position Bauer criticises as an attempt to return to the transcended standpoint of the Reformation, to regain the particularistic independence of the Churches that history has annulled. In congealing spirit in the form of religion, Stahl's position implies further a fundamental derogation of the genuine spirituality of the state, which is grasped "only as a police force, at most as an institution which has to assure the uninfringed preservation of formal rights."[58] In Stahl's construction, the state would be only "the external unification of particular rights and freedoms, and in relation to the Church its power [would be] only a means for upholding the orthodox order."[59]

Bauer develops the oppositions, grounded historically, between various forms of the state and the unfolding claims of reason. He denounces not only the Christian state that Stahl advocates and that Friedrich Wilhelm IV seeks to implement, but also, in a historically differentiated vision, he attacks both absolutism and the formal *Rechtsstaat*, or liberal constitutionalism. While Bauer uses the term *Rechtsstaat* indiscriminately in the text, a number of contemporary usages should be distinguished. The term might refer to the Prussian fundamental law of 1794, or to the form in which this concept is developed by Stahl in the 1830 and 1837 editions of his *Philosophie des Rechts*.[60] Stahl argues for the compatibility of the *Rechtsstaat* with the monarchical principle and the traditional social order, governed by differential rights, privileges, and immunities. In contrast, the usage of the term by German liberals like Welcker and Rotteck is directed against traditional power and historically grounded right; in this case, the *Rechtsstaat* represents a state of juridical equality and popular representation (if restricted by property and education), which is still to be realised.[61] For Bauer, the commonality of these positions is that they define freedom as private interest, religious or economic. They cannot rise to Hegel's view of freedom as universality, even if Hegel's own account is inconsistent or incomplete. This will be Bauer's provocative claim at the Welcker banquet of September 1841.

This insight permits Bauer to identify religious particularism and the egoism of the private individual in civil society, whose political expression is the liberal constitutionalist *Rechtsstaat*. This equation is fundamental for the concept of universal self-consciousness, as Bauer will explain it shortly in the *Posaune*. Free activity is opposed to the tutelage that the absolutist state exerts, and to the religious consciousness; but autonomy is also opposed to possessive individualism or atomistic egoism, and to the liberal order that corresponds to it. The latter seeks to freeze individual privileges as private rights. The partisans of the old order comprise all those who are incapable of rising above immediate interests and therefore unable to grasp the principles of universal self-consciousness. Bauer takes the religious consciousness and the possessive individualist assertion of private right to be identical insofar as interests seek to preserve themselves immobile against criticism and history.[62] The problem will be at the heart of Bauer's political interventions between 1842 and 1849, and is sharply delineated in the *Posaune*.[63] The equation of religious consciousness and private economic interest receives its first formulation in the Stahl review.

Instead of absolutism and the *Rechtsstaat*, Bauer advocates what he calls the free state saturated with reason, whose prerequisite is the elimination of egoistic atomism by the moral self-consciousness of the individual citizen. He traces the development of this new state, whose threshold the current era is, in a dialectic which re-enacts the passage from immediate unity of opposites to immediate opposition, and finally to mediated unity, subsequently repeated at higher levels of concreteness. The first stage is the immediate unity of church and state, the former as abstract ideality, the latter as raw constraint: This is the primitive form of the genuinely Christian state, the Byzantine state.[64] Next there appears, in the mediaeval period, not an authentic Christian state but rather the immediate opposition of moments. Church and state constitute themselves as two distinct hierarchies locked in insoluble contradiction. Third, the Protestant state is the product of the defeat and rebirth of the state at the dawn of modernity: This is the second and higher form of Christian state, where the duality of the immediately preceding stage is retained, but now as moments of the state's own development.[65] Here Bauer attempts to ground historically the position elaborated in the *Landeskirche*, transforming into an entire historical-philosophical problematic what he had earlier depicted as tendencies contrary to the state's free development.

At the same time, the argument becomes more theoretically nuanced. Whereas in the earlier text the Protestant principle is still taken to be a principle of freedom, Bauer now stresses its opposition to emancipated self-consciousness. In absolute monarchy, the Protestant principle, which Stahl still defends, permeates the political order. The state therefore assumes in reality the attributes that the Protestant theory ascribes to it, spiritlessness and godlessness. It becomes the realm of external coercion, the spurious infinite repelled from the real particular contents, which are left untouched in the pursuit of their egoistic religious and material interests. But in its very alienation from spirit, the state becomes the real but not yet conscious generality, dissolving the Church as an outer and independent barrier to its own true infinity. This is the perspective in which Bauer now situates the Union of the churches: "It is the highest work of the absolute monarchy, but also its last... then the State itself passes over into a new form, and the distinctions in which it moved are left free to restore unity through free movement."[66]

The state, however, having subordinated the Churches to itself, is not yet fully the true universal: Its own form is still irrationally limited in absolutism, and the world itself, civil society, is not yet permeated with reason. The Enlightenment and the French Revolution represent the dawning of universality and the moral self-consciousness:

> The Revolution, the Enlightenment, and philosophy have... elevated the state and transformed it into the comprehensive appearance of moral self-consciousness.... Self-denial is the first law, and freedom the necessary consequence.[67]

The dialectic of particular and universal, intimated here, is developed in *Die Posaune* later in 1841. The Enlightenment is depicted in the present text as the moment of retreat of spirit into itself out of its entanglements with positivity.[68] The new form of externalisation is not yet elaborated in its determinateness; the content of Enlightenment is self-certitude, but not yet self-knowledge:

> It was belief in itself, but belief in that free, human form in which it could no longer allow self-consciousness to remain in the form of its worldly reality... rather it was the belief which introduces self-consciousness into its own essential world through its own free development.[69]

With self-consciousness now permeating the world, the vestiges of the formal *Rechtsstaat*, having become purely positive, must be eradicated. Here opposition breaks out between science, representing progress and illumination, and the Church, advocating a regression to transcended historical stages. Bauer now states overtly the thesis he had articulated in his private correspondence of February 1840. The state, representing earlier forms of self-consciousness and clinging to its positive existence, now attempts to resurrect and promote the church not as an independent institution, but only as a moment in its struggle against its own further development, although objectively this standpoint is long since transcended. The state is not yet purely determined by its own concept. What is at stake is the dissolution of its irrational form and its reconstruction by free self-consciousness, its transformation into the republican state.[70]

In view of the position he develops on the social question in the *Allge-meine Literatur Zeitung* and the *Norddeutsche Blätter*, Bauer's assessment of the theoretical and practical situation of the workers in early 1841 is also extremely significant. The solution of the social question is the culmina-tion of the state's own development. In emancipating the workers, the state frees itself from its own historical limitations and the dominance of particular interest. Bauer also distinguishes genuine political from spuri-ous religious solutions.

> The final, but also admittedly the most difficult task which remains for the state in this respect [its own liberation] is the freeing of the civil helots [*bürgerlichen Heloten*], who must struggle daily with matter, who must con-quer sensuousness for the universal, without becoming truly personally conscious in this struggle of the universal which they serve. It was the state, not the Church, which could destroy serfdom; so also the Church cannot free those helots, cannot educate the cyclopes to ethical manhood, if it can only elevate them from time to time to the infinite, and after the flight from this life leave them to sink even deeper in their struggle with matter.[71]

While the literature on Bauer frequently equates *die Masse* with the industrial working class, this is much too narrow a definition. His cat-egory of the masses after 1842 includes the liberal bourgeoisie with its narrow material interests. As his critique of the masses sharpens, it in-creasingly colours his view of the state and of the revolutionary process. The contradictions within that process threaten it with defeat.

Bauer concludes his analysis, still supremely confident of the victory of science over the forces of positivity. By the time he writes the *Posaune* in summer 1841, having criticised both absolutism and Hegelian con-stitutionalism, he will attribute the function of universality not to the state itself, but to individual citizens, whose republican institutions allow them constantly to reshape the political sphere. Bauer thus opposes the principle of republicanism to possessive individualism, or the duties of citizenship to chrematistic. The elements of the theory of universal self-consciousness attain their first explicit formulation in Bauer's political criticism of 1840–41.

III

THE EMANCIPATORY PROJECT

"ONLY THE OUGHT IS TRUE": HEGEL, SELF-CONSCIOUSNESS, AND REVOLUTION

Among Bauer's numerous texts of 1841, *Die Posaune des jüngsten Gerichts über Hegel, den Atheisten und Antichristen* (*The Trumpet of the Last Judgement upon Hegel, the Atheist and Antichrist*) [1] is the most significant formulation of the ethic of historical perfectionism, and of its relation to the Hegelian system. It applies this ethic in defence of the revolutionary task of the present. The doctrine of infinite self-consciousness defines the relation of subjectivity to the world as an affirmation of human freedom against all transcendent powers. It asserts the claim to the conscious reshaping of the self, the state, and society, in the light of universal purposes. These purposes are now conceivable in their generality and scope because of the progress of history and philosophy, securing the vantage point from which the present may be submitted to apodeictic judgement and criticism. The experience and limits of the French Revolution, and the systematic achievements of Hegel, open new horizons for an enlarged *Sittlichkeit* and authentic individual autonomy. Bauer's text outlines a political programme, the critique of the church, the existing state, and conciliatory liberalism, in the interests of republican transformation, with constant reference to the Jacobin example. In describing the ethics of the revolutionary process, the text stresses the principled and ruthless critique of all existing relations; the refusal to compromise; the need to provoke escalation of conflict in order to generate a clean and decisive break between opposed principles, culminating in the revolutionary overthrow of the old order. [2] The antithetical character of this ethical programme is rooted in the historical process of self-consciousness. What the present demands is opposition to alienation and heteronomy in all their forms.

The text, published anonymously in October 1841, is redolent of Luther's polemical style. [3] In it, Bauer assumes the guise of an arch-conservative, pietist opponent of Hegel. In this imposture, he rails against the Hegelian system as a thinly veiled atheism and Jacobinism, thus substantiating the criticisms of Hegel's conservative opponents. [4] He acknowledges Heinrich Leo, author of *Die Hegelingen*, [5] as a precursor of his pietist critique. Leo's defect, says Bauer, is that he restricts his criticism to members of the Hegelian school and does not attack the master himself. Bauer satirically commends Leo's unfamiliarity with philosophy as an appropriate stance for a pious Christian, but claims that such an attitude is an inadequate basis for a thorough indictment. One must be prepared to enter upon the adversary's own terrain in order to contest him effectively. Bauer contends that Hegel's revolutionary conclusions derive from a conception of spirit that elevates human subjectivity to the status of the demiurge of history.

The form of the work is conditioned by the exigencies of censorship. The proclamation of the revolutionary principle could only occur under the pretext of its denunciation; but the device is transparent, and Bauer clearly revels in his theatrical disguise. He sets about his task with great relish, exuberantly displaying his biblical erudition together with his Hegelian scholarship. His ironical fire is directed primarily against Hegel's *Philosophy of Religion*, the second edition of which he himself had just prepared.[6] The irony is often unmistakable, and Bauer manipulates Hegel's dialectical categories with a virtuosity that bespeaks a lengthy and painstaking apprenticeship. There is evidence that the conservative forces in Germany initially welcomed the work,[7] though Bauer's intent was to expose them to public execration; it is no testimony to their acuity that they did not immediately penetrate the façade. Among Left-Hegelian circles, Arnold Ruge, editor of the *Deutsche Jahrbücher*, participated wittingly in the charade, as his correspondence with Bauer demonstrates.[8] Otto Wigand, the publisher of the book and a well-known supporter of Left-Hegelian causes, also circulated an ironic apologia for the work, claiming that its publication was an attempt to redress the balance of his editorial house, which had formerly been hostile to pietist writers.[9] The authorship and genuine intent of the work, however, were soon discovered, and the book did not escape the censors' grasp. It was banned and confiscated in Prussia in December 1841. Bauer publicly acknowledged his authorship in *Die gute Sache der Freiheit und meine eigene Angelegenheit* (*The Good Cause of Freedom and My own Affair*), of June–August 1842.[10]

The sustaining irony of the text not only lies in the author's assumption of a pietist identity, but operates at a deeper philosophical level. Bauer attributes to Hegel himself theoretical and political positions he has developed from within the Hegelian system, but that, in their revolutionary ethics and historical perfectionism, are not consonant with Hegel's own views of the historical process. The *Posaune* interprets the Hegelian problematic as a theory of infinite self-consciousness, and as a call for revolution. Bauer seeks to show that Hegel judges and condemns the existing order in its twin pillars, church and state; and that Hegel's conservative opponents are right to claim that the concept of spirit, far from signalling a quiescent resignation, is fired by what Bauer calls Hegel's berserk rage against all existing statutes.[11] Bauer is not attempting to be consistent with Hegel's own explicit intentions, nor merely to liberate unchanged a supposedly esoteric doctrine concealed in an exoteric husk.[12] The Hegelian system requires inner revision, but it also offers resources that enable this revision to be made. Nor are differences due to errors or misreadings of the Hegelian text, as has also been proposed.[13] The *Briefwechsel* confirms that in 1840–41 Bauer did not consider Hegel an atheist, and that he was "scarcely still able to read the book [the *Philosophy of Religion*] through again,"[14] characterised as it was by the "crude juxtaposition of the most complete critical developments with the most orthodox manner of speech."[15]

Bauer's revolutionary Hegel is not, however, an entirely fictitious creation.[16] For Bauer, Hegel lends himself to such an interpretation, once his central concepts are critically appropriated and transformed. It is not simply a matter of liberating the esoteric from the exoteric, as the hidden essence is itself contradictory and must be purged of its positivity. In freeing the Hegelian system of its inner limitation, Bauer formulates the classic leftist reading of Hegel. The *Posaune* consciously develops these critical elements. The result differs from the Hegelian system, both theoretically and practically. But the text denies this difference, and makes Hegel himself a Jacobin. In defence of his claims, Bauer cites mainly the *Philosophy of Religion, History of Philosophy*, and *Philosophy of History* lectures, as well as the *Phenomenology*, though, as we have observed, Hegel does voice elsewhere arguments that lend a certain credence to Bauer's reading.[17]

The *Posaune* presents itself as an appeal to all Christian governments,

> so that they might finally acknowledge what a deadly danger threatens everything existing and particularly religion, the *only basis of the state*, if they do not immediately extirpate the root of the evil. There will be nothing fixed, certain and lasting any longer, if the cunning error of that philosophy continues to be tolerated in the Christian state. . . . All divine and human authority is denied by [the Hegelians]. Once they have destroyed religion and the Church, so will they certainly also want to destroy the throne.[18]

In his pietist guise, the author claims to write anonymously because he seeks only a heavenly reward. The absolute opposition between faith and reason is the basis for his supposed indictment of Hegel; this tension he had already indicated in his 1829 manuscript. "The Christian well knows that it is the pride of the flesh for man to attempt to justify God and to prove his revelation to be true."[19] Mimicking pietistic fideism,[20] Bauer asserts that the claim of reason, even if it begins to stir innocuously enough in the defence of religion,[21] leads inevitably to atheism and republicanism. Faith, church, and state form an indissoluble bond based on the rejection of reason, the repudiation of human autonomy, and the humble acceptance of tutelage and domination. Hegel's system, says Bauer, drives the contradiction of faith and reason to an extreme, where it necessarily collapses. Bauer describes Hegel as the authentic heir of the "devilish" work of the French Revolution. He depicts Hegel's struggle for self-consciousness as a direct continuation of the revolutionary strivings of the French, and a deeper interiorisation of their principles, so that church and state in Germany are now staggering under the assault.[22]

> The hour has struck, in which the evilest, the proudest – the final enemy of the Lord will be hurled to the ground. But this enemy is also the most dangerous. The French [*Wälschen*][23] that people of the Antichrist – with shameless flagrancy, in broad daylight, in public, in the face of the sun which never before had beheld such an outrage, and before the eyes of Christian Europe, reduced to nothingness the Lord of Ages, just as they had murdered the consecrated of God; they committed blasphemous adultery with the whore, Reason; but Europe, full of holy zeal, choked the horror and united into a holy Alliance to fetter the Antichrist in irons and to set up again the eternal altars of the true Lord.
>
> Then came – no! then was summoned, cherished, protected, honoured, and endowed the enemy, who had been externally defeated, in a man who was stronger than the French people, a man who elevated again the decrees of that hellish Convention to the force of law, a man who gave them a new, more solid basis and who made them available under the flattering title, particularly beguiling for German youth, of Philosophy. Hegel was summoned and made the centre of the University of Berlin! This man – if he can still be called by a human name – this man of corruption filled with hate for everything divine and sacred, now began under the shield of philosophy an attack on everything which should be elevated and sublime for man. A flock of young people attached themselves to him and never – in all history – was seen such obedience, dependency, blind trust, as his young followers displayed toward him. They followed him where he led, they followed him in the struggle against the One.[24]

Concealed in Bauer's hyperbole is a serious philosophical point. Bauer attributes to Hegel of a theory of absolutely free and universal self-consciousness, in which the invocation of substance and of a transcendent absolute is merely a necessary but self-annulling illusion. Substance is both assimilated and opposed to subjectivity, and in absolute spirit, properly understood, all religious pretensions dissipate, while the absolute itself dissolves into the critical activities of conscious individual subjects. Bauer asserts that Hegel situates the dialectic of particular and universal exclusively within the individual self-consciousness. Nothing transcendent remains.

Bauer's exposition of Hegel's *Philosophy of Religion* begins with the critique of immediate consciousness, in the subjectivism of Schleiermacher and Jacobi. Schleiermacher and pietist orthodoxy appeal to the

immediacy and particularity of the subject in face of the ineffable principle of the absolute, which can be grasped not through reason, but in
feeling. For Bauer in his authentic voice, the practical consequence of
pietism is the renunciation of reason as an instrument of liberation, the
freezing of the historical movement, and the imprisonment of the spirit in
its own alienated works; donning his pietist mask, he commends this attitude. These consequences flow from the profound error of hypostatising
the universal outside the reach of self-consciousness, and of derogating
the subject to pure particularity. Rigid particularism and transcendent
universality are mutually sustaining.

Against particularity and sentiment, Bauer shows how Hegel initially
stresses the objectivity of substance, as a domain transcending the immediate, particular self. A theory that fails to recognise an objective universal
remains trapped in the circle of particular, uncriticised feelings and conceptions, which cannot possess truth-value, but only subjective certainty,
as the *Phenomenology* demonstrates. In contrast, the Hegelian synthesis of
particular and universal moments endows the concept with being, and
raises the individual from the plane of certainty to that of truth. Immediate particularity cannot be the criterion of theoretical validity or worldly
order; rather, individuals must, in the first instance, "sacrifice themselves
to the substance," internalise it as the substance of their own life. In
contrast to Schleiermacher, here the individual renounces immediacy
in order to gain back as a new content the contents of the absolute, to
become the organ through which the universal attains conscious form.[25]

The first shape in which this objective universal appears is the substantiality relation, the assimilation of the many into the One, which exists
through itself, and which alone possesses true reality. Unlike the particularistic feelings on which Schleiermacher bases religious subordination to
the deity, substance originally implies a kind of pantheism, which recognises only a single, all-encompassing being, without inner differentiation.
Substance is a mode of universality in which the moment of distinction
or individuality is not yet developed; it cannot accommodate the internal
negative power of form that imparts structure and determinacy by reworking the given in light of an end or concept, as in a realised aesthetic work.
Though it undergoes various mutations, the religious consciousness according to Bauer is a paradigmatic expression of substance. Its historical
role is to discipline and absorb the particulars, to point beyond the bare
immediacy of the self towards a realm of universal interests; but it is an
inadequate manifestation of the universal, and Bauer traces its deficiency
through its diverse configurations. The critique of religion assumes a central place in judging the historical process, because it identifies and traces
the substantiality relation.

In this dialectical movement, the universal or substance exists as "absolute content"[26] in which all particularity, including the particular ego, is

subsumed. This initial, Spinozist moment, invoked against the rigid assertion of mere particularity, creates in Hegel an appearance of pantheism.
It is this appearance that misleads some critics and interpreters, such as
D. F. Strauss, who, according to Bauer, never surpasses this standpoint.[27]
In Bauer's depiction, however, Hegel now proceeds to dissolve substantiality itself as a power independent of consciousness. This is not to renounce all objectivity. It is rather to show that substance, once it has
demonstrated to the particular consciousness the need to transcend itself, may not claim an immediate validity either. Bauer contends that
Hegel invokes the moment of substance at the earlier stage of the argument in order to elevate the immediate consciousness to universality,
to purge it of its particularities, and to reveal to it the identity of self-
knowledge and knowledge of the world, the condition of the apodeictic
judgement. It is by transcending the dialectical illusion of substance that
the unity of concept and objectivity can first be glimpsed. The subject
must appear as potentially universal, and the objective must show itself
as a purposive order, responding to the subject's striving for rational
freedom.

The next development, then, is to transform substance into the record
of the acts of conscious spirit. Substance must be seen as involving an inner relation of self-consciousness to itself. In reconceiving substance, subjectivity assimilates the principle of universality, and renders substance a
moment of its own becoming. It subsumes its other to itself. That is, subjectivity now contains universality as its own character, not as something
alien to it. But this relation is not confined to an inward experience; it
has not dispensed with externality, because reason must realise itself in
the world. This externalisation produces a historical sequence, including
the forms of alienated life. The stages in this sequence can be grasped
as moments in the unfolding unity of thought and being. As Bauer had
argued in the *Johannes*, the completion of philosophy in the present allows this process, for the first time, to be comprehended in its totality.
Self-consciousness, conceived as an immanent and subjective universality,
is the motive force of history, encompassing and generating all content,
as the given is taken up and transformed. The Spinozist attributes of
thought and extension are reconciled when extension or substance is
seen to be formed by the activity of thought. As Bauer's first manuscript
of 1829 declares, what is at stake is not only the subjective realisation
of the concept, but the fate of the idea, the unity of thought and being; and this now requires that the objectivity of the historical process
be equally emphasised. This historical and critical idealism, which the
Posaune attributes to Hegel, is revolutionary: It affirms the rights of free
self-consciousness against any positive institution that cannot justify its
existence before rational thinking, against state, religion, hierarchy, and
subordination.[28]

In Bauer's interpretation of Hegel, the movement from absolute sub-sumption of subjectivity under an abstract universal substance to the free-dom of infinite self-consciousness follows a complex course. In its first appearance, the absolute represents the undifferentiated, pure univer-sal, including even the self. This is Spinoza's substance, but its twin at-tributes of thought and extension must not be seen as merely correlated. They must be led back to their common source in active thinking. "The universal is nothing other than thought, no object external to thinking, but rather the activity of thinking as the undifferentiated, self-subsistent [bei sich selbst Bleibende] act and essence of self-consciousness."[29] This pure unity "is the universal precisely in this, that it is identity with itself, in all things,"[30] encompassing all distinction. Appearing first as an inert sub-stance, it reveals itself to analysis as an active self, and reveals to the self that it must abandon its own particularism.

The universality of substance, once it is understood as activity, attains expression in and through the individual consciousness, as its funda-mental property. A new struggle between the universal and particular moments within the self now ensues. The universal here reappears in a subjective form, as feeling. These are not the purely subjective feel-ings and intentions of Schleiermacher's immediate consciousness, but a higher and contradictory feeling, the contradiction, situated within the self, between universal and particular moments, "between myself in my pure fluidity and in my determinateness."[31]

Bauer characterises this contradictory feeling as alienation, in that the universal, thought in and for itself, appears to negate the particular em-pirical being, to reduce it to a nothingness whose truth lies beyond it, only in the universal. The self is unable yet to synthesise the two moments of its existence, and lives in the tension between them. This is the origin of the unhappy consciousness. "In feeling the moment of empirical existence, I feel that side of the universal, negation, as a property falling outside of myself, or if I am this property, I feel myself alienated in my empirical ex-istence, denying myself and negating my empirical existence."[32] It is this fundamental diremption that is the basis of religious alienation. Religion gives expression to this tension, and drives it to a new pitch.

This experience of alienation is transformed but not yet abolished by a new activity of the self, positing its determination outside itself and thus externalising itself. This externalisation appears in art, as the sensuous in-tuition of unity-in-diversity, but the artistic object is an inadequate vehicle for the contents of this new consciousness. Consciousness does not grasp its own essence in the material object of art; concept and objectivity are not yet synthesised in the materiality of the aesthetic object. This object must be re-integrated into consciousness: Thinking itself must appear as the object of consciousness.[33] The next stage consists, then, in cancelling the externality of the object through the form of subjectivity. This is the basis of the religious consciousness as representation or *Vorstellung*, the world of sentiment perfected in a higher subjective awareness, but one that has not yet attained conceptual clarity. Here the products of the struggle between particular and universal moments of consciousness are still inextricably entwined with sensuous intuition or perception. Thus the unity of certainty and truth, particular and universal, assumes concrete but inadequate forms: as specific historical episodes or incidents (hence the form of Revelation, analysed in Bauer's critiques of the *Synoptics*), or as the separate traits of the divine Being, the unity of many properties.

At this point in the text, Bauer adopts the classical Hegelian configuration of the absolute. Yet in an earlier discussion of art in the *Posaune*,[34] he reverses the priority of religion to art within the system of Absolute Spirit, showing art and philosophy to have a much closer affinity. In religion, self-consciousness is alienated and seemingly passive, whereas art reveals the activity of spirit, though still in a material element. This latter argument is consistent with the position Bauer adopted in 1829, and with his claims in *Hegels Lehre* of 1842. The seeming inconsistency here can be resolved if we consider the present account to be a description of the process of subjective *Bildung* or self-formation that remains faithful to Hegel's account, while the restructuring of absolute spirit, placing art and philosophy in intimate contact, is a logical or systematic operation of Bauer's own devising. He thus does not accept the assertion that the materiality of the artwork diminishes its value as a depiction of the absolute, but sees it rather as emblematic of the formative power of the idea.

Having traced some of the forms of self-alienated spirit, Bauer next vindicates the historical role of the Enlightenment. It represents the critique of the religious consciousness, the transcendence of representation or *Vorstellung* in favour of the concept, and the purification of all positivity from self-consciousness.[35] Bauer interprets Hegel as grasping and concretising the truth of the Enlightenment, and thereby radically undermining all religious pretensions. It is Hegel who makes possible the transition from the infinite judgement of the Enlightenment to the apodeictic judgement of the present. The substantial is finally dissolved in its independence of consciousness; but this position is not equivalent to a radical subjectivism. Thought must comprehend and be reconciled to the historical forms of its being, and subjects must act in light of objective contradictions. Bauer's Hegel stresses the form-giving activity of practice as the source of objectivity, but only after consciousness has elevated itself above immediacy can this creative process be fully comprehended. In producing itself as universal consciousness, it engenders and judges the historical world, a theme to be elaborated in the *Entdeckte Christenthum*.[36]

In Bauer's reading of Hegel, religious consciousness is always alienated, in all its manifold forms of appearance – whether as immediate feeling, as the immediate grasp of the absolute, or as the immediate sensuous depiction of the unity of universal and particular. Bauer here develops the themes that had activated his religious critique in *Herr Dr. Hengstenberg* and the *Johannes*. Although philosophy appears at the summit of a phenomenological process in which "the religious relation is the dialectic and movement of self-consciousness,"[37] philosophy as the self-knowledge of historical development is absolutely opposed to the religious consciousness, which grasps its own deed as the deed of another. Here arises a frequently remarked antinomy in Bauer's thinking. Critical consciousness grows out of the deepening and universalisation of alienation. A dialectical rupture intervenes both conceptually and objectively at the moment of most extreme alienation. As in his *Entdeckte Christenthum* and other writings of 1842–43, Bauer describes Christianity as the perfect religion, the purest representation of the religious consciousness and its limits. He asserts that all human and artistic interests that give life and content to other religions, all human determinateness that persists in the interstices of their doctrinal systems, are completely deficient here. The negation of this purely abstract religion is the practical task that philosophy must now undertake.[38] The attack on Christianity is at the same time a direct assault on the ideological bases of the restoration state[39] and on all irrational social institutions.[40] The philosophy of self-consciousness is the birthplace of the new world and the critique of everything existing. The new principle appears at once in theory and practice, in direct relation to reality as act, a practical opposition between interests.[41] The practical relation is the genuine form of existence of the theoretical principle: "the opposition must be serious, sharp, penetrating, ruthless, and the overthrow of the existing the principal aim."[42] Philosophy is the consciousness and practice of freedom, and its major enemies Bauer identifies as Christianity and the Christian state. Both must be overthrown.

Bauer's theory of revolutionary self-consciousness, here attributed to Hegel himself, must not be seen as a simple reversion to a Kantian or Fichtean opposition of being and concept. It is rather an inner engagement with the principles of the Hegelian system, with the intent of producing a theory of self-determination in history. It develops on the terrain of Hegelian philosophy, through an immanent reformulation and critique of Hegel's principal categories, in response to the rhythm of the historical process and its revolutionary crisis. The central contention of the *Posaune* is that Hegel succeeds in reconciling substantiality and self-consciousness because he grasps the former, first, as a necessary dialectical illusion, whereby the particular subsumes itself under a universal; and second, as a self-annulling illusion, because the particular then recognises that the production of substantiality is its own work, that there is no universal which enjoys a transcendent status. The absolute, too, has its roots in the rational and conscious activities of subjects, and expresses nothing other than the immanent rationality of their deeds and reflections. A year later, in December 1842, while engaged in a controversy with Marx and Ruge over the editorial direction of the *Rheinische Zeitung* and the *Deutsche Jahrbücher,* Bauer delivered to the latter a text that clarifies his criticism of the Hegelian system, shedding the ironic mask he assumed in the *Posaune.*[43] He asserts in this article that Hegel depicts the absolute either as an external object of consciousness, or as movement that opposes to itself another sphere, that of finite spirit, and is therefore itself limited and finite. Bauer no longer holds, as he did in 1829, that the Hegelian Idea effectively realises the synthesis of objectivity and concept. He directs at Hegel the same criticisms he had made of Kant's unreconciled opposition between finite and infinite. The Idea as the unity of thought and being must be developed beyond the form in which Hegel left it; the Hegelian system signals the correct solution, but does not achieve it. Hegel did not succeed in eliminating the transcendent appearance of the absolute,[44] and illegitimately retained religious presuppositions.[45] Bauer offers infinite self-consciousness as the genuine unity of opposites, secured without transcendence.[46] He will elaborate further in 1845, arguing that the Hegelian synthesis of Spinoza's substance and Fichte's self is incoherent. Hegel fails to take the second step that Bauer had attributed to him in the *Posaune,* showing substantiality to be self-annulling. Instead, Hegel leaves substance and subject as distinct and heterogeneous principles. Bauer already believes this to be the case in 1841, but he argues that the correct development is also indicated by the proper deployment of Hegel's categories. The later criticism runs as follows:

> Hegel combined Spinoza's substance and the Fichtean ego. The unity of both, the tying together of these opposed spheres, the oscillation between two sides, which permit no rest and yet in their repulsion cannot get clear of each other, the breaking out and prevailing of the one over the other and of the second over the first, constitute the particular interest, the epochal and essential, but also the weakness, finitude, and nullity of Hegelian philosophy. While for Spinoza, all reality is substance, "that which is thought or comprehended in itself and through itself, that is, whose concept does not require the concept of another thing from which it can first be constructed"; while Fichte posits the absolute self, which develops out of itself all the activities of spirit and the manifold of the universe; for Hegel the point is "to conceive and express the true not as substance, but also as subject." On the one hand, he takes seriously the sublation of the finite. . . . He demands above all, that the self in its finitude "renounce itself in deed and reality [*Wirklichkeit*]," "as the particular against the universal, as the accident of this substance, as a moment or a distinction which is not for-itself, but which has renounced itself and knows itself as finite." On the other hand, though, absolute spirit is nothing but the concept of spirit, which grasps and develops itself in the only spiritual realm that there is, that long train of spirits in history. "Religion, political history, the constitutions of

states, arts, sciences, and philosophy" are nothing but "works of thought";
the work of previous history has no other purpose than "to recognise self-
consciousness as the only power in the world and in history," "the strivings
of spirit through almost 2500 years of its most serious labour" have no
other aim than [for spirit] "to become objective to itself, to recognise itself:
tantae molis erat, se ipsem cognoscere mentem."

This contradiction, that the absolute is the best and highest, the whole,
the truth for man, the measure, the essence, the substance, the end of
man, but that again man is the substance, is self-consciousness, is the result of his own activity and owes his existence to his deed, his historical
struggles, therefore necessarily making the absolute into something limited [*beschränkt*] – this contradiction, in which the Hegelian system moved
back and forth, but from which it could not escape, had to be dissolved
and annulled. This could only occur if the posing of the question of
how self-consciousness relates to absolute spirit, and absolute spirit to self-
consciousness, were not silenced with half-measures and fantasies, but were
made for ever more impossible. This could be done in two ways. Either self-
consciousness has to be consumed again in the fire of substance, that is, only
the pure substantiality relation can persist and exist; or it has to be shown
that personality is the creator of its attributes and of its essence, that it lies
in the concept of personality in general to posit itself as limited, and to sub-
late again this limitation, which posits itself through this universal essence,
since this very essence is only the result of its inner self-differentiation, of
its activity."[47]

The irony of the *Posaune* is to claim that Hegel does not suffer from
this defect, when Bauer had already identified and sought to remedy
it through the concept of infinite self-consciousness. Later still, after
the revolutions of 1848, Bauer will contend that Hegel succumbs completely to the Spinozistic element in his thinking, so that substance engulfs
subjects.[48]

In 1841, the unity of thought and being is still the central insight
that Bauer attributes to Hegel. Yet this unity does not enjoin political
resignation. It must be shown to be compatible with the exercise of radical criticism, one that identifies deep discrepancies between what is and
what ought to be, without reverting to an impotent Kantianism. The theoretical problem is to resolve that which, by analogy with the aesthetic
judgement,[49] we may call the antinomy of the critical judgement, namely,
to reconcile two affirmations that appear to be contradictory. The thesis
of this antinomy can be formulated as follows: Being and the concept
do not correspond. The antithesis reads: Being and the concept are in
essence united. In general, the Enlightenment sustains only the first affirmation. This unilateral affirmation of the thesis of the antinomy provides
the structure of the infinite judgement, the logical form upon which Enlightenment social criticism is predicated. Contrastingly, in intent if not
faultlessly in execution, Bauer's critical theory maintains both thesis and

antithesis, transforming the infinite judgement into a new, apodeictic, form. The solution to the antinomy involves taking being in two distinct senses, as positivity, and as the realisation of the rational idea. Not all externalisation is positivity, but only that which stands opposed to the higher development of freedom. Positivity is the outcome of a historical, developmental process in which spirit generates the forms of substance and then retreats from them, leaving them fixed and rigid, devoid of rational justification. It is these forms that the critical judgement exposes and challenges. On the other hand, being corresponds to the concept in that objectivity records the history of thought, the realisation of reason through alienation and struggle. Critical judgement identifies determinate negations, specific contradictions in the current configuration of being that necessitate transformation. Ethical subjects then act to secure this conformity. The ought is not merely opposed to being, but is inscribed in it as its immanent movement.

In the *Posaune*, the dialectic of history as self-production makes possible a critical judgement that demonstrates an intolerable disparity between the concept of freedom and the current forms of its actualisation. In these circumstances, the practical application of dialectic to mediate or balance contradictions, and not to remove them, is at best a spurious reconciliation. Bauer thinks that Hegel attempts such a fruitless solution when, for example, in his constitutional doctrine he conjoins the monarchical principle with some transfigured and concealed elements of popular sovereignty; but the critical judgement, informed by Hegel's own system, shows these two principles to be incompatible. Here Bauer's antithetical approach is again evident. Dialectic dissolves all positivity, calls everything stable into question, but Bauer believes (when not concealed behind his pietist mask) that Hegel's usage allows it to become frozen in the configuration of the present; it seems to justify the positivity of the existing order, to demonstrate the rationality and necessity of what is patently false. For Bauer the dialectic must be restored to its critical and revolutionary role, to become the theoretical instrument completing and transcending the work of the Enlightenment and the French Revolution, temporarily arrested by the Restoration. This entails a critique of the state and religion, the foundations of the old order, and of atomistic egoism and particularism, the characteristics of modern civil society. Thus both pseudo-objectivity and immediate subjectivity are to be transfigured in a new dialectic of free universal subjectivity or self-consciousness. The *Posaune* directly develops the critique of positivity and egoism (here, the clinging to immediate particularity, as in the religious conscience) that a number of subsequent texts will elaborate. It justifies the overthrow of the existing forms of objective relations through a critique of the doctrine of the Absolute, insofar as this appears to transcend the powers of rational subjects, and to occupy an ontologically distinct realm.

Bauer's notion of self-consciousness in *Die Posaune* is a reworking of Hegel's concept of Absolute Spirit, the *dynamis*, propulsive force and goal of the historical process. Bauer takes as his guiding motifs two central Hegelian doctrines: the efficacy of reason, its ability to shape objectivity, and also the return to self from this externality, the archetype of the life of spirit that reintegrates the objective form as a subjective awareness. With Bauer, this duality expresses the movement of individual self-consciousness. He strips the absolute of its transcendent character, while elevating individual consciousness above its immediacy and opening the realm of free self-determination. Spirit is not a hypostasis, separate from the intellectual production of individuals, but is the very product, constantly renewed, of intellectual activity itself. The historical realm of finite spirits is the only spiritual realm.

It is not, however, any undifferentiated activity that can be the locus of *Selbstbewußtsein*. Self-consciousness is free creation, positing and negating of the given. Its content is the culmination of the strivings of the Enlightenment and the French Revolution: liberty, the possibility of universal participation in the construction of reality; equality, the ultimate identity of all self-consciousness and the suppression of all irrational privileges; and fraternity, the creation of a new republican community of self-determining rational individuals.[50] While infused with the content of modern subjectivity, infinite self-consciousness is designed to overcome the antinomic formulations of Enlightenment materialism, the unsublated difference of substance and subject, is and ought.[51] To justify the political revolution as an ongoing task, Hegel's own resolution of the opposition of substance and subject in the realised totality of objective and absolute spirit must likewise be submitted to revision.

Despite his ironic counter-claims, Bauer believes that Hegel's notion of Absolute Spirit depicts the historical process as essentially complete. Reason has realised its dialectical progress and now encloses its products in a totality that imbues each element with true infinitude. In confronting being, it confronts its own self and knows itself in this reflection. It has grasped the stages of its own becoming as a necessary dialectical progression, and the patterns of the present as its own true incarnation. Objective spirit is structured by syntheses wherein the passive universality of substance becomes determinate, and the active but negative universality of the subject becomes concrete. Here subjects have made themselves substantial in the community of rational intersubjectivity, and substance is pervaded by subjective deed, has become the translucent product of subjective activity. Hegel contrasts being at this level of realisation, where objective spirit has overcome its contradictions, with transcended historical stages of being, understood as positivity. Where the *telos* of freedom has not yet infused matter with its absolute form, being can indeed become positive and fixed in opposition to spirit, thus standing in need of fundamental transformation. Though they are always the product of reason, the forms of being can block the further unfolding of reason, can represent fetters and limits that must be overcome in a new movement of spirit. But Hegel cannot leave unresolved this opposition of being and the ought. His own solution to the problematic of thought and being is not Bauer's apodeictic judgement. Hegel propounds the doctrine of absolute spirit as the overcoming of positivity in a realised and rational totality.

Bauer finds Hegel's solution theoretically and practically unacceptable. His new formulation of the dialectical categories precludes the possibility of subjectivity's coming to rest in a totality of its creations where it finds itself perfectly reflected. Only the self is the true synthesis, but the objective process remains permanently open. Behind his ironic pose, Bauer's argument against Hegel is that the principle of substantiality is not fully assimilated to that of subjectivity. Hegel's absolute idealism is therefore to be transformed into an ethical idealism whose agent is the individual consciousness, reflecting on the conditions of its genesis, but excluding all elements of transcendence. In Bauer's formulation, the constant positing and negating of the given is the free activity of self-consciousness. Yet this is not an arbitrary activity, but one conditioned by objective historical requirements.

Bauer fuses teleology and freedom and situates them in the rational subject, in opposition to the sphere of positive, irrational institutions. This, again, does not entail a repudiation of objectivity, but a liberation of its potentialities. Freedom is the inner liberty of the will, attained through the purging away of particularity in favour of universality; but it is also the will in act, changing its objective manifestations. As self-consciousness, the determinate will breaks through into existence in unending transcendence of the given, generating form and also, in the same movement, an opposition between this new form and its own creative power and infinitude. Enriched by its dialectical movement through objectivity into self and back into the outer order, it can then engender new and more complex objective forms. The historical process is the constant reproduction of this movement. Self-conscious subjects submit the given to radical critique, free themselves from the grip of the positive, and dissociate themselves from the social relations that constitute the existing totality.[52] Bauer seeks to realise the concept both in individual self-consciousness, and in the totality of objective history. He retains Hegel's insistence on the identity of concept and being; but he takes being as an unending process, not as a consolidated result. While subjects recognise the rationality of history, they cannot find themselves confirmed in the current political and social structures, which are condemned as positive and reified institutions, having forfeited their right to exist. Hegel's judgement on past, positive forms of ethical life is the same judgement that Bauer issues on the present. Together with Hegel, Bauer insists that being is a necessary, affirmative moment of the rational idea. The concept cannot remain fixed in abstract isolation, but must encounter and modify objective relations, must attain *Wirklichkeit* or causal efficacy. But only in constant transformation of the self and its products does individual self-consciousness establish identity with the universal. The Hegelian system implies as much, but, Bauer believes, Hegel did not draw out the full implications of his theory.[53]

Truth never lies in existing structures, but objectively, in the historical process as a struggle for freedom, and subjectively, in the enlightened self-consciousness, in individuals as the autonomous subjects of their own world and their own relationships. All positivity, all conditions that militate against this absolute freedom, that seek to perpetuate themselves against the further development of reason, are immediately illegitimate. Consciousness retreats out of the products of its previous activity back into the pure domain of subjectivity, but then breaks forth afresh as a new principle enriched by its struggles with a higher dialectical content. It opposes the given with unbending resolution, and in this confrontation destroys its opposite, creating a new totality as its own manifestation. With Bauer, the process is endless. The newly created products of spirit themselves become positive and must be annulled in turn. The future republican state must be in constant transformation, in permanent revision of its structures and principles. We have witnessed this position already in the *Landeskirche*, and it constantly informs Bauer's thinking in the *Vormärz*. The political consequences drawn from this formulation in the *Posaune*, the critique of the Christian state and the call for the continuation of the French Revolution, are developed and generalised in the texts of 1842–45.[54]

While the ever renewed contradiction between self-consciousness and reality, positing and positivity, appears to reproduce the Kantian and Fichtean contrast of *Sollen* and *Sein*, "ought" and being, the Hegelian motif of the unity of thought and being is still the decisive element in Bauer's presentation. This unity is achieved in the objective historical process, when subjects make its momentum their own. Subjectively, it is secured in individual self-consciousness, where universality vanquishes particularity, and where autonomy is attained in opposition to positivity. The beautiful self and its sublime struggles are evocative of the aesthetic judgement, while the motive to act is furnished by the ethics of perfectionism. This judging and rational self-consciousness is the power of *Wirklichkeit* or effective reality, in contrast to that which simply is, and is to be annulled. The ought and true being are equated in history. Bauer differentiates his own position from Fichte's, criticising as ahistorical the latter's radicalisation of Kantian practical reason.[55] Accordingly, he understands externalisation through the prism of a Hegelian phenomenology of consciousness, now identical with the philosophy of history. In the *Landeskirche*,[56] he had simply eliminated religion from an otherwise unmodified absolute spirit, and recognised the state as universal determination, the highest form of objective spirit. Bauer now comes to more radical conclusions, both on the absolute and on the conditions of political and social emancipation, which are worked out in subsequent texts. Moreover, he elaborates his critique of immediate subjectivity, whose forms, religion, and possessive individualism he also repudiates as expressions of the old principle. They are simply substantiality aroused to a rudimentary awareness – alienated, impure forms of consciousness.[57] They represent the heteronomous subordination of consciousness to matter. Against immediacy, Bauer stresses the universality and free determination of infinite self-consciousness. This is the lesson learned in the passage through substance.

As we have seen, this notion of self-consciousness contains both a subjective and an objective dimension. In the latter respect, it translates the Hegelian conception of substance mediated by consciousness and therefore infused with dynamism. In its objectivity, infinite self-consciousness refers to the totality of the operations of consciousness viewed in their outward structure and necessary sequence. The first moment is the determinate but constricted universality of antiquity, wherein individuals are subordinate to the community and have not yet understood themselves as free subjectivity. The next stage is that of the religious consciousness, which grasps the universality of subjectivity in opposition to substance, but then posits this subjectivity outside itself, in an alien domain wherein the product of its own deed is estranged from it and appears as the deed of another.[58] In its transcendent character, this moment of self-abasement, where the subjects lose themselves and worship their own loss, still represents the dominance of substantiality or pseudo-universality over subjectivity, which in turn is constricted into the forms that the unhappy consciousness now assumes. Finally, the Enlightenment and the French Revolution regain subjectivity for itself, permitting it to grasp its own universality and to posit it in the world. Here the liberated consciousness encounters another aspect of substantiality as its mortal foe: possessive individualism, particularity, the immediate consciousness that clings to its own limitation as its essential content. The principle of freedom, enunciated in the French Revolution, now needs to be theoretically and practically elaborated in order to sweep away the vestiges of positivity and alienation, religion, absolutism, and egoistic particularism.[59]

Besides this objective dimension, infinite self-consciousness evokes the intersubjectivity of Hegelian spirit. The phenomenological process of this critical consciousness is the work of enlightened individual subjects, whose activities form a diachronic nexus. If the community of free self-consciousness is the *telos* of spirit, it has also been its *energeia*, the means of historical progress. Here the material cause or *dynamis*, on its subjective side, is the empirical individual consciousness, which can either attain determinate form and universality through its permeation with *energeia* or sink into heteronomous positivity and inertia. In this sense it is the individual consciousness itself that is the decisive battleground of history, though the victories there secured by the vanquishing of particular interest must be carried into objectivity. Whether Bauer adequately accounts for synchronic connections among subjects as they struggle for liberation is a question we must examine. It will recur in the discussion of the masses and of the Jewish question.

Bauer' s explanation of the process by which the particular consciousness becomes universal self-consciousness corresponds to his programme of ethical idealism. The need to describe the dynamics of conscious self-determination poses the problem of reconciling freedom with the operation of necessity in society and history. Bauer's problem is this: How is it possible to retain a dialectical foundation for the historical evolution of freedom without admitting any elements of transcendence outside the formative power of individual self-consciousness? How can being and concept be equated in history?

If in Bauer the process of self-determination always has the same form, the elevation of particularity to universality, the specific contents of its articulation arise from two possible sources, each attested in different places in Bauer's work: from judgements either on the inner resources of subjectivity, or on the historical present, and its immanent possibilities. In the latter case at least, it is clear that objective limits constrain the patterns of spirit, positing a precise task to be fulfilled, though neither the manner of its fulfilment nor the agent of the transformation can be prescribed. This is the meaning of Bauer's denial that substance can exert any causality which is not itself mediated through individual consciousness. Bauer's texts nowhere sustain the view of one commentator, according to whom self-consciousness can change the world at will, entirely unhindered by real conditions.[60] He recognises that the teleology of subjective action is conditioned by necessary immanent contradictions in history. Genuinely free activity must be spontaneous or self-causing; those actions that exemplify infinite self-consciousness must be exempt from determination by external causes in respect to their end; though the range of possible ends is also limited by the historically given material, as the doctrine of apodeictic judgement implies. In the process of objective execution, teleology must encounter and work through external causality if the proposed end is to be realised, but even in this dimension, Bauer wants consciousness to reflect on the causal mechanisms. It is in this sense that he repudiates as mythological any notion of causality that is taken to be operative without having first been raised to consciousness.[61] As Bauer also argues in his critique of Strauss, substance as universal cannot be taken to have an immediate impact but must be mediated through individual critical reflection. The passage from heteronomy and necessity to autonomy can occur only in the full consciousness of freedom. But how do subjects secure the vantage point from which such critical judgements can be made? There appear to be two distinct models in Bauer, one in which subjects reflect on history and their place in it, the other in which they confine their attention to their own subjectivity. In referring to classical antiquity and the origins of the gospel narratives, for example, he argues that it is not by reflection on substance as constituted, or on the historical record, that the immediate awareness rises to self-consciousness. By abstracting from any objective universal, this type of judgement could not claim apodeictic status. In these cases, Bauer describes the process of engendering the new as complete interiority and self-reflection, combined with the practical sundering of connections with the existing order. Yet elsewhere, Bauer delineates historically specific, contradictory totalities that bear the seeds of their own immanent negation, through contradictions revealed to the critical consciousness.[62] Such a stance must be possible if there are to be any apodeictic judgements. Analyses of the early Fichte point to a similar duality, identified as the struggle of rationalist and historical principles.[63]

The answer to this difficulty is provided by Bauer's *Johannes* text. In the past, the function of judgement is like that of the owl of Minerva, invoked by Hegel in the *Philosophy of Right*. The true meaning and potentialities of historical forms of life are occluded from their members, who experience them as immediately given. Their genuine significance is grasped only subsequently, as a judgement conferring unity on a manifold of discrete historical occurrences.[64] Bauer had expressed a similar idea in his 1829 manuscript, when he describes situations where externality and the idea are discordant, because the idea is not yet grasped in its purity.[65] In these circumstances, a self-consciously prospective and apodeictic judgement, which Bauer advocates for his own times, is not yet possible. The *Johannes* text argues that the present is the great nodal point, permitting a transition to a new kind of historical awareness, as the achievement wrought by Hegel's philosophy. Some months previously to the *Posaune*, in *I. Synoptiker*,[66] Bauer explains that previous critical judgements lacked such a universal perspective on the objective chronicles of spirit. Here reflection on the self, not on substance, is the criterion of judging.

> Only the subject, the single self-consciousness, can bring substance to form, to pattern [*zur Gestalt*] and therefore also to the determinateness of content [*Bestimmtheit des Gestalts*]. Nevertheless self-consciousness is not active in this creative endeavour as a pure isolated ego, and it does not create and form out of its immediate subjectivity, at least not in the case when its work is taken up, recognised by the people or the community and considered for centuries as the form of its own intuition [*Anschauung*]. Without always knowing how far it has found itself in connection with its general environment, self-consciousness has stood in opposition with substance, it has been

fructified by this contradiction and driven to activity, or rather: the deeper the work is, the greater its success in gaining general recognition, so much more certainly can we assume that the originator, far from all reflection on the universal, has worked in pure impartiality and that the influence of his life-substance on his work has revealed itself in the deep intensity with which he worked.[67]

As the *Johannes* shows, the ethical status of the present is fundamentally different. The opposition to constituted, determinate forms of ethical life can either be based on subjective withdrawal and self-reflection, as in Stoicism; or it can be sustained by reflection on history as a universal product of self-consciousness, the post-Enlightenment form. The apodeictic judgement of modernity secures the correspondence of thought and being more fully and consciously than any previous attempt. This is the glory of the world to which Hegel introduces us.

Individuals can now grasp their freedom and universality in opposition to, and in critical judgement upon, existing positivity.[68] Lying behind being as its hidden essence and hidden negative, consciousness breaks through into new forms of existence as theoretical principle and as practical act. It is never a question of pure theory: The practical bearing of the principle is precisely its honour.[69] It entails real opposition, the clash of diametrically opposed interests. As Bauer argues in the *Landeskirche*, the new principle is at first accessible to relatively few who have succeeded in opening themselves to the movement of history. At its nodal points, society is divided into the bearers of universal consciousness and those imprisoned in positivity.[70] Free activity is opposed to subjugation, state tutelage, and atomistic egoism. Besides outright feudalist reactionaries, the partisans of the old order comprise all those who are incapable of rising above immediate individual interests and therefore unable to grasp the principles of infinite self-consciousness. This includes both liberal constitutionalism and incipient socialism. The *Posaune* anticipates the sharp critique of reformism in the texts of 1842–48. Precisely because it is no longer suffused with spirit, the principle of the old order is initially incapable of offering vigorous resistance to the new. It is indolent, cowardly, "massy" [*massenhaft*].[71] Its spokesmen seek compromise and conciliation, seek to minimise the difference between the old and the new. The new principle, however, requires the complete overthrow of the old; it develops most rapidly through the exacerbation of contradictions.[72] The very stridency of opposition energises the new form of consciousness to overthrow the old world. Radical critique becomes an arm of practice, practice the vehicle of the new theoretical principle.

The *Posaune*, then, effects the transformation of Hegel's dialectic in the interests of republican renewal: Because of their positivity, the religious, political, and social institutions of the Restoration have forfeited their right to exist. They have been condemned by the apodeictic judgement, whose purview encompasses all the essential moments of history. Reality is to be remade in the light of the new, higher consciousness of freedom, both as idea and as practice. Religion is to lose its grip, and political power is to be exercised by the community of free and equal citizens. Bauer presents his dialectic as the theory of the liberation of individuality from previous historical forms, and the completion of the revolutionary process initiated by the French. As he hyperbolically asserts, "Philosophy wants revolution, revolution against everything positive, even against history."[73] In Bauer's depiction, Hegel repudiates the past in favour of the freedom of the concept, and its ability to reshape the world according to its rational insight.[74] Hegel's system is the terrorist regime of the Jacobins.[75] It teaches "atheism, revolution, and the republic."[76] For Bauer, revolution and the philosophy of self-consciousness are one. This radical form of the unity of being and concept is blazoned forth in the *Posaune*.

6

"TO THE PEOPLE BELONGS THE FUTURE":
UNIVERSAL RIGHT AND HISTORY

After the pseudo-pietistic hysteria of the *Posaune*, Bauer's texts of late 1841 to mid-1842 analyse the concrete political and ideological conjuncture. They also examine further the relation between autonomous consciousness and the forms of its historical genesis, particularly the Enlightenment and the French Revolution. Bauer depicts the Revolution as the struggle for the emancipation of self-consciousness, and probes its connection to the progressive movement in Germany. He clarifies his relation to Hegel. Renouncing the ironic guise of the *Posaune*, he now explicitly argues what he had stated privately in his earlier correspondence, that Hegel's doctrine of Absolute Spirit retains elements of transcendence, antithetical to the claims of autonomy. Yet he continues to defend the Hegelian system and its progressive orientation, both against Hegel's own defective execution of his principles, and against the criticisms and attempted appropriations by the conservative forces. With the *Posaune*, Bauer's theoretical system is essentially complete. The problematics of thought and being, and of ethical idealism, remain the determining context of reflection in the subsequent period. The texts of 1841–42 offer elaboration and clarification, but no fundamentally new departures. They do, however, make manifest tensions in Bauer's conception of the revolutionary process, which have significant theoretical consequences. The publications can be grouped into three categories: two books, eighteen journalistic articles, and six theoretical essays.

In his anonymous continuation of the *Posaune*, entitled *Hegels Lehre von der Religion und Kunst* (*Hegel's Doctrine of Religion and Art*),[1] written between December 1841 and February 1842[2] and published on June 1, 1842, Bauer demonstrates the connection between Hegel's critique of religion and of the state.[3] The attack on religion is the opening salvo in the political revolution.[4] *Hegels Lehre* develops ideas that, in varying degrees, the *Posaune* had already outlined,[5] but Bauer's account incorporates his 1829 critique of Kant, with its stress on aesthetic freedom and the proximity of art to philosophy. Its importance in illustrating the continuity of Bauer's thought has already been shown.

Hegels Lehre restates the critique of religious alienation. The categories of religion "invert the laws of the real, rational world, alienate the universality of self-consciousness, rend it violently away or bring it back to representation as an alien, limited, sacred history."[6] As in his critique of theological pragmatism in 1840, Bauer stresses that theology is determined by material interests, in opposition to the aesthetic disinterestedness of universal self-consciousness.[7] The freedom of self-consciousness is its universality, its qualitative liberation from any particular interest. As he also argues in *Das entdeckte Christenthum*, the material interests that theology defends are opposed to the forces of progress, while infinite self-consciousness is free of positivity and open to constant change and transformation.

The affirmation of political revolution forms the core of another important text of June–August, 1842. Bauer composed *Die gute Sache der Freiheit und meine eigene Angelegenheit*[8] on the occasion of his dismissal from the University of Bonn in March 1842. It is a stinging indictment of his opponents, and of the political and religious edifice of the Restoration. In it Bauer assesses the theoretical status, roots, and consequences of the *Vormärz* crisis, and the prospects of human emancipation. He reemphasises that the revolution, as a necessary vehicle of social emancipation, is the task of liberated individuality.

The dominant motif is the universality of alienation, and the struggle to overcome it. At stake is a rebirth of ancient Greece, but in a modern guise. Although they could not succeed in this project because they lacked a concept of free and universal individuality, the Greeks strove to liberate humankind from the power of nature: Their gods are humanity triumphant. "We, on the other hand, have to win man back from the heavens, that is, from spiritual monstrosities, invented spirits, ghosts, indeterminateness, intellectual illusion, lies."[9] After its definitive loss of self, humankind is now to regain its freedom in infinite self-consciousness.

Bauer thus repeats the assessment of the Greeks he had offered in his 1838 *Religion of the Old Testament.* It is his evaluation of modernity, and of the place of Christianity in it, that has undergone a substantial revision. In 1838, Bauer depicts Christianity as a liberation with respect to the slavishness of the legal-religious consciousness. This it remains in the present account, but it is a dialectical progress, being at the same time the summit of alienation, the perfectly abstract and abject religion. In *Die gute Sache*, Bauer gives an account of the development of his political and religious radicalism.[10] Already in his 1838 text, he had subjected the dogmatic representations of religion to criticism, showing to what extent they are incompatible with reason. The deficiency of this early text, according to Bauer now, is that he still partly shared these religious presuppositions. He identifies his complete break with apologetics, the birth of his radicalism, as occurring in his text of 1839, *Herr Dr. Hengstenberg*.

Bauer also reflects on his theoretical development in relation to contemporary sources.[11] In a chapter originally intended as a separate essay for the *Deutsche Jahrbücher* but rejected by the censors, he restates his opposition to Strauss's tradition hypothesis: Strauss's defect is that he allows the universal to act directly and immediately in the collective consciousness of the community. This for Bauer represents substance without subjectivity, without the formative and creative energy of the individual, who aesthetically appropriates the amorphous conceptions of the community and endows them with a determinate shape. Bauer again links the principle of substantiality with that of the abstract universal. He explicitly denies that he wishes to retain only the moment of subjectivity at the expense of the objective; rather, he insists that what he proposes is a dialectical synthesis.[12] As in his early texts, Bauer's aim is to realise the unity of thought and being. The nebulous preconceptions of the community constitute the moment of abstract universality. In the singular consciousness originate new, determinate forms of these representations. When these new forms successfully capture the aspirations of the age, they mark a new stage in the historical process of self-consciousness.[13] In describing this creation, Bauer also utilises some of the language of Aristotelian causality. The singular consciousness is the source of energy, the being-at-work of form, while the abstract universal (the community's vague needs and aspirations) is the matter to be formed. As such, it is both the passive recipient of form, and also the necessary element for its realisation. Substance, here standing for the material cause, cannot be simply suppressed, though we have already seen a subjective material cause in the individual consciousness which is required to transcend itself. *Die Gute Sache* is Bauer's own defence against the charges of abstract subjectivism. Our previous considerations of Bauer's ethical idealism help us to understand the course of the argument here. The unity of thought and being entails two moments: The historical process sets the task but predetermines neither the mode nor the agents of transformation. Creative subjectivity must prescribe its own forms of resolution, and these must be freely acted upon.

This significant section of the *Gute Sache* also recalls the description of the work of art in Bauer's 1829 text, which forms its theoretical basis. Aesthetic creation is the first mode of transformation of substance into subject, the penetration of matter by thought; but it comes to fruition in philosophy, or critique, which explains the still unconscious movements of artistic creativity, and its limits. This argument is also consistent with that of *Die Posaune* and of *Hegels Lehre*. A second element in the exposition, the syllogism of universal and particular, is similar to the dialectic of citizenship that Bauer had developed in his political critique of 1840–41. *Die gute Sache* describes the process of creation within the bounds of the alienated religious relation, while "Der christliche Staat" outlines the possibilities of self-determination in a free, republican community, whose time is dawning.

The advent of such a community is now a concrete possibility. Standing opposed to the process of emancipation are religion and the state. Protestantism now represents to Bauer the completion of human alienation.[14] Catholicism is not yet the culmination of the religious consciousness, because it still recognises a source of development and change in tradition, even though the contents of tradition are held to be unaltered from time immemorial. But Protestantism has eradicated even this feeble source of determination, in favour of rigid determinateness and positivity.[15] Its principle is the pure constriction and dependency of spirit, and thus it perfects the religious consciousness. By upholding the letter of the Bible as the only source and norm of truth, it breaks with history and denies the possibility and right of free historical development. It imprisons spirit in the letter.[16] For Bauer no principle may lay claim to eternal validity; to do so is to fetter the unfolding of true human universality.

This perfection of the religious consciousness is simultaneously the manifestation of the imperfection of concrete human activity in politics, art, and science, those spheres that Hegel had designated as objective and absolute spirit. The incomplete character of free self-activity is the very ground of religion. Its basis is the alienation of the concrete domains of human life. As the product of this alienation, religion then sets itself up as an exclusive sphere and rules over the other domains of intellectual activity.[17] Religion

> is nothing but the expression, the isolated appearance and sanction of the incompleteness and sickness of existing relations. It is the general essence of all human relations and strivings, but an inverted essence, an essence rent away from them, and therefore the distorted expression of their inessentiality and alienation.[18]

Despite the weight that Bauer attaches to religion in this conjuncture, it would be erroneous to interpret the crisis as fundamentally religious. Bauer is explicit on this point. "It is not the church which is a burden to us, nor we to it – but it is the state which oppresses us with its Christian demands."[19] If the method of theology is to proceed from dogmatic presuppositions that are exempt from criticism,[20] it is the power of the state that commands compliance with these beliefs and that sets limits beyond which it forbids philosophy to venture.[21] Bauer's expulsion from the university for heterodoxy is evidence of this power, but simultaneously of the weakness of the state, its subservience to a particular and historically transcended interest. Bauer identifies criticism as the consciousness of a millennial struggle, the struggle for a state emancipated from the grip of private interest. It is the articulate voice of a political striving. He expresses with the greatest clarity the political content of his religious critique.

> What is of general [importance] in this collision, is that the ecclesiastical and religious interest wants to prevail at the expense of the concept of the state, while the state must finally free itself from ecclesiastical and religious tutelage, and constitute itself as a true state. *Criticism is the presupposition for this striving of the state* [emphasis added. DM], since it explains the power of church and religion, and completely dissolves their pretension to be a supernatural, superhuman power. [Criticism] thus initiates the political crisis which assigns to church and religious power, as purely human, its appropriate place in the circle of other human powers. The collision at this moment is therefore only this: whether the government will judge criticism according to the principle of the genuine, free state, or of the state which is dominated by the church.[22]

The dissolution of religion is not merely its theoretical substitution by philosophy, but is part of a cultural transformation in which humanity attains its potential for autonomy and creativity. As in the *Landeskirche*, critical theory figures as the authentic voice of political liberation, identifying the crucial tasks posed by the historical moment, and pressing for their solution. It represents a unity of thought and being, the rehumanisation of the species.[23]

> The collective goods of mankind, state, art, and science, form a whole, a system, and among these none counts as absolute and exclusive. None should dominate exclusively, lest it become an evil in its turn. Against these goods, religion has fought a life and death struggle, so that they might be controlled by the expression of their own imperfection. They must finally become free and freely develop. Mankind wants nothing exclusive any more. It can no longer accept religion as a universal, ruling power, since religion has up till now hindered men from being all that their potential [*Bestimmung*] is.[24]

In giving voice to one of the central demands of the republican movement, the separation of church and state, Bauer makes evident his demarcation of a public and a private sphere. This demarcation is not a simple co-existence of spheres having equal value, but is an opposition or a hierarchical ordering. Bauer accords priority to the public arena, and to citizenship. The eradication of religion is, first, its elimination from the public stage, marking the liberation of the state from ecclesiastical power and from the defence of particular interests. The free state is the expression of universal human rights, to which religion is impervious.[25] Among its other attributes, the republic has relegated religion to a merely private status. This is only an initial result of republican transformation, however. Once religion has lost its public sanction and authority, and as the conditions of social life are increasingly humanised, the roots of religious alienation are attacked, and it withers away. This is the argument that Bauer will take up, with some modification, in his two texts on Jewish emancipation of late 1842 and early 1843. Bauer does not defend a narrow idea of political emancipation against a broader account of human freedom, as Marx accuses him, but he does attribute greater weight to the overcoming of religious alienation.

> [Emancipated mankind] thus excludes religion, not in the way in which religion must exclude art and science, by trying to eliminate them root and branch. Rather, [free humanity] recognises [religion], and lets it exist as what it is, as a need of weakness, as a punishment for indeterminacy, as the consequence of cowardice – as a private affair. Art, state, and science will therefore still have to struggle against the incompleteness of their development, but their imperfection will not be elevated to a transcendent essence, which, as a heavenly, religious power, hems their further advancement. Their imperfections will be recognised as their own, and, as such, in the progress of history, they will be easily enough overcome.[26]

Bauer develops the critique of the Christian state and the Restoration he had been consistently advancing since 1840. The basis of this state is a positive principle that claims exemption from change or historical critique, and that justifies the exercise of power irrationally and irresponsibly. Because the Christian state transposes the essence of humanity into the beyond, it imposes on real human relations an order of raw constraint, a life indifferent to rights and to the rational, ethical bonds among persons.[27] It thereby reduces individuals to an amorphous mass of pure particulars, confronting an external and irrational universal. The true synthesis of universal and particular in self-consciousness and in the republican community is thus, momentarily, precluded.

Still more fundamentally, this configuration reposes upon the egoism of private interest. Particularism is the real content of the religious consciousness, but also of the possessive individualist form of assertion of private right. As does the state in clinging to its religious basis, here other private interests seek to preserve themselves immobile against history.[28] This intrinsic connection of the two forms of egoism, religious and economic, and their common opposition to the true universality of self-consciousness, is a *Leitmotif* in Bauer's work throughout the 1840s.[29]

> Universal self-consciousness [is] the conquest of egoism, which wants to uphold itself in opposition to the world, to history, to the development of history and its results. . . . Theory, which has thus far helped us [to recognise and reappropriate our essence] still remains our only aid to make us and others free. History, which we cannot command and whose decisive turns

are beyond purposive calculation, will destroy the appearance and raise the freedom which theory has given us to a power which gives the world a new shape.[30]

Bauer depicts the existing relation of the state to civil society as essentially feudal. It consists in the preservation of monopolies, and the bestowal of differential rights and privileges.[31] This relation is founded in a dialectic of consciousness. The tutelage that the state exercises is made possible by the immaturity and cowardice of its subjects, who externalise their essence in the state and thereby distort and lose that essence. The history of the state is that of the still imperfect development of self-consciousness. With fear and trembling, the subjects of the absolutist state have sought to be patronised, to be handled with suspicion and distrust by the figure of authority.

> We are simply immature: the power which has turned our essence into its own privilege thinks, speaks, acts for us, or rather for itself, and can only succeed because we belong to it as private property. We are only private property and serfs of another because we have bestowed our essence on him as his exclusive privilege.[32]

If the previous history of self-consciousness is the ground of serfdom, it also creates the conditions for its overthrow. Already church and state are reduced to pure positivity, without a commanding force or intellectual presence.[33] Their dominance of all aspects of life is only an appearance, a rotten husk. The present crisis, the concentration of the forces of progress and spirit against reaction and privilege, proves that humankind has finally attained maturity, that the decisive verdict on historically given forms may be pronounced. The state attempts to restrain its subjects, while within the conservative coalition the church still seeks to uphold the religious interest at the expense of the concept of the free state.[34] Bauer observes further that when Hegel declared constitutional monarchy to be the very concept of the state, he had not grasped the essence of freedom. Freedom and unfreedom had not yet completely crystallised out as opposing moments, but now, in the Restoration period, only unfreedom rules. Can the state be freed of religious tutelage and transformed into a true state of liberated humanity?

> Is not a principle transcended when its consequence emerges? ... Is not the feudal state overcome by its consequence, absolute monarchy; is not this overcome by its consequence the Revolution and restoration and constitutional monarchy, and this not by its consequence, the Republic?[35]

The immediate resolution that Bauer foresees, then, is the emergence of a republican state representing the interests of universal and enlightened self-consciousness. *Die gute Sache der Freiheit* expresses unequivocally the aspirations of German republicanism.

This attitude is exemplified further in a second category of texts in early 1842, a series of brief articles written for the *Rheinische Zeitung*. Ernst Barnikol gives the following assessment of these writings:

> The importance of the eighteen political-historical essays is that Bauer here represents above all the standpoint of the French Revolution of 1789 and its meaning for the future. This is in diametrical opposition to his Russian orientation of about a decade later.[36]

While Bauer's post-1848 transition will only be alluded to in the Epilogue, Barnikol's judgement about the revolutionary orientation of these texts is fully substantiated. They have attracted little critical attention. Of them, one commentator observes that Bauer's critique of constitutionalism is based upon his republican convictions, but that these remain vague and unelaborated.[37] But like Marx subsequently, methodological principles prevent Bauer from articulating a precise institutional structure for a future republican society. To do so would be to freeze the historical movement in one positive, determinate form, and to deny the rights of self-consciousness to constant evolution. The texts are not without important theoretical content.

The *Rheinische Zeitung* articles begin the evaluation of the French Revolution and its impact upon Germany, which will preoccupy Bauer until 1849. They develop three principal themes. First, Bauer compares the English and French Revolutions, to the advantage of the latter. In England, the Cromwellian Revolution was accomplished in the guise of religious fanaticism and hypocrisy, whereas in France "political questions were posed purely as such, in the sunlight of reason, humanity, and their essential content [*der Sache selbst*]."[38] The historical significance of the French contribution to emancipation far surpasses that of England, where, as a legacy of an incomplete revolution, private interest and indeterminacy continue to reign, and are sanctioned by the state as the authentic content of politics.[39]

The second principal theme of Bauer's *Rheinische Zeitung* articles is the course of the Revolution and its consequences. On the one hand, "The French Revolution destroyed the feudal Middle Ages completely: theoretically, thus with free consciousness; and legislatively, thus organising through the general will for the general good."[40] On the other, it also gave rise to aberrant phenomena like Napoleon, who was entirely alien to the spirit of the Revolution, and to incoherent attempts at reform by absolutist governments, who sought modest changes in the old order without sacrificing the principle of the absolute state itself.[41] These developments are only indicated here. They become thematic in Bauer's detailed studies of the Revolution after 1842.

The third major theme is the current state of politics in Germany, as moulded by its experience of the French Revolution. Under this rubric,

Bauer addresses in turn a number of specific issues. First, he asserts that the religious appearance of the Restoration state is mere illusion. Behind this outward guise lurks a new set of political contradictions, between the old feudal order and emergent modern society. The question of survival will have to be fought out as earnestly as it was in France.[42] This position is consonant with Bauer's declarations on the relation of church and state since 1840. As he also contends in the *Gute Sache*, it is not the church but the state that is the source of oppression. Next, he characterises the existing order in Germany as based upon the defence of narrow private interests. He stresses that egoism is to be understood in a material sense, entailing the possessive individualism of economic concerns. The dominance that the state accords to private material interests implies a contempt for the spiritual achievements of the nation, and a repudiation of universal rights, which the French Revolution had heralded.[43] Finally, Bauer begins an assessment of the oppositional movement. He argues that thanks to philosophy, the Germans occupy a higher theoretical standpoint than the French, and thus can more completely dispose of the vestiges of the old order.[44] Their critical judgement is more radical, apodeictic. At the same time, the liberal, constitutionalist movement in Germany fails to understand this heritage. It shares the same terrain as the existing feudal order. It proposes a solution that would merely perpetuate the rule of private interest, and sustain within the state itself the oppositions that constantly issue from egoism.[45] Bauer develops the metaphor of Germany as the heart of Europe. The contents of this heart, political and cultural emancipation, must pass into words, and then into action.[46] He thus advocates the continuation and completion of the French Revolution, enriched by the cultural heritage of German philosophy. He stresses the fundamental unity of these two movements.

The *Rheinische Zeitung* articles articulate the opposition of private and public interest, which Bauer signals in various forms of state and society. The defence of private interest, and the denigration of the common good or universal right, is the property both of the feudal state and of the inconsequent opposition to it, mounted by the English Puritanism of the seventeenth century, and by contemporary German liberalism. As he had done in the Welcker banquet of September 1841, Bauer argues that Hegel develops a theory of universality that transcends these particularisms and that demonstrates their place in the history of self-consciousness. Bauer depicts the opposition between public and private in very broad strokes, so that the specific content of private interest and the significant variations in its form do not always clearly emerge. In these texts, the contradiction in which self-consciousness stands to its previous historical development is not developed in a carefully nuanced phenomenological account. Two points, however, retain particular attention here. First, Bauer makes it clear that egoism is to be understood as economic and political, as well as religious, private interest. This runs counter to a long line of interpreters who depict Bauer as an exclusively religious critic.[47] Secondly, Bauer adopts a controversial tactical perspective. The revolution forges ahead through the exacerbation of contradictions: It is thus necessary to assume a provocative stance in order to crystallise the oppositional consciousness and to undercut the possibility of compromise. Bauer's adamant stance provokes a conflict with Marx over the editorial direction of the *Rheinische Zeitung* in late 1842.[48]

The third category of publications of early 1842 contains a number of substantial theoretical essays. These address, among other themes, the revolutionary tactic of accentuating contradictions, and the dialectical problem of determinate negation. They represent a defence of Bauer's revolutionary perspective against the incipient criticisms of other republicans, like Ruge.[49] Bauer's texts on reaction and revolutionary struggle evince the same historical dialectic already evident in the *Posaune* and *Hegels Lehre*. Against positivity, or substance rigidified, the determinateness of the subject is the birthplace of the new. As spirit deserts it, even that positive fixity which substance had once possessed now melts into indeterminacy. Here the task of the new principle is to provoke, to exacerbate the contradiction, to force the positive to assume again a momentary determinate stance that is necessary before it can be definitely overthrown. Only thus can the complete incompatibility of the new and the old be manifest, can all reconciling, mediating positions be undercut, can the new appear in its purity. It is in texts dating from the summer of 1842 that Bauer gives fullest expression to this principle, which is crucial for his conception of revolutionary struggle through the accentuation of contradictions.

> In those periods when the times fundamentally separate from each other, when interests break with one another and the past condemns the future, this rupture, this solution of the vital questions, is only possible because the old feels itself incompatible with the new, but still has only an unclear, if infallible, feeling of this incompatibility. It does not dare to examine the new impartially and to understand it, since it fears its own loss in this understanding, and in any case will already have denied itself should it even unashamedly examine the new. It simply does not want the new and applies all the power of its will to repel the future and the new principle from itself. But in the first moment of the struggle, it cannot even comprehend the new. Before the break, when the new principle still lay in the womb of the past, both principles, which the crisis rends apart, had still penetrated each other in an unclear fashion, limited each other, but also supported and borne each other.[50]

Though he takes it to be a principle of general historical validity, this description is especially applicable as Bauer's characterisation of the period of the 1830s, when the contradictions within the old order, and between it and the emancipatory demands of philosophy, had not yet attained clear and universal recognition. It is also a self-critical account of his own early career as a speculative theologian, a criticism he also formulates in his *Synoptiker* series. In the next phase of transition, the old principle seeks compromise with the future, seeks to profit from that moment of unclarity, of indeterminateness in which the new and old co-exist, to reconcile itself with the husk but not the essence of the new principle. "When the snake of eternity has rejuvenated and is resplendent in its new attire, then the old draws on the discarded snakeskin."[51] Bauer's critique of theological rationalism within the camp of orthodoxy, and of proponents of substance among the progressive forces, appears to correspond to this description. Theological rationalism attempts to mitigate the contradiction between faith and reason by purging the most obviously irrational elements of religious belief, but retaining the essential relation of alienation and subordination upon which the old order depends. The reason it admits is emasculated and disfigured. The metaphysic of substance in Strauss and Feuerbach, likewise, inadvertently offers a prop to the collapsing old order by minimising the autonomous, formative power of self-consciousness. This configuration sets the task for criticism, and determines its tactics. Through the elaboration of its form and content, through its conscientious defence of itself and unrelenting critique of its adversary, the new principle forces the contradiction to be resolved.

> Always, when a new principle has prevailed and has really elevated itself above its presupposition, there appears in the first moment of its victory an instant in which the defeated principle rises up again, offers resistance to the new, but through the exhaustion, indeed the impotence of the attempt proves its complete overthrow even to those who did not yet believe it.[52]

As it grapples with the new order, the old is itself transformed. Bauer here adverts to his critique of Stahl, whose defence of the *ancien régime* cannot pretend that that order is immediately valid. What now defines it is a fundamental opposition between incompatible principles. As the defence of positivity, all conservatism is burdened with a contradiction. When it attempts to justify itself against a rational opponent, it denies itself.[53] The old can no longer invoke tradition to defend its existence, because, in confrontation with its adversary, its existence is no longer immediate. Its opposition to the new principle imparts to it a new shape:

> The old which opposes the new is no longer genuinely the old, rather, through the contradiction, it has itself become a new configuration of spirit: its rights lie no more in the past, but are first to be proven.[54]

Still, this new configuration momentarily adopted by the outmoded order is rooted in the past, in the positivity of spiritless forms of life. The opposition of the new principle to the old brings to clarity what was merely implicit before. It reveals "the consequence of the old, its correct meaning and execution, the secret of the old,... the confession which its contradiction with the new has wrested from it."[55] Only when the old is forced to assume a momentary and final determinateness can it be practically vanquished. This is Bauer's justification for the provocative character of his writing. He is the herald of the new, summoning the opponents to the field to exert themselves in a decisive battle; but he is also a partisan of the new, preparing the terrain for the overthrow of the adversary.

The theoretical essays of late 1841 and early 1842 clarify the oppositions that are fleetingly outlined in the contemporary journalistic articles. Though Bauer here traces inner relations more carefully, his language is equally provocative. In "Theologische Schamlosigkeiten," Bauer undertakes a highly political defence of his critique of the gospels. As confirmed by his correspondence with Ruge,[56] the text was written in October 1841, as the *Posaune* was about to be published. It appeared in Ruge's *Deutsche Jahrbücher* in November 1841. With its acute polemical tone, the piece demonstrates an intense sharpening of contradictions among the different currents of religious reaction on the one hand, and, on the other, the critical opposition, which Bauer explicitly relates to the process of social transformation.[57] Bauer's publication of his biblical criticism was a political act around which raged a heated controversy, and he now undertakes the work of critical characterisation of the opposing positions, carrying forward the struggle outlined in historical perspective in "Der christliche Staat." He simultaneously moves from an attack on the Church and theological doctrine to a more comprehensive attack on faith and its irrational, antirational forms of expression.

Bauer contends that the modern age is characterised by the perfection of faith, with the consequent degradation of humanity, reason, and morality, and the perfectly antagonistic contradiction and mutual repulsion of faith and reason. Bauer outlines five variants of fideistic conservatism, dubbed *Schamlosigkeiten* or shamelessness because of their unabashed repudiation of reason. First, the orthodox-pietistic direction of Hengstenberg simply refuses to deal with or recognise the results of criticism; but this neglect merely highlights the muteness and impotence of faith.[58] Hengstenberg no longer appears as the worthy adversary of 1839; he is now an ineffectual onlooker in a struggle that has passed him by. Second, the historical school of Leo advocates "love and patience" towards outworn social conditions; here Bauer is particularly eloquent in advocacy of revolution.[59] Third, he identifies among his critics opportunists who merely follow shifts of power.[60] Fourth, Schleiermacherian pseudo-criticism strives to combat science with certain scientific weapons, but thereby turns defence into deceit and hypocrisy.[61] Finally, theological rationalism attempts merely to expunge the contradictions and absurdities of religious belief while still asserting it as a positive force.[62] These various attitudes represent distinct moments of transition between the old and the new principle: Hengstenberg the initial moment of rejection, Schleiermacher and the theological rationalists the moment of untenable compromise, and Leo the recognition of the incompatibility of the old and the new.

By far the most significant section is that on Leo, the third major proponent of Restoration politico-religious orthodoxy after Hengstenberg and Stahl to become the object of Bauer's criticism. Already satirised for his ignorant pietism in the *Posaune*, Leo now appears as a representative of the historical school of law, for whose forerunner, Haller, Hegel himself had reserved his severest polemics in the *Philosophy of Right*.[63] In his criticism, Bauer makes a clear affirmation of the republican revolution. Free self-consciousness will guide and partake in the victory of a previously excluded class, the partisans of the emancipatory principle. This victory will mean a profound political transformation, the creation of a new state based on the principle of universal freedom. This is consistent with his critique of liberal reformism and his defence of republicanism in "Der christliche Staat." The Restoration's tutelary state must be completely reorganised to secure freedom and autonomy. The virulent polemical tone is indicative of the intensifying political struggle. Leo demands

> that one should show "love and patience" towards historical institutions which have become outdated, that one should not destroy them by depicting them as defunct and dead. Love and patience! Leo demands this in a tone befitting a rabid hound who should demand mildness and tranquillity of one on whom he springs howling and gnashing his teeth. Herr Leo barks, howls, snaps and bares his fangs as though he were himself rabid when he demands that philosophers should treat with love and patience the corpse whose stench already makes the air unbearable....
>
> Free science is today proscribed and repudiated by the state, it stands outside the power which the government possesses and to which it allows access to the faithful, the mute variety as well as the vocal [a reference to Bauer's characterisation of Hengstenberg and Leo, respectively. DM]. If it were purely a question of power and its enjoyment, does Herr Leo really believe that we would have no part in it if we were willing to renounce our principle and to convert to one or other of the forms of faith? But it is not simply a question of power as such, but the power of a principle; not a matter of pure recognition, but of recognition for and because of the principle; not a matter of enjoyment of the state, but of the enjoyment of a state which is based on the principle of free self-consciousness. It is not just a question of freedom of the person and of conscience, which no one yet need guarantee us, but of freedom based and dependent on the public recognition of the principle of free self-consciousness. A new principle only attains its end when it passes from its theoretical ideality into the immediacy of power....

Yes, we want to participate [*mitgeniessen*], just as all new principles with their drive for participation have unsettled and finally destroyed the privileged classes. When first this hunger is awakened, it is no longer possible for the privileged class to permit only the leaders to partake of its advantages – its privilege must become a universal right. So the Hussites did not want to leave the wine only to the parsons, and their thirst was still not quenched when the priests allowed a few crowned laymen to partake of the wine. They wanted everyone to be able to enjoy, and it was not long until everyone could drink who wished. So has every excluded class in all of history wanted to participate, and to none who has earnestly desired has it been denied. "Take ye all and drink," it is written.

Free self-consciousness too will come to participate, and its time is not far off.[64]

The article "Leiden und Freuden des theologischen Bewußtseins" ("Suffering and Joys of the Theological Consciousness"), written in January 1842,[65] simultaneously with *Hegels Lehre*, makes a further contribution to the analysis of the ideological currents of the time. Having attained for a moment a clear conception of a worthier future for humankind and respect for the French Revolution, the Germans have sunk back into torpor, mysticism, and theology. The analysis of the theological consciousness is thus precisely the analysis of the mind of the Restoration.[66] Political critique entails moreover a self-clarification of the relation of the German progressive movement to the French Enlightenment and the Revolution. The French had not only initiated a struggle against the personal representation of the religious consciousness as faith and superstition, but had even challenged this consciousness in its generality,[67] its objective manifestation and pivotal role in a system of political and social oppression. It has now become the norm, Bauer contends, to dismiss the work of the Enlightenment as frivolous and unethical, even when it is scarcely known or studied; but the result of this thoughtless repudiation is that Germany is plunging further into the abyss of reaction. It is necessary to recall the heroic struggle of Enlightenment figures against the power of absolute monarchy and the clergy, the fight for emancipation and the assertion of autonomy.[68] The Germans must once again learn from the French and, enriched by the highest acquisitions of dialectical thought, develop the relation of the alienated theological consciousness to the universal activity of self-consciousness. This entails the demonstration of the nature of religious alienation and of the possibilities of its transcendence.[69] Both aspects are fundamentally political.

Bauer argues that the theological consciousness emerges from a rupture within self-consciousness between the miserable individual self and the universal, true self. This split constitutes the religious relation in its immediate form of existence. Consciousness becomes truly theological when it enlists reflection, the power of the understanding, in its service.

The activity of reflection produces the world of concrete religious representation, but it does so by denying its own creativity and attributing it to another. Its activity appears to it as the passive reception of truth and value from an alien source.[70] At the same time, this consciousness undergoes a phenomenological progression (described by Hegel) that evinces various distinct attitudes. The contradictory unity of universal and particular first evokes anxiety: The feeling of subjective unity with the divine dissipates, because the self is ceaselessly jostled back and forth between each element of the contradiction. Next appears self-deception, the conscious refusal to recognise the contradiction as one's own work; then the futile labour to eliminate the contradiction within the bounds of the religious relation. In all these and other forms of suffering and gratification,

> Theological consciousness cannot exist without a split and diremption of self-consciousness. Free, human self-consciousness recognizes and always unifies in its own inner, universal and ideal world all the general determinations which unite and count for mankind, considering these as a witness of its own development and as the only worthy witness of its life. But the religious consciousness has rent these away from man's own self, has transposed them to a heavenly world, and so it has created a contradiction between the individual self, which has become infirm, staggering and miserable, and the only self which deserves the name of man.[71]

This unhappy religious consciousness, which construes the highest forms of human activity as the deed of another, thus debases and deforms its particular bearers. It places universality in an inaccessible "beyond," denying the claims of the subject to self-transcendence. It is always a spurious infinite suspended over a mass of particulars, without ever achieving genuine integration of its moments. But as an unattainable universal, it also reveals its own nullity. A One beyond all particulars, it is therefore without content; but its claim to be All leaves the many submerged hopelessly in their immediacy.

Against this static configuration, Bauer asserts the rights of free self-consciousness. "The movement surges ahead precisely because it serves the general interest."[72] Its proponents, "citizens in the republic of self-consciousness,"[73] are capable of self-determination and autonomy. The unity of the empirical self with the highest determination of universality is now a concrete, objective possibility. The task of the present is to bring this possibility to fruition. It is precisely this which religion denies, seeking to restrain humankind at the level of brute particularity, to make it a mass. Hence the necessity of confrontation. Bauer stresses throughout the political character of the revolution and of the crisis. His intent is the unification of universal and particular in a new form of autonomy grounded in history. This position is consistent with his interpretation and critique of Hegel in the *Posaune*.

The clash of religion and philosophy is also the theme of Bauer's review "Bremisches Magazin für evangelische Wahrheit gegenüber dem modernen Pietismus,"[74] which appeared in the *Anekdota* of 1843. The text describes the dialectic of pietism and rationalism as modern theological currents bringing to completion the process of abstraction that has characterised the history of Christianity. It is a document of particular importance, however, in determining the development of Bauer's relation to Hegel. Bauer argues that Hegel had retained religion as a positive power outside the realm of self-consciousness, and had sought to reconcile the diametrically opposed principles of religion and philosophy.[75] The religious interest has refused such a compromise, seeing in the power of reason not an ally, but the deadly adversary of faith. This position regarding Hegel accords with the views that Bauer expresses in his correspondence in 1841, though it is at odds with the argumentation of the *Posaune*. Bauer contends that

> the true refutation is the elaboration of philosophy and its liberation from all positive presuppositions, which up till now it has seemed to share with its religious opponents. . . . Precisely on the point which has been most contentious in recent years, the Hegelian system approaches its completion, and the impetus which it has thereby received will also complete the system in the other disciplines and construct it according to its own eternally true principle. In its positive aspect, it still seems to separate the universality of consciousness from self-consciousness itself as a substantial power; but criticism will draw this into self-consciousness and its movement, which encompasses everything because self-consciousness is the unity and power of the universal.[76]

The immanence of the universal is the final result of philosophical criticism. In this text, Bauer develops above all the theoretical implications of this position for reconstituting philosophy and the particular scientific disciplines. Other contemporary articles emphasise the role of practical reason and the political meaning of autonomy.

In his review of Theodor Kliefoth's *Einleitung in die Dogmengeschichte*,[77] Bauer again stresses the fundamental unity of his critique of religion and state: Both are rooted in the critique of substantiality as a positive power. Allegedly lying outside free self-consciousness, the forms of positivity claim universality for themselves and deny it to the particulars. Bauer's demand for free self-determination is a radical critique of oppressive and irrational relations of power. He exposes the fundamental unity, the transcendent character of the church and the absolutist police state, a unity of principle that is much more than a merely tactical alliance against the progressive forces.[78] Consistent with his argument in "Der christliche Staat," Bauer does not exempt the "formal constitutionalist state" from this criticism, because it seeks to perpetuate "its determinate positive form, which it considers eternal and definitive."[79] Bauer's dialectic of the formative power of self-consciousness clearly underlies his republican stance.[80]

> In any case the formal constitutional and the police state are not the only forms of state. States will arise – their time draws near, as the existing states already sense in the premonition of their dark and uncertain future – states will come, which will base themselves confidently on the freedom of self-consciousness.[81]

The review of Kliefoth is also the occasion for a further specification of Bauer's relation to Hegel. Hegel grasps subject as substance, but also provides the critique of this standpoint, because he derives substantiality from the movement of self-consciousness. He does so in principle, if not always in execution. The Hegelian principle itself supplies a correction to the defective formulations in the system. Bauer acknowledges his continuing adherence to this philosophy, which is now, in the storm of struggle, undergoing further development in his own work.[82]

In "Bekenntnisse einer schwachen Seele" ("Confessions of a Weak Soul"),[83] composed in April 1842, Bauer takes issue with the reformist, constitutionalist faction of the oppositional movement. He describes the liberal position as a cowardly retreat before the tasks of social transformation, an attempt to reconcile diametrically opposed principles, to preserve the rotten carcass of the old order. Against this, he expressly favours a principled revolutionary stance. Consistent with the *Posaune* and *Das entdeckte Christenthum*, he situates the agent of the revolution in self-consciousness.[84] Criticising the weak soul of the title, the reformers of the *Berliner literarische Zeitung*, Bauer encapsulates his own political position.

> "Reform, not revolution!" right from the beginning (No. 2, p. 34) is their campaign cry. "Reform" but no revolution, and no reaction either (No. 4, p. 85).
>
> "The revolutionary," our reformer teaches us, "struggles against the existing relations and institutions not purely because they are inadequate or because a change seems objectively necessary, but according to wholly abstract ideals, or because the institutions do not correspond to his maxims and tendencies." "Abstract, dead, negative, arbitrary" is the "content" of the revolution. How "noble," knightly, baronial, indeed princely – even if not spiritual – is in contrast the "pattern of an organic political development, making progress through objectively necessary reforms." (No. 13, p. 298)
>
> When however the "objective" relations are rotten through and through and demand transformation from top to bottom, may revolution then raise its head? When existing relations entirely contradict the idea, where else can the idea exist but in pure self-consciousness, which has saved itself from the decay and at first bears within itself as an ideal the true forms of its existence? But has not self-consciousness the right to desire that its inner determinations be replicated [*wiederfindet*] in the existing laws and institutions?[85]

Bauer's text also notes critically the changing evaluation of Hegel by the supporters of the old order.[86] Whereas in the 1830s Hengstenberg had denounced Hegel himself as a revolutionary, he is now praised as a champion of religion and monarchism against the strident demands of the Left. Bauer continues to claim the authentic Hegelian heritage, "atheism, revolution and the Republic,"[87] for the cause of progress and political change. The necessary and destructive work of scientific critique has transformed the vapid German oppositional movement into a determinate movement on the French model. Criticism announces the turn from theoretical to political revolution.[88]

Bauer leaves no doubt that the revolutionary struggle he envisages is no mere abstract clash of principles. In his review of von Ammon's *Leben Jesu*,[89] of June 1842, he contends,

> The crisis is no longer a theoretical one of principles, but a practical one: whether a defeated principle, which proves its defeat by its speech and by its whole appearance, should still rule in the real world, in a world which it no longer intellectually governs and is no longer able to govern; or whether the new victorious principle shall obtain practical recognition. . . .[90]
>
> To the people belongs the future; but the truth is popular, because it is open, undivided, relentless and unafraid. The truth will thus share the possession of the future with the people, or rather both, the people and the truth are one, and the one, all-powerful ruler of the future. The curial style of tutelage will no longer be understood by the people: they want the style of truth, courage and simplicity – they desire the popular style, which they alone understand.[91]

This affirmation of the unity of popular strivings and theoretical emancipation is characteristic of Bauer's political position in 1842. He here identifies the people as *das Volk*, a revolutionary subject who can attain to universal aspirations and can topple the existing order. By 1844 he stresses the danger to *das Volk* posed by *die Masse*, pure particularity that stands opposed to the progress of spirit. While maintaining his republican aspirations, he increasingly finds the various social classes that compose the movement to be inadequate representatives of the principles of freedom. The tension between the faltering objective movement and the critical subjective consciousness becomes extreme.

IV

JUDGING THE REVOLUTIONARY MOVEMENT

"THE FIRE OF CRITICISM": REVOLUTIONARY DYNAMICS, 1843–1848

The critical judgement that Bauer effects upon the present entails determining the relation of consciousness to the moments of its historical development. The essential issues are to grasp the historical forms of alienated spirit, and to recognise and distinguish the phases of their overcoming, of which the most significant are the Enlightenment and the post-Hegelian period. While describing a historical sequence, these phases also represent a logical progression, a shift from the infinite to the apodeictic judgement. These questions are addressed in a text that Bauer composed in winter 1842–43, *Das entdeckte Christenthum*. The censors confiscated this book directly from the publishing house, and only a few copies are known to have circulated. It is among the many merits of Ernst Barnikol's research to have discovered a copy of this text, long believed lost.[1] The opposition of self-consciousness to the constituted forms of religious alienation is Bauer's central theme. Continuing his presentation of religion and philosophy as antinomies, Bauer draws the consequences of his earlier pronouncements on a range of subjects, including the materialist current of the Enlightenment in relation to his own thought.

For Bauer, religious consciousness is the static, internally antagonistic expression of particularity, which freezes the historical movement. It perpetuates the opposition of particular against particular by occluding the true universality of the species. Each religious party claims for itself the status of the universal, of the final and authentic essence of humankind. From its fetishistic vantage point, each is compelled, in order to preserve its own form, to reject identical claims of other particular groups; hence ensues a mortal combat among factions. But this is a struggle without progress, without resolution. The conflicts do not lead beyond themselves to a new level of being and consciousness that reconciles or overcomes the differences; instead, they merely heighten and intensify the existing oppositions. Hegel's dialectic of master and slave might appear to have a similar foundation, in that each party initially wishes to have its own claim of freedom prevail; but for Hegel this relation leads directly to transformation, first in a unilateral recognition in which one party surrenders its claim to independence, and then in a higher consciousness wherein each acquires a new self-definition.[2] In contrast, according to Bauer the struggle among competing religious factions, which is typical of the post-Reformation world, engenders no mutual recognition, but simply results in the perpetuation and infinite repetition of the conflict. Each particular wants to count immediately as the universal. No party surrenders its independent claim to absolute validity, but, while knowing that the others make identical assertions, each clings rigidly to its own self-sufficiency; no internally motivated evolution or change of vantage point is possible. The religious consciousness has as its basis not the natural self, as in the master–slave relation, but an already constituted form of *Sittlichkeit*, however defective this might be. Thus it is unable to renounce itself, because it can command the resources of its members, or call on the power of the state to guarantee its prerogatives. The closer analogy is perhaps with the relations among sovereign states as outlined in the *Philosophy of Right*, though these must defend their autonomy because they represent concrete realisations of the ethical will,[3] while the religious consciousness is mere particularity. Bauer himself suggests that such a comparison is not entirely misplaced when he claims that the Jewish question, for example, is to be understood as a national question, concerning the mutual compatibility of different forms of *Sittlichkeit*.[4] He describes the sterile antagonisms of the religious consciousness:

> Each [religious] party believes itself to be the true expression of the human essence, each must therefore deny the other, declare it to be inhuman, and in its estrangement from it go so far that each becomes as alien as one species of animal to another. Each party believes itself alone to be eternal, each must therefore exclude the other from eternity or rather damn it for eternity, thereby giving the eternal impression of its unique, exclusive justification. But while one party damns the other, it must always bear the consciousness that it is also damned by the other. Each party damns and is forever damned.[5]

In the variety of its manifestations, religious consciousness thus tends towards a self-perpetuating totality. While each element of this unity stands in a contradictory relation to the others, this contradiction bears no inner principle of development. It contains no determinate negation. "Religious consciousness cannot freely express and recognise this contradiction as such, because it is its own self."[6] If progress is impossible from within the static totality of religious representations, consciousness cannot ultimately remain satisfied with this configuration. Transformation does occur, but wrenchingly, through great revolutionary upheavals. The seeds of the new and higher form are not to be found in the system of constituted forms, consisting of opposed but formally identical particulars. Only when these forms are freed from their immediacy and led back to their common origin in alienated self-consciousness does an immanent solution appear. When, through theoretical critique and historical experience, the content of these forms is undermined, there appears a radically new constellation of ethical life, predicated on a new fundamental principle. Self-consciousness liberates itself from its previous limitations, and sets to work creatively. The foundation of the religious consciousness is attacked first by the infinite judgement of the Enlightenment; and then by the post-Hegelian apodeictic judgement, which, appropriating the results of previous philosophical and historical labour, shows the way to true resolution.

For Bauer, the rigidity or positivity of existing forms of consciousness, this static configuration, has constituted itself out of objectively negative processes, expressing the limits and unclarity of previous human endeavour. He claims that religion represents the defects of social life and historical self-awareness. The divine attributes are not, as for Feuerbach, the permanent, universal properties of the species, which stand in contrast to the finite individual.[7] Nor are they demanded by practical reason, as in Fichte. Bauer sees them rather as historical products, the expression of an objective deficiency in the level of thought and self-consciousness.

> God is the non-being of all real being, . . . the limit or rather the restrictedness [*Beschränktheit*] of thought, the objectified limitation of thought elevated to an independent essence. God is the passivity of man, the highest suffering, poverty and emptiness of spirit.[8]

This negativity is the cause as well as the effect of religious alienation. The religious consciousness comprises both subjective and objective dimensions. The various forms of subjective belief are each grounded in the objective limitations that produce and sustain them. The static character of this consciousness is the crucial factor. The solution to religious alienation cannot therefore consist solely in reintegrating the divine into the human, as Feuerbach proposes, but in negating the limitations that are its roots. Marx adopts a similar position to Bauer's in his writings of 1843.[9] Bauer insists that both particular and universal are to be transformed, the former overcoming the practical deficiencies that constrict and deform it, the latter abandoning its transcendent character and its timeless, substantial appearance. Feuerbach's naturalism remains alien to history; only if both terms are absorbed in the flux of historical becoming can the assimilation of the universal with the particular be complete.

Knowledge of the true relationship, the discovery of alienated self-consciousness and the means to overcome it, is also a historical achievement, but this insight is attained only gradually, through protracted critical struggles. The Enlightenment is the first moment in this process of definitive awakening and self-mastery. As in Kant, Enlightenment is the dawning of moral maturity, when tutelage is cast off, but for Bauer the enlightened moral subjects are not yet fully aware of their freedom. "The French did not go too far when they taught that lack of knowledge, misery and misfortune and fear gave men their first ideas of divinity."[10] The Enlightenment critique of religion as fraud, however, is superficial. It does not engage with the profound issues of alienation that religion presupposes.

Unlike Holbach, for example, Bauer does not hold that religion is based upon duplicity. As he shows in the third volume of the *Synoptics*, where he describes the literary origins of religious representations, this process is less the expression of intentional deceit than of immature and alienated self-consciousness. When he distinguishes these naive representations from the process of theological ratiocination in John's gospel, this further refinement of which the religious consciousness is capable is not deceit, either, but the entrapment of reason by representation or *Vorstellung*. Bauer sees this emergence of the theological from the religious viewpoint as a necessary historical passage, where the irrepressible higher strivings of spirit, for clarity and determinateness, are applied to an inferior, unevolved, alienated content. This synthesis, which marks the transition from immediate religious sentiment to reflective theological conception, however, is no genuine progress, but is the deeper self-abasement of consciousness, its enslavement before a deficient content. It leads nowhere but into servile apologetics.

As a more recent adaptive strategy, the religious consciousness attempts to respond to Enlightenment critique by internalising the opposed rational principle, but in an entirely anodyne manner. Bauer claims that, like the eighteenth-century deistic current, his contemporary theological-rationalist opponents try to secure a conformity between religious precepts and reason, by eliminating miraculous elements, and offering plausible or banal explanations of other essential doctrines. For Bauer, this is not a true development or an authentic synthesis of faith and reason, because here is still no free, unfettered examination, but an apologetic justification of a given content. In abasing reason as an instrument of faith, however, theological rationalism does demonstrate the necessity of a fundamental break. The Enlightenment claims that faith and reason simply do not (contingently) conform; this claim theological rationalism rebuts, but both antagonists share the same fundamental presuppositions. For essential progress to occur, the opposition must be grasped more radically.

The solution is given in Bauer's conception of history. The post-Enlightenment self-consciousness now asserts its right to absolutely free and untrammelled enquiry, and critically appropriates for itself the results of its previous development. After the work of the transcendental philosophy and its further development by Hegel, self-consciousness now knows itself as the movement of reality and its reflection in knowledge. It recognises that the constricted forms of its past existence were necessary stages in its evolution; no essential content is lost in this recognition. In Bauer's language, self-consciousness thus posits the world, in the sense that it is the movement of the world brought to consciousness, become truly for itself.

> To what end does spirit exist? Why self-consciousness? As if self-consciousness, in positing the world, that which is different from itself [*den Unterschied*], and in engendering itself in its products – for it again sublates the difference between its products and itself, it is itself only in engendering and in movement – as if it did not have its purpose and first possess itself in this movement, which is itself![11]

The historical process, so understood, is the objective side of the union of concept and objectivity. The self-consciousness here invoked is no hypostasis, but is the record of the achievements of concrete subjects who acknowledge a common task. The subjective side also requires elaboration through a new concept of agency that transcends the fixed Enlightenment perspective.[12] The Enlightenment discovers the general concept of humankind, which had been obscured and denied by religious differences and social hierarchy. In a related text, Bauer criticises the view of universal human rights as innate and eternal. Instead, he offers a defence of rights based on the historical development of self-consciousness.

> These human rights are first a product of modern history. Earlier they were not accessible. They are only a product of freedom and self-activity, and not a gift of nature. So too there have only recently been men. Man is a product of history, not of nature. He is the product of himself and of his deed. The revolutions of the modern age were necessary for human rights to prevail against natural drives and the natural determinations which guided and ruled men in the life of the estates. Thus too the same revolutions were needed, so that men could finally come to themselves and become men.[13]

But this initial concept of universal human rights remains vacuous, because the Enlightenment counterpoised to it a rigid and particular view of the individual as a creature of necessity, dominated by material need, and not as a free and self-determining subject. Bauer does not simply conjure need away, but he invites subjects to conceive of their potentialities more broadly, and to struggle to establish social and political forms that actualise this potential, though there are significant tensions in his account of freedom, as we will observe. Now, he claims, what is required is to understand the self too in its universality, as fluidity and becoming, thus overcoming the rigidity of the Enlightenment standpoint. This is the logical progress from the infinite to the apodeictic judgement on its subjective side, corresponding to the historical experiences of revolution.

For Bauer the subject in its truth is not a particular, contingent synthesis of given traits and dispositions, alongside the determinateness of the objective world. Such is the case with that subjectivity which is heteronomous, a particularity that has not grasped its freedom and elevated itself to universality. Nor is the subject, in Bauer's view, an aggregation of material and economic interests, a possessive individualist.[14] The materialist utilitarianism favoured by the Enlightenment constricts the universality of spirit through the domination of objects, as means of satisfaction or material appropriation. This philosophical conception does not rise from empirical to pure practical reason, from the hypothetical satisfaction of desires to the disinterested striving for freedom. Bauer rejects the corresponding view of activity as the simple rearrangement of natural elements into new constellations. Activity must engender the new out of the inner resources of free subjectivity, by negating the positively given, and liberating the repressed possibilities of the present. Even when it turns to the question of relations among subjects, Enlightenment subjectivity remains essentially particular. Echoing Hegel's criticisms of Rousseau,[15] Bauer argues that it rests on the private calculation of the common good, but this common good is not conceived in its true generality. It is what Hegel names a universal judgement, a summation of private individual interests. Enlightenment formulations dissolve and atomise the genuine universal, both in its objective existence, and in its being for consciousness. Bauer himself does not satisfactorily resolve the question of intersubjectivity, as his ethics of revolution will make plain; but his intent is to defend a universal that has no transcendent status, while being irreducible to a mass of mere particulars.

The emergence of the new principle of freedom entails the purging away of the religious consciousness, and self-identification with the objective movement of history. "The impartial man recognises this contradiction, the necessary consequence of the religious consciousness, and when he recognises it purely and openly and without secret egoistic reservation, so he has freed himself from it."[16] The results of a century of implacable criticism, and the rapid advance in the critical standpoint under the experiences of political and philosophical revolution, have eroded the totality of religious representations. Spirit has already abandoned this stage of its development. Though still locked in futile combat, the religious contestants are exhausted, and incapable even of sustaining their mutual hostilities without outside intervention. As Bauer also argues in the *Landeskirche* and *Die gute Sache*, the state has become the essential prop of the religious consciousness. The independent existence of religion is a mere sham, says Bauer, and it exists now as an arm of political repression and tutelage. But this is a post-Enlightenment judgement, available only once we have grasped the role that political, religious, and other alienations have played in history.

The argument of *Das entdeckte Christenthum* is the basis of the position Bauer assumes on the Jewish question. His revolutionary stance is far more problematic in these two texts, dating from October 1842 and early 1843. *Die Judenfrage (The Jewish Question)*[17] and "Die Fähigkeit der heutigen Juden und Christen, frei zu werden" ("The Capacity of Present-Day Jews and Christians to Become Free")[18] elaborate Bauer's critique of the religious consciousness and of political reformism.[19] The immediate consequence of their publication, however, was that Bauer forfeited his leading position in the opposition movement, as he was seen to reject one of its central demands. The question was whether the Prussian state, with its explicitly Christian foundation, could eliminate longstanding restrictions on Jewish participation in civil institutions.[20] Conservative opponents of Jewish emancipation denied this possibility, for in that case the state would have to renounce its confessional allegiance and become a lay state. This would undermine the religious basis of its sovereignty, which supported the hierarchical social order. Liberal and republican forces were generally united in their advocacy of emancipation for the Prussian Jews. Bauer subjects all parties in the dispute to criticism. He attacks the state for its defence of irrational privilege, and claims that it uses religion as a mask for its interests in maintaining relations of subordination. He criticises liberalism for its view of freedom as particular interest. He criticises the Jewish religion for its immutability, its opposition to change and progress; and its practitioners for claiming freedom on the basis of their particular identity. His position on Jewish emancipation is that the precondition for genuine political and social freedom is the renunciation of all particularistic ties with the past; thus, to be free, Jews must renounce their religious allegiance, as indeed must Christians. Both of Bauer's texts are the object of criticism by Marx in 1843. From his newly acquired socialist perspective, Marx dissects Bauer's notion of political liberty, and opposes to it an idea of full human liberty. He argues that Bauer's concept of revolution does not transcend the horizon of bourgeois society.[21] For all the weaknesses of his analysis in this case, Bauer, however, clearly maintains a distinction between political and human emancipation, which Marx claims as his own. He rejects Marx's accusations, and asserts that his objective is social as well as political freedom; he will continue to defend this position throughout the revolutionary years of 1848–49.[22] For all their contentious character, Bauer's texts on the Jewish question contain critical observations that shed additional light on the relation of politics and religion and on his vision of modern society.

The method and scope of Bauer's texts have only recently received close critical attention.[23] Critics of his position have insufficiently recognised that his argument must be understood from the standpoint of *Das entdeckte Christenthum*, which was written at about the same time as his first intervention on the Jewish question. Bauer's argument that a renunciation of religion is a prerequisite to political emancipation re-states his consistent critique of exclusivity and particularity. Bauer fuses exclusiveness and egoism as principles of the old order, in opposition to the universality of free self-consciousness, and depicts the attempt to up-hold those principles unchanging as a blind assertion of positivity against the historical movement of emancipation.[24] His practical stance is thus in many respects coherent with the theoretical dialectic of the *Posaune*, but it now involves him in opposition to a concrete demand of the progres-sive movement. While he continues to insist that his is indeed the correct revolutionary position, his adamant opposition has serious consequences for his republican credibility.

Bauer distinguishes the nature of oppositions as they appear within the fixed constellation of the religious consciousness, and the real relation, as it exists for the scientific consciousness that has developed beyond it. His method is to uncover the basis of religious views, then to order them as developmental stages, and finally to connect them with forms of ethical life that give rise to them. The religious consciousness cannot itself grasp these distinctions. They are moments in the historical emancipation of subjectivity from the weight of particular interests and from heteronomy. His description of the relations of Christianity and Judaism is virtually identical to passages from his *Entdeckte Christenthum*. For the sects defined by the religious consciousness,

> Neither can let the other exist and recognise it; if one exists, the other does not exist; each of them believes itself to be the absolute truth. If it therefore recognises the other and denies itself, it denies that it is the truth.... Religion is exclusivity itself, and two religions can never conclude peace with each other as long as they are recognised as religions, as the highest and the revealed.[25]

For the scientific consciousness, the matter presents itself differently. This critical consciousness is able to uncover the basis of religion in par-ticularity, egoism, and estrangement from universal human concerns, and demonstrate the roots of religious alienation in the insufficiencies of constituted ethical life. As in *Das entdeckte Christentum*, Bauer sees in religion a mirroring of empirical contradictions.

> Men have never yet done anything in history purely because of religion, undertaken no crusades, fought no wars. [Even] if they believed that they acted and suffered only to do God's will... it was always political in-terests, or their echoes, or their first stirrings, that determined and led mankind.... Religious prejudice is the basis of social [*bürgerlichen*] and po-litical prejudice, but the basis which this latter, even if unconsciously, has given itself. Social and political prejudice is the kernel which religion only encloses and protects.... Religious prejudice is the reflection created by

men themselves of the impotence, unfreedom, and constriction of their social and political life, or rather dream.[26]

Next, the scientific consciousness distinguishes, within religious attitudes, grades of historical evolution. In judging the place of various religions in the historical sequence, Bauer draws on his earlier work on the history of revelation. There he had claimed that Judaism represents a lower level of consciousness, that of the external relation of humankind and God, mediated though law or arbitrary will; as in Hegel's view of Oriental society, only the one is free (though this One is transcendent), while the particular subjects are subordinate to irrational command. Christianity demonstrates a higher degree of consciousness, as in it all are free, and the externality of the deity is cancelled. But this is not a unilateral progress upon Judaism, because Christianity and especially Protestantism universalise alienation to encompass all aspects of social life. The superiority of Christianity consists only in its unendurable negativity, making requisite a transition to a new and higher form of ethical life.[27] By the exacerbation of the contradiction between self-determination and self-abasement, the way is cleared for an epochal resolution; this position we have witnessed in Bauer's writings of 1841–42.

The essential political question raised by Jewish emancipation is not, for Bauer, the integration of particulars, which maintain their particularity, into a more comprehensive whole, but rather a change in character, or self-transcendence of the particulars themselves. The whole, too, takes on a new conformation, not as the summation and defence of private interests, but as the conscious universal end. Only this, for Bauer, is the plan of the republic. Hence, he concludes, it is impossible to become a citizen of the republic while protecting a particularistic identity. Nor may one even claim rights within the existing state on this basis. The first reason is exactly as the proponents of the Christian state maintain, that this state is fundamentally committed to one particular sect, and must therefore deny recognition to others. Second, even as addressed to the existing state, and not to the future republic, such a rights claim is theoretically inadmissible before the court of self-consciousness, because it confuses universal right with a privilege or exemption claimed in virtue of some given feature or identity. Only by subjects' renouncing this identity is access to freedom open to them.

While Bauer continues to subscribe to historical perfectionism and the sublime struggle for emancipation, he now enters into conflict with important elements of the political opposition. Bauer sees his position on the Jewish question as entirely consistent with his ethical idealism and republicanism, and we have identified significant parallels with his other writings. Yet, even if we adopt the republican criteria Bauer has devised, his critical position on Jewish emancipation is not the only possible mode of judging the revolutionary movement. What is not inevitable, nor essentially inscribed in his republican programme, is the conflation of right and morality that occurs in Bauer's thinking on this question. He demands that subjects adopt a certain moral attitude, or set of maxims, as a precondition for political action and juridical equality. Such an attitude may be a criterion for full adherence to the republican movement, but this is to confuse the present question, that of eliminating irrational restrictions on access to public institutions, within the context of a defective form of state. Bauer does not prove that his is a necessary standard for the concession of juridical rights, which, in the tradition of Kant, abstract from motivation, and concern only outward action. Nor does he prove that for groups to claim such rights would be inimical to the larger revolutionary project, though he clearly believes this to be the case. He asserts that to make demands on this state is to legitimate it, and this is unconscionable; but it is not merely the state to which it is addressed, but the character of the demand itself that Bauer takes to be illegitimate, in that it is a particularistic identity claim. Bauer denies what other German republicans and liberals aver, namely that the Jews are making a universalistic claim, while it is the state that acts as a mere particular. He rejects the argument that the Jews are not claiming rights in virtue of a particular identity, but rather that the state itself has acted irrationally and particularistically in excluding them from civic life on the basis of their identity; thus they would be seeking only rights already generally enjoyed by other subjects. His response is that the Jews have consistently excluded themselves from public affairs, and the state in excluding them is only executing their own will.[28] Nor, according to Bauer, can this will change: It is immutable as long as they practise their religion. Bauer's critical judgement here focuses on a putatively inflexible form of subjective consciousness, not on analyses of concrete objective possibilities. While admitting that such changes may occur, as nothing is impossible for spirit,[29] he overlooks his own analyses, in 1838, of the transition from the legalistic to the prophetic consciousness in Judaism.[30] He adopts instead from his *Entdeckte Christenthum* the idea that religious representations are absolutely static.

More fundamentally, we witness here a slippage within Bauer's republican model, where the subjective and objective aspects come into tension. The subjective unity of the free self, as a precondition for effective historical action, is overshadowed by another figure, emancipation achieved by the solitary efforts of the self-sufficient subject. It is the adoption of the appropriate republican maxims that Bauer here deems essential, and to which he is prepared to sacrifice concrete advances in the scope and exercise of rights. Bauer's position can be properly described as sectarian, using the definition he himself furnishes in the *Entdeckte Christenthum*, namely, the refusal to extend recognition to those of other persuasions.

It is another case of his antithetical approach, but this time less well grounded in a dialectical theory, because it does not follow necessarily from his premises. It can be best understood not as a repudiation of his republican model but as an example of republican rigorism. It has recently been suggested, with reference to Cicero, that we can distinguish two strands in republican thinking. One is a minimal or rights-based approach, aiming at security and protection of the person, and corresponding to negative freedom. The second is a positive injunction to promote the good of the community, beyond its merely protective functions. In Cicero, this is the purview of the active citizen, placing more stringent demands on his ethical decisions and political deeds.[31] It is this rigoristic attitude that colours Bauer's thinking on the Jewish question. Citizenship and equality can be claimed only when all particular interest has been sacrificed. But Bauer fuses the juridical with the ethical.

This repudiation of recognition is a failure to work out the intersubjective relations that link juridical subjects and that Fichte, for example, had seen as a necessary step towards full moral recognition.[32] This thwarted intersubjectivity also has consequences for the coherence of Bauer's own synthesis of the subjective and objective, and of ethics and aesthetics. The beautiful unity of the self begins to be asserted against the objective process, and as an alternative to it, though Bauer believes that he is contributing positively to the contest, and not defending the status quo. This deviation from the objective unfolding of the political struggle is not, however, an inevitable consequence of Bauer's version of republicanism. It is a costly error in judgement on Bauer's part.

The texts on Jewish emancipation contain other important theoretical motifs that recur in Bauer's later writings. He reiterates the critique of liberalism he had developed throughout 1842 in the pages of the *Rheinische Zeitung*, describing it as a system of monopolistic privilege. "Constitutional liberalism is the system of privileged, limited, and [self-]interested freedom. Its basis is prejudice, its essence still religious."[33] By deploying private interests against each other, constitutionalism seeks a mechanical balance among them; this arrangement is antithetical to the republican community, which consciously pursues its positive freedom. "Egoism is to check egoism? For a while at least the law can preserve its privileges against unprivileged egoism. But there is not just egoism in the world, but also a history, which, against privileged self-seeking, will procure the right of the universal interest of humanity and freedom."[34] This universal interest continues to guide Bauer's republicanism, even when his assessment of the concrete situation is faulty.

Bauer had regularly claimed that religion has its roots in the limits of concrete ethical life. Among the significant theoretical developments in the texts on the Jewish question is Bauer's growing concern to describe more concretely the forces shaping modern social life, to give an account of the specific contradictions that condition current expressions of consciousness and current forms of alienation. His characterisation of the dynamics of civil society is significant here. This depiction lacks the power of Hegel's Jena writings,[35] or the description of civil society and its contradictions in the *Philosophy of Right*, with its compelling account of overproduction and polarisation of wealth and poverty in the modern world.[36] Nonetheless, it is illustrative of Bauer's conception of modern economic development.

> Need is the powerful mainspring which sets civil society in motion. Each uses the other to obtain satisfaction of his need, and is used by the other for the same purpose. . . . But where need rules with its accidental caprices and moods, where need is dependent for its satisfaction on accidental natural events, the individual can maintain his honour but cannot prevent the possibility of a sudden, unforeseen, incalculable change of status. Need, the very basis which assures the existence of civil society and guarantees its necessity, poses constant dangers to its existence, maintains an element of uncertainty in it and brings forth that mixture, contained in constant exchange, of poverty and wealth, misery and prosperity.[37]

For Bauer, the principal contradiction of the modern capitalist economy, based on universal commodity exchange, is the insecurity of property. He does not yet explore class conflict or structural contradictions, though this subject will feature in his writings of 1845. At the same time, he affirms the development of industry as the conquest and humanisation of nature.[38] Bauer defends the mediating function of occupational estates, which in France and England the Industrial Revolution swept away, and which were undermined by the Prussian reform movement in the wake of the Napoleonic wars.[39] The argument is similar to Hegel's in the *Philosophy of Right*.

> The member of the estate has the duty to pursue not only his private interest, but at the same time the general interest of his estate, which poses a necessary limit to his own. He knows himself to be honoured, since as a member of an estate he looks not only to his particular self, but to the interest of civil society generally.[40]

The mediating role of corporations operates through the individual consciousness, as its honour and its striving for universality. Bauer emphasises the fragility of this position, based on capricious shifts in the sphere of circulation. In stressing the dissolving effects of possessive individualism, Bauer anticipates a theme that recurs in his critique of *die Masse*, and in his histories of the revolutionary process.

After 1842, Bauer's republican commitment does not waver, but continues to be affirmed through an engagement with the French Revolution and its aftermath. If reflection on the historical process reveals the emancipatory potential of the present, the history of the immediate past also instructs us strategically how this result is to be achieved. The contradiction between genuine autonomy and possessive individualism is decisive for his conception of the republic. The republic as a self-determining community is an alternative to a society that derives its principles and its form of organisation exclusively from the market. In Bauer, this critical idea of the republic has its origins in the Hegelian theory of objective spirit, which, while upholding the principles of competitive market society, also seeks a distinct and irreducible role for the state. The Left-Hegelian critique of this position opens the possibility for the transformation of social life and suggests new horizons of liberty. The existing Prussian state, with its absolutist pretensions, rests on interests opposed to enlightenment and progress. A positive institution in the Hegelian sense, it stands over and against its individual subjects; it does not stem from their own free act but from the dead weight of historically transcended forms of life. It seeks to congeal the historical flow in forms from which reason has retreated.[41] From the republican perspective, the practical defects of the Hegelian state are apparent as well, though Hegel is not seen as an apologist for the existing order: His constitutional state appears as an untenable compromise between absolutist tutelage and popular sovereignty, an inconsequent thing of *Halbheit*, a half-measure.[42] Bauer criticises, further, the inconsequence of liberal, reformist, or constitutionalist thought. He excoriates the German bourgeoisie for its inability to adopt an undeviating oppositional position towards the absolutist state, its lack of revolutionary fervour, exertion, and sacrifice. The basis of this group in private interest promotes a readiness to compromise with the reactionary state whenever those interests appear in jeopardy. It is this weakness that Bauer sees as the very essence of constitutionalism.[43] For Bauer, bourgeois egoism is the root of the failure of previous revolutions, and mortally endangers the current movement. Only an undeviating republicanism based on free self-consciousness can sustain a principled opposition to the existing state, the necessary condition for its overthrow.

In Bauer's writings on the French Revolution, the distinction of *Masse* and *Volk* plays a key role; we will reexamine this question in Chapter 8, in conjunction with his critique of liberalism. The people appears as an ambivalent concept. A common origin in the dissolution of a society based upon feudal estates gives rise to two possible forms of national life, depending on the orientation of its members towards autonomy or towards the accumulation of property. As in Aristotle, chrematistic militates against the possibility of a good form of state. On the one hand, the people can appear as the *Volk*, to the extent that it exemplifies the ideas of freedom and constant self-transformation whose historic embodiment is anticipated in Jacobin France and is now, again, a concrete possibility. On the other hand, and much more commonly, the people can renounce its liberating claims, to wallow instead in the immediacy of self-interest. This mass society corresponds to various historical forms, either apolitical, or imperialistically voracious: the France of the Gironde, of Thermidor, and of Napoleonic expansionism; the majority tendency in Germany under the Restoration; contemporary England, etc.

For Bauer, the need to forge a unity out of the welter of tiny states whose power rests on the submissiveness of their populations sets the political agenda for Germany of the 1840s. The national and the republican struggle are one. Only by constituting themselves as a revolutionary people can the Germans overthrow the old order and liberate themselves from the enervating effects of egoism, possessive individualism, and the religious consciousness. With its stress on the absolute autonomy of the individual subject, the republican community is the result of individual ethical decisions. Membership in the national community is the result of free adherence; the nation is not a hypostatised universal. This position yields a nonparticularistic concept of nations, in mutually educative and collaborative relationships.[44] Nor is the nation based in irrational particularities of race or destiny, as in the romantic concept. In seeking alternatives to possessive individualism, Bauer advocates republicanism as a bulwark against the encroachments of liberal self-interest. His interest in the social question is fundamental to his republican commitment.

Bauer explores in detail and with great concreteness the course of the French Revolution itself, and the transition to the new vantage point of critique in the post-revolutionary period. His studies of the Revolution[45] represent a consistent defence of the Jacobin position; by implication they also prescribe the correct stance in the current German crisis. Bauer shows himself to be a partisan of Robespierre, criticising him only when he deviates from the purity of the revolutionary line.[46] The Jacobins are the party of the *Volk*, of exertion and sacrifice to the ideal.[47] It is they who consolidate the revolution, who make fast its principle, while the Gironde would indulge in facile conquests and egoistic expansion outside the national frontiers.[48] Their actions reflect their social bases, as well as their understandings of freedom: While the Jacobins are the most advanced elements of the *Volk*,[49] the Gironde is characterised as the party of commercial interests,[50] whose principle is the enjoyment of private interest, of particularity and positivity.[51] They are the party of the *Masse*. The Jacobins represent Paris, the heart of social contradiction and therefore of progress, while the Gironde's support rests in the provinces, isolated from and inimical to the dynamic movement of the revolution.[52]

In defending the Jacobin tradition, Bauer is extremely critical of the possessive individualism of the bourgeoisie, their clinging to property that ties them to the positivity of the old order. Of the middle class, "which lives by industry, manufacture, and trade," he writes,

> Jacobinism indeed pushed them back into the obscurity which they love,
> for they do not care to trouble themselves about general matters, but they

did not therefore have any less weight in political affairs. Sooner or later the state would be rebuilt according to their opinion, and they would determine its fate.[53]

This is Bauer's explanation of Thermidor,[54] the reassertion of private interest by the bourgeoisie, combined with the exhaustion and inability of the republican elements to sustain their revolutionary commitment:

> The time which followed the overthrow of the old monarchy belonged to the bourgeoisie. The bourgeoisie itself destroyed the reign of terror and harvested the golden fruits which sprang from the blood-drenched seed of the eighteenth century. They alone benefited from the revolutionary idea, for which not they but unselfish or passionate men had sacrificed themselves. They turned spirit into gold – of course only after they had emasculated the idea, depriving it of its consequence, its destructive earnest, its fanatical opposition to all egoism.[55]

Nonetheless the very dedication and revolutionary zeal of the Jacobins permitted them for a moment to prevail even as a minority faction,[56] a moment fraught with great consequence for the revolution. The destruction of the bastions of feudal privilege was the necessary condition for the victory of the principle of freedom. Feudal privilege and universal right are diametrically opposed, and the greatness of the Jacobins was to recognise and realise this absolute opposition.[57] Thus, under the leadership of the Jacobins, "with a single stroke the mass, deprived of rights, transformed itself into a people [*Volk*], which through its heroic strivings attained force, courage, and the capacity to destroy all privileges."[58]

But the revolution went aground on the national question. It betrayed its own legitimating principle; thereby it was undone. The defeat of the Jacobins meant that the revolution would be carried beyond the frontiers of France, no longer as the march of freedom, but as a war of conquest. "The French wanted to destroy privileges, including that of nationality, but they conquered as a nation, as an exclusive people."[59] Through their particularistic nationalism, the French too renounced their liberty to a brutal military ruler,[60] and fell back into somnolence and servitude.[61] The overthrow of the Jacobins also strengthened the reactionary forces outside France, even if their power was momentarily threatened. The German "wars of liberation" consolidated the grasp of these retrograde elements, and the servitude of the German people.[62] Here the *Volk*, in contrast to the *Masse*, is taken to have no exclusive, particularistic interests; it is opposed to external as well as internal manifestations of egoism. Though possessing a national form, its republicanism has a cosmopolitan orientation.

The revolutionary wars became a protracted trade war between France and England for the dominance of Europe and the world market[63]; the question was the defence of private interest, not of the principle of emancipation. Lacking political and economic unity and "spiritual capital,"[64]

Germany became the passive victim and battlefield of these wars. In fact Germany did not exist: It was a mere welter of private interests,[65] each asserting itself at the expense of the others with no conception of the common good. Bauer ridicules the restrictive character of the petty German states, the absurd pretensions of the tiny aristocratic courts and their claims to unquestioning obedience.[66] No principle, no leadership was to be found here. He criticises too the torpor of the German bourgeoisie, which could not respond to the ringing call for freedom. Bauer describes this bourgeoisie as backwards and philistine, concerned only with the narrow sphere of its private advantage,[67] which precluded all thought of a political community. The peasantry, too, were restricted and cut off from the great events of the time. Their servitude and isolation prevented their participation in the struggle; rather, they sought recourse in sanctity, where, only in imagination and under the favour and protection of their lord, they could "purify themselves of the filth of slavery."[68]

The French Revolution could not rally any of these elements to its cause, and moreover it betrayed its own legitimating principle. Thereby it was undone. The subsequent reaction was the reassertion of the old principle of positivity, which was not yet fully transcended.[69] Even the Enlightenment thinkers themselves were not yet free of the old presuppositions. By stressing the contingency of the human essence, its composition as a manifold of particular determinateness, they were unable to rise to the notion of free self-consciousness, of pure universal determination.[70] Their critical judgement was constricted in its form. The world existed for the subject, but the Enlightenment subject could fully understand neither itself nor its world, just as Bauer's 1829 manuscript had contended. The principle of infinite self-consciousness alone is the ground for universal emancipation, Bauer maintains, and it alone overcomes the limitations of Enlightenment thought. It alone prepares a worthy future of freedom. Meanwhile its representatives must confront the consequence of the revolution, its transformation into a new absolutism, even the absolutism of the so-called constitutionalist states,

> a system in which the government acts purely from "raison d'etat," and confronts a mass of individuals possessing rights equally, i.e. equally little, and determines the worth of the individual according to the monetary contribution which his taxes make to the maintenance of the state machine.[71]

The cause of freedom demands the critique of vacillating and merely positive political forces that, Bauer contends, are not true partisans of *die gute Sache*. As late as 1850, Bauer is still attacking the German constitutionalist opposition for its inconsequence.[72] Rather than opposing the state or recognising its incapacity for change, the reformists continued to make specific political demands on it,[73] thereby legitimating its existence and its right to act as arbiter of political questions. Bauer contends on the contrary that severing all the bonds of positivity is the precondition for the new world. The reformists merely retain the presuppositions of the old, positive power, and demand the transformation of a state whose essence Bauer had already demonstrated to be resistance to change.[74]

But in engaging with reform tendencies, the sectarian and antithetical character of Bauer's critique is again in evidence. He cannot envisage an alliance of diverse progressive forces to attain immediate goals as part of a larger revolutionary struggle. Indeed he denies absolutely to the constitutionalist faction any progressive function whatsoever. It is simply part of the old order, something to be unequivocally opposed. This tactical refusal has deep theoretical roots, because revolution for Bauer entails the unqualified affirmation and realisation of a new principle. This principle can in no way be compromised, even for seemingly immediate gains. We have already encountered this position in *Die Judenfrage*.

Bauer also criticises the overt aspirations of the public as insufficiently clear, determinate, or revolutionary,[75] contending that insofar as this is so, it is the duty of the press to oppose the public, not to depict itself as its spokesman and representative.

> It must also be unconditionally admitted that the press really expressed what was alive and mighty in the popular spirit, but it only expressed what was at hand in this latter, i.e. the little it contained of general and indeterminate demands and stirrings. The press did not have power or courage enough to advance to new creations and judgments which would dissolve the indeterminacy and would alone have made possible an honourable resolution, if it also gained the support of a great portion of the public. The public no longer lived with naive faith in the old forms, but it was also not yet beyond them. While the government vainly endeavoured to alleviate suspicions against its own attempts at reform and at touching up the old order, the spokesmen of the public gave literary expression only to an indeterminate dissatisfaction with this restoration. In this confused tangle a decisive, destructive, living power capable of new creations showed itself nowhere.[76]

In *Vollständige Geschichte der Parteikämpfe* (*Complete History of Party Struggles*),[77] Bauer criticises not only the constitutionalist but also significant elements of the republican political movement as being insufficiently radical.[78] Attacking the *Rheinische Zeitung*, which as early as fall 1842 had been rejecting his articles because of their provocativeness,[79] Bauer contends "Even in the fight against the existing order, they want to struggle only under the surveillance of the existing law, that is, they do not want struggle, progress, development!"[80] He ridicules Ruge's defence of the *Deutsche Jahrbücher* before the Saxon Second Chamber in 1842, where Ruge claimed the journal to be harmless.[81] He censures Ruge's inconsequent bearing in minimising the political effects of the opposition. It is instructive to compare the defence conducted by Bruno Bauer's brother,

Edgar, against charges of *lèse-majesté* in 1844. The accused says that he does not act before the bar as a Prussian subject, nor ask who might be offended by the publication of his findings. He rather adopts the standpoint of emancipated humanity, and shows how his work contributes to this end. He turns his trial into a scientific argument. He lost the contest, but used the trial as an act of civil disobedience, an occasion to defend the cause of freedom, in which he did not accept the legitimacy of the law that repressed him, but succumbed unbendingly to its irrational coercive force.[82] So Bruno Bauer understands his own self-defence upon his dismissal in 1842, and in his own contests with the censors. So, he believes, must all republicans act.

With approval ("entirely agreed: if the struggle were so widely flourishing"),[83] Bauer cites the liberal paper *Der Pilot*, whose first issue of 1843 had argued, "Peaceful coexistence between revolution and the state is impossible, according to the fundamental basis of the State."[84] The struggle must end in the destruction of one or other of the parties. This is Bauer the Jacobin. But he now also claims that recourse to terrorism proves that consciousness is not yet universal, that it seeks to perpetrate itself by force.[85] This is a new note that did not sound in the *Posaune* blast, nor did it explicitly figure in the characterisation of the Jacobins in the *Denkwürdigkeiten*. Its importance should not be exaggerated, as Bauer was quick to defend the barricade fighters in 1848 against conservative critics; he does not repudiate revolutionary struggle. But it is clear that Bauer's relations with the opposition movement have become more conflictual and problematic. His aesthetic self-sufficiency tends now more often to assert itself at the expense of the sublime, of his Jacobinism. The antithetical character of Bauer's thought tends to preclude even strategic alliances among opponents of the Restoration, in the name of the purity of principle. While he continues to attack political inconsequence, and thus strikes the same stance as in 1842, he stresses the immediate, personal, conscious unity of the individual with the universal, the subjective side of the ethical and aesthetic models. And yet his interest in the objective process in no way diminishes. The social question now comes most prominently to the fore, as one of the defining factors of the revolutionary situation.

8

"THE REPUBLIC OF SELF-CONSCIOUSNESS": REVOLUTIONARY POLITICS IN 1848

The revolutions of the old style are at an end. That is especially what the course of the movement of 1848 shows. The great social movement of modern times is revolutionary too in its thought content, and avoids the beaten paths which the vanished bourgeois parties had trodden. It sets itself new goals and travels on new ways.[1]

This appraisal of the Revolutions of 1848, written at the end of the nineteenth century by a follower of Marx, encapsulates Bauer's own estimation of the emancipatory prospects of the movement, despite the vehement disagreements between these former allies. The nature of the new goals and the new ways has remained a subject of controversy, and widely divergent assessments have continued to be produced.[2] Among the array of issues raised by the Revolutions of 1848, the participants themselves agreed on the vital political importance of the social question, the existence of new forms of poverty and resistance linked to the end of the old agrarian order and the beginnings of capitalist industrial production.[3] They disagreed violently on its causes and its solution.

It has not been recognised to what extent the social question shapes the work of Bruno Bauer, especially in the later years of the *Vormärz*. Since 1843, Bauer had posed the relation of political and social emancipation as an object of critical theory. Even before the polemics occasioned by the publication of Marx's *Holy Family*,[4] Bauer was responding to the emergence of the social question, which was a determinant of political debate in Germany, as elsewhere in Europe. In Buonarroti's widely disseminated writings on the French Revolution, as reported by Lorenz von Stein in 1842,[5] for example, the opposition between egoism and community is the central theme. While rejecting Buonarroti's socialist conclusions, Bauer may here find parallels to his own views in the *Posaune*. In the first issue of the *Allgemeine Literatur-Zeitung*, in December 1843, Bauer already contends, without elaboration, that the real meaning of political questions is social.[6] The French, he continues elsewhere, have correctly raised the social question, but have no valid solution to offer.[7] They have a deficient grasp of the new theory of freedom, which emerges from an inner engagement with Hegel.

The social question as Bauer sees it presents two distinct aspects. It occasions the criticism both of liberalism and of socialism. One facet of the problem is the emergence of mass society in the wake of the French Revolution; liberalism unconsciously gives voice to this development, seeking to define freedom as acquisition. The second is the birth of modern socialism, which, according to Bauer, shares much of the same terrain as liberalism but proposes inconsequent and unacceptable solutions to the conditions that liberalism simply affirms. Bauer's critical struggle against particularity encompasses these two aspects, while continuing to be unstinting in its attack on the irrational privileges, exemptions, and corporate monopolistic interests of the Restoration regime. The tradition-bound world of the old order and liberal, atomistic, possessive individualism mirror each other as expressions of particular interests, religious in the one case, economic in the other. Both militate against the rational self-determination of the subject, the elevation of consciousness from particular to general interest, though they occupy distinct places in Bauer's evolutionary historical scheme. Criticising the abstract individualism and egoism of civil society, he calls for a new, liberated individuality that subordinates accumulation as an end of action, in favour of a freely chosen identification with the progressive and revolutionary thrust of the historical process. Such a transformation, he contends, is not limited to politics, but infuses all social relations with dynamism and justice.[8]

As the *Vormärz* crisis deepens, Bauer's republicanism defines itself more clearly as an oppositional current distinct from liberalism and socialism. The break between liberal and republican positions is not an original feature of 1848. Bauer had already analysed this hostile configuration as it had developed during the French Revolution, and his discussions of Cromwell and Puritanism in the *Rheinische Zeitung* of 1842 alluded to it in the English case. He now interprets this ideological split as a social distinction, opposing the partisans of the people to those of the mass. This opposition is all encompassing: There exist on the one hand the masses, who represent inertia and stagnation, and whose inarticulate consciousness constitutes the real bulwark of the status quo, and on the other, the genuine revolutionary forces, who have assumed with ethical courage the tasks of liberation. The distinction takes on the character of an absolute antithesis between free self-activity and passive sentience, between autonomy and heteronomy.

Bauer argues that *die Masse* is the outcome of the French Revolution: The dissolution of the feudal estates gives rise to a purely atomistic society, characterised by the assertion of individual property right.[9] The mass is a vision of emergent civil society, dominated by the market: "What gives this mass an appearance of collective movement is only the movement of the individual atoms with their particular interests and needs; what struggles within them is only the struggle and competition of this infinity of individual interests."[10] While the secondary literature on Bauer frequently equates the masses with the industrial working class, this definition is far too narrow and distorts his social criticism, misconstruing its real object.[11] The concept must be understood instead in relation to Bauer's ideas on post-revolutionary modernity, and on social and political struggle and transformation within it. Despite Bauer's pessimism about the capacity for autonomous action of the proletariat at its present level of consciousness and organisation, his category of the masses refers particularly to the vacillating liberal bourgeoisie, and to civil society shaped by private economic interests. Bauer's republicanism offers a critique of liberal rights in favour of a new doctrine of virtue; we have already observed some of the consequences of this position in the Jewish question. Bauer claims that rights, as liberalism construes them, are privileges or exemptions, in essence no different from feudal immunities. For Bauer the ultimate right is that of self-transcendence, the ability to withdraw the will from any particularity in favour of an ethical universal. While conceding to liberals that personal independence requires a measure of individual property, he rejects the liberal idea of rights as rigid, immutable, and inimical to genuine autonomy. Such rights merely sanction particularity and resist historical change. Consolidating differences in wealth and social position, they are positive in the Hegelian sense, in that they seek to hold fast against historical development.[12] Bauer sees liberal rights as claims to immunise some portion of the objective world from rational scrutiny and revision. He does not reject rights, but their liberal justification. Liberalism derives rights exclusively from empirical practical reason and material satisfaction, sacrificing to this the higher idea of autonomy prescribed by pure practical reason; but unlike the juridical account of freedom retained by Kant, Fichte, and Hegel, Bauer again treats these two forms of reason as antinomies. His reticence to admit particular rights, and his tendency to moralise the juridical relation, have already been noted in his attitude towards Jewish emancipation.

What is noteworthy now is the application of Bauer's critique to the social question, and his identification of liberalism with chrematistic or immoderate accumulation. The liberal definition of freedom as the possessive individualist assertion of private right has marked social consequences. Bauer's indictment of liberalism is that it dissolves the bonds of ethical life, reducing society to an aggregate of competing atoms. Itself the effect of revolutionary changes wrought by the French, liberalism in its progressive moment contributes to the release of individuals from the traditional relations of subordination that had characterised the *ancien régime*. But it promotes a sham liberty, one that reveals itself as a form of heteronomy. The determining principle of liberalism is private property, and proprietary attitudes and relations dictate the behaviour of their bearers. Behind the mask of liberty and equality, liberalism thus sanctions monopoly and privilege for those who have amassed wealth; its doctrine of rights is as exclusive and anti-historical as the feudal defence of rank. The shattered *Sittlichkeit* of modernity cannot be restored by the mere summation of private interests. The culture of diremption that had already preoccupied Bauer in 1829 is fully manifest in the liberal programme. The state, potentially the agent of historical transformation (as Bauer had argued in 1841), becomes for liberalism the guardian of the status quo, of the existing distribution of goods. As the sanctity of possession is the supreme liberal principle, any state that guarantees property (at minimal cost) will suffice; consequently, Bauer concludes, liberals are incapable of sustained opposition to the existing political order and will hasten to compromise with it in order to win security. This lesson had been amply demonstrated in the French Revolution and threatens to be repeated in Germany. The Jacobins had valiantly opposed this attitude, but had signally failed to overcome it, and it emerged even more potent from the revolutionary crucible.

Bauer's alternative is the republic, based on the recognition of a genuine common interest and on the self-transcendence of individual citizens, who cease to be determined by property, but acknowledge themselves as *tele* and *energeiai* of historical change. This conclusion of the *Posaune* and *Hegels Lehre* underlies all Bauer's analyses of the French and German revolutionary movements in the 1840s. Bauer delineates the common interest broadly, as the eradication of privilege and inequality, and the assertion of the people's right to refashion their political and social institutions consonant with their deepening understanding of freedom. Infinite self-consciousness assumes its proper shape in the republic, in constant revision of its own forms of existence. In the present circumstances, the foundering of the old order and its desperate quest for irrational legitimation, the critical judgement articulates the decisive historical question: The right of popular sovereignty must be defended categorically against monarchical arrogations and liberal vacillation. Because of its reflexive and self-revising character, this right differs fundamentally from liberal privilege. Once it is secured, its forms and content can be further elaborated and renewed. The possibility of a rational modern ethical life depends on the ability of individuals to make themselves the agents of universal interests and to affirm their autonomy in new, republican institutions.

In contrast to the freedom of property in liberalism, Bauer invokes ethical perfectionism and the uncompromisingly sublime struggle to transform political relations and institutions. Once the republican state is attained, further social changes become possible. Bauer's republicanism differs from older republican appeals to the virtue of the past, but is rooted in the specific character of modern development.[13] It continues to seek objective orientations for its critical judgements through the comprehension of the social question.

Bauer's criticisms of mass society have contributed to the impression in the recent secondary literature, as also among many of his contemporaries, that he had abandoned the revolutionary cause prior to the violent confrontations of 1848–49.[14] According to his own account, however, his criticisms of the opposition movement, in a series of articles in the *Allgemeine Literatur-Zeitung*[15] and the *Norddeutsche Blätter*,[16] do not represent a deviation from his commitment to political revolution, as manifested in the texts of 1839–43. They are a judgement on its social bearing. Bauer continues to defend a republican position, despite his intense criticisms of the elements participating in the struggle against the Prussian regime. Even at its most extreme, however, Bauer's criticism is directed against the inconsequence, vacillation, and unclarity of the demands of the progressive party. His social critique is a repudiation of both liberalism and socialism, while unwavering in its opposition to the Restoration order.

In his 1844 polemic against mass society in "What Is Now the Object of Critique?" Bauer argues that the crisis of 1838–44 has been conceived by the masses and their spokesmen not as an inner combat of self-consciousness against its previous contradictions and limits, but as a struggle tied to immediate material interests, and hence not transcending the horizon of the old system of relations and of egoism; but for Bauer there can be no particular that, unreconstructed, bears the seeds of the future in itself. The identification of his criticism with the struggle of the masses, he says, was only illusory. There occurred rather a temporary confrontation of criticism with the political presuppositions of its opponents. As the confrontation unfolds, criticism draws out into completeness and openness the political essence whose previous limitation had checked the egoism of parties, estates, and corporations. Thus, on the one hand, in its historic development, this egoism now knows no bounds, and on the other, the results of the clash show the necessity of grasping man's imperfection and of its overcoming as the course and movement of self-consciousness, while these were previously imagined to be alien and beyond his powers.[17] In this and related texts, Bauer's critique of the masses adopts a supercilious tone that justifies Barnikol's description of his intellectual arrogance[18]; it bespeaks his tendency to present oppositions as antitheses, for which he has been much, and rightly, criticised. The formal and material causes of change, republican criticism and the mass base it must touch and transform if it is to be successful, now appear in a new and antagonistic relationship. In the *Landeskirche*, as we have seen, Bauer presents the mass as the necessary basis – though dull and resistant – of any objective historical transition; he is now contemptuously dismissive of it. The creative and critical intellect now has adopted an antithetical attitude towards the masses as the bulwark of the existing order. This attitude evinces again the tension between the subjective and objective sides of the historical process. As the objective political forces prove recalcitrant to change, Bauer's criticism appears to take refuge in pure subjective self-certainty. The "ought" and being are now in violent opposition, which the critical judgement seems increasingly unable to bridge. The impending defeat of the revolution heightens the pathos of Bauer's interventions after 1844.

This tone must not mislead us, however, into the view that Bauer is re-treating from active engagement in the political process. He equates the merely political revolution with liberalism, the freeing of the elements of mass society to pursue their restrictive course. Republicanism proposes new goals and new ways, transcending the liberal horizon. Bauer points to the antithesis between people and mass and concludes that this oppo-sition must now be traced through its contemporary forms.

Other texts by Bauer's collaborators help to elaborate the distinction of political and social revolution, though these texts must always be used with great caution as evidence for Bauer's own positions. Here they merely give further evidence for a distinction that occurs in Bauer's own writings, such as those on the French Revolution. Edgar Bauer, for example, pub-lished in 1844 a text entitled *Der Streit der Kritik mit Kirche und Staat (The Contest of Criticism with Church and State)*. In 1845, this publication earned him a lengthy prison sentence for sedition, from which he was released only by the popular uprising three years later. He argues in this text that for the revolution to realise itself completely, freedom must be more universally conceived than in a purely political form.[19] The political con-ception is necessary, but insufficient. Freedom requires the humanisation of the living conditions and of the work of the least favoured elements of society. He links pauperism and private property, and attacks mere reformist palliatives that do not grasp the root of the evil.[20] Edgar Bauer here describes his own position as communism, and defines the workers, including the unemployed and the marginalised, as the revolutionary class. "It is not fitting for the free man to have private property. For the free man should cut himself off through nothing from his fellow men, should have nothing for himself [*an sich*] which limits the freedom of the other."[21] In 1849, rejecting private property as a politically privileged monopoly that has held society in a state of war,[22] he contends that in the true society it is no longer force that binds its members together, but a common interest, "forever newly arrayed."[23] The positions of the two brothers cannot always be assimilated, and Bruno Bauer never identifies so closely with the socialist programme; indeed, his anti-socialism is the-matic, but it emerges through his own diagnosis of the social question and its solution. Unlike his younger brother, he views private property as in part constitutive of personal independence and initiative, but he attacks its tendency to overspill its proper boundaries. There are nonetheless important parallels between Bruno Bauer's and Edgar Bauer's assaults on particularism and reformism, and the former's critique of the masses is illuminated when it is seen as an attack on the dominance of the market over all social relationships. This idea is confirmed in writings by other members of Bauer's Berlin circle after 1844. In 1846, Szeliga, for example, published a booklet entitled *Organisation der Arbeit der Menschheit (The Organisation of the Labour of Mankind)*. In it, along with a critique of the insufficiencies of the political movement from the eighteenth century to the present, the author stresses the distinction between the masses and *das Volk*, the inorganic multitude of possessive individualists as opposed to the people embodying the values of liberated humanity.[24] The republican community differs fundamentally from the proprietary state.

In the concept of the masses lies a key to Bauer's distinction of political and social revolution.[25] The social revolution constitutes the republican people, while the merely political revolution, as ultimately in France, liberates the elements of mass society. Bauer defends a notion of *das Volk* as transcending the horizon of liberalism. But he opposes it to the idea of the masses. This position is consistent with Bauer's dialectic of particular and universal interests, and explains his participation in the revolution of 1848: He is not repudiating political emancipation, but rather advocating a broader form of social liberation, and criticising the limits and egoism of the oppositional movement. The alliance of criticism with the highest aspirations of the revolutionary movement is not yet broken. Bauer's understanding of liberation requires us to examine in particular his contentious relations with socialism.

One of the significant results of the Revolutions of 1848 is the break between republican and socialist currents. Bruno Bauer grasps this development clearly, while in Edgar Bauer's work, cited previously, it remains more ambiguous. The revolutionary movement of the 1840s reveals not the continuity of the Jacobin tradition, but its rupture. Political groupings in the popular alliance crystallise as each attains a clearer consciousness of its own specific goals, and defines itself in part against its former allies. For Bruno Bauer, this is a necessary process, because through it, inchoate oppositions are refashioned as principled and self-conscious contradictions, and in this form they can be resolved. Earlier Jacobinism itself had not presented a solidly united front on social, political, and military issues, as the tempestuous course of the French revolutionary government of 1793–94 vividly demonstrated.[26] In 1848, differences in the movement attain clear theoretical formulation. Bauer's anti-socialist polemics, before and during 1848, attest to this transformation. As we have already observed, Bauer considers that the older Jacobinism cannot simply be revived, but must be purged of the positivity of its principle, its clinging to a materialist view of the self and to a mimetic conception of virtue. It must also be challenged for the insufficiency of its results, its incapacity to overthrow the old order in all its manifestations, and its defeat under the crushing weight of egoistic particularity. The new republicanism, he claims, is far in advance of its precursor in its understanding of freedom and its critical judgements on history. Despite the vacillations and confusions of its apparent allies, it remains confident of its ultimate victory.

Further specifying differences with the older Jacobinism, Bauer asserts plainly that the objective of the new republicanism is not merely political, but social, emancipation.[27] This he offers in reply to Marx's characterisation of his position in "The Jewish Question,"[28] though his differentiation of political and social liberation precedes these polemics. Since 1841, Bauer had maintained that the solution of the social question was among the most pressing political tasks. As we have also seen, Bauer's critique of capitalism focuses not on the oppression and resistance of workers, as Marx's does, but primarily on the instability of the sphere of circulation, and its tendency to reduce the state to its servant and watchman.[29] Bauer also stresses the need to reconceive the nature of labour, not linking it to the egoistic fulfilment of need, but making of it a vehicle of creativity. He had maintained since 1841, against Hegel's more sceptical assessment, that the solution of the social question was now a concrete possibility. He argues that the state accomplishes its historic mission only when it achieves the liberation of the proletariat.[30] For Bauer, this process is fundamentally propelled by the rational state's striving for its own completion, under the guidance and urging of critical theory.[31] It is the culmination of the millennial struggle by which the state emerges from domination by particular interests and privileges, to assume its proper republican shape as the manifestation of universal and rational freedom. The freeing of the workers involves primarily education, the humanisation of their living conditions, and the acquisition by them of new types of self-consciousness. Bauer anticipates that these reforms will have wide-ranging effects, not only in eliminating pauperism but also in permeating all social relations with justice, and in stimulating new forms of social and cultural creation. The Restoration state, tied to particular interests that history has long transcended, has failed in its necessary work. Instead, it falls to republicans to take the decisive steps towards genuine emancipation.

In defending his position, Bauer understands this liberation to be a requirement of social justice that will be fulfilled by the republican state as a consequence of popular self-rule. It is not the state that grants emancipation; freedom cannot come as a gift from above, but must be won by the efforts of all, including the workers themselves. From autumn 1843, Marx takes the self-emancipation of the working class to be the hallmark of his own specific form of socialism. Bauer shares the view of self-activity, but denies that its political consequence is the socialist state. For Bauer, too, this new consciousness is a prerequisite for effective revolutionary action. But for Bauer the revolutionary subjects are not predetermined by their social position, though he underlines the vigorous opposition of those whom the present social order marginalises. In his view, revolutionaries must rise to the challenge, and redefine themselves, not by defending particular interests, but by transcending them. This is a consistent demand in Bauer's work. He opposes Marx on the grounds of the heteronomy that he takes to characterise the latter's position. For Bauer, the dialectical process in which the particular transcends itself may not be seen as the unconscious working of necessity (as in Marx's description of class formation), but as an act of ethical freedom.

A growing awareness of the tensions within the oppositional movement also develops in the socialist camp. Marx's polemics with Bauer date from late 1842, when, as editor of the *Rheinische Zeitung*, he objected on tactical grounds to the overly provocative character of writings by Bauer and the Berlin *Freien*; at this time, however, Marx and Bauer shared a republican orientation.[32] After autumn 1843, when Marx adopts a socialist position, these polemics assume a new character, as a difference of principles. The differences are compounded by Marx's break with Arnold Ruge in summer 1844 over the editorial direction of the *Deutsch-französische Jahrbücher*. Here lines of demarcation between socialism and republicanism are clearly drawn.[33] *The Holy Family* and *The German Ideology* then work out the theoretical differences in greater detail from the socialist side, though the latter text remained unpublished until the 1930s.[34] In their polemics, each side accuses the other of the same defects: For Bauer, socialism is the generalisation but not the transformation of the proletariat; for Marx, republicanism consolidates but does not transform bourgeois civil society. In responding to Bauer in his text "On the Jewish Question," Marx describes the fetish character of the republican state. It sets up a sphere of political universality that leaves intact the individualistic and egoistic strivings of civil society. Republicanism, as advocated by Bauer, is less an option than a complement to possessive individualism, less a challenge than a confirmation of the hegemony of property. In Marx's analysis, the republican state is impotent against the power of capital, and its universalist ideology masks real contradictions in concrete social life. These weaknesses stem from the inability of republicanism to create a sphere of genuine common interest in conditions where civil society remains divided by class. Marx's text on the Jewish question also criticises the Jacobinism of the French Revolution as a futile attempt by the state to assert its independence from its own material basis, from the bourgeois society that generates it.[35] The theoretical rupture of republicanism and socialism does not imply the impossibility of strategic alliance; in late 1848, Marx attributes a growing role to the republican and democratic movement among small property holders, as he finds that the German bourgeoisie fails to carry out a consistent anti-feudal programme.[36] But republicans are viewed as unreliable allies, and their ideal of political freedom is discarded, with significant consequences for the future of the socialist movement.

Marx's bitter parody of Bauer in *The Holy Family* takes aim mainly at the *Allgemeine Literatur Zeitung* articles. It does not present a comprehensive conception of Bauer's political or theoretical position. The unrelenting severity of Marx's judgement is rooted in the practical break between the republican and socialist revolutionary movements. In his three broadsides against Bauer as an adversary of socialism, in "On the Jewish Question," *The Holy Family*, and *The German Ideology*, Marx claims that Bauer lacks a concept of social emancipation, that he translates all social questions into religious questions, and that he confuses political and genuinely human emancipation. If we examine the whole spectrum of Bauer's writings prior to 1848, these claims appear untenable. Marx is correct to denounce the overly stringent character of Bauer's critical judgements, the absolute opposition he maintains between particular and universal interests, as in the Jewish question. Marx also reconstrues the relation of critical theory to its mass base in a way that avoids the more sectarian implications of Bauer's *Allgemeine Literatur Zeitung* articles; theory becomes a material force when it arouses the masses to political action.[37] In this Marx is closer to Bauer's own formulation of the problem in the *Landeskirche*.

In response, the republicanism in 1848 expresses itself in a conscious hostility towards socialism, one of the major features of Bauer's thought in the late 1840s. If it is incorrect to equate the proletariat exclusively with the masses in Bauer, it is nonetheless true that after 1844, he devotes particular attention to criticising socialist and communist theories. This opposition focuses on the conception of labour, and on different versions of freedom as a universal, and not a particularistic, claim.

The emancipatory potential of labour is central to Marx's idea of socialism. Marx formulates his theory of labour partly in response to what he sees as the illusory community of the republican state, which would merely co-exist ineffectually beside the possessive-individualist sphere described by liberalism. For Marx, civil society is not to be preserved unchanged within a state that claims to represent conscious freedom and universality. Civil society is, rather, to transform itself by incorporating universality into the relations that sustain and reproduce material social life. In his "Theses on Feuerbach," Marx's concept of labour highlights the insufficiencies of previous philosophical traditions, in ways parallel to Bauer's reading of the history of freedom. While Bauer describes the split between materialism and transcendent versions of idealism, Marx criticises the bifurcation of modern philosophy into mechanistic materialist and subjective idealist currents. In Marx's reading, the former, including Feuerbach,[38] defends receptivity but denies spontaneity, whereas the latter, such as Bauer, confines activity to its spontaneous, conceptual side, the setting of goals, but abstracts from the processes of their realisation, which entail engagement with material causal processes. Marx proposes a new, activist materialism, whose central concept is labour. The synthesis in labour of teleology and causality, purpose and process, is to integrate the subjective and objective dimensions that modern philosophy has sundered.[39]

Bauer has his own, independent theory of alienated labour. Labour appears as duress and command as a consequence of other forms of alienation, especially religious and political.[40] Thus it is not the primary manifestation of estrangement. In its current, alienated form, labour, "sunken in matter,"[41] lacks the moment of free subjectivity. Bauer does not spare workers criticism for the narrowness and particularism of their present consciousness.[42] The alienated labouring consciousness remains at an immediate, rudimentary level, unable to grasp the principle of its own self-determination, because, for Bauer, it confronts only brute nature as its opposite, and cannot reflect on the lessons of the historical process as the conquest of autonomy. Bauer contends that the power to shape history in the pattern of free self-consciousness belongs to intellectual creation, not to the cramped and constrained labour of the proletariat, which, in its current form, lacks autonomy and determinacy. He also denies the intersubjectivity of labour, which will be central for Marx: the realisation that the otherness which workers encounter is not only the world of material objects, but also other subjects involved as collaborators in a common task.[43] To Bauer, alienated labour does not provide its own solution by generating new forms of solidarity. These must come from a free identification with the republican community, by critical reflection on objective processes, and not by necessity. The *praxis* with which Bauer identifies is neither labour nor contemplation, but political action, especially revolutionary opposition to the status quo.

Bauer's is not a purely negative account of labour, however. This is evident when he compares the workings of self-consciousness through industry and art with the negation of nature wrought by miracles, according to the religious conception.[44] The former operate through natural laws to effect the transfiguration or spiritualisation of the given; the latter merely suspends these laws, and treats nature with derision. Here Bauer speaks in a characteristic and modern accent. From this perspective, labour is not merely the loss of purity by the idea as it becomes contaminated by matter, but it is the transformation or elevation of nature in light of the idea. This view he shares with Hegel, for whom labour as well as art is a symbol of his idealism.[45]

The sharpest confrontation between socialism and republicanism occurs on the terrain of particular interest, and its connection with universality. Bauer rejects socialism for being what Marx claims it is, the ideological expression of a particular class and its immediate interests. This for Bauer is to condemn socialism as irredeemably heteronomous; unlike Marx, he denies the relation of this particular to the universal, to historical progress. Bauer sees in the proletariat only pure particularity, and denies that this particularity can transform itself into a genuine universal unless it first renounces its own sectional interests.[46] The incipient socialist movement, he claims, seeks only the immediate satisfaction of material wants. It thus shares the same basic principle as its liberal adversaries. It wants to organise the workers as they are, in their immediate, particular existence, and not to transform them, as he insists his own theory envisages.[47]

Bauer also anticipates the negative effects of a socialist organisation of labour. While criticising capitalism for its irrational competitive forms, he defends the principle of competition itself as a necessary condition for progress, the independence of persons, and the possibility of conscious, free self-determination. Linking competition and innovation, Bauer contends that under socialism the freedom of creation and experimentation would be cramped and withered; by seeking to eradicate competition, socialism shows that it lacks confidence that the struggle of competing powers can promote freedom and creativity. Instead, a single monopoly of capital would be substituted for the more diffuse monopolies of privilege and wealth favoured by liberalism, but without changing the basic principle of egoistic (rather than aesthetic) production. He recognises a hidden affinity between liberalism and socialism in their anti-historical positivity and particularism. Against the flow of history, which requires the permanent and fundamental revision of all maxims, socialism would set up one single dogma as an eternal ruling truth; a narrowly conceived, positive principle, the primacy of manual labour, would dominate and deform all domains of life. Socialism privileges the workers as the only suffering class, and would amputate the other segments of society in favour of an absolute equality, secured by a tyrannical constitution. Its political consequence would thus be the generalisation of the proletariat as a particular interest, not a higher universal community. Generalising proletarian status would only generalise need and poverty. Here, Bauer claims, is no road to freedom.[48] None of his criticisms are strikingly original; they are parallel to those voiced against socialism and communism from various political perspectives by contemporaries such as Proud'hon and Lorenz von Stein. Some of them are not dissimilar, even, to Marx's own strictures against crude communism in the *Manifesto* of 1848; but Bauer admits no fundamental distinction between Marx's socialism and that of rival schools. In some respects, Bauer anticipates John Stuart Mill's views on historical experimentation and perfectionism, and his critique of conformism.[49] Bauer's positions are, however, entirely consistent with the theory of revolution and self-determination he had been advancing since 1841.

Like his brother Edgar in *Streit der Kritik*, Bauer also turns his attention to bland, reformist versions of socialism that do not escape censure; Marx devotes the latter portions of the *German Ideology* to similar adversaries, and in similar tones.[50] In *Die Parteikämpfe*, for example, Bauer challenges the insipidity of "true socialist" proclamations. He studies the incorporation of the social question into the ideology of dissident intellectuals, who, defeated in the foregoing political struggle, now seek another object for their attention. Their lack of courage and their inability to rise to universality are merely transposed to the social sphere.[51] He wishes to distinguish his own engagement with the social question from such expedient dabbling, but he produces in this text no cogent analysis of the causes of the present economic crisis.

How he conceives this crisis, and the dynamics of the competitive market, raises a significant problem, which is treated most explicitly by some of his collaborators, notably Faucher.[52] Like Marx himself, the republican circles around Bauer tend to support free trade rather than protectionism.[53] This position stems, in the case of Bauer's associates, from opposition to monopoly and to direct state involvement in production; the latter is a significant difference from Marx's rationale for free trade. There is an important commonality, however. The free trade position derives, both in Marx's case and in Bauer's circle, from the idea that the opening of international markets for manufactured goods accelerates production and, with it, the development of oppositions and struggles between capitalists and workers: a version of Bauer's principle of exacerbating contradictions. These stances are in marked contrast to Fichte, for example, who, in 1800, in his *Closed Commercial State*,[54] had defended protectionism and national economic self-sufficiency as necessary to guarantee the fundamental right of all subjects to live by their labour. They are atypical, too, of *Vormärz* republicanism. Recent research on 1848 has identified a correlation in the German territories between support for free trade and the constitutional monarchist and liberal currents, whereas republican and democratic tendencies appear in general to favour protection.[55] The distinct position occupied by Bauer's collaborators on economic issues is entirely consistent with his views of freedom and competition, and his attacks on tutelage and domination, though we cannot provide direct textual evidence of his own stance on free trade.

There is, however, an intriguing, revolutionary defence of free trade, "Das Wohl der arbeitenden Klassen" ("The Welfare of the Working Classes"), which appeared in Bauer's *Norddeutsche Blätter* in March, 1845. This is an anonymous text, attributed to Bauer neither by Barnikol nor by Zanardo,[56] but discussing themes contained in Bauer's electoral addresses of 1848–49, and echoing some of Bauer's own arguments about the inevitably monopolistic consequences of untrammelled competition.[57] Its publication in *Norddeutsche Blätter* implies an endorsement by Bauer of the positions taken in this article, even if he is not himself the author. The text is close to Edgar Bauer's diagnosis of the causes of pauperism and the uselessness of bourgeois moralising reform,[58] and Edgar may be the author, as he had not yet begun to serve his prison sentence at the moment of its publication. While we must be careful to distinguish the brothers' positions when they publish texts independently, here we can be more confident that, because of his editorial supervision, the views expressed are consonant with Bruno Bauer's own. The text is of sufficient interest to warrant citation here.

> It will be difficult for our bourgeoisie to acquire political importance, a share in legislation. As the rump of a political body which bears only too clearly the marks of its origin in the Holy Roman Empire, it has to suffer constantly from its involvements with the other layers of society. Before it has overcome one of them, it already becomes embroiled with a new one. On all sides threatened, jostled, opposed, it is incapable of concentrating its powers, of drawing together into a phalanx.
>
> The French bourgeoisie was victorious in a similar struggle. But why? Because the ruins of the old feudal aristocracy no longer stood in its way; because it was not yet entangled with the proletariat. Principally, though, victory had to come to it because it was itself able to make the effects of competition, of freedom of trade [*Gewerbefreiheit*], in a word: the rule of big capital, take hold.[59]

The Prussian case differs from the French, according to the text, because the German bourgeoisie was unable to conquer power for itself, but thrives parasitically on concessions from the state. Besides its Marxist-sounding thesis about the sequence of classes and their mutual struggles, the text fundamentally addresses the question of free trade. Like Marx, it argues that protective tariffs are a subsidy to the bourgeoisie, a means of forcing workers to purchase expensive, poorly made domestic products.[60] It defines labour power as the inexhaustible, eternally renewed source of capital.[61] It also suggests an explanation of surplus-value or capitalist profits, deriving from circulation and inflated prices, and not directly from production. This explanation differs from the one later adduced by Marx, who in 1845 had not yet worked out his own position on the question.

> Now consider that on average the worker buys back his product, at the moment when it leaves his hands, at about a fifth above the costs of production, because it belongs to a private proprietor and must bring him a profit. In this fifth you reckon the rest of the costs necessary to maintaining the national wealth, which the worker must bear almost alone, for example, the indirect taxes, ground rents, customs duties, etc. Through this prosaic calculation you will find that ultimately the working classes in France have to pay almost all that its national economy costs the bourgeoisie.[62]

The real justification for free trade is its progressive historical role in exacerbating oppositions, and thereby resolving them. It creates monopoly through the ruin of small producers (as Bauer had argued about the insecurity of circulation in *The Jewish Question*); but it also creates the conditions in which monopoly can be overthrown. Hegel's thesis of polarisation, deployed here, is now seen as signalling a solution to the contradictions of civil society. Here is a republican response to the social question, in new though ill-defined organisational forms, instituting a humane relation between labour and capital. "At first, naturally, labour power can triumph only in the form of its alienation [*Entäusserung*], as capital."[63] Subsequently it will be possible for humankind "to consider labour and capital as its life-content, as the basis and manifestation of its life."[64] As Bauer himself puts it, all relations are to be infused with justice. The anonymous text continues:

> So the French bourgeoisie certainly founded its political rule through freedom of trade, free competition. But could it do this without at the same time exhausting the consequences of these revolutionary principles? One of the main consequences of free competition consists in the rule of capital! The largest capital was at the disposal of the bourgeoisie. Through this it created an industrial power, which was immediately decisive in all political, legislative, and economic [*staatsökonomischen*] questions. It is this power which rules, represents, polices France, and gives it its laws. This power prepares now before the eyes of an astonished Europe the frightful spectacle of twenty million workers, in the midst of abundance, suffering from want of everything that men need. But it is also this power that will conquer competition through competition, destroy the bourgeoisie, oppose a large mass of capital to the large mass of workers, and perhaps restore a tolerable relation between capital and labour power [*Arbeitskraft*].[65]

Here the republican programme confronts an antinomy. On the one hand, in Bauer's writings, competition is a necessary element in personal independence. On the other, Bauer's journals recognise untrammelled competition as a cause of the supremacy of capital, and thus of the concentration and centralisation of wealth. Competition undermines the conditions of its own existence, and promotes monopoly on a national scale. We have also seen that Bauer, in *The Jewish Question*, stresses the tenuousness and insecurity of property-holding in the modern competitive struggle. Lacking more explicit evidence, we might tentatively reconstruct his social and economic ideal in the 1840s as a form of simple commodity production, where small independent producers co-exist without extremes of wealth or poverty. This classic republican vision, expressed in Rousseau's *Social Contract*, would not be inconsistent with Bauer's view of the infusion of justice into all relations, and of the dignity of unconstrained labour, in the future revolutionary state. It is open to question whether such an ideal of relatively stable productive relations is in contradiction to Bauer's overall view of constant transformation, and his critique of liberal rights. It may be that republican proprietary rights would not be absolute, but subject to a greater degree of political jurisdiction and redistribution than liberalism allows (as in the Jacobin example, which Bauer explicitly approves); state interventions could be justified insofar as they maintained competition in a dynamic balance, restoring conditions of relative equality, without subordinating production to direct political control. It may be, too, that Bauer believes an egalitarian market society would be most conducive to citizenship, and to the political transcendence of private interests that is the heart of his republicanism; though this argument runs the risk of re-inscribing heteronomy into the political sphere, unless the economic conditions are seen to be merely contributory, but not determinant of individual actions and attitudes. On another aspect of the social question, Bauer is reticent on the issue of the peasantry, who still constituted 80% of the population of Prussia. He merely observes its enervation under the historical effects of servitude (only recently and problematically ended); he contends that the peasantry is devoid of political initiative, and, as a bulwark of the religious consciousness, props up the status quo. Despite this assessment, his critique of feudal dominance is unrelenting.

Beyond certain theoretical similarities on the question of free trade, the opposition to socialism retains its centrality for Bauer. His critiques of liberal and socialist currents do not cause him to renounce the necessity of political transformation or struggle, even at the height of reaction in 1849. He offers a vigorous defence of the right of insurrection in the March days of 1848 in Berlin, and especially of the barricade fighters against the monarchical regime. He distinguishes the revolutionary goals shared by the workers and republicans, excluded from the old order, from the limited objectives of the bourgeoisie, determined by their proprietary interests. Responding to the conservative claim that the fomenters of discord and struggle were aliens, he maintains:

> Yes, they were aliens who undertook the real struggle against the military: workers and a few intellectuals, who were cast out of official, privileged society, and to whom the indignation [*Empörung*] of the bourgeois served as a support in their struggle against this hard and spiritless society. The bourgeois let these small companies defend barricade after barricade ... but what did [the bourgeois] want in this struggle, which they approved of in their indignation, and in which even a few of the bourgeoisie took active part? Those outcasts who bled on the barricades struggled against the existing [order] in general, which laid on them only the duty of deprivation, and which rewarded them for the exercise of this duty only with contempt – these victorious fighters believed they had the monarchy in their hands and that they were making a revolution. But the bourgeois' only target was the absolute monarchy. The bourgeoisie wanted to deprive the monarchy

of its exclusive position, to reduce it to itself, to the mass, to which it [the monarchy] was already long akin through its lack of creative power, through the death of its conquering spirit [*Geistes*], through the poverty of its ideas. The bourgeoisie wanted to treat with the monarchy on the basis of equality and equal right.[66]

Here Bauer signals again the opposition between the limited struggle against absolutism and the more radical revolutionary aims of the popular movement. This text is coincident with Marx's own denunciation of liberal compromise with the monarchy and the Junkers in "The Bourgeoisie and the Counter-Revolution."[67] In similar terms, Bauer too voices the thesis that the revolution has been betrayed because of private economic interests. Despite their convergent diagnoses, their political projects remain distinct.

Extremely significant for his analysis of the political situation are Bauer's two public addresses in the revolutionary crisis of 1848–49, when he unsuccessfully stood for election to the Prussian National Assembly as a candidate for Charlottenburg.[68] Together with his brother Edgar, newly released from imprisonment for his subversive writings, he was a founding member of a local branch of the Democratic Society in Berlin.[69] In his electoral speeches, Bauer denies the impression created by his *Parteikämpfe* and his writings on the Jewish question that he was ever opposed to the party of progress.[70] He describes his career as a fifteen-year-long trial against the government, the sustained critique of its intentions, powers, and interests. If he is not a man of the party, he says, it is because he seeks to represent first of all the universal interest of freedom, and must criticise the party when it falls short of this ideal or misconstrues it.[71] "My struggle against the theological and corporate interests [i.e., of the *Stände* or estates of the old order] had as its goal political and social liberation, just as my critical struggle was a social struggle."[72] He attacks the state for attempting to restore feudal distinctions between estates,[73] for denying the rights of popular representation, for striving to stultify political and social life. These reactionary attempts prove only the powerlessness of the old order to embody the demands of self-consciousness, the nullity and positivity of a principle of tutelage that can no longer triumph of its own inner strength. Through sustained and implacable criticism, he affirms, "I thereby prepare the organisations which firmly and certainly will establish themselves upon the real relations, upon the noblest power of our representations, upon our entire world of thought and feeling."[74] Hence, he concludes, it is impossible for him to work against the party of progress.

His electoral addresses articulate with full clarity the fundamental political issue. The great question of the 1848 revolutions, already posed in the first outbreak of fighting in March, though not clearly seen by the parties, is "whether the people have the right and the power to give themselves their own laws, or whether they can calmly accept that a state power, which can always only be absolute, can prescribe their constitution to them."[75] Opposing steadfastly all compromise with the feudal regime, he stresses the incompatibility of popular sovereignty with rule by divine grace [*Gottesgnadentum*].

> Some popular leaders demanded of the monarchy that it issue the electoral law of the Constituent Assembly from the fullness of its own power, they demanded of the monarchy that it concede these important laws which would determine the participation of the people in legislation.... The rights which the people believed *they* had won were derived in these addresses from grace from above [emphasis added. DM] ... These addresses wholly forgot the struggle through which the Prussian people had acquired its rights.... Those very rights which the people conquered in March must now be newly assured for ever. It must be shown that these rights are truly the property of the people.... What we desire now is the creation of a constitution on the basis of equal right, which must have great social consequences, since such a constitution must introduce the principle of justice into all relations.... Only with this league of equal right will the unqualified freedom of the person be created.[76]

The league of equal right, created through heroic exertion and uncompromising struggle against the old order, expresses the historically progressive potential of the present moment. To attain this end, the revolution has cast off the yoke of tutelage and must now, with unflinching courage, carry out the work of liberation in all spheres of life. The old order is not yet extirpated; the danger of a reactionary coup persists.[77] Only the dedication of the revolutionaries will preserve and broaden the conquests of March. The work of creating a new constitution is only beginning; its aim must be to eliminate all obstacles that hem in the movement, that restrict human freedom.[78] There are tasks of an intensely practical order to be accomplished:

> The government, the statesman must win esteem and respect for the country, so that we can procure outlets for the products of our industry. He must bridge the seas and build fleets which can transport our labour to other parts of the world; he alone has the duty to eliminate all obstacles.[79]

This is not an imperialist proclamation, but a Smithian one: The obstacles to trade are still essentially internal, stemming from the dominance of landed interests. As is also clear from his critiques of Napoleon, Bauer is not advocating foreign conquest or the pillage of other lands,[80] but rather the elimination of all barriers to the free development of the economy and of industrial production in Germany. We have also seen that support for free trade is a distinctive feature of the republicanism advocated in Bauer's circle, though he does not elaborate here.

Bauer's first electoral address deals explicitly with the seizure and exercise of sovereignty by the progressive forces. He asks: "Has the nation already the power to determine this future for itself, to create for itself a government which can assist it in this shaping; has an organ been formed which can seize the initiative?"[81] Bauer outlines the revolutionary political situation, wherein two opposed principles of sovereignty co-exist, and have assumed institutional shape in the two houses of assembly. The untenability of Hegel's own political compromise between monarchy and people has been practically demonstrated. The Prussian upper chamber, reserved for the Junkers as an unelected body, exists as a permanent, institutionalised veto and censorship over popular initiatives. To counter the illegitimate power of this chamber, Bauer proposes what he calls an effective, not merely a symbolic, protest, in which the popularly elected lower house would prove its victory and affirm the supreme right of the revolution by taking real control and exerting power, both legislatively and politically. The lower house should immediately create a constitutional committee, whose task would be the redrafting of the constitution in accord with universal right, and the rallying of popular support for this work, so that when the inevitable confrontation with the upper house occurs, the entire weight of progressive public opinion would already be mobilised on the side of the revolutionaries.[82] No compromise between the two sources of legitimacy can be admitted, but the contradiction must come to a head in conditions where the republican principle has maximised its chances of victory. Only clear and decisive political initiatives will secure this outcome.[83]

While alluding to forms of modern civil society that endanger freedom by their monopolistic claims and limitlessness,[84] Bauer in his electoral addresses does not directly attack the liberal opposition, except to criticise, as a tactical perspective, its readiness to compromise with feudalism. He seems more willing now to entertain a common front with liberals than in his stinging pre-revolutionary polemics. While stressing that he proposes not only political but also social justice, Bauer does, however, differentiate his republican position sharply from that of the socialists, whom he sees as advocating a political alliance with and strengthening of the existing state apparatus. This he understands as a consequence of their basic authoritarian doctrines, and not just as a tactical error. Assimilating all variants of socialism to a single political position, Bauer here disregards (or may be unfamiliar with) polemics within the socialist camp over alliances, tactics, and strategies. It is clear that in 1848 one socialist faction, to be revived by Lassalle in the Bismarck era, did appeal to the existing state for protection against capital; others eschewed political struggle in favour of humanitarian reform. Some, but not all, tendencies equated socialism with the defence of the industrial proletariat. Among these, in turn, some pressed for immediate confrontation with the capitalist class,

while the group represented by Marx and Engels argued for the immanent necessity of eradicating feudalism as a precondition for the struggle
against capital.[85] Bauer's criticism would apply mainly to the first tendency, insofar as he describes the state that the socialists invoke as the
very state that has just been shaken by the revolutionary movement; and
we know that, in his characterisation of republicanism, and even of certain varieties of socialism,[86] the distinction between participation in the
existing state and the creation of a new state is one that Bauer himself
recognises. But he does not make these differentiations here.

Instead, he contrasts his republican league of equal right, whose goal
is the unconditional freedom of the person,[87] the self-rule of the people, and the self-organisation of society and of the workers,[88] with the
authoritarian nature of state socialism.

> In the social interest one party goes so far that it would screw up into
> the highest place the authority of the government, that it desires that the
> government should take the national labour into its own hands and regulate
> and manage it, even take it over. While for us the outcome is to shake off the
> yoke of tutelage, this party elevates the power of government to a mystical
> height, so that state and government rule over all relations with an iron
> sceptre, even though the absolute government was overthrown in March
> because work had outgrown it, because it no longer had the power to shape
> [*gestalten*] the national labour, this enormous labour.[89]

On the public platform, Bauer now elaborates his earlier critiques of
socialism. As government is the representative of that which exists against
change and progress, a victorious state socialism would exert a papal in-
terdiction upon invention and discovery. On the contrary assumption
that the government did sponsor innovation, it would risk fiscal ruin,
because progress depends upon experimentation and repeated failure
before the correct solution is found. The overseeing of these processes
would require an army of civil and military officials, and costly but un-
productive investments.[90]

> If you want to have a true picture of such state works, turn your gaze,
> gentlemen, to those of Asia, to those colossal building works, the pyramids
> of Egypt. These are the state works of despotism, which the despots have
> imposed on their subjects, to employ them for their advantage, to make the
> seething masses harmless. They are the labours of these nations, the docu-
> ments of the anxiety of their despots, who in these memorials have delivered
> to posterity a permanent testimonial to their despotism and to the slavery
> of their people.[91]

The first electoral speech thus identifies the principal opponent to be
the remains of the feudal order, but also warns that socialism is seeking
to revive this very despotic state for its own ends. In his second electoral address, of February 1849, Bauer defends himself against three

accusations,[92] versions of which have also characterised much of the subsequent interpretative literature on his thought. The scope and contradictory nature of these charges are testimony to the difficulty of an unam-
biguous reading of his work. The first is that his extreme revolutionary
attitude would jeopardise the progressive movement by rashly exacerbating contradictions.[93] The second is the converse accusation, arising from
his writings on the Jewish question, that he would rather defend the existing order against the opposition.[94] The third is that of being a merely
abstract theorist, divorced from the movement and seeking to undermine
all parties in order to assert his own intellectual superiority.[95] He claims
the right of a public defence on the basis of civic responsibility, mutual
respect being the foundation of citizenship in a rational political order.

> Indeed we do not yet live in a free state, but we all want to bring it into
> existence, and we will most certainly bring it into existence if we discharge
> the duties that such a state imposes on its members.[96]

Defending his interventions on the Jewish question as politically progressive, Bauer says that he merely shows that privilege is the essence of
the old order, hence no concession of freedom by that order is possible;
nor can the Christians concede freedom to others when they themselves
have not yet attained it. "Freedom can only be conquered by common
work, not given as a gift."[97] Responding to his critics, Bauer gives the
following self-characterisation:

> Criticism is nothing other than the correct [*wirkliche*] use of the eye. It
> is genuine [*wirkliche*] seeing, unhindered, undistorted by representations
> [*Vorstellungen*] and interests which are alien to the object that I will to see;
> undeceived by wishes, hopes, and fears which the parties carry about and
> which often do violence to the object. The corporate and government
> interest will not admit that the object be seen as it is. Criticism dissolves
> this will, this interest, and frees the object from a pressure which violently
> constricts or extends it. It restores to the object the right to be what it
> wills to be according to its nature, gives it back its freedom and allows it
> to pronounce its judgement and its decision upon itself.... [Criticism] is
> based on knowledge of the present [form] of the resolutions [*Gegenwart
> der Beschlüsse*] which lead us to a secure future.[98]

This passage utilises the metaphor of unimpaired seeing, reminiscent
of Feuerbach's account of the proper use of the senses against the distor-
tions and inversions of idealism. Here it links instead to Bauer's defence
of ethical idealism, and to his 1829 manuscript; after 1848 this idea will
come to play a different role, as the Epilogue notes. Nothing is added to
the object by criticism, no extraneous standard is invoked, but criticism, in
its aesthetic disinterestedness, merely allows the object to undergo its own
fate. Disinterestedness is not indifference, and Bauer affirms his alliance
with the party of progress. Declining to share its illegitimate enthusiasms,

and exercising the right of criticism against its insufficiencies, Bauer defines himself as the true friend of the good cause of freedom and of the progressive movement. "Criticism is the means and the power [*Kraft*] to eliminate the impossible and to bring the necessary to recognition."[99] The task of criticism is to make manifest the real contradictions, to pose the issues sharply and without distortion by subjective preconceptions and extraneous considerations. Its judgement is sustained by reflection on the course of history, and the contradictions of the moment. It is the necessary presupposition for effective action; it is not abstract, but grapples with concrete issues in the emancipatory struggle. As the first electoral address also shows, criticism must identify the key issues and press for their resolution in the most favourable possible conditions; these conditions are brought about by the courage and decisiveness of the revolutionaries' own act. This constitutes Bauer's restatement of republican virtue in the service of political and social transformation.

Bauer's political position in 1848 is thus complex. He castigates the bourgeoisie and its liberal spokesmen as deeply compromised with the old order. The primacy of property deforms their view of freedom. He identifies with the struggle of the unprivileged and the excluded, but is highly critical of socialism for reviving the authoritarian state as its organising principle. He appears closer to liberalism in his defence of competition (however dialectical, and not purely affirmative, this view may be); and he seems prepared now to entertain a strategic alliance with the liberals against the vestiges of feudalism. But the revolutionary forces prove inadequate to the tasks of republican transformation, as Bauer prescribes them, and indeed as he predicted. This failure accentuates the tensions in Bauer's thought between its subjective and objective dimensions. Bauer distinguishes both his ethics of perfectionism and his aesthetics of the sublime from the spurious infinite, in which thought and being never coincide. Hence he requires the idea of the beautiful self, the return of consciousness into interiority after its engagements with objectivity. This subjective unity, the self-certainty of the revolutionary consciousness that has grasped and internalised the historical process, comes to appear as an antithesis to the claims of all other consciousnesses. This attitude accounts for the sectarian tone of Bauer's criticisms of the mass, of Jewish emancipation, and of the workers' movement; and his isolation vitiates his claims to objectivity. Yet even this deficiency is only one side of Bauer's thinking and political activity in 1848. His two electoral addresses encapsulate many facets of the struggle against feudal retardation, proposing the doctrine of equal right and the expansion of a new industrial order. As a dedicated partisan of this struggle, Bauer regains his stature as a protagonist of freedom in the moment of revolutionary confrontation itself.

In characterising Bauer's *Vormärz* republicanism, we revert to the themes of his prize manuscript of 1829. "The light of truth advances only by division and opposition and movement,"[100] thus by the exacer-bation of contradictions, posing them without compromise or mediation so that they appear in their purity, and can thus be overcome. This truth is the unity of thought and being, not as a closed and completed identity, but as a process, in which, through subjective efforts, the concept of free-dom breaks through into existence, and refashions objective relations. Bauer stresses the objectivity of thought, both in its comprehension of historically possible ends, and in the need to realise these ends in political and social relations. "Thought conscious of itself cannot be limited to an internal sense, but is both in itself and in objectivity, and finds itself in its other."[101] Thus thought is infinite, as self-consciousness. Subjects now enjoy a unique vantage point on history as a process of alienation and recovery of reason. The philosophy of Hegel evokes a new kind of critical judgement, and a new republicanism. Engagement with the inner limi-tations of the Hegelian system, as well as with its formidable strengths, opens the possibility of an ethical and aesthetic idealism, wherein subjects transcend their particular interests and identities to become the vehicles of the universal. "Only as sublated do they truly exist."[102]

When we read Bruno Bauer's defence of the barricade fighters of Berlin in 1848, we know that this is not his last word. The rupture in Bauer's thought supervened after the defeat of the revolutionary strug-gle. He succumbed to the pessimism of the 1850s, holding that Europe was exhausted and incapable of creative self-renewal. Rebirth, he now held, will come from Russia. The coherence and stability of premodern life now represent an alternative version of the unity of thought and be-ing, though Bauer no longer found this terminology appropriate. As a cultural and literary historian, and a prophet of imperialism and global-isation, the later Bauer was uninterested in the problems of republican-ism that have concerned us here. After the failures of 1848, the "friend of freedom" severed his links with the philosophical project of emanci-pation and with the concrete political movement. He became known as the "hermit of Rixdorf." His personal fate is not the decisive refutation of his earlier republican commitments, which retain their relevance as a struggle to fashion humane and liberating social institutions, recognising and generalising the claims of autonomy. The unity of thought and being does not mean the collapse of all such efforts into a premodern substan-tiality, as the later Bauer believed, nor the end of history in the ubiquity of the market, but evokes the necessity of further transformations. The rediscovery of republicanism, in the variety of its forms, has its historical import here. Bauer's ethical idealism in the *Vormärz* makes an original and significant contribution to this republican tradition.

EPILOGUE: AFTER THE REVOLUTION: THE CONCLUSION OF THE CHRISTIAN-GERMANIC AGE

In Bauer's late judgement, the failure of 1848 attests to the bankruptcy of the European metaphysical tradition, of which, formerly, his own ethical idealism was to have been the culmination.[1] While he continues to proclaim his fidelity to his basic pre-revolutionary insights, his thought undergoes a profound change. He abandons his republicanism, but his abiding anti-liberal stance now induces him to contribute to conservative causes. After 1848 the ethics of perfectionism can no longer be sustained, but the aesthetic idea proves more durable in Bauer's thinking. Something of the metaphysical idea of the unity of thought and being persists, greatly transfigured, in both individual and social forms. Individually, this unity is no longer secured through sublime and ceaseless struggle, but in private self-cultivation, or disinterested aesthetic contemplation of the inevitable processes of cultural decay and regeneration. Socially, after 1848, Bauer looks particularly to Russia as a revivifying force for an exhausted and impotent Europe, sunk under the weight of particularism. Though the European legacy of reform and revolution is pressing upon it, and though he describes it as filled with repugnance for its own shameful and unacknowledged past, Russia unites political and ecclesiastical powers in all-encompassing absolutism. A premodern society now appears to hold out the prospects for a new beginning, as a stimulus to change, if not as a model to be emulated.

After 1848, Bauer no longer believes that the immediate future is one of republican progress. He now foresees an age of multinational or global imperialism, in which Russia will play a prominent part. The German political movement of all complexions is exhausted,[2] and it is uncertain how much of its cultural patrimony will survive. Any hope of a revival must now lie in a fundamental reorientation towards Europe. Until 1848, Bauer's reflections on history focused on the international implications of the Enlightenment and the French Revolution. The decisive question after 1848 is the assertion of Russian power, and the inflection of all major European policy issues by Russian involvement. Bauer predicts that

European union will be hastened through the encounter with Russia. Whereas his pre-revolutionary thought stressed the amorphousness of emergent civil society, it is now states that will shed their particular characters in a move towards a European and global absolutism. He considers such union to be inevitable, though its form will vary depending on whether these new relations involve active collusion with Russia, or a decisive battle against it,[3] as two distinct types of absolutism are at stake. The crisis of 1848 had been insufficiently radical, because it upheld the independence of individual states, and even imparted renewed energies to particular nations. The crisis is now to become universal through the struggle awakened by Eastern despotism; Bauer affirms that this was already his basic idea in 1848.[4] Anticipating Nietzsche, he predicts that from this generalised catastrophe of European civilisation will emerge a new era of liberation, breaking with the old historical forms and values, together with their metaphysical and religious sanctions.[5] Even Bauer's late work heralds a revolution in a new key. Despite his renunciation of historical perfectionism and his collaboration with conservative forces after 1848, he continues to repudiate traditionalism, and sets a new course for anti-liberal thinking. The way is fraught with perils; Bauer becomes a harbinger of anti-Semitism, and is claimed as an ancestor by some National Socialist authors, though Barnikol disputes this connection.[6] The late writings set his historical criticism on a new footing.

For Bauer, the revolutions of 1848 represent a crisis of reason. They were so inextricably connected with the transcendental project that their failure meant the final ruin of metaphysics. Philosophy culminates in the ineffectual struggles of 1848, and at the same time proclaims its own demise. The realisation of philosophy is its end, though in a sense other than that intended by Marx in 1843[7]; it leaves behind merely a rubble of dashed hopes and impossible aspirations. The crucial moment in Bauer's post-revolutionary intellectual development occurs in 1852. In that year, he still depicts his own work as the completion of the Kantian and Hegelian programme,[8] but then rapidly distances himself from Hegel. His late critique assimilates Hegel with Strauss and the standpoint of substance. Bauer's final verdict on Hegel echoes parts of his 1829 manuscript, with its insistence that substance is the negation of form and subjectivity.[9] The victory of substance means the effacement of individuality. While this claim is consistent with Bauer's early criticism, he now extends it to describe the Hegelian system as a whole. Here systematic unity is won only by submerging all particulars under undifferentiated, formal, and abstract thought determinations, losing the living detail in an amorphous substantiality.[10] Hegel subsumes the individual under a chimerical universal, thus succumbing to the Spinozist impulses in his thought,[11] whereas in 1845 Bauer had identified a creative tension in Hegel between Spinoza and Fichte, between inert substance and formative striving. Now the transcendent character of the rational idea is no longer an incidental formulation, which Hegel's own system rectifies, but is inscribed in the very substantiality in which the system is embedded. This change of perspective requires a new political assessment of Hegel. While prior to 1848 he believed that Hegel had taught "the republic and the revolution," Bauer now decries the absolutist tendencies of traditional metaphysics.[12] The oppressive unity of metaphysics parallels the historic trend towards an all-encompassing despotism, and even anticipates it, because the philosophical movement, the assimilation of particulars under abstract thought, is already complete. The late Bauer appears to offer no self-criticism of his own ethical idealism of the *Vormärz*, merely attributing to Hegel the discounting of individuality in favour of conformity. This intonation has a surprisingly contemporary resonance.[13]

Methodologically, Bauer advocates the transition from metaphysics to critique, understood as a positive science. In his new characterisation, his method involves research into historical details, working through them until their own intrinsic relationships become apparent, but with no *a priori* systemic concern. Only a careful empiricism permits the observer to follow the real movement of history without distortion or partiality. It is no longer requisite that we view the totality of historical phenomena as revealing a common intellectual essence, or as displaying a connected series of emancipatory strivings. Not all links with his previous work are lost, however. As he had argued in the *Landeskirche*, the best scientific research retains its independence from ecclesiastical and political tutelage. Its objective is to determine the relation of rights and freedom of the will (neither of which the late Bauer denies, though they now lack metaphysical grounding) to humankind's natural basis.[14] The relation of nature and freedom remains among the central theoretical issues, as it had in the 1829 manuscript,[15] but reason does not direct us to intervene in order to affect the course of change. The friend of freedom now describes himself as the detached friend of research. The echo is clearer in German, where the "Freund der Freiheit" becomes the "Freund der Forschung."[16]

What this research reveals is that the future belongs not to the people[17] or to separate national destinies, but to a transnational imperialism, involving the confrontation of two distinct absolutist programmes. One, the German, retains the principle of private interest; political absolutism arises over modern mass society as its necessary complement. This description, recalling Bauer's earlier polemic against antiquated and outmoded forms of state, now applies to an ongoing process of development, whose completion is yet to come. The other absolutist form is that of Russia, whose cohesiveness is based on the fusion of political and ecclesiastical power, and the retarded development of the modern principle of personality. Hegel, like Kant and Fichte, had excluded this zone from the scope of world history, but its significance can no longer be denied.[18] Russia owes its original political foundations to Germany.[19] Here Bauer anticipates the thesis of the anarchist Bakunin, who, however, inverts Bauer's meaning, finding in Russia's lack of spontaneous political productivity a proof of its superiority over the West.[20] In Bauer's view, Russia has, however, remained largely immune to western philosophical influence, adopting only what served its immediately practical ends. It thus represents a separate path of development, but Russia too is ambivalent, enigmatic. If western metaphysics found no fertile ground in the Russian spirit, the influence of religious movements like the Quakers did penetrate it through the reforms of Peter the Great. The czar's personal experiences of religious renewal during his sojourn in England inspired his westernising programme.[21] Bauer also speaks of 10 million Russian sectarians (*Raskolniki* and Dukhobors, believers in inner revelation and the invisible church) locked in conflict with Panslavists, who bolster the throne and the Orthodox Church, and reject all reform attempts. The issue of this conflict is unclear. Despite the coherence it derives from the interlocking power of church and state, Russia is animated by a violent hatred and shame of its own past. Its power cannot be contained, but threatens to engulf the Balkans and Constantinople.[22]

In texts on Russia that precede the Crimean War,[23] Bauer contends that the solution to the contemporary crisis is not directly provided by Russia, but properly belongs to Europe, and especially to Germany.[24] Despite his repudiation of metaphysics, it is the model of elicitation devised by Fichte that best describes Bauer's view of the influences flowing from the East. In Fichte's model, applied at both interpersonal and international levels, the encounter with the other summons, but does not compel, recognition and renewed effort in the self.[25] As Bauer tacitly applies this model, Europe, depleted of inner resources, confronts the vigour of an alien adversary, and must rise to the task of changing itself if it is not to succumb utterly. Russia thus elicits the struggle whereby the basic historical issues can be solved. In a phrase adopted by Löwith, Bauer refers to this question as the conclusion of the Christian-Germanic age.[26] This process involves the full extension of imperialism to encompass Europe and the globe, and the clash of rivals for dominance within the new empire. World war is on the historical agenda.

Bauer anticipates some of the socialist Karl Kautsky's theses on ultra-imperialism, though he does not share the latter's optimism that this trend heralds a resolution of conflicts between contenders for hegemony.[27] The historic function of this globalising programme is the disciplinary crushing of particularity,[28] grinding down national identities and creating the basis for an eventual cosmopolitan rebirth. Bauer downplays the significance of nationalism as a political force. The issue is less the defence of national interests than the vying of different centres for supremacy within a transnational order. The growing centralisation of political power, driving peoples together, is abetted by the levelling power of the socialist movement, though the latter is far from realising its internationalist pretensions, and thus poses no immediate danger to the existing order. This trend also corresponds to what Bauer calls the emergence of a political pauperism,[29] a generalised disability to intervene in political affairs. The problem for the future to resolve is how to unite equality with personal worth and independence. This will be the key to any cultural revival, but at present the solution cannot be foreseen.[30]

Bauer finds the present crisis reminiscent of the end of the classical world in Roman imperialism. His religious criticism is recast in this respect. In a series of studies published in the 1850s, he resumes his investigations of the New Testament.[31] He locates the origins of Christianity only in the second century, concluding that the first gospel was written under Hadrian (A.D. 117–138), though the Pauline epistles are slightly earlier. Paul's letters express the unembellished core of Christian belief, the resurrection. Bauer traces the evolution of Christian doctrine from the Hellenistic heritage, primarily from Stoicism and other sources in the eclectic culture of the Roman Empire. Of particular interest is the *logos* doctrine of John, which Bauer derives from Philo and neo-Platonism. His intent is to foreclose a direct relationship or dependency of Christianity upon Judaism. That the two religions must not be seen as a continuous development had also been Bauer's position in *Herr Dr. Hengstenberg*, but now he argues more emphatically for the belated historical appearance of the Christian community. Compared with his *Vormärz* position, he also offers a more positive assessment of Christianity as a source of liberation for the underclasses of the Roman Empire, accentuating the revolutionary character of this religion as a form of recognition that the poor and the slaves extracted from the ruling orders. Continuing this line of thought in his final work of 1882, he stresses the socialist conclusion of Greek and Roman history in Christianity, contrasting the world-shaking power of the early Christian religion with its modern role as mere solace to the bourgeois conscience.[32] It is this element that Engels celebrates in his very positive obituary of Bauer.[33] In 1908, Karl Kautsky develops Bauer's thesis in his own *Origins of Christianity*.[34]

As the role of rational and ethical self-determination subsides in Bauer's late work, he gives a more positive assessment of feeling in contributing to the formation of modern subjectivity. This attitude is exemplified in his extensive studies of the international influence of the Quakers and similar movements.[35] In this account, the inwardness and passivity of pietism appear as the dominant characteristics of the eighteenth century, at least in Germany. The rationalist Enlightenment is tributary to it, and pietism leaves its impress on Kant and Fichte, whose practical reason translates the inner voice of conscience into another, rationalist, idiom.[36]

Bauer conflates the primacy of practical reason with pietist sense- or feeling-certainty, against which he had earlier reserved some of his most violent polemics.[37] But he also sees pietism as the culmination and the end of Christianity, because it destroys dogmatic assertion in favour of inward illumination, and dissolves statutory religion into moral rectitude.[38] Bauer argues here consistently with his *Entdeckte Christenthum*, according to which religions are defined by their fetishistic clinging to exclusive dogmas and symbols. The direction of history is still that of dissipating these illusions, but Bauer now finds that the motive force lies more in inarticulate sentiment than in autonomous reason. The comparison with his position in the *Posaune* is instructive. There he had denounced as regressive Schleiermacher's efforts to restore dogmatic Christianity through an appeal to feeling, and had held sentiment and rationality to be diametrically opposed. Now he claims that the force of sentiment is precisely contrary to Schleiermacher's supposition. It works to undermine the validity of all doctrinal claims; even rationalist critique derives its strength from this basic force. If the Roman Empire ended in the triumph of Christianity, the new world empire will end with the dissolution of dogmatic religion into personal conviction.

In judging the contemporary political situation, Bauer offers a critical assessment of Bismarck's military and state socialism, which subordinates all productive activity to narrowly conceived political ends. Barnikol rightly observes that Bauer was never a pro-Bismarckian National Liberal, as he is sometimes depicted.[39] Bauer describes the domestic roots of Bismarck's policies, perpetuating the militaristic efforts of the early eighteenth-century Prussian kings, that he had long before described in the *Landeskirche*. Bauer also notes the external impetus provided by what he calls Disraeli's romantic imperialism, the attempt to level English society before a paternalistic monarchy. The political form that Bismarck imparts to the inevitable globalising trend is different, marked by intense efforts to organise all production at the behest of the state, and to place the population under the strictest tutelage, choking off the sources of innovation and independence. Bismarck's policies perfect state socialism, but his political manoeuvrings cannot appease the workers or silence his Catholic adversaries. Assessing Bismarck's contributions to world imperialist tendencies, Bauer judges him ultimately a failure.

Underlying Bauer's critique of Bismarck is a defence of German culture against its partial manifestations in the Prussian and Austrian regimes, and against its arrogation by any state. This attitude is combined with a harsh critical judgement on the insufficiencies of that culture, even in its highest exemplars such as Goethe.[40] The metaphysical tradition is in part responsible for these failings, but Bauer stresses, as in his earlier work, that the German spirit is a product of thought, and not of nature. Germany is not a racial but a historical artefact. The danger lies in the extinction of the German spirit of individual spontaneity in favour of the state,[41] though the irresistible progress of imperialism may make this an unavoidable fate. Bauer's late reflections are marked by a stringent anti-nationalism, which makes a National-Socialist appropriation of his thought questionable.

In this respect, it is also noteworthy that Bauer stresses the positive value of racial mixing, not racial purity, though, like Max Weber, he is preoccupied with the Slavic influx into Berlin and eastern Germany. Mixing requires assimilation and balance, and its positive effects are lost through a sudden and disproportionate increase of one element. It is clear, however, that the anti-Semitism for which Bauer was taxed in the 1840s becomes a much more prominent feature of his later thought. An anonymous 1882 article, of which Barnikol suspects Bauer is the author, describes the Jewish question as the new form of the social question. The history of Western Europe is now presented as a process of decline, in which efforts at renewal have been constantly aborted.[42] The author claims that the political significance of the Jews throughout the political spectrum is testimony to this general weakness. He describes the Jewish character as usurious, seeking quick and effortless gain at the expense of productive labour and the workers. This text, like similar ones undoubtedly of Bauer's authorship,[43] contributes powerfully to the arsenal of anti-Semitic rhetoric in Germany.

In Bauer's last texts, surprisingly perhaps, the voice of the *Vormärz* republican is not entirely silenced. His final verdict on 1848 is that the people's elected representatives failed to entrust its constitutional future and its collective freedom to the progress of the revolution; rallying instead to the king of Prussia, they subverted the popular cause.[44] He describes the opposition between the old feudal right of conquest, and the new right of the free personality and pacific labour, which might one day animate the uprising of countless masses [*Scharen*] against the existing order.

> With a similar uprising and liberation Greek and Roman history ended before the triumph of imperialism.... The formerly oppressed and burdened found then in Christianity their point of convergence, and over the course of centuries wrenched recognition from the empire. Up till now the prospects are quite slim for a fraternisation among the particular national workers' circles like that which Christianity offered to their Greco-Roman precursors, and because of the failures of their efforts, governments need not disturb themselves over an alliance against a single, all-threatening worker's league.[45]

However, if not the socialist dream of a brotherhood of workers, another form of unification is impending:

> Beneath their superficial national costumes, [the peoples] have become *Europeans*, and common imperialistic experiences will make them feel ever

more *European.* When the end comes, when the struggle of emperors [*Imperatorenstreit*] breaks out over the composition of the European fatherlands, the members of these nationalities will provide the armed rivals with valuable military material.[46]

Unlike Kautsky, the ultraimperialism that Bauer foresees is not pacific, but spawns large-scale internecine wars. Neither does it stimulate, but hampers economic growth. Bauer declares that perpetual political unrest and military preparedness undermine productive activity.[47] In the all-embracing catastrophe brought on by world imperialism, the old order will reach its apocalyptic climax. Only then will new cultural possibilities emerge. Hegel has been fully eclipsed; Nietzsche is on the horizon.[48]

Bauer's late work merits further study. It reveals the vicissitudes of a failed republicanism, contains prescient observations on globalisation and world war, and manifests possible connections with a variety of twentieth-century forms of thought. The elements of this complex intellectual legacy are strewn on the left and the right, reappearing in Kautsky, Nietzsche, extreme German nationalism, and elsewhere. What remains constant throughout Bauer's work is a categorical imperative, never to be a liberal.[49]

APPENDIX: BRUNO BAUER, "ON THE PRINCIPLES OF THE BEAUTIFUL" (1829)

Dissertation on the principles of the beautiful, which Kant exposed in that part of his philosophy which he intended as a critique of the faculty of judgement.

Motto: "Seriousness in Art is its Serenity."[1]

(66 [b]) After two millennia of the labour of spirit [*ingenii*], the philosophy of Kant arose, and through a great revolution opened the way to the new philosophy. In order to ascertain the power and movement of this philosophical system, we must briefly indicate the antecedent principles of philosophical science, for the system can only be understood through its antecedents.

Every philosophy wanted to examine the principle of thinking and being, and to discover their

(67 [a]) common source. For this indeed is the eternal idea, that in God being and thinking are not separate. Thus philosophical thinking is divine thinking, since it endeavours to examine that unity, that source, as it is in God.[2] But since Greek philosophy derived from the immediate unity of being and thinking, the opposition [between these terms] could neither be overcome nor abolished. Now Parmenides very simply enunciated this immediate unity: *to einai esti* and *to einai esti to noein*.[3] His teaching will remain forever true, [but] not because he penetrated as far as division and opposition, nor because he correctly mediated the truth by means of these [distinctions]. The philosophy of Plato,

(67 [b]) as well, is founded upon the concord of things and idea: for according to his teaching only the notion or the idea *is*, and the idea is the truth of things. And next Aristotle, too, says: the thing is the passive *nous*, and thought the active *nous*. Thus things are thought, and led back and elevated to concepts.

In the Middle Ages this opposition became most serious. Christian teaching opened to mankind the heavenly world, through which the minds of men might find refuge from the contention of this world. For this world was bound by the utmost barbarism and division, which it wished to mediate and remove, and all life was striving in every field to rise up by means of the sharpest strife to the species and form

(68 [a]) of the new age. For the light of truth advances only by division and opposition and movement. Faith, to be sure, consoled men in the face of the uproar and tumult of earthly life, and taught them that the truth of this life is only found in the world beyond. Therefore, since philosophy was in the service of faith, it retained that separation and un-reconciled opposition. Reconciliation was indeed desired, and scholastic philosophy even secured unity, but only as belief, and not truly as something known. For faith excludes all doubt. Thus since faith was already given and became the object of philosophical thought, the truth of this thought

(68 [b]) is already given, and thought is not its own object. Thought was known by the power of faith, and for this reason it was not free. Since, therefore, thought is identical with faith, thought cannot be that truth which mediates its own object. For this reason, it is necessary that they be separated, and only that mediated unity which has come about in our own age will be true knowledge.

That separation which had already arisen was elevated to its highest point when Kant attempted to resolve it.[4] For from the second part of his metaphysics on, he was endeavouring to demonstrate the truth and freedom of thought; but since the entire finite world

(69 [a]) was in opposition to it, he was unable to bring about a true reconciliation. Empiricism manifested this defect, and concerned itself with the finite world alone. Its metaphysic was even destitute of the truly philosophical idea, in opining about the finite world. But since the finite world was opposed to the unity of the divine world, the separation was [to be] explained as much as possible, because it was necessary to advance to a true unification. Kant, then, discovered these two distinct moments and undertook the great work of resolving them, a task which, in fact, has at last been accomplished by the new philosophy.

Thus the necessity and truth of the Kantian philosophy repose upon

(69 [b]) the great work of reconciling the opposition between realism and idealism, advanced by Locke and Hume of the realist faction, and by Descartes, Spinoza, and Leibniz of the idealist faction.[5] But since the critical philosophy strives to maintain both realism and idealism, it shows

that there is truth in both of them. Since, however, the truth cannot be present in contrary positions, Kant turns his attention to the thing-in-itself. This, however, since it does not truly join both of those factions to itself, remains an infinite obstacle; because if indeed we perceive something by means of our senses, our mind [*animus*] is affected by an external force, and the knowledge which we acquire through this is neither

(70 [a]) necessary nor universal. Although we perceive things by means of our senses, we nevertheless retain spontaneity of thinking, which does not come to us from without, for the reduction to unity of the manifold characteristics of any thing can only be the spontaneous action of the mind. Therefore, since we admit our receptivity for an impression only in that we are affected by some thing, knowledge must be distinguished from that affection. For we obtain the forms of Quantity, quality, relation etc., which are functions of our judgement, from our mind alone, and we do not owe them to the things themselves. Therefore, because it is by means of those forms alone that we reduce the plurality of things to unity, and because in the things themselves there is no

(70 [b]) reality, idealism is restored to its rights. However, because our thinking is only able to operate if it discovers the different characteristics of things which it reduces to unity, and without that manifold it would be nothing at all and empty, to the extent that thinking must necessarily be affected by things, thinking depends upon things. Therefore, since reality necessarily exists by means of things, realism too is re-instated. Since, then, realism and idealism are necessary and reality exists in both, and since, nevertheless, they are opposite to each other and at the same time each depends on the other and they do not truly mediate each other, some other thing must be understood as effecting their unity. This is the thing-in-itself, which,

(71 [a]) however, since it is being without appearance, is unknown and absolutely nothing.

Thus Kant derives that which affects the senses from one faction, but from the other, thought or the idea; the former, he says, can only be known in theoretical philosophy, while we attain to the latter in practical philosophy. Both, however, are still divided, and pertain to different powers which limit each other and do not yet achieve their own unity. For theoretical philosophy is able to know its objects by means of representation, not however as the thing-in-itself, but only as appearances; while practical philosophy, on the other hand, which possesses the notion of freedom,

(71 [b]) in its objects knows the thing-in-itself, but is unable to demonstrate it in a representation. Induced by these considerations, Kant posits an infinite supersensual power which, however, we are unable to penetrate by means of our thought. But although there is an immeasurable distance between the sensible, or the concept of nature, and the concept of freedom, or the non-sensual – a distance which cannot be bridged – nevertheless, as Kant says, this notion [of freedom] *ought* to have force and movement in that domain [of nature], that is, the concept of freedom or the idea ought to effect its purpose or its interest in the world of the senses.[6] Therefore the unity of the sensible and the supersensible, the passage from the concept of nature to

(72 [a]) the concept of freedom must be achieved. Thus Kant reaches the summit of his philosophy when he recognises the conjunction of concept and objectivity, and we shall consider how he hastens along this lofty path. Just as there exists a passage from the concept of freedom to the concept of nature, so it is necessary too that there exist an intermediate between understanding and reason, which is the faculty of judgement. But there is also another reason by which we are led to accept the faculty of judgement as intermediate between reason and understanding. For all the faculties of the mind [*animi*] can be reduced to three; which are the faculty of knowing, the sense of pleasure and of aversion, and the faculty of

(72 [b]) desiring. Understanding alone imposes law upon the faculty of knowing by means of the *a priori* concepts of nature, while reason alone imposes law upon the faculty of desiring.[7] Since, therefore, the sense of delight or of aversion is intermediate between the faculty of knowing and the faculty of desiring, and the faculty of judgement is intermediate between understanding and reason, Kant concludes that there inheres in the faculty of judgement too an *a priori* principle, and that this faculty constitutes the passage from the concept of nature to the concept of freedom.[8]

Now the faculty of judgement is that by which we subsume the particular to the universal. If the universal has already been given and the particular is subsumed under it, then the faculty of judgement is determinative.[9]

(73 [a]) However, there exists such a variety of forms of nature which are still indeterminate, that we must investigate their laws as well. Thus the faculty of judgement arises as reflective, [when] by means of it, the necessary ascent from the particular to the universal occurs.[10] Yet, in order to accomplish this, it lacks a principle, which we ought neither to deduce from experience nor attribute to nature itself, since nature does

not depend upon those conditions by means of which we strive to grasp its concept, which [concept] extends to it not at all. Thus Kant proposes that, since the universal laws of nature depend upon the understanding which attributes them to nature,[11]

(73 [b]) the particular and universal laws, in respect to those things which remained undetermined by them, ought to be regarded according to such a unity *as though* the understanding had produced them. From this it surely follows that the faculty of judgement imposes laws upon itself, but not upon nature.

But to approach the matter more closely, what is that subsumption? It is the form of finality. The end is the general concept, and in that individual things correspond to this end, they are purposive. In fact, the realisation and satisfaction of this interest [of the end] has been linked with the sense of pleasure.[12] Therefore, when we perceive that the particular is in agreement with the universal, we are moved with pleasure, which contains neither covetousness

(74 [a]) nor longing. Since, therefore, pleasure has been connected to the apprehension of the form of some object without reference to distinct knowledge determined by concepts, the representation is referred not to the object but to the subject alone, and the pleasure which derives from this is nothing other than the agreement of the object with the faculty of knowing.[13] For when we grasp that form in apprehension, it necessarily occurs that the reflective faculty of judgement, even if it is unconscious of itself, compares that representation

(74 [b]) with its own faculty of referring representations to concepts. If, therefore, pleasure is caused by the agreement of the faculty of imagination (which is the *a priori* faculty of representations) with the understanding, the object is in agreement with its end. Such a judgement, which neither depends on the concept of the object nor provides its concept, is called the aesthetic judgement. Now the object, whose form necessarily gives birth to pleasure through mere reflection on it, is the beautiful, and the faculty of judging of this pleasure is taste.[14]

Since, as we saw above, understanding and reason were hindered in every common force and in every movement which they might reciprocally have toward each other by the immeasurable distance between

(75 [a]) the sensible and the supersensible, and since the contemplation of the supersensible in the sensible must be attributed neither to understanding nor to reason, Kant posited the intuitive understanding in order to grasp the beautiful, and thus attained to truth.[15] But this [accomplishment] is once again diminished, since Kant demotes the

notion of the faculty of judgement to [the rank of] a constitutive principle in respect to the sense of pleasure and of aversion, that is, to a subjective rule.[16]

Kant advances these considerations before proceeding to the actual criticism of the faculty of judgement and his doctrine of the beautiful in order to show the place and position of the beautiful in philosophy.

(75 [b]) But before we proceed to a criticism of his doctrine of the beautiful, let us carefully consider this introduction, in order that we may see whether the true nature of the beautiful and its idea can be grasped in this way. Kant proceeded to a consideration of the beautiful and to the critique of the faculty of judgement after he completed two other chapters of his philosophy, namely the critique of practical and of theoretical reason. Philosophy, he says, is synthetic judgement, the binding together of different reasons [*rationes*], and not their separation, as Wolff taught in his metaphysics. But in addition, this judgement must not be derived from experience, as empiricism did, but must necessarily depend on the concept and thought, for which reason,

(76 [a]) synthetic judgement is *a priori*. But before we may examine and construct this synthetic system, Kant says, the faculty of knowing must be determined and subjected to criticism. In accordance with this principle, he accomplished the critique of pure reason. The spontaneity of the understanding is in opposition to sensibility. Its activity consists in reducing the manifold of sensual representations to universal concepts. Understanding, therefore, is the action of judgement. Thus Kant appropriates the four categories from ordinary logic without having demonstrated their necessity.[17] But these categories are empty and abstract, and in order that

(76 [b]) they be may filled, they must be applied to objects and appearances; but they do not apply to the thing-in-itself. For we know the thing-in-itself by means of our reason alone; but since cognition is nothing other than the application of the categories, and since the categories can accomplish nothing in the domain of reason, reason falls into contradiction, which is the object of the transcendental dialectic. The great merit of the critical philosophy is that it dared to advance toward contradiction; but it was unable to contain it and to proceed to the true solution and to the truth of the concept, because it never considered the internal plenitude and concreteness of the concept. Thus the philosophy of Kant

(77 [a]) remains wholly a subjective idealism, since it does not penetrate to the developed truth and to the developed idea, and since abstract subjectivity alone remains. Since, therefore, in that part of his philosophy

which we are considering, Kant posits such a mutual relationship of universal and particular that the particular is determined by the universal, this constitutes another, superior relationship to that which he studied in the critique of pure reason, where the concept or universal fell into contradiction if it were applied to things. In the beautiful, however, the universal is immanent in the particular, and the idea has been made manifest and realised. Thus

(77 [b]) in this part of his philosophy, Kant arrives at the knowledge of the idea. However, that knowledge is not united with the knowledge that the idea alone is the truth, and that truth exists only in the knowledge of it [the idea].[18] Kant therefore diminishes it, since he shows that it appears only in sensible things and in experience, and demotes the knowledge of it [the idea] to [the rank of] subjective sense. For we discover the knowledge of that relationship through the intuitive understanding. But Kant discovers this intuitive understanding in the harmony of sensible intuition or in the free play of representations and the law-imposing understanding.

(78 [a]) This sense of harmony excites in us a certain pleasure, and [Kant] calls taste this subjective faculty of judging of such a pleasure. Thus the general knowledge of that which manifests itself in the object is an indefinite sense only, which cannot claim for itself objective value and truth, because it is accidental with respect to its objects, just as the truth and being and nature of an object cannot be expressed by its concept. Therefore, when Kant erected, as it were, the critique of the faculty of judgement upon this sense of delight as its foundation, he remains in a mere subjectivity

(78 [b]) which lacks all objectivity. For this reason, if one considers the individual moments of the beautiful, one will be examining nothing other than that sense which is set in motion in the subject, and one will be able neither to penetrate to the true knowledge of the beautiful nor to discover its concept. For if we grant that there exists so much beauty in this [sense] that it causes pleasure, we understand what it causes in the subject, but not what its true concept is. For, to cite an example, surely we have not grasped the movement and concept of Greek art if we say only that the Greeks, contemplating works of art, were affected by the height of pleasure and that they reposed in this pleasure?

(79 [a]) The nature of art consists rather in this, that it is the dissolution of the highest contradiction between freedom and necessity, and the resolution of this contradiction is truth and idea. If this idea appears in objectivity or in external form, and if the idea itself is true, then the form

as well will be adequate to the idea and will be, as it were, entirely suffused with the idea. If, therefore, we say that a work of art is beautiful, we do not suppose that the concept alone is beautiful, nor that the form alone is beautiful, but we grasp both together, because the work of art joins both together harmoniously in itself. Indeed, it is true that the mind [*animum*],

(79 [b]) when contemplating the beautiful, is affected by peace, repose, and blessed tranquility and serenity, which Kant seems to understand as coming under [the power] of pleasure, but by means of the word pleasure we signify only a power which the beautiful compels in us, but not the being of the beautiful itself. And, because subjectivity alone is being considered, we shall always see this defect in the four moments of the beautiful which Kant judges according to the four categories. Now, following Kant, let us examine those four moments.

First moment, with respect to the category of *quality*.[19] That the beautiful is that which excites pleasure, which latter does not de-

(80 [a]) termine the will, i.e. it does not pertain to the faculty of desiring. If our will is determined by some thing, this occurs not on account of the thing itself, but because of its relationship with our experience [of it]. Kant, principally in order to explain this moment, distinguishes the beautiful from the agreeable and the good. For the pleasure derived from the good and the agreeable determines our will.[20] If I call some object agreeable, I am not free from desire [*concupiscentia*], for my desire [*cupiditas*] is moved by a sense of the pleasing, because the pleasure of the agreeable indicates the relationship of the existence of some thing to me. For in the sensible thing which exists, there inheres only that value

(80 [b]) which is related to our want and its satisfaction. Such, therefore, is the relation [*ratio*] here that there is on the one hand the object, and on the other hand the interest or end to which we refer the object, and from which the object is distinct.[21] For example, because I consume some object, the interest is mine alone, and does not exist in the thing.[22] But the good is such because through the reason it pleases by means of the concept alone. For since the concept of the end is present, the relation of reason to the will is present, i.e. the desire for the existence of an object or an action. Therefore the relation to the faculty of desiring is present in the good and the agreeable, and both excite pleasure, which [pleasure] is indicated not only by representation but

(81 [a]) by the conjunction and connection of the subject with the object. Hence it follows that the aesthetic judgement is contemplative only.[23] For this reason Kant says correctly that among these three kinds of pleasure, only the pleasure of the beautiful can be free. For in the beautiful,

the end [*destinatio*] is not distinct from the object. Hence we define the object as free, for it pleases us by itself alone, since it contains within its own self its purpose or its end.[24]

Second moment according to the category of Quantity.[25] Since the pleasure of the beautiful is linked with no desire [*concupiscentia*], it must be assumed that the beautiful is immediately pleasing to all. For that

(81 [b]) pleasure does not depend on any desire [*cupiditas*] of a judging subject; but rather [the] judging [subject] is himself free and bound by no affection [or affect, *affectione*]. Nor can he adduce any reasons, which might inhere in him as an individual subject, why the beautiful should be pleasing to himself [alone]; rather, he thinks that his own judgement is only confirmed and supported by what it is possible to posit also for other subjects, just as he believes that everyone will be affected by the same pleasure.[26] Thus, judgement of the beautiful may appear to be logical, i.e. determined by the concept of the object.[27] It is, however, aesthetic, and contains in itself the relation of the representation of the object to the subject. It is similar to the logical judgement only because it must be valid for everyone.

(82 [a]) However, this universality of the aesthetic judgement cannot arise from concepts, since there can be no passage from the concepts to the sense of pleasure, because in this judgement only subjective universality can subsist.[28] Hence in the aesthetic judgement nothing is required except the common sense without the mediation of concepts. If, therefore, the cause of the judgement is subjective only, without, indeed, the concept of the object, then the cause, or that which subsists in the judgement, is only that condition of the mind [*animi*] which is discovered in the relationship of the powers of representation among themselves. In such a way the powers of cognition exist in free play, because no distinct

(82 [b]) concept contains them in a single rule of knowing. In producing knowledge of some object, the power of imagination pertains to the representation of the object, and the understanding pertains to the unity of the concept. This free play of the faculties of knowing must be communicated in common, because knowledge is the only manner of representation which is valid for all.[29] Subjective judgement, therefore, is the cause of that pleasure which we experience from the harmonious play of the cognitive powers, and upon the universality of these reposes the common force of the pleasure by which we are affected in contemplating the beautiful. Therefore, since the aesthetic judgement depends on the subjective sense, we are conscious of neither the distinct concept

(83 [a]) nor the subsumption under the universal. Because [the aesthetic judgement] is nothing else than [this, that] in the pleasure of the beautiful the separation which occurs in the logical judgement does not occur, therefore the second moment of the beautiful is: that the beautiful is that which is pleasing to all immediately, i.e. without the mediation of a concept.[30]

Third moment according to the category of *relation*.[31] In this section Kant considers how the form of finality can be attributed to the beautiful. The end is the object of the concept, if the concept is taken as the cause of the object.[32] Therefore, when that which is being thought is not only the knowledge of an object, but the object itself as the effect of the concept of some thing, the end is necessarily being thought. The object,

(83 [b]) however, is congruent with the end, even if the representation of the end of some thing is not necessarily posited. Therefore, the form of finality can be without an end if we do not place the cause of this form in any will.[33] Hence we are able to contemplate the form of finality according to the form alone, even if we do not grant that a distinct end subsists in it. Thus, in the beautiful, [there is] nothing other than the subjective form of finality in the representation of some object without any [specific] end; therefore the form alone of the form of finality can determine the will. But the objective form of purposiveness is able to be known only by means of the relation of the manifold to a distinct end, therefore only by means of a concept. For this reason the beautiful, in the judgement of which only the formal form of purposiveness

(84 [a]) subsists, is entirely different from the representation of the good, in which the objective form of purposiveness subsists.[34] Rather, the formality of the representation of some thing, i.e. the reduction of the manifold to unity, produces no objective form of finality, because it is wholly abstracted from unity as from its end [or cause], and only the subjective form of purposiveness of the representations remains in the mind [*animo*] of the one who is contemplating. Therefore the judgement is named aesthetic, because its cause and principle is not a concept, but the sense of that agreement in the play of the powers of the mind [*ingenii*].[35] Thus Kant arrives at the following conclusion: that there is no objective rule of taste which by means of con-

(84 [b]) cepts indicates and determines what the beautiful is.[36] For every judgement about the beautiful is subjective, and no concept of the object subsists in it.[37] Therefore the attempt to seek the principle of taste is sterile, because it would give a common criterion of the beautiful by means of distinct concepts.[38]

But if we inquire, is there therefore absolutely no principle of the aesthetic judgement except the subjective sense? Kant answers that the normal image of taste is the mere idea.[39] Kant names idea the rational concept, and ideal the representation of some thing congruent with the idea.[40] For this reason the normal image of taste which, even though it depends on an indefinite idea of reason,

(85 [a]) nevertheless can be demonstrated not by concepts but by the single representation of the beautiful, is better named the ideal of the beautiful.[41] [There is] however, only one genus of the beautiful appropriate to the idea, namely that alone which contains in itself the end of its own existence, man.[42] Thus we come to the truth of this moment. An object is beautiful if we do not possess the concept of its end in such a way that the end differs from reality. In the finite form of finality, the end is distinct from its medium, since the end possesses an external relation with respect to the material. Here the representation of the end has been separated from existence itself. The beautiful, however, contains its own end in its

(85 [b]) very self. The end is life and life exists in all the members, and in life the end is not distinct from the entire matter, but both have been conjoined without mediation, for something is an existent if its own end is immanent in it. In the beautiful, therefore, this form of finality inheres, just as the end is the immanent nature of the thing itself.

Fourth moment, according to the category of *modality*[43]: the beautiful has a necessary relationship to pleasure. This necessity of pleasure, however, is not theoretical, objective, such that it could be known *a priori* that everyone would be moved by the same pleasure by an object which I might call beautiful; nor is it practical, as though this pleasure could be

(86 [a]) deduced as the necessary consequence of an objective law. Rather, this necessity of the agreement of all in the same judgement is seen as exemplary of some rule which cannot be demonstrated. Hence it follows that this necessity cannot be derived from a distinct concept. It is the aesthetic judgement, from which one expects that the thing which is called beautiful ought indeed to be designated beautiful. But this "ought," however, is not pronounced absolutely in the aesthetic judgement. Since aesthetic judgements do not possess a distinct objective principle, while yet necessity is attributed to them,

(86 [b]) they may not be destitute of every principle. It is necessary that they have a subjective principle which determines generally what is beautiful, not by means of concepts, but by the subjective sense. However, such a principle can only be contemplated as a common sense, under

which common sense is understood the effect of the free play of the faculties of knowing. This common sense leads us to judgements in which the "ought" inheres; it does not say, however, that everyone will share in our feeling, but that they ought to. Thus we come to the subjective principle of the necessity of aesthetic judgements. For this reason we call the beautiful that which,

(87 [a]) without a concept, is the object of necessary pleasure.[44] _____ Since now we are about to pass over to our criticism of these moments of the beautiful, first of all it must be asked why Kant enumerates only four moments. It is clear that he affirms four moments of the beautiful because in the transcendental logic he exposed four categories as determinations of thought. Through these as the basis of all concepts, he posited the transcendental unity of self-consciousness. In the transcendental aesthetic, he recognised that representations which are given by sense are combined from the manifold, as much in their internal plenitude [*copia*] as in their form. When the subject

(87 [b]) refers this manifold to himself and unites it in self-consciousness, this manifold is reduced to unity. Now the categories are the distinct principles [*rationes*] of that referring of the manifold to the subject. Kant posited twelve basic concepts of the human mind, which he divided into four categories. It was Aristotle who first studied and listed those concepts, but by no means did he explain them as well as Kant. These, as a bad totality, Kant took over from Aristotle and ordinary logic, and he did not, in fact, show why of their own nature they exist nor by what necessary manner one comes into being out of the other. Although he had derived them empirically from contemporary logic and had not

(88 [a]) grasped them philosophically, he nevertheless maintained that they are the determinations of thought and the foundation of all knowledge. But these categories, which are the unity of the subjective consciousness only, are empty in themselves; they find their employment and internal richness and truth in experience. Thus, in this part of his philosophy which we are considering, Kant refers them to the beautiful and to the judgement of the beautiful. But since we must doubt the truth and totality of these categories, in that they have not been demonstrated according to their own necessity but only accepted empirically, no necessity can exist in those

(88 [b]) four moments of the beautiful, either. Here Kant wished to escape the longing of discerning and the fortuitousness of thinking, but it is not better if the idea of the beautiful be ascribed to the inertia of thought and judged according to four bare formulas. Logic has no

slight [*haud parvam*] force and weight in philosophical thought; [but] if the logical determinations of thought are accepted empirically from experience and are not deduced from thought itself, its determinations are empty and futile shadows.

Now then, logic can be active and a true moment of philosophy, if in the logic the concept

(89 [a]) itself can demonstrate, in the process of its own unfolding [*excultionis*] and determination, those forms and determinations of knowing together with its coherence [or proof: *argumento*] and internal plenitude. In the critique of the faculty of judgement, these categories, therefore, discover in the beautiful their concrete richness as the unity of the subjective consciousness, just as we see this in experience. Since a part of its sense and representation are determinations as something only subjective, we remain in abstract subjectivity, and do not advance to true objectivity.

(89 [b]) Now Kant gives the following definition of the first moment of the beautiful, that in the judgement of the beautiful we leave it [the object] free for itself, for this [object] is immediately pleasing, and divorced from all desire. For in the judgement of the beautiful we cannot know the beautiful, but by the power of the imagination we only refer the representation to the subject alone, and to the subject's sensual pleasures. For this reason, since the aesthetic judgement determines only the subjective, it cannot produce knowledge, and the object is not perceived by the subject.

Thus, on the one hand we see that the object

(90 [a]) stands free for itself, and on the other hand [we see] the aesthetic judgement, the determining cause of which can only be subjective, since it depends upon the sense of pleasure. Thus the aesthetic judgement, too, is free, and is not determined by the object itself. But is it thus that we discover what the beautiful itself is? We hear only of some sense which remains [enclosed] in its own self and does not refer itself to its object, nor does it penetrate this [object] by thinking. Since it leaves the object indifferent, it maintains itself in its own abstract subjectivity. The aesthetic judgement is nothing other than this abstract sense, which can be understood not from the object

(90 [b]) itself, but from the pleasure which the contemplation of the object excites. But if Kant posits the aesthetic judgement, he must also suppose the object which is judged, and the thinking intellect, which judges. This thinking intellect must not remain outside the object, but [must] escape from the sense which the object excited; and it [must]

penetrate the object by thinking. If, therefore, that internal subjective sense turns toward the object and refers itself to it, feeling [*affectio*] is excited. In feeling, therefore, we have not only that internal sense but also the external object; not only subjective knowledge,

(91 [a]) but also the objective thing. This is necessary to excite feeling, because feeling depends on the object. But because it depends on the object, which is beyond feeling, and [because] that object is finite, so feeling itself is finite, and as finite may not remain it itself.[45] For since, in judging, the judgement must be made about the object, and [since] judgement essentially pertains to the power of thinking, then thought must underlie the aesthetic judgement. In thinking, neither does the object stand free for itself, nor indeed do we abstract ourselves from it, but we perceive the object by thinking, and we draw it up out of itself to thought as to its truth. Thought

(91 [b]) conscious of itself is no longer [*non amplius*] that internal sense which limits itself to its own subjectivity, nor is it only affected by that [sense], but is both in itself and in the other, and finds itself in the other; and we may even say that we find the object in ourselves.[46] Thus thinking cognition is truly infinite. Hence it follows that feeling and thought must necessarily be ascribed to the aesthetic sense, for it consists of both and is composed of both, and this identity of feeling and thought we discover in the representation. In this unity of representation, feeling passes over into thought and thought into feeling; finite and infinite have been united in one and the same thing,

(92 [a]) the infinite passes under the form of the finite, and the finite receives the infinite into itself and unites itself with it transcendingly [*auctissime*]. This transcending [*aucta*] connection and composition produces at length the aesthetic sense, in which every opposition has been removed, and in which peace, happiness and the highest serenity inhere.

From this union of feeling and thought which we have discovered in the judgement of the beautiful, it follows that neither of these moments of the contemplation of the beautiful must be posited without the other, that neither must be separated from the other, and that neither must the one be denied and only the other accepted. Therefore, when

(92 [b]) Kant posited the determining cause of the aesthetic judgement as being subjective only, he limits himself solely to the sense of feeling and pleasure, and utterly denies the moment of thought. In the successive moments of the beautiful we shall see this error further unfolding.

Thus the second moment of the beautiful is exposed, that the beautiful is represented without concepts. Yet, to be sure, in the introduction to the critique of the faculty of judgement, Kant admitted [that there was] a territory between the concept of nature and reason, where by that reason the sensible is determined by the supersensible, matter by the idea, and both are drawn together in a concrete identity.

(93 [a]) But since Kant calls reason merely an indefinite idea [existing] in us which cannot be known, from Kant's doctrine the aesthetic idea can never be known either. Since in the beautiful the opposition of feeling and thought has been transcended, Kant understands this transcendence as negation, as though the intelligible indeed were not positively present in the beautiful. For this reason Kant always arrives at the same result, that the beautiful cannot be known, that we are able to posit no concept of it, and that it pleases without any concept. And thus, since the beautiful depends on the sole

(93 [b]) desire of sense and on the sense of delight, and on the harmonious play of the imaginative powers, it is necessary that the beautiful itself be subjective and finite, and that there exist in it no objective truth. Thus, when Kant says that the beautiful is universally pleasing, this universality can be nothing other than subjective, i.e. it does not have its foundation in the object itself, and it is not from the concept of the object itself that it exists. The error and emptiness of this subjective universality is evident too from the fact that the aesthetic judgement is unable to commend the assent of everyone, for this would only occur if that judgement arose not from subjective pleasure alone, but

(94 [a]) from the object itself and from its concept.

Thus, while we are held fast in subjective feeling, and [while] universality is ascribed to this subjectivity, we have not yet discovered how this empty subjectivity has been filled, and we seek its concrete internal plenitude. The answer to this is given to us in the third moment of the beautiful. Here Kant arrives at the notion of the idea. Before Kant this term was very often grotesquely and incorrectly presented both in ordinary life and in philosophy, and was all the more degraded in that nothing was understood by it other than a subjective, indefinite representation.

(94 [b]) Kant defended this notion again as the notion of reason, and tried to restore it to its rightful place.[47] But the idea is truly a universal, and at the same time the totality of all particulars. The idea is essentially action, and that which is particular to it, and exists at first only implicitly [per se] in it, must be posited. Thus the idea which contains the particular

implicitly [*per se*] in itself alone is the concept.[48] But this concept is not something merely subjective in us which is distinct from the thing itself, but is the very soul, truth, and essence of the thing. In the prior form [as implicitude], the idea is the concept. But the concept must unfold itself and emit itself into objectivity. Indeed, the concept and objectivity

(95 [a]) are not two distinct things which exist without any mutual relationship, but essentially a single totality, the idea itself. For this reason, the idea is the objective truth, that which truly is, and that in which external responds to internal, and concept responds to objectivity. The idea as existent is life entirely, for the idea is truth, and truth inasmuch as it exists is life. Now the truth, inasmuch as it is life, is the beautiful, whence beauty and life are one. The beautiful is the concept which inheres in objectivity, just as objectivity appears only in the concept, and the entire concept is

(95 [b]) contained in objectivity. Thus the idea is, in itself, life; or life in its truth, in its substance, is precisely the beautiful. For that reason, the beautiful and life are identical to idea and truth. For the truth is the idea as it is thought and known, the beautiful is the idea as it exists in representation. It is necessary, however, that life become essentially something living and subjective, for it must not remain the substance of Spinoza, in which all subjectivity is lacking. In this subjectivity, all distinctions have been joined together, and this unity effects the determination of negation and infinity.

(96 [a]) This subjective unity is an infinite self-relation, or true freedom. By this unity alone is life an actually living thing. Now this unity unfolds itself into an organism, and in the beautiful we seek that [unity] before all else. Thus, when it passes over into external existence, the idea becomes a real idea, and in this subjective unity it becomes an ideal. Now in this ideal as concrete idea we see concrete freedom, blessedness, and peace.

We said above that Kant again reconciled the idea to the notion of reason. One asks therefore, what Kant

(96 [b]) understood by rational notion? The notion of reason, he says, is the notion of the absolute, but it is transcendent with respect to appearances. Reason, as empty action, as the bare notion of the infinite, is retained in opposition to the finite. Since, according to Kant himself, that infinity must be absolutely free, a most serious contradiction arises, because [for him] the absolute does not exist without abstraction from something opposed to it; indeed, it is nothing at all without that opposition.[49] Thus the infinite or the absolute itself becomes relative,

since it does not refer to an objectivity which has been posited through its own self.[50] Instead,

(97 [a]) [objectivity] remains outside it, and stands over against it indifferently. The idea, however, as we have just explained, is [genuinely] absolute because it does not refer to something which, as alien to it, stands over against it; but from its very self it emits objectivity and bears itself along in this [element]. As this totality of objectivity and concept, it is truly rational.[51] And thus both concept and objectivity must be contained in the idea as in their unity, and must not be separated; and the idea must not be held to be solely the subjective concept. For if this occurs, the idea itself is reduced to something

(97 [b]) fortuitous.

Nor is it less perverse if, as Kant does, the objective truth of the idea is denied, [on the grounds] that it is transcendent with respect to appearance, and that no object can be discovered in the sensible world which would be congruent with it. But surely, I ask, it is not those appearances which are vain, weak, fleeting, perishable, and false that constitute the true objectivity of the idea?[52] Surely it is not in them that the true idea is to be sought? But if the idea is true, it will also have a worthy, real, and rational objectivity; and if objectivity is real, the idea is also immanent in it. Kant, moreover, holds the idea to be the limit or, as it were,

(98 [a]) the boundary according to which, as its normative image, reality is to be contemplated. This doctrine arises from the Kantian determination of the idea, that the idea is transcendent with respect to things, just as that idea is transmundane which nothing at all can approach, and to which absolutely nothing is adequate. This opinion, however, clearly must be rejected, since the idea itself is already the whole of the concept and objectivity. Since the identity of both is already present in it, it is not in fact necessary to postulate whether they may be congruent with each other. For something is beautiful only if the idea is truly immanent in it.

(98 [b]) If, therefore, Kant says that the normative image of taste is an idea according to which objects are judged, and that an object cannot be found which is truly congruent with this idea, the idea becomes a merely subjective rule, a canon by which we measure objectivity, and examine whether an object approaches the idea or not. But since the idea is found in the subject alone and the beautiful stands over against it, what, I ask, is the beautiful, or what can it be, in which the idea itself is not immanent, and which does not contain in its very self the idea as witness to its own truth? It is absolutely nothing. But the work of art in itself is a totality. Since [for Kant] the concept is only cast back

(99 [a]) upon the subject, the art-object therefore falls back into itself, and the formless matter remains, as it were, like a death's-head. Indeed, Kant so advances in this opposition that he says that everyone must fashion this idea in himself.[53] But this follows necessarily from Kant's opinion, merely stating differently what was already contained in the foregoing. But thus the idea of the beautiful clearly becomes subjective. It opposes objectivity as being foreign to it, and to it this [objectivity] does not respond. For this reason, the idea of the beautiful is nothing other than an indefinite transcendental idea

(99 [b]) in us which, however, cannot be known. However, Kant himself provided its concept when he said that the idea of the beautiful is nothing other than the identity of the concept of nature and reason. Thus, because he considers abstract subjectivity alone, Kant arrives at the opinion that an idea of reason can never become knowledge, since the supersensible contains in itself the concept, with which no reality or representation could ever be found congruent. Nevertheless, an idea of reason is demonstrated in the beautiful, and the concept is shown forth in the representation. For the idea of reason is seen and represented as identity of the sensible and the supersensible,

(100 [a]) but under the idea is not to be understood the supersensible, which the sensible as foreign opposes, just as the supersensible transcends knowledge. If, however, Kant says that the idea of the beautiful or the aesthetic idea cannot be known because no concept is congruent with the representation, he did not consider that the aesthetic idea is revealed in the idea of reason. For the beautiful is the concrete composition and mutual penetration of the real and the ideal, the annulling of the highest opposition, and the identity of the finite and infinite in representation. But in philosophy that opposition

(100 [b]) sublates itself in pure identity. Thus both art and philosophy converge at the highest point of knowledge. So it happens that nothing penetrates further into the true nature of art than philosophy, and that in philosophy, art necessarily becomes the object of knowledge, especially as nothing can be known absolutely about art except through philosophy. Only intellectual laziness claims that the beautiful cannot be known, that it can be grasped by feeling alone, and that no concept is adequate to it. Only the barren reflection of subjectivity separates finite and infinite[54] and casts the infinite or the absolute, [as something] above all human

(101 [a]) ... knowledge, back into that empty and vast infinity which in reality cannot be demonstrated. So the idea, the absolutely true and real

is reduced to subjective judgement [*arbitrium*], by which the subject contemplates things in his own reflection.

Let us now advance to the fourth moment. Kant says here that the beautiful is the object of necessary pleasure without a concept. Necessity is an abstract category. Necessity is truth, in which possibility and reality are one. The necessary is immediate, pure Being, and at the same time reflection into itself, because both have been joined

(101 [b]) together.[55] Insofar as the necessary is reflection, it has a foundation and condition, but it owes its foundation and condition to itself alone. For the necessary rests upon its own self. Thus the necessary in itself is internal organisation, so that when we attribute necessity to the beautiful, nothing other must be understood by that than the organism[56]: that necessity by which the beautiful rests on itself, and manifests itself, and that necessity by which, in the beautiful, concept and objectivity become only one. So, too, the concept manifests itself through objectivity, and objectivity at the same time receives into itself the entire notion and is its witness. But this internal harmony, this peace with itself,

(102 [a]) is at the same time absolute negativity and the freedom of its own being. Thus necessity is that freedom and free love with which the idea manifests itself in the beautiful, emitting itself forth into the concept and objectivity. Joining both with the bond of its love, it reconciles them in concrete unity.

But Kant posited this necessity of the beautiful as subjective. For he assumes a "common sense" by which all men are affected by the beautiful in the same way, so that it necessarily happens that everyone might concur in the judgement of the other. But clearly perceiving the weakness of this subjective necessity,

(102 [b]) he was compelled to posit this necessity as relative, and to maintain that whenever one makes a claim in the discernment of the beautiful, others ought to concur with his judgement. On account of his subjective principle, Kant does not advance beyond this "ought," indeed the incapacity of thought abides and acquiesces in this abiding. This determination of the beautiful is very like that which we explained above, that the idea only *ought* to manifest itself in reality, since Kant most stubbornly retained the separation of concept and objectivity, and believed that he had thereby already accomplished enough.

But now let us attain the pinnacle of our

(103 [a]) critique. In the reflective faculty of judgement, Kant discovered the intermediary between the concept of nature and reason;

between objective or empirical multiplicity, and the abstraction of the understanding.[57] But this identity is essentially reason, about which idea Kant speaks more or less formally in this part of his philosophy. Although Kant had given the notion of reason together with that identity of the concept of nature and freedom, nevertheless it is nothing other than the supersensible idea in us which is not accessible in any case to knowledge.[58] Just as the idea of reason cannot be known because it contains in itself the notion of the infinite, so the aesthetic idea, too, cannot become

(103 [b]) knowledge, because the power of imagination underlies it, and to this no concept can be adequate. Thus Kant divides the idea into the sensible and finite, and into the supersensible, because it transcends every experience and cognition, although the idea is truly able to be known in the absolute identity of objectivity and concept. Therefore, when the beautiful was explained as the identity of the concept of nature and freedom, but [at the same time] the supersensible can neither be known nor represented, aesthetic judgement is referred to abstract subjectivity, and becomes the supersensible principle of the judgement of the beautiful. But if it becomes the supersensible principle of the beautiful, nothing

(104 [a]) about it is known, since neither is its representation explained by a concept, nor is its concept demonstrated by a representation. Thus the beautiful is referred to subjective feeling and to the pleasure of the subject alone, which pleasure is born out of the relation of the beautiful to reflection; and thus the beautiful has clearly become subjective and fortuitous. Although Kant has posited an intelligible moment in the beautiful, nevertheless he has remained in this subjective and finite cognition, and he holds it to be absolute. Kant advanced to the notion of the idea, but its true notion was not to be accommodated in his system: if he had shown the idea

(104 [b]) as true principle and end of his philosophy, he would have violated his own doctrine. It is [therefore] necessary that the idea be disparaged, diminished, and corrupted, and that subjective reflection and finite cognition be held to be true. Thus the Kantian philosophy remains formal knowledge, for absolute multiplicity together with opposition opposes the formal identity of the subject. Therefore if, in this opposition, that abstract identity passes over into multiplicity and determines it, it nevertheless remains alien to it. It is no less alien if multiplicity passes over into that identity and fills it, because the synthesis of both is only formal.[59] The mediation of this opposition, by which it is absolutely removed, in fact remains transcendental

(105 [a]) . . . reason, [and] it can only be believed and not truly known, just as the infinite desire for it is born. Therefore, when Kant discovered in the beautiful the mediation of this absolutely finite and absolute infinity, in which it is necessary that both be joined, he does not transgress that "ought." We are, on the contrary, unable to attain true identity, and the true idea becomes the subjective principle. _____

Let us now proceed to the second part of the critique of the faculty of judgement, namely to its dialectic.[60] Kant defines understanding as the synthesis of the manifold through the unity of self-consciousness. This synthetic

(105 [b]) action rests essentially on the categories. But reason, when compared with this understanding and with that by which this [understanding] has been filled and with the particularities which inhere in these categories, is abstract unity. Since this abstract unity is retained as the concept of the infinite in opposition to the finite, the Kantian philosophy falls into the contradictions which are demonstrated in the antinomies. But that opposition by which, as Kant says, the absolute or the infinite opposes the finite necessarily becomes determination and therefore negation. That Kant remains in this negation is the greatest defect which dominates in his system. It is indeed the new philosophy, which, having advanced beyond this negation, arrived at the positive end, eliminating the oppositions and discovering the truth in their unity.

(106 [a]) For opposition and contradiction and the dialectical movement of the notion constitute the essential path to truth. But the separated oppositions must not oppose each other, as though each one had some value in itself, but they are only able to be truly eliminated [inasmuch] as they discover their truth only in their resolution [*sublatione*]. Their true dialectical contemplation consists in this, that each part of the contradiction be shown to contain the other in its very self, that neither is possible without the other, and that only as sublated do they truly exist. We have just said that this absolute opposition necessarily leads to the determination and negation of the infinite, to the negation of the true idea. We see this in those three types of antinomies which Kant

(106 [b]) posited. He adopted three types of antinomies because he posited three faculties of knowing: understanding, the faculty of judging, and [that] of desiring; and each of these possesses its own *a priori* principle.[61] Kant says that when reason judges about those principles and their use, it necessarily seeks an absolute for everything relative and finite[62]; this, however, as absolute or the idea, he says cannot be known. This Kant expounded as the result of his entire philosophy. Thus, by this absolute opposition, the idea and reason have been destroyed. Subjective

reflection triumphs, having been made into an absolute which determines all things. In the dialectic of the faculty of judgement Kant therefore propounded a dialectic of the aesthetic judgement as to

(107 [a]) its principles. Kant says that this dialectic is possible if the antinomy of the principles of this faculty can be discovered which would make doubtful their legitimacy and authority. But Kant acts rather casually in exposing this antinomy, since it does not follow from the motion and rhythm of the concept itself, which he was concerned to demonstrate in the analytic.[63] Kant considers [instead] two commonplaces, and the dialectic of the faculty of judgement follows from their contradiction. The first commonplace is contained in the dictum that everyone has his own taste, i.e. that the determining cause of the aesthetic judgement is only subjective, and that it is not necessary to postulate objective necessity.[64]

(107 [b]) The second commonplace is this: there is no disputing [*disputari*] about taste,[65] i.e. the determining cause of the aesthetic judgement can indeed be objective, but it cannot be reduced to a distinct concept, whence it follows that judgement cannot be discerned by any demonstration, although it is possible to argue [*certari*] about it.[66] But this opinion, that it is possible to argue about aesthetic judgements, is clearly opposed to the previous commonplace. The antinomy involved in the principle of aesthetic judgements is posited thus:
Thesis: the aesthetic judgement is not based upon concepts.
Antithesis: the aesthetic judgement is based upon concepts.[67]
    Kant correctly understands that this contradiction can only be eliminated by showing that the concept to which the object is referred in the aesthetic judgement is used in a double sense or, rather, in both cases is derived from only one part, and that the truth consists only in the unity

(108 [a]) of the opposition. Kant discovered this solution of the contradiction in reason. Thus, indeed, reason alone removes all the contradictions which abstract understanding sets forth and opposes to each other. But what does Kant understand here by reason? Nothing other, as we heard above, than the indefinite idea of the supersensible which underlies objects as appearances. But this notion is such that it can neither be demonstrated by representation, nor can anything be known through it. By this notion of the supersensible, by this idea of reason, which cannot be known, the entire antinomy is eliminated. Indeed, judgement reposes on the concept, by which, however, nothing

(108 [b]) in respect to the object can be known. In this way or, rather, by this sophism, the contradiction has been removed. For when Kant says in the thesis that the aesthetic judgement does not depend upon

concepts, this indeed is true according to its opposition, since it reposes on the infinite concept only, by which nothing can be known; nor does what is said in the antithesis, that the aesthetic judgement depends upon concepts, contradict the thesis, since this notion is indefinite and not distinct. Thus the entire solution of the antinomy consists in this, that these two opinions stand together, and both can be true, although, as Kant says, the definition or the declaration of the possibility of their concept exceeds our power of knowing. Thus, when he ought to have eliminated those oppositions in the true idea, Kant returned once more to that subjective principle,

(109 [a]) that is, to the indeterminate, supersensible idea in us which can neither be understood nor grasped. Thus, at the end of the critique of the aesthetic faculty of judgement, where it was to be expected that all oppositions would be truly sublated, and that the true idea of the beautiful would be advanced, the contradiction which had been born from subjective reflection is retained. For at the end we hear again that the idea of the beautiful cannot be known, although Kant himself had provided the definition of it, namely that it is the identification of the concept of nature and freedom.[68] Nothing less than this is the culmination of the Kantian philosophy, that neither can the rational notion be known, since the supersensible in itself contains the notion

(109 [b]) and exceeds all cognition; nor can the representation be congruent with it, as if the rational idea were not demonstrated in the beautiful, [nor] the concept in the representation. But this entire defect has arisen out of a false understanding [*cognitione*] of the idea, which we have explained above. For Kant did not recognise in the idea the unity of concept and objectivity, but rather he divides them both. He sets the sensible and the supersensible, as he says, against each other as direct opposites, just as the supersensible stands outside all knowledge and transcends it. Because, therefore, in the beautiful as in the represented idea the opposition of concept and objectivity has been negated, Kant thinks that so indeed the concept itself has been negated and, as it were, absorbed. For this reason

(110 [a]) Kant always returns to that sad transcendental result, when he says that the idea can neither be known nor represented. But since the idea cannot be known, we are not even able to grasp the beautiful by cognition, nor is there an objective principle of taste and beauty, i.e. there cannot be a philosophy of art. But art itself is the highest thing for the philosopher, because art leads him into that sanctuary where the bond of the idea harmoniously unites that which in nature and in thought [*ingenio*] have been separated, objectivity and concept, which

always seem to be fleeing from each other. Just as in philosophy the opposition of knowledge is raised to concrete identity, so in art the opposition of concept

(110 [b]) and objectivity has been transcended immediately. Art is thus a kind of symbol of philosophy, and no-one, including the artist himself who remains in immediacy, can study art more profoundly than the philosopher. Nothing can be known absolutely about art except by philosophy; from this it follows that the philosophy of art indeed exists. For, I ask, why should philosophy, which discovers in the concrete idea the resolution of every opposition, not be able to recognise the idea as it emits itself into objectivity. Yet a philosophy which claims that the idea is transmundane and transcends all knowledge, is equally unable to recognise the idea as it immediately offers itself to representation. When it ought to have recognised the idea

(111 [a]) as the soul of the beautiful, it elevated instead that abstract subjectivity to [the rank of] sole principle of the beautiful, and renders beauty itself finite, fortuitous, and vain. Indeed, we see in history from the artistic achievement of individual peoples that the idea alone is truth and is, in the beautiful, both animating and active. For where the idea has not yet been recognised in its truth, the desire nevertheless has been born to demonstrate this idea by representation, just as the idea itself lacks taste and genius [*ingenio*]. But where the idea has arisen in its true genius [*ingenuitate*] and truth, there indeed arises the beautiful, there [arises] the external or objectivity coloured by the idea, and it is nothing other than the expression of the idea.[69] But this in-

(111 [b]) sight Kant indeed was unable to surmise, since he made subjectivity the sole principle of the beautiful.

Just as the result on the one hand was that the idea cannot be known, so Kant on the other hand says that the idea is not representable. But what is art other than the demonstrated and represented idea?[70] If therefore the idea cannot be represented, art is not possible, or it becomes something fortuitous, i.e. the sort of thing which refers itself only to the feeling of pleasure, therefore to that sorry subjectivity.[71] Kant understood in the concept of the beautiful the identity of the concept of nature and freedom;[72] he accepted the intelligible as substrate and foundation of the beautiful, and even recognised this as rational. He saw

(112 [a]) that cognition of the beautiful does not abide in sensory appearance, but must essentially depend on that rational substrate. Nevertheless this intelligible, this rational, even reason itself is denied, and finite cognition is held to be absolute.[73] Although Kant was led to the

notion of the intuitive understanding as the medium of his philosophy, in which concept and representation are joined, nevertheless, in the course of this part of his philosophy, this notion did not win through to its truth. Although finally the notion of the idea has been more or less distinctly enunciated in this part of the Kantian philosophy,

(112 [b]) and the idea has been recognised as foundation and substrate of the beautiful, nevertheless it is cast down by subjective reflection into an unknowable, empty, vast, transmundane region. The beautiful, bereft of its soul, becomes wholly finite. In place of absolute knowledge, finite subjective reflection rises up, and triumphs on the grave of the idea and of reason.

– *translated from the Latin by Douglas Moggach, with Peter Foley*

NOTES

Introduction: "The Friend of Freedom"

1. Edgar Bauer, *Bruno Bauer und seine Gegner* (Berlin: Jonasverlagsbuchhandlung, 1842), 4–5. [Unless otherwise indicated, all translations of passages cited are my own. DM.]
2. Bruno Bauer was born on September 6, 1809, in Eisenberg in Thuringia, and died on April 13, 1882, in Berlin-Rixdorf. His father was a porcelain painter, who moved with his family to Berlin in 1815, as director of a factory. Of his three brothers, Edgar and Egbert were close collaborators with him in the *Vormärz*, the former as a writer, the latter as the publisher of a number of his texts, most importantly on the French Revolution and the social question. One reference describes his third brother, Egino, as an apprentice carpenter, but nothing further could be discovered about him. Bauer's family and early education are described in Ernst Barnikol, *Bruno Bauer, Studien und Materialien*, ed. P. Reimer and H.-M. Sass (Assen: van Gorcum, 1972), 6–20.
3. Karl Marx, Frederick Engels, "The Holy Family, or Critique of Critical Criticism. Against Bruno Bauer and Company," *Collected Works*, vol. 4 (New York: International Publishers, 1975), 5–211; "The German Ideology," *Collected Works*, vol. 5 (1976), 19–539.
4. Albert Schweitzer, *The Quest of the Historical Jesus. A Critical Study of Its Progress from Reimarus to Wrede* (Baltimore: Johns Hopkins University Press, 1998), 137–60.
5. Expressing the disappointments of liberalism after the failures of 1848, Rudolf Haym, *Hegel und seine Zeit* (Berlin: Gaertner, 1857), sees Hegel as an apologist of the old order, but also contends that his philosophy gave rise to the utopian abstractions of the Hegelian Left, which allegedly brought moderate liberalism into disrepute and led to its collapse before the Prussian reaction. Hans Rosenberg, *Politische Denkströmungen im deutschen Vormärz* (Gottingen: Vandenhoeck und Ruprecht, 1972), 86–96, cites this interpretation approvingly.
6. Robert Tucker, *Philosophy and Myth in Karl Marx* (Cambridge: Cambridge University Press, 1961), 73–77. The premise of self-deification, upon which Tucker's account is based, was already advanced against Hegelians by orthodox and pietist opponents as early as 1834. Ernst Barnikol, *Bruno Bauer*,

Darstellung und Quellen, ca. 1965, unpublished ms. (International Institute for Social History, Amsterdam), Bd. III, No. 25, p. 1, records a letter from the conservative bishop Neander to Baron von Kottwitz in 1834 regarding the Hegelian presence in Prussian universities: "Shall this illusion of self-deification be ever more promoted?" This accusation must have been current. Bruno Bauer responds to it directly in *Das entdeckte Christenthum* (Zürich und Winterthur: Verlag des literarischen Comptoirs, 1843), 105–06:

> Modern criticism has finally brought man to himself, it has taught him to know himself, has freed him from his illusions, and has taught him to know self-consciousness as the single creative power in the universe – as the universe itself.
>
> And could it now think of deifying man, that is, of losing itself and leading man to adore his chimerical, denuded, distorted image? It has rather proven that it is precisely in religion that man deifies himself, that is, has lost himself and worships his own loss.

7. One influential version of this thesis is Karl Löwith, *From Hegel to Nietzsche* (Garden City: Doubleday, 1967). Löwith depicts Bauer's position in the *Vormärz* as a thoroughgoing nihilism, incongruously combined with faith in the historical process. He fails to recognise that Bauer's optimism is founded on the view that human beings can make their own history, liberating themselves from the weight of historical traditions that are the objects of critique. This is the sense of Bauer's concept of infinite self-consciousness. A different approach to the cultural crisis, stressing the philosophical independence of the Young Hegelian movement, and resisting the view of an unbroken line of descent from Hegel to Marx, is that of Horst Stuke, *Philosophie der Tat. Studien zur 'Verwirklichung der Philosophie' bei den Junghegelianern und den Wahren Sozialisten* (Stuttgart: Klett, 1963), 38–39.

8. Heinz und Ingrid Pepperle, *Die Hegelsche Linke. Dokumente zu Philosophie und Politik im deutschen Vormärz* (Frankfurt a. M.: Röderberg, 1986), 5–44.

9. M. C. Massey, *Christ Unmasked: The Meaning of the Life of Jesus in German Politics* (Chapel Hill: University of North Carolina Press, 1983).

10. Charles Rihs, *L'école des jeunes-Hégéliens et les penseurs socialistes français* (Paris: Anthropos, 1978).

11. E. Lange et al., *Die Promotion von Karl Marx. Jena 1841. Eine Quellenedition* (Berlin: Dietz, 1983).

12. See Quentin Skinner, *Liberty Before Liberalism* (Cambridge: Cambridge University Press, 1998); and "Two Concepts of Citizenship," *Tijdschrift voor Filosofie* 55/3 (1993), 403–19. While Bauer defends a positive conception of freedom as the acquisition of a universal perspective, undistorted by private interest, Skinner links republicanism to negative liberty, understood as freedom from domination.

13. Bauer himself employs the military metaphor for his work, in the second edition of his *Norddeutsche Blätter*, published under the title *Beiträge zum Feldzuge der Kritik. Norddeutsche Blätter für 1844 und 1845. Mit Beiträgen von Bruno und Edgar Bauer, A. Fränkel, L. Köppen, Szeliga u.s.* (Berlin, 1846).

14. W. Bolin and F. Jodl (eds.), *Feuerbachs Sämmtliche Werke* (Stuttgart: Fromann, 1904); Werner Schuffenhauer, ed., *Feuerbachs Kleinere Schriften* (Berlin: Akademie Verlag, 1970).

15. Bruno Bauer (anon.), *Die Posaune des jüngsten Gerichts über Hegel den Atheisten und Antichristen. Ein Ultimatum* (Leipzig: Otto Wigand,1841), 163.

16. E. Barnikol, *Bruno Bauer. Studien und Materialien*, 1–5.

17. Copies of these letters are contained in E. Barnikol, *Bruno Bauer, Darstellung und Quellen*, unpublished manuscript, *Quellenteil.*

18. E. Barnikol, ibid., #95, pp. 19, 26, suggests that Bauer assumes the mask of anonymity to conceal the narrowness of the circle of contributors to the *Norddeutsche Blätter*, but also to avoid the overzealous attention the censors would surely devote to any article signed by Bauer himself.

19. See, for example, the discussion of Marx's possible collaboration on *Hegels Lehre* in Chapter 1. We owe the most extensive catalogues of Bauer's works in the 1830s and 1840s to Aldo Zanardo, "Bruno Bauer hegeliano e giovane hegeliano," *Rivista Critica di Storia della Filosofia*, 1965, 1–57.

20. See Chapter 8.

21. The exception is E. Barnikol, *Bruno Bauer. Studien und Materialien*, 249–73, who offers an overview of this material but does not directly address the social question.

22. David Koigen, *Zur Vorgeschichte des modernen philosophischen Sozialismus in Deutschland* (Bern: Stürzenegger, 1901); Wolfgang Eßbach, *Die Junghegelianer. Soziologie einer Intellektuellengruppe* (München: Wilhelm Fink Verlag, 1988).

23. G. A. van den Bergh van Eysinga (1874–1957), *Bruno Bauer*, unpublished manuscript, International Institute for Social History, Amsterdam, 210.

24. Ibid., 212.

25. Sass, H.-M. "Bruno Bauer's Critical Theory," *Philosophical Forum* 8 (1978) 93–103.

26. Daniel Brudney, *Marx's Attempt to Leave Philosophy* (Cambridge: Harvard University Press, 1998), 129–30.

27. Max Stirner (anon.), "Bruno Bauer," in *Wigands Conversations-Lexikon*, Bd. II (Leipzig: Otto Wigand, 1846), 78. Stirner misses here the connection of the two phases, and the political and social character of Bauer's earlier religious critique. He had recognised the latter explicitly in his articles of 1842, especially "Königsberger Skizzen," *Leipziger Allgemeine Zeitung*, July 9 and 20, 1842.

28. Ingrid Pepperle, *Junghegelianische Geschichtsphilosophie und Kunsttheorie* (Berlin: Akademie Verlag, 1978), 68–70; Hans und Ingrid Pepperle, *Die Hegelsche Linke*, 11–12, 19, 35–36.

29. Mario Rossi, *Da Hegel a Marx III: La Scuola hegeliana. Il giovane Marx*, 2nd edition (Milan: Feltrinelli, 1974), 71–97, 115–16, 120.

30. G.W.F. Hegel, *Lectures on the History of Philosophy*, volume II, trans. E. S. Haldane (London: Kegan Paul, 1892), 1. Chapter 1 analyses Bauer's 1829 manuscript.

31. G.W.F. Hegel, *Logic, Encyclopedia of the Philosophical Sciences*, Part I, trans. William Wallace (Oxford: Clarendon Press, 1975), §142, pp. 200–02.

32. The Greek and German terms are etymologically related, as Attic *energeia* had, by Aristotle's time, lost the digamma before its root vowel.

33. G.W.F. Hegel, *Lectures on the Philosophy of World History. Introduction: Reason in History*, translated by H. B. Nisbet (Cambridge: Cambridge University Press, 1975), 147.

34. Ibid., 149.

35. G.W.F. Hegel, *Science of Logic*, translated by A. V. Miller (London: Allen and Unwin, 1969), 227–34.

36. Dieter Henrich, "Logische Form und reale Totalität. Über die Begriffsform von Hegels eigentlichem Staatsbegriff," in D. Henrich and R.-P. Horstmann, eds., *Hegels Philosophie des Rechts* (Stuttgart: Klett-Cotta, 1982), 428–50.

37. By assuming a determinate existence beside its conditioning elements, the synthesis can thus be described as real, in contrast to merely formal or implicit unity. This methodological principle will play an important role in distinguishing republican from Marxist conceptions of the state in the later 1840s, as Marx would have civil society fully absorb the universality to which the state pretends. On the distinction of formal and real power, see Stephen Houlgate, "Substance, Causality, and the Question of Method in Hegel's Science of Logic," in Sally Sedgwick, ed., *The Reception of Kant's Critical Philosophy. Fichte, Schelling, and Hegel* (Cambridge: Cambridge University Press, 2000), 237.

38. G.W.F. Hegel, *Enzyklopädie der philosophischen Wissenschaften im Grundrisse* (1830), hrsg. Friedhelm Nicolin und Otto Pöggeler (Hamburg: Meiner, 1969), §382 Addition, in the translation cited by David Kolb, "The Particular Logic of Modernity," *Bulletin of the Hegel Society of Great Britain*, 41/42 (2000), 42 n. 8.

39. G.W.F. Hegel, *Elements of the Philosophy of Right*, edited by Allen W. Wood, translated by H. B. Nisbet (Cambridge: Cambridge University Press, 1991), §356, pp. 378–79.

40. C. B. Macpherson, *The Political Theory of Possessive Individualism* (Oxford: Oxford University Press, 1962).

41. J. G. Fichte, *Grundlage des Naturrechts, Gesamtausgabe*, Bd. I/3 and I/4 (Stuttgart: Fromann, 1966 and 1970); Hansjürgen Verweyen, *Recht und Sittlichkeit in J. G. Fichtes Gesellschaftslehre* (Freiburg/München: Alber, 1975), 90–92, 123; Ludwig Siep, *Anerkennung als Prinzip der praktischen Philosophie* (Freiburg und München: Karl Alber, 1979), 22–36.

42. Charles Taylor, *Was ist Liberalismus? Hegelpreis 1997* (Frankfurt: Suhrkamp, 1997), 25–54.

43. Hegel's complex, modern notion of a social good requires that, as Brudner puts it, the priority of the good be suspended in a private sphere that recognises the autonomy of particular purposes. Alan Brudner, "Hegel and the Crisis in Private Law," in Drucilla Cornell et al., eds., *Hegel and Legal Theory* (London: Routledge, 1991), 131.

44. G.W.F. Hegel, *Science of Logic*, 170–78.

45. G.W.F. Hegel, *Philosophy of Right*, 20.

46. Michael Theunissen, "The Repressed Intersubjectivity in Hegel's Philosophy of Right," in Cornell et al., eds., *Hegel and Legal Theory*, 3–63, argues that subjectivity here exhausts itself, and Hegel finds himself compelled to begin a new movement, from the side of substance, that has only a negative relation to the preceding. Hegel thus reproduces a version of classical substantiality,

sacrificing subjectivity and modernity to it; but, corresponding to our own reading, Giuseppe Bedeschi, "Il pensiero politico e giuridico," in Claudio Cesa, ed., *Guida a Hegel* (Rome: Laterza, 1997), 157–200, argues in favour of continuity in the construction of Hegel's argument. This issue cannot be examined here.

47. K.-H. Ilting, "Die 'Rechtsphilosophie' von 1820 und Hegels Vorlesungen über Rechtsphilosophie," in G.W.F. Hegel, *Vorlesungen über Rechtsphilosophie 1818–1831*, ed. K.-H. Ilting, vol. I (Stuttgart: Fromann-Holzboog, 1973), 25–126. Many of the Left Hegelians had direct access to Hegel's Berlin lecture material, which Ilting rediscovered.

48. This view is anticipated in the 1830s by Eduard Gans, who took over the teaching of Hegel's *Philosophy of Right*. On Gans, see Michael H. Hoffheimer, *Eduard Gans and the Hegelian Philosophy of Law* (Dordrecht: Kluwer, 1995).

49. Contrasting his own approach to that of the anonymous author of the *Posaune*, Ludwig Feuerbach stresses the opposition of materialism and idealism, and the need not to revise but to reject Hegel. See E. Barnikol, *Bruno Bauer*, Ms., *Quellenteil* 23, 2, 23 [a].

50. Ludwig Feuerbach, "Zur Kritik der Hegelschen Philosophie" [1839] in W. Bolin and F. Jodl (eds.), *Sämmtliche Werke* II (Stuttgart: Fromann, 1904). K. Marx, "Contribution to the Critique of Hegel's Philosophy of Law," in Karl Marx, Frederick Engels, *Collected Works*, vol. 3 (New York: International Publishers, 1975), 3–129.

51. Karl Marx and Frederick Engels, "Manifesto of the Communist Party," in Karl Marx, Frederick Engels, *Collected Works*, vol. 6 (New York: International Publishers, 1976), 479.

52. G.W.F. Hegel, *Science of Logic*, 661–63.

53. See Chapters 2 and 3.

54. Bruno Bauer, "Johann Christian Edelmann oder Spinoza unter den Theologen," *Deutsche Jahrbücher*, November 24–25, 1842, nos. 302–03, pp. 205–12.

55. For a contrary assessment, see Ruedi Waser, *Autonomie des Selbstbewußtseins. Eine Untersuchung zum Verhältnis von Bruno Bauer und Karl Marx (1835–1843)* (Tübingen: Francke Verlag, 1994).

56. Bauer's later idea of the disciplinary erosion of particularity is not without anticipation in his *Vormärz* texts. See, for example, Bruno Bauer (anon.), *Die evangelische Landeskirche Preußens und die Wissenschaft* (Leipzig: Otto Wigand, 1840), 19–33, especially in reference to the policies of Friedrich Wilhelm I. See, in addition, Bauer's *Die bürgerliche Revolution in Deutschland seit dem Anfange der deutsch-katholischen Bewegung* (Berlin: Hempel, 1849), 295, also cited in E. Barnikol, *Bruno Bauer: Studien und Materialien*, 308; and Bauer's letter to Arnold Ruge, August 17, 1842, in the Barnikol manuscript, *Quellenteil*, #14, 25. In *Bruno Bauer. Studien und Materialien*, 352–53, Barnikol describes Bauer's late links with Hermann Wagener and the *Staatslexikon*, which he characterises as conservative but not traditionalist.

57. In his obituary, "Bruno Bauer und das Urchristentum," *Sozialdemokrat* (May 4 and 11, 1882), Friedrich Engels stresses, however, the value of Bauer's late work for the socialist understanding and critique of religion.

58. Despite postmodern criticisms of this procedure, on which I refrain from comment here, Bauer's "grand historic narrative" of the rational progress of freedom will simply be retained as a fundamental Hegelian element in his work.

59. E. Barnikol, *Bruno Bauer, Studien und Materialien;* and *Bruno Bauer, Darstellung und Quellen,* unpublished manuscript, IISH.

60. Bruno Bauer, ed., *Acktenstücke zu den Verhandlungen über die Beschlagnahme der "Geschichte der Politik, Kultur und Aufklärung des achtzehnten Jahrhunderts" von Bruno Bauer.* Teil I (Christiania: Verlag von C. C. Werner, 1844), 53.

1. "The Idea Is Life": Bauer's Aesthetics and Political Thought

1. In the course of his extensive research on Bauer, Ernst Barnikol discovered, but did not publish, Bauer's 1829 Latin manuscript on Kant's aesthetics. In the posthumous selection from his archive, Ernst Barnikol, *Bruno Bauer, Studien und Materialien,* ed. P. Reimer and H.-M. Sass (Assen: van Gorcum, 1972), 18 (see also p. 425, n. 1 and 3), indicates that a review of Bauer's work by Eduard Schläger, in *Schmeitzner's* [*sic*] *Internationale Monatsschrift,* Bd. I (1882), 380, first alerted him to the existence of the prize manuscript. Barnikol also reproduces Hegel's comments, pp. 18–19, n. 42; but not the Bauer manuscript itself. Comments on the manuscript by the adjudicators Tölken and von Raumer appear on pp. 19–20, n. 43. Hegel's comments are also published in G.W.F. Hegel, *Sämtliche Werke,* Bd. XI, ed. J. Hoffmeister, Bd. XI (Hamburg: Meiner Verlag, 1956), 670–72. In referring to his discovery, Barnikol made a substantive claim that must be disputed here, that Bauer's early text remained without influence on his subsequent work. E. Barnikol, *Bruno Bauer,* 20, states that Bauer did not follow up critically his 1829 text, and mentioned it in none of his publications. For Barnikol, the text stands only as a testimonial to Bauer's self-confidence, his intellectualistic approach, his Hegelian allegiance, and the limits of his thinking.

2. Lawrence Stepelevich, "Translator's Introduction," in Bruno Bauer, *The Trumpet of the Last Judgement against Hegel the Atheist and Antichrist. An Ultimatum,* trans. L. Stepelevich (Lewiston, N.Y.: E. Mellen Press, 1989), 18.

3. Bruno Bauer, *Über die Prinzipien des Schönen. De pulchri principiis. Eine Preisschrift,* hrsg. Douglas Moggach und Winfried Schultze (Berlin: Akademie Verlag, 1996). Barnikol's own unpublished transcription, of which my own is independent, is located in his archive at the International Institute for Social History, Amsterdam. It contains some inaccuracies. Many of these are morphological, but occasionally they bear upon the sense of the document. Thus, for example, on p. 70b (or p. 11, according to his pagination), Barnikol reads *officiat* for *efficiat,* reversing the meaning of the passage from "effecting the unity" to "obviating the unity." On p. 95b (Barnikol's p. 61), he reads *sine vita,* "without life," for *sive vita,* "or life."

4. On this annual competition and the regulations governing it, see Winfried Schultze, "Bruno Bauer und die Aufgaben der Philosophischen Fakultät der Berliner Universität für den Königlichen Preis," in B. Bauer, *Über die Prinzipien*

des Schönen, 105–09. The regulations are there reproduced in full, "Anlage 1," 113–16.

5. The question, written by Hegel, is preserved in the archives of the Humboldt-Universität, Berlin. It is published in G.W.F. Hegel, *Sämtliche Werke*, Bd. XI, 670.

6. The text was submitted anonymously, as required by the regulations for the competition. Bauer's authorship is confirmed by his written acknowledgement of receipt of the prize, retained in the archives of the Humboldt-Universität.

7. On March 15, 1834, Bauer defended twelve theological theses to obtain a licentiate. His habilitation in Berlin followed in November 1834, but no *Habilitationsthesen* have been recorded. See G. A. van den Bergh van Eysinga, *Bruno Bauer*, manuscript, IISH Amsterdam, 13, 17. Among Bauer's twelve Latin theses, reproduced in the Barnikol manuscript, the most intriguing is the first, "The concept of the person resolves all controversies about the dual nature of Christ." Though it is unknown how Bauer might have defended this thesis, we can speculate that there may be an anticipation here of the duality of particular and universal moments within self-consciousness, which is fundamental to his later thought. The significance of some of the other theses, such as the eleventh, that Darius was a Mede, cannot be established. This description of Darius is given in the Book of Daniel, for example, at 5.31 and 9.1.

8. F. von Raumer, in E. Barnikol, *Bruno Bauer. Studien und Materialien*, 20, n. 43.

9. Hegel, *Glauben und Wissen* (1802), *Gesammelte Werke*, Bd. 4 (Hamburg: Meiner Verlag, 1968), 323ff.

10. G.W.F. Hegel, *Vorlesungen über die Ästhetik, I , Sämtliche Werke. Jubiläumsausgabe*, ed. H. Glockner, Band 12 (Stuttgart: Fromann-Holzboog, 1964); *Enzyklopädie der philosophischen Wissenschaften im Grundrisse* (1827), *Gesammelte Werke*, Bd. 19 (Hamburg: Meiner Verlag, 1989).

11. Immanuel Kant, *Kritik der Urteilskraft, Kants gesammelte Schriften*, vol. 5, Königlich Preußische Akademie der Wissenschaften (Berlin: de Gruyter, 1908); *Critique of Judgment*, trans. and ed. Werner Pluhar (Indianapolis: Hackett, 1987).

12. On the Hegelian provenance of this criticism, see B. Tuschling, "Intuitiver Verstand, absolute Identität, Idee. Thesen zu Hegels früher Rezeption der *Kritik der Urteilskraft*," in H.-F. Fulda and R.-P. Horstmann, eds., *Hegel und die "Kritik der Urteilskraft"* (Stuttgart: Klett-Cotta, 1990), 180.

13. *Geist* or spirit in its full Hegelian sense is usually rendered in the manuscript by *ingenium*. Kant in "Critique of Judgement" §46 uses *ingenium* for innate mental aptitude as a characterisation of genius. Descartes uses *ingenium* to mean the mind, taken more empirically as the individual consciousness. In the latter sense, Bauer tends to use *animus*, but not invariably.

14. B. Bauer, *Prinzipien*, 97b.

15. Ibid., 94b–95b.

16. Ibid., 102b–103a.

17. D. S. Stern, "A Hegelian Critique of Reflection," in William Desmond, ed., *Hegel and his Critics. Philosophy in the Aftermath of Hegel* (Albany: State University

of New York Press, 1989), 178–90; H. S. Harris, *Hegel's Ladder*, vol. 1, *The Pilgrimage of Reason* (Indianapolis: Hackett, 1997), 474–615.

18. G.W.F. Hegel, *Vorlesungen über die Geschichte der Philosophie*, III, 355.

19. On the concept of universal self-consciousness, see G.W.F. Hegel, *Enzyklopädie der philosophischen Wissenschaften im Grundrisse* (1830), hrsg. Friedhelm Nicolin und Otto Pöggeler (Hamburg: Meiner, 1969), §436–37 (pp. 353–54).

20. Cf. G.W.F. Hegel, *Glauben und Wissen*, 316.

21. Hegel, *Vorlesungen über die Geschichte der Philosophie*, III, 332, 350–51, 381–82.

22. G.W.F. Hegel, *Enzyklopädie der philosophischen Wissenschaften im Grundrisse* (1827), *Gesammelte Werke*, Bd. 19 (Hamburg: Meiner Verlag, 1989), §37–§60. See also Hegel, *Glauben und Wissen*, 321.

23. G.W.F. Hegel, *Vorlesungen über die Geschichte der Philosophie*, III, 332–33.

24. Hegel, *Enzyklopädie* (1827), §21–§31.

25. For a recent discussion, see Beate Bradl, *Die Rationalität des Schönen bei Kant und Hegel* (München: Fink, 1998).

26. G.W.F. Hegel, *Vorlesungen über die Ästhetik*, I, 92.

27. B. Bauer, *Prinzipien*, 79b–81a, 89b–92b.

28. B. Lypp, "Idealismus und Philosophie der Kunst," in Fulda and Horstmann, eds., *Hegel und die "Kritik der Urteilskraft,"* 110, 118.

29. B. Bauer, *Prinzipien*, 97b.

30. Ibid., 91b.

31. G.W.F. Hegel, *Science of Logic*, translated by A. V. Miller (London: Allen and Unwin, 1969), 647–50.

32. B. Bauer, *Prinzipien*, 81a–83a, 92b–94a.

33. Ibid., 83a–85b, 94a–101a.

34. Ibid., 96b–97a.

35. Ibid., 85b–87, 101a–02b.

36. Hegel, *Vorlesungen über die Ästhetik*, I, 88, 90–91.

37. For discussions of the end of art thesis, see Anne-Marie Gethmann-Siefert, "Ästhetik oder Philosophie der Kunst," *Hegel-Studien*, Bd. 26 (1991), 103; Dieter Henrich, "Zur Aktualität von Hegels Ästhetik," *Hegel-Studien*, Beiheft 11 (1974), 295–301; A. Hofstadter, "Die Kunst: Tod und Verklärung," *Hegel-Studien*, Beiheft 11 (1974), 271–85; T. M. Knox, "The Puzzle of Hegel's Aesthetics," in W. E. Steinkraus and K. I. Schmitz, eds., *Art and Logic in Hegel's Philosophy* (Sussex: Harvester Press, 1980), 1–10; H. Kuhn, "Die Gegenwärtigkeit der Kunst nach Hegels Vorlesungen über Ästhetik," *Hegel-Studien*, Beiheft 11 (1974), 251–69; and R. D. Winfield, "Rethinking the Particular Forms of Art: Prolegomena to a Rational Reconstruction of Hegel's Theory of the Artforms," *Owl of Minerva*, 24/2 (1993), 131–44.

38. Hegel, *Vorlesungen über die Ästhetik*, I, 30–31.

39. These two claims are made by Anne-Marie Gethmann-Siefert, *Die Funktion der Kunst in der Geschichte, Untersuchungen zu Hegels Ästhetik* (Bonn: Bouvier, 1984), 325; "Die Rolle der Kunst im Staat," *Hegel-Studien*, Beiheft 27 (1986), 69–74; "Einleitung: Welt und Wirkung von Hegels Ästhetik," in A. Gethmann-Siefert and Otto Pöggeler, eds., *Welt und Wirkung von Hegels Ästhetik* (Bonn, Bouvier, 1986), XI–XIII, XXVIII. See also, by the same author, "Ästhetik

oder Philosophie der Kunst," 92–110; "Die Idee des Schönen," in Otto Pöggeler et al., eds., *Hegel in Berlin, Preußische Kulturpolitik und idealistische Ästhetik* (Berlin: Staatsbibliothek Preußischer Kulturbesitz, 1981), 182–87; and, edited by her, *Phänomen versus System. Zum Verhältnis von philosophischer Systematik und Kunsturteil in Hegels Berliner Vorlesungen über Ästhetik oder Philosophie der Kunst* (Bonn: Bouvier, 1992). Cf. Bauer's discussion of the barbarism of the mediaeval period, *Prinzipien*, 67b–68b.

40. Anne-Marie Gethmann-Siefert, "H. G. Hotho: Kunst als Bildungserlebnis und Kunsttheorie in systematischer Absicht – oder die entpolitisierte Version der ästhetischen Erziehung des Menschen," in Otto Pöggeler and A. Gethmann-Siefert, eds., *Kunsterfahrung und Kulturpolitik im Berlin Hegels* (Bonn: Bouvier, 1983), 229–62. The author claims that Hotho's edition of Hegel's lectures on aesthetics distorts their systematic structure and misrepresents individual judgements on works of art. The Bauer manuscript offers no basis for assessing these claims.

41. B. Bauer, *Prinzipien*, 110a, b.

42. G.W.F. Hegel, "Vorrede zur zweiten Ausgabe," *Enzyklopädie* (1827), 5–18; Hegel to his wife, Oct. 12, 1827, *Briefe von und an Hegel*, Bd. 3, ed. J. Hoffmeister (Hamburg: Meiner Verlag, 1961), 202.

43. On the politics of Prussian pietism, see Erich Jordan, *Die Entstehung der konservativen Partei und die preußischen Agrarverhältnisse vor 1848* (München: Duncker und Humblot, 1914), 144.

44. B. Bauer, *Prinzipien*, 102b.

45. This is the theme of Bruno Bauer, *Herr Dr. Hengstenberg. Ein Beitrag zur Kritik des religiösen Bewußtseins. Kritische Briefe über den Gegensatz des Gesetzes und des Evangeliums* (Berlin: Dümmler, 1839), a text that marked Bauer's shift to a Left-Hegelian position and that occasioned his transfer from Berlin to Bonn. See Chapter 3.

46. E. Barnikol, *Bruno Bauer*, 33, rightly emphasises the political character of the theological disputes of the time, including Bauer's own atheism.

47. Bruno Bauer (anon., 1st ed.), *Die evangelische Landeskirche Preußens und die Wissenschaft* (Leipzig: Otto Wigand, 1840); "Der christliche Staat und unsere Zeit" [1841], in *Feldzüge der reinen Kritik*, ed. H.-M. Sass (Frankfurt/M.: Suhrkamp, 1968), 9–41. The former text is often taken as a defence of the existing state against religious arrogations; for an interpretation of its polemical intentions, see Chapter 4.

48. Cf. Daniel Brudney, *Marx's Attempt to Leave Philosophy* (Cambridge, Mass.: Harvard University Press, 1998), 129–30.

49. Bruno Bauer (anon.), *Die Posaune des jüngsten Gerichts über Hegel, den Atheisten und Antichristen. Ein Ultimatum* (Leipzig: Otto Wigand, 1841), 167.

50. Ibid., 140, 146–48.

51. I. Kant, *Grundlegung zur Metaphysik der Sitten, Werke*, Bd. 4, ed. A. Buchenau and E. Cassirer (Hildesheim: Gerstenberg, 1973), 302.

52. I. Kant, *Kritik der Urteilskraft*, 260–66; *Critique of Judgment*, 119–26.

53. In *Die Septembertage 1792 und die ersten Kämpfe der Parteien der Republik in Frankreich*. 2e. Abteilung (Charlottenburg: Verlag von Egbert Bauer, 1844), 5, Bauer describes the French Revolution as not yet attaining freedom, but

as imparting the sublime feeling of struggle, attempting to clear away all hindrances to freedom in public and private life.

54. Hegel, *Science of Logic*, 227–34.

55. B. Bauer, *Prinzipien*, 85a.

56. Ibid., 96b, 111a.

57. B. Bauer, *Posaune*, 95–105.

58. L. Feuerbach, *Das Wesen des Christentums* (1841), hrsg. Werner Schuffenhauer and Wolfgang Harich (Berlin: Akademie Verlag, 1973).

59. B. Bauer (anon.), *Hegels Lehre von der Religion und Kunst von dem Standpuncte des Glaubens aus beurtheilt* (Leipzig: Otto Wigand, 1842). Zvi Rosen, *Bruno Bauer and Karl Marx* (The Hague: Nijhoff, 1978), 62, erroneously places *Hegels Lehre* in 1843. The new edition of *Hegels Lehre* (Aalen: Scientia Verlag, 1967) attributes to Karl Marx much of this text, the section entitled "Hegels Haß gegen die heilige Geschichte und die göttliche Kunst der heiligen Geschichtsschreibung," 67–227, without justifying this attribution, which is almost certainly incorrect. Bauer's letters to Ruge, of December 6 and 24, 1841, do report that he and Marx were collaborating on a continuation of the *Posaune* (the letters are reproduced in the unpublished Barnikol manuscript, *Quellenteil*). *Hegels Lehre*, 2–3, indicates that two authors each wrote one part of the manuscript. It is clear that Marx and Bauer discussed the projected text towards the end of 1841, but it is unlikely that Marx actually completed or submitted his portion of the book. In his letters to Ruge of February 10, March 5, and March 20, 1842, Marx expressed doubts about the feasibility of the project, constantly deferred completion of his manuscript, and eventually expressed an intention to submit (though apparently never delivered) an essay on Christian art to Ruge's *Deutsche Jahrbücher für Wissenschaft und Kunst*, and not a text for Wigand, publisher of *Hegels Lehre*. See David Rjazanov and Viktor Adoratskij, eds., *Marx Engels Historisch-kritische Gesamtausgabe*, III/1 (Frankfurt/M.: Marx-Engels-Verlag, 1929), 21, 22, 24, 26. Bauer himself claimed authorship of *Hegels Lehre* slightly later in the year, in *Kritik der evangelischen Geschichte der Synoptiker und des Johannes* (Braunschweig: Fr. Otto 1842), 316. The content of Marx's promised contribution is uncertain, but the published text deals only with the literary arts, poetry, drama, and the composition of the Gospels. Visual art is merely skimmed on pp. 138–39. There is possibly a lacuna here, where a chapter by Marx might have been inserted. The reference to dual authorship of *Hegels Lehre* might be explained, as the editors of *MEGA* suggest, by the fact that Bauer wrote the introduction (and delivered it to the printer in February 1842) before Marx's demurral became evident.

60. Cf. B. Bauer, *Posaune*, 163n.

61. B. Bauer, *Hegels Lehre*, 69–70. Claudio Cesa, *Studi sulla Sinistra hegeliana* (Urbino: Argalia, 1972), examines the *Posaune*, *Hegels Lehre*, and *Entdeckte Christenthum*, demonstrating the coherence and development of Bauer's relation to Hegel and his position on history, theory and practice, and idealism and materialism.

62. B. Bauer, *Hegels Lehre*, 61.

63. Ibid., 48–49.

64. Ibid., 162–63.

65. Ibid. 166–67.
66. B. Bauer, *Prinzipien*, 68a.
67. B. Bauer, *Hegels Lehre*, 196.
68. Ibid., 225, citing Hegel, *Aesthetic* I, 136.
69. B. Lypp, "Idealismus und Philosophie der Kunst," 105.
70. B. Bauer, "Das Kölner Quartett," *Rheinische Zeitung*, No. 60, March 1, 1842.
71. Karl Marx and Frederick Engels, "Manifesto of the Communist Party," in Karl Marx, Frederick Engels, *Collected Works*, vol. 6 (New York: International Publishers, 1976), 477–519.
72. B. Bauer, *Posaune*, 61.

2. "Free Means Ethical": Idealism, History, and Critical Theory

1. G.W.F. Hegel, *Elements of the Philosophy of Right*, edited by Allen W. Wood, translated by H. B. Nisbet (Cambridge: Cambridge University Press, 1991), §356 (pp. 378–79) This image differs from the modern figure of the beautiful soul described in *Phenomenology*, a pure interiority of consciousness that disdains to realise itself in objectivity. See G.W.F. Hegel, *Phenomenology of Mind*, translated by J. B. Baillie (New York: Harper & Row, 1967), 658–60, 665–66.
2. Hegel, *Philosophy of Right*, 20–21.
3. G.W.F. Hegel, *Enzyklopädie der philosophischen Wissenschaften im Grundrisse* (1830), hrsg. Friedhelm Nicolin und Otto Pöggeler (Hamburg: Meiner, 1969), §436–37 (pp. 353–54); for an analysis, see Andrew Chitty, "Recognition and Social Relations of Production," *Historical Materialism*, no. 2 (Summer 1998), 57–97.
4. Bruno Bauer, *Kritik der evangelischen Geschichte des Johannes* (Bremen: Carl Schünemann, 1840), 182–83.
5. G.W.F. Hegel, *Science of Logic*, translated by A. V. Miller (London: Allen and Unwin, 1969), 661–63.
6. Douglas Moggach, "Absolute Spirit and Universal Self-Consciousness: Bruno Bauer's Revolutionary Subjectivism," *Dialogue, The Canadian Philosophical Review* 38, 2 (1989), 235–56, is wrong on this point, though providing material that sustains the interpretation presented here. Bauer's 1829 prize manuscript makes the unity of thought and being thematic. See Bruno Bauer, *Über die Prinzipien des Schönen. De pulchri principiis. Eine Preisschrift*, hrsg. Douglas Moggach und Winfried Schultze, mit einem Vorwort von Volker Gerhardt (Berlin: Akademie Verlag, 1996).
7. Bruno Bauer, "*Das Leben Jesu, kritisch bearbeitet* von David Friedrich Strauss. Erster Band. Fortsetzung," *Jahrbücher für wissenschaftliche Kritik*, No. 111, December 1835, 891.
8. Bruno Bauer, *Kritik der evangelischen Geschichte der Synoptiker*, Erster Band (Leipzig: Otto Wigand, 1841), 81.
9. Bruno Bauer (anon.), *Die Posaune des jüngsten Gerichts über Hegel, den Atheisten und Antichristen. Ein Ultimatum* (Leipzig: Otto Wigand, 1841), 146–48, citing Hegel's *Vorlesungen über die Philosophie der Religion*, Bd. 1, 2nd ed. (Berlin, 1840), 63–65.

10. Bruno Bauer, *Das entdeckte Christenthum. Eine Erinnerung an das 18. Jahrhundert und ein Beitrag zur Krisis des 19*. (Zürich und Winterthur: Verlag des literarischen Comptoirs, 1843); Karl Marx, "Theses on Feuerbach," in Karl Marx, Frederick Engels, *Collected Works*, vol. 5 (New York: International Publishers, 1976), 3–5. Hegel's 1802 essay on natural law distinguishes modern philosophy into empiricism and formalism. Bauer and Marx treat this distinction in their characteristic ways. See G.W.F. Hegel, *Natural Law. The Scientific Ways of Treating Natural Law, Its Place in Moral Philosophy, and Its Relation to the Positive Sciences of Law*, trans. T. M. Knox (Philadelphia: University of Pennsylvania Press, 1975).

11. G.W.F. Hegel, *Lectures on the Philosophy of World History. Introduction: Reason in History* (Cambridge: Cambridge University Press, 1975). Bauer's critique of Hegel sharpens in 1845. See Chapter 5.

12. B. Bauer, *Das entdeckte Christenthum*, 161.

13. Max Stirner, *Der Einziger und sein Eigentum* (Leipzig, 1845). Bauer criticises Stirner, along with Feuerbach and Marx, in "Charakteristik Ludwig Feuerbachs," *Wigands Vierteljahrschrift* III (1845), 123–24. Stirner's work is a defence of a particularism, which Bauer repudiates theoretically, despite maintaining amicable personal relations. To this extent his connection to Stirner is unlike his relations to Marx and to Arnold Ruge. Stirner in turn rejects Bauer's ethical rationalism, based on a principle of universality that Stirner regards as a "spook," like the fetishistic objects of religious belief.

14. D. F. Strauss, *Das Leben Jesu, kritisch bearbeitet*, 2 vol. (Tübingen, 1835; second edition 1836; third 1838; fourth 1840); B. Bauer, "Charakteristik Ludwig Feuerbachs," 102–23.

15. Douglas Moggach, "New Goals and New Ways: Republicanism and Socialism in 1848," in Douglas Moggach and Paul Leduc Browne (eds.), *The Social Question and the Democratic Revolution: Marx and the Legacy of 1848* (Ottawa: University of Ottawa Press, 2000), 49–69.

16. Bruno Bauer, "Rezension: *Die christliche Glaubenslehre in ihrer geschichtlichen Entwicklung und im Kampf mit der modernen Wissenschaft*. von D. F. Strauss. 2 Bde. 1840–1841," *Deutsche Jahrbücher*, January 25–28, 1843, nos. 21–24, 82 (also cited in van den Bergh van Eysinga manuscript, 221Q).

17. See Chapter 5.

18. B. Bauer, *Posaune*, 82.

19. J. G. Fichte, *Grundlage des Naturrechts*, Gesamtausgabe der Bayerischen Akademie der Wissenschaften, ed. R. Lauth et al., Bd. I/3, §§3–4 (Stuttgart, 1966); Douglas Moggach, "Reciprocity, Elicitation, Recognition: The Thematics of Intersubjectivity in the Early Fichte," *Dialogue, The Canadian Philosophical Review*, 38/2 (Spring 1999), 271–96.

20. Bruno Bauer, letter to Arnold Ruge, October 27, 1842, v.d. Bergh van Eysinga ms., §14/26.

21. Hegel, *Science of Logic*, 662 (trans. A. V. Miller).

22. B. Bauer, *Johannes*, 178.

23. Bruno Bauer (anon.), *Hegels Lehre von der Religion und Kunst von dem Standpuncte des Glaubens aus beurtheilt* (Leipzig: Otto Wigand, 1842), 162–63.

24. Hegel, *Science of Logic*, 642–43. The infinite judgement is also distinct from the universal judgement (647–50), an empirical summation of particulars. On the infinite judgement of the Enlightenment, see H. S. Harris, *Hegel's Ladder*, vol. 2: *The Odyssey of Spirit* (Indianapolis: Hackett, 1997), 364, 384, 494.

25. H. S. Harris, *Hegel's Ladder*, vol. 1, 452.

26. Paul-Henry Thiry d'Holbach, *Le christianisme dévoilé, ou Examen des principes et des effets de la religion chrétienne* (London, 1756), *Oeuvres philosophiques*, tome 1, Préface de Jean Claude Bourdin (Paris: Editions Alive, 1998), 1–120.

27. B. Bauer, *I. Synoptiker*, 25; cf. 240–41, 307n. Published in March 1841, Bauer's argument that religion hypostatises the universality of the human spirit is independent of Feuerbach's analogous claim in *Das Wesen des Christenthums*, of June 1841.

28. For example, H.-M. Sass, "Bruno Bauer's Critical Theory," *Philosophical Forum* 8 (1978), 93–103.

29. Bruno Bauer, *Die Religion des alten Testaments in der geschichtlichen Entwicklung ihrer Prinzipien dargestellt*, Bd. I (Berlin: Dümmler, 1838), 160–61, here applied to Judaism and pagan deities.

30. B. Bauer, *Das entdeckte Christenthum*, 161.

31. Bruno Bauer, "Der christliche Staat und unsere Zeit," in H.-M. Sass, ed., *Feldzüge der reinen Kritik* (Frankfurt a.M.: Suhrkamp, 1968), 26.

32. This polemic is reviewed in Moggach, "New Goals and New Ways," 54–57, stressing the rupture between republican and socialist ideologies in 1848.

33. Bruno Bauer, "Die Gattung und die Masse," *ALZ* X, 1844, 42–48.

34. B. Bauer, *Religion des Alten Testaments* I, 183.

35. As Rawls puts it: "Heteronomy obtains not only when these first principles are fixed by the special psychological constitution of human nature, as in Hume, but also when they are fixed by an order of universals, or of moral values grasped by rational intuition, as in Plato's realm of forms or in Leibniz's hierarchy of perfections." John Rawls, "Themes in Kant's Moral Philosophy," in Eckart Förster, ed., *Kant's Transcendental Deductions* (Stanford: Stanford University Press, 1989), 97.

36. Immanuel Kant, *Critique of Practical Reason*, trans. L. W. Beck (New York: Macmillan, 1956), 33–42; *Groundwork of the Metaphysics of Morals*, trans. H. J. Paton (New York: Harper & Row, 1964), 10–11.

37. B. Bauer, *Hegels Lehre*, 166–67.

38. B. Bauer, *I. Synoptiker*, 311.

39. David Koigen, *Zur Vorgeschichte des modernen philosophischen Sozialismus in Deutschland* (Bern: Stürzenegger, 1901), 48.

40. Bruno Bauer, "Leiden und Freuden des theologischen Bewußtseins," in Arnold Ruge (ed.), *Anekdota zur neuesten deutschen Philosophie und Publizistik*, vol. II (Zürich und Winterthur: Verlag des literarischen Comptoirs, 1843), 111.

41. Quentin Skinner, *The Foundations of Modern Political Thought*, vol. 1, *The Renaissance* (Cambridge: Cambridge University Press, 1978), 156–86.

42. On the fundamentally political, not religious, character of the crisis, see Bruno Bauer, *Die gute Sache der Freiheit und meine eigene Angelegenheit*

(Zürich und Winterthur: Verlag des literarischen Comptoirs, 1842), 218, 219.

43. B. Bauer, "Leiden und Freuden," 111.

44. Bruno Bauer, "Rezension: *Einleitung in die Dogmengeschichte* von Theodor Kliefoth," in A. Ruge, *Anekdota* II, 135-59.

45. Bruno Bauer, "Theologische Schamlosigkeiten," in Sass (ed.), *Feldzüge*, 54-56.

46. See, for example, Istvan Hont and Michael Ignatieff (eds.), *Wealth and Virtue. The Shaping of Political Economy in the Scottish Enlightenment* (Cambridge: Cambridge University Press, 1983).

47. Cf. Robert Nola, "The Young Hegelians, Feuerbach, and Marx," in R. C. Solomon and K. M. Higgins (eds.), *The Age of German Idealism. Routledge History of Philosophy*, vol. VI (London: Routledge, 1993), 298-99; Bruno Bauer, "Was ist jetzt der Gegenstand der Kritik?", *Allgemeine Literatur-Zeitung* VIII (1844), 18-26.

48. Bruno Bauer, "Organisation der Arbeit," *Norddeutsche Blätter* V (1844), 76-85.

49. Bruno Bauer, *Die Septembertage 1792 und die ersten Kämpfe der Parteien der Republik in Frankreich*, I. Abteilung, *Denkwürdigkeiten zur Geschichte der neueren Zeit seit der französischen Revolution* (Charlottenburg: Egbert Bauer, 1844), 5-6; *Geschichte der Politik, Kultur und Aufklärung des achtzehnten Jahrhunderts*, Bd. III: *Die Politik bis zum Frieden von Basel* (Charlottenburg: Egbert Bauer, 1845), 256.

50. Bruno Bauer, "Erste Wahlrede von 1848," in Ernst Barnikol, *Bruno Bauer, Studien und Materialien*, hrsg. P. Riemer und H.-M. Sass (Assen: van Gorcum, 1972), 526-29.

51. Bruno Bauer, "Rezension: *Die Geschichte des Lebens Jesu* von Dr. von Ammon. Erster Band," in A. Ruge, *Anekdota* II, 185.

52. B. Bauer, *Prinzipien des Schönen*, 66a.

53. See, for example, Bruno Bauer, *Vollständige Geschichte der Parteikämpfe in Deutschland während der Jahre 1842-1846* (Charlottenburg: Egbert Bauer, 1847); *Die bürgerliche Revolution in Deutschland seit dem Anfange der deutschkatholischen Bewegung* (Berlin: Hempel, 1849); *Untergang des Frankfurter Parlaments* (Charlottenburg: Egbert Bauer, 1849).

54. Bruno Bauer, "Die Judenfrage," *Deutsche Jahrbücher*, October 27–November 4, No. 274-82, (1842): 1093-126; and "Die Fähigkeit der heutigen Juden und Christen, frei zu werden," in Georg Herwegh (ed.), *Einundzwanzig Bogen aus der Schweiz* (Zürich und Winterthur: Verlag des literarischen Comptoirs, 1843), 56-71. See Chapter 7.

55. Cf. Harris, *Hegel's Ladder*, vol. 2, 741, 752-53, 760 n. 44.

56. Bruno Bauer, *Geschichte der Politik, Kultur und Aufklärung des achtzehnten Jahrhunderts. Erster Band. Deutschland während der ersten vierzig Jahre des achtzehnten Jahrhunderts* (Charlottenburg: Egbert Bauer, 1843), vii: under the leadership of the Jacobins, "with a single stroke, the mass, deprived of rights, transformed itself into a people [*Volk*], which through its heroic strivings attained force, courage, and the capacity to destroy all privileges."

57. Eric Gamby, *Edgar Bauer, Junghegelianer, Publizist und Polizeiagent* (Trier: Karl-Marx-Haus), 1985, 23-29, describes an attack by a royalist mob on Bruno Bauer and his brother Edgar on August 20, 1848, at a founding meeting of the Charlottenburg Democratic Club. Gamby also outlines Edgar Bauer's

post-revolutionary career as an informant for the Danish government among the London exile community.

58. Bruno Bauer, "The Present Position of the Jews," *New York Daily Tribune*, June 7, 1852. This article asserts a racial distinction between Jews and Germans, differing significantly from Bauer's earlier treatment of the question as essentially historical, cultural, and religious. The new position stresses a permanent divide.

59. On Bauer's late works, see Barnikol, *Bruno Bauer*, 310–424. van den Bergh van Eysinga, ms., 221, distinguishes in Bauer's later phase his ongoing critical work in religious history, and his reactionary politics.

3. "The Other of Itself": The Critique of the Religious Consciousness

1. See, for example, Bruno Bauer, "Rezension: *Das Leben Jesu, kritisch bearbeitet von David Friedrich Strauss. Erster Band*," *Jahrbücher für wissenschaftliche Kritik*, December 1835, no. 109, 879–80; no. 111, 891; no. 113, 905–12; "Die Prinzipien der mosaischen Rechts- und Religions-Verfassung nach ihrem innern Zusammenhange" entwickelt von Lic. B. Bauer. *Zeitschrift für spekulative Theologie*, 1837, vol. II, no. 2, 297–353.

2. Zvi Rosen, *Bruno Bauer and Karl Marx* (The Hague: Nijhoff, 1978), 41. Rosen, 39–41, stresses the continuity in Bauer's thinking, taking issue with W. J. Brazill, *The Young Hegelians* (New Haven: Yale University Press, 1970), 179.

3. For a discussion of these issues in the *Phenomenology*, see H. S. Harris, *Hegel's Ladder*, vol. 1, *The Pilgrimage of Reason* (Indianapolis: Hackett, 1997), 395–436.

4. J. G. Fichte, *Versuch einer Kritik aller Offenbarung*, in *Fichtes Werke* V (Berlin: de Gruyter, 1971), 9–174 [first edition 1792, second 1793]. See Hansjürgen Verweyen, "Offenbarung und autonome Vernunft nach J. G. Fichte," in K. Hammacher and A. Mues, eds., *Erneuerung der Transzendentalphilosophie* (Stuttgart: Klett, 1979), 436–55. See also Graziella Rotta, *Applicazione del punto di vista kantiano e sviluppi originali nel "Saggio di una critica di ogni rivelazione" di J. G. Fichte*, Tesi di Laurea, Università degli Studi di Pisa, 1987-88; Graziella Rotta, *L'Idea Dio. Il pensiero religioso di Fichte fino allo Atheismusstreit*, Tesi di Dottorato, Università di Torino, 1992–93, 74–121. I am grateful to Claudio Cesa for making these latter references available to me.

5. G. Rotta, *L'Idea Dio*, 97–98, indicates the presence of some historical considerations in Fichte's text, however.

6. On this subject, see David Kolb, ed., *New Perspectives on Hegel's Philosophy of Religion* (Albany: State University of New York Press, 1992).

7. Bruno Bauer, *Herr Dr. Hengstenberg. Ein Beitrag zur Kritik des religiösen Bewußtseins. Kritische Briefe über den Gegensatz des Gesetzes und des Evangeliums* (Berlin: Ferdinand Dümmler, 1839).

8. E. Barnikol, Bruno Bauer (Manuscript), International Institute for Social History, Amsterdam, Bd. III, #30, pp. 29, 30. Auguste Cornu, *Moses Hess et la Gauche hégélienne* (Paris: 1934), attributes this book to April 1839, but the last letter in the text explicitly states that it is not yet new year.

9. Barnikol ms., Bd. III, #29, pp. 7–12. Hengstenberg, editor of the *Evangelische Kirchenzeitung*, is identified by Barnikol as the most conservative professor

in Prussia (ibid., Bd. III, #27, p. 1) and a major exponent of "Restoration ecclesiastical orthodoxy" (ibid., Bd. III, #27, p. 1), and "political Restoration-Christianity" (ibid., Bd. II, #30, p. 58). Tholuck's *Literarische Anzeiger* represented the same theoretical and political currents (ibid., Bd. III. #27, p. 4). Leo was a member of the Historical School of Law, which opposed the "arid rationalism" of liberal constitutionalism in favour of "unconscious organic development," leaving feudal privilege intact as long as possible. See also Karl Marx, "The Philosophical Manifesto of the Historical School of Law" in Karl Marx, Frederick Engels, *Collected Works*, vol. 1 (New York: International Publishers, 1975), 203–10; and E. Rambaldi, *Le origini della sinistra hegeliana* (Florence: Nuova Italia, 1966), 6–14.

10. On the Kamarilla, see Erich Jordan, *Die Entstehung der konservativen Partei und die preussischen Agrarverhältnisse vor 1848* (München: Duncker und Humblot, 1914), 144, where he identifies the "neo-orthodox party" as a union of landed proprietors and clergymen. See also Gustav Mayer, "Die Anfänge des politischen Radikalismus im vormärzlichen Preußen," *Zeitschrift für Politik* (1913), Heft 1, Sonderdruck, 51. Hengstenberg's and Leo's texts are summarised in Barnikol Ms., Bd. III, #27 and #28; also indicated here is Hengstenberg's polemic against Strauss in the *Literarische Anzeiger* of August 1838, in a review of E.C.J. Lützelberger, *Die Gründe der freiwilligen Niederlegung meines geistlichen Amtes* (1839). It is noteworthy that Barnikol, whose own interest in Bauer was originally theological, came in the course of his studies to emphasise the political character of the theological disputes of the time. See, for example, E. Barnikol, *Bruno Bauer: Studien und Materialien*, 33. Barnikol himself published some of his conclusions on Bauer in his introduction to a new edition of Bauer's *Das entdeckte Christentum*, entitled *Das entdeckte Christentum im Vormärz. Bruno Bauers Kampf gegen Religion und Christentum und Erstausgabe seiner Kampfschrift* (Jena: Eugen Diederichs, 1927), and in "Bruno Bauer, der radikalste Religionskritiker und konservativste Junghegelianer," *Das Altertum*, Band 7, Heft 1 (1961), 41–49. Barnikol's interpretation of Bauer directly occasions that of Karl Löwith, *From Hegel to Nietzsche* (Garden City: Doubleday, 1967), except for the former's greater stress on the political dimension of the Left-Hegelian movement. On Barnikol's relation to Löwith, see Lothar Koch, *Humanistischer Atheismus und gesellschaftliches Engagement. Bruno Bauers "Kritische Kritik"* (Stuttgart: Kohlhammer, 1971), 16–21. A survey of six Bauerian texts (the critiques of John and the *Synoptics*, *Das entdeckte Christentum*, and *Christus und die Cäsaren*), Koch's book does not engage deeply with the theoretical questions Bauer raises.

11. D. F. Strauss, *Das Leben Jesu, kritisch bearbeitet*, 2 vol. (Tübingen: 1835).

12. On Strauss, see M. C. Massey, *Christ Unmasked: The Meaning of the Life of Jesus in German Politics* (Chapel Hill: University of North Carolina Press, 1983); and E. Rambaldi, *Origini*, 229–57. Rambaldi, 120, summarises Strauss's work (in my translation): "In practice, what Strauss does is to withdraw from the Christian *Vorstellung* the right to reflect on the religious level the mysteries of speculative logic. He therefore denies the absoluteness of the Christian religion, and reduces Christianity to a historically and phenomenologically transient form of religion."

13. D. F. Strauss, *Streitschriften zur Vertheidigung meiner Schrift über das Leben Jesu und zur Charakteristik der gegenwärtigen Theologie.* Erstes Heft (Tübingen: 1837), 9–19.

14. Ibid., 39ff.

15. Ibid., Zweites Heft, 205–14.

16. G.W.F. Hegel, *Enzyklopädie der philosophischen Wissenschaften im Grundrisse* (1827), *Gesammelte Werke,* Bd. 19 (Hamburg: Meiner Verlag, 1989), §6.

17. B. Bauer, *Herr Dr. Hengstenberg,* 4.

18. D. F. Strauss, *Das Leben Jesu, kritisch bearbeitet,* 2 vol., 4th edition (Tübingen, 1840).

19. The suggestion of encouragement by Schulze is made in the Barnikol ms., Bd. III, #27, p. 2. On Altenstein, see Terry Pinkard, *Hegel. A Biography* (Cambridge: Cambridge University Press, 2000), 412ff.

20. Barnikol ms., Bd. III, #27, p. 2.

21. Bruno Bauer, *Die gute Sache der Freiheit und meine eigene Angelegenheit* (Zürich und Winterthur: Verlag des literarischen Comptoirs, 1842), 23.

22. B. Bauer, *Herr Dr. Hengstenberg,* 15.

23. Ibid., 96.

24. Ibid., 47–48.

25. On this fundamental question see especially E. Rambaldi, *Origini,* 6–14; Jacques Droz, *Le romantisme allemand et l'État: Résistance et collaboration dans l'Allemagne napoléonienne* (Paris: Payot, 1966), 225ff, 299; J. Droz, *Europe Between Revolutions, 1815–1848* (London: Fontana, 1967), 9–17; Eric Hobsbawm, *The Age of Revolution, 1789–1848* (New York: Mentor, 1972), 255–276. Note also the letter of Bettina von Arnim, associated with Bauer's Freien circle in Berlin, to her son Ferdinand, October 27, 1841, where she critically observes, "There is no greater danger for young people than pietism.... Church affairs are now the secret drive shaft of the wheel of state, through these shall the great state machine be set in motion again" (cited in Barnikol ms., Bd. VIII, no. II, #11, p. 2).

26. B. Bauer, *Herr Dr. Hengstenberg,* 81.

27. Ibid., 57–58.

28. Barnikol, *Bruno Bauer. Studien und Materialien,* 136–92, 479–505. This inquiry was authorised on August 20, 1841, by the Minister of Education, J.A.F. Eichhorn, who had replaced Altenstein on the latter's death in 1840, under the conservative regime of Friedrich Wilhelm IV.

29. On the composition of the *Johannes,* see Bauer's five letters to the publisher Ferdinand Dümmler from January 5, 1840, to April 18, 1840, in Barnikol ms., Bd. III, #39b, pp. 2–3. Bauer's atheistic position dates from the end of 1839, prior to the composition of this text. On this question see *Briefwechsel zwischen Bruno Bauer und Edgar Bauer während der Jahre 1839–1842 aus Bonn und Berlin* (Charlottenburg: 1844), letters 1–4 (October 21, 1839 to November 30, 1839), pp. 8–18; Barnikol ms., Bd. IV, #38; and Barnikol, *Bruno Bauer: Studien und Materialien,* 30–46. Further on the composition of the *Johannes,* see *Briefwechsel,* letters 7 (January 20, 1840) and 19 (May 8, 1840).

30. See *Briefwechsel,* letters 28 (August 7, 1840), 33 (January 23, 1841), and 35 (March 10, 1841).

31. See *Briefwechsel*, letters 40 (May 17, 1841), 43 (July 11, 1841), and 44 (August 16, 1841).

32. See *Briefwechsel*, letter 55 (mid-April, 1842).

33. See *Briefwechsel*, letter 7 (January 20, 1840); also cited in Barnikol, *Bruno Bauer: Studien und Materialien*, 37–38.

34. See *Briefwechsel*, letter 8 (February 4, 1840), 34–36.

35. B. Bauer, *Kritik der evangelischen Geschichte des Johannes* (Bremen: Carl Schünemann, 1840), 182.

36. Ibid., 406.

37. Ibid., 178.

38. The *Johannes* makes a relatively favourable mention of Strauss, v–vii.

39. Bauer had previously published the following reviews of Strauss's work in the *Berliner Jahrbücher*. 1. Review of *Leben Jesu*, volume I: December 1835, no. 109, pp. 879–80; no. 113, pp. 905–12; 2. Review of *Leben Jesu*, volume II: May 1836, no. 86, pp. 681–88; no. 88, pp. 697–704; 3. Review of writings on Strauss: March 1837, no. 41, pp. 321–28; no. 43, pp. 337–43; 4. Review of Strauss's *Streitschriften* (1837): November 1837, no. 101, p. 837; no. 103, p. 838. On Bauer's critical self-characterisation of these reviews, see his *Landeskirche*, 3.

40. B. Bauer, *Johannes*, 5 ff.

41. Ibid., 5.

42. Bruno Bauer, *Kritik der evangelischen Geschichte der Synoptiker*. Erster Band (Leipzig: Otto Wigand, 1841), ix.

43. B. Bauer, *Johannes*, 178–79.

44. B. Bauer, *I. Synoptiker*, vii–viii.

45. Ibid., vi.

46. G.W.F. Hegel, *Science of Logic*, 735–54.

47. B. Bauer, *Johannes*, 178.

48. George Lukacs, *The Young Hegel* (London: Merlin Press, 1975); H. S. Harris, *Hegel's Development*, vol. I: *Towards the Sunlight* (Oxford: Clarendon Press, 1972).

49. B. Bauer, *Johannes*, 182.

50. Ibid., 181.

51. Karl Obermann, *Deutschland von 1815 bis 1849* (Berlin: DVW, 1967), 130ff.

52. See Chapter 4.

53. B. Bauer, *I. Synoptiker*, xiv.

54. Bauer recognises as a source the work of Christian Hermann Weiße, who refutes Strauss by showing that Messianic expectations were not at hand in the first century; thus the gospels cannot be rooted in a preexisting tradition of the early Christian community. Weiße also demonstrates the chronological priority of Mark to Luke and Matthew, as Bauer (and his contemporary Ferdinand Wilhelm Wilke; see B. Bauer, *I. Synoptiker*, xiii) will also show. The deficiency of Weiße is that he accepts the authenticity of the verbal reports of the Gospels, and explains miracles as parables. He remains mired in positivity. B. Bauer, *I. Synoptiker*, v.

55. Ibid., 388.

56. Ibid., 388.

57. B. Bauer, *Kritik der evangelischen Geschichte der Synoptiker und des Johannes.* Dritter und letzter Band (Braunschweig: Fr. Otto, 1842), 6, 8. On the Messiah as a pure literary product who never existed as a concrete individual, see ibid., 14.

58. B. Bauer, *I. Synoptiker*, 25. Cf. ibid., 240–41, 307n.

59. B. Bauer, *I. Synoptiker*, 42; cf. 81.

60. B. Bauer, *III. Synoptiker*, 310, presents a dialectical demonstration of the necessity of alienation as a stage in the development of self-consciousness.

61. Bauer attributes the increase in positivity and the greater conciliatory tone of the third edition of Strauss's *Leben Jesu* to the substantiality of the basic principle, the hostile power retained within Strauss's critical theory (B. Bauer, *I. Synoptiker*, ix; 66n.). Rambaldi ascribes the changes in this edition to accidental factors, particularly the (disappointed) possibility of a chair in Zurich. Bauer's interpretation cannot readily account for the more radical fourth edition of Strauss's text.

62. In his obituary of Bauer, Engels recognises the superiority of Bauer's more radical conception, the ruthless critique of the historical pretensions of religion: Bauer "exposed the utter lack of scientific spirit of Strauss' vague myth theory according to which anybody can hold for historical as much as he likes in the Gospel narrations." F. Engels, "Bruno Bauer and Early Christianity" (May 4 and 11, 1882) in *Marx and Engels on Religion* (Moscow: 1957), 195. Arnold Ruge expresses the same opinion in *Zwei Jahre in Paris. Studien und Erinnerungen.* Zweiter Teil. (1846), 50–56. This section of Ruge's text is reproduced in Barnikol ms., Quellenteil Bd. VII, no. II, #53, pp. 1–4.

63. B. Bauer, *I. Synoptiker*, vi.

64. Ibid., vi.

65. Ibid., 69.

66. Though not the earliest. Bauer distinguishes the gospel reports from the still earlier epistles, which depict the Christian message in its essential character, revolutionary with respect to the Old Testament consciousness: namely, the unity of human and divine as enacted in the death and resurrection of Christ. See B. Bauer, *II. Synoptiker*, 45. See also B. Bauer, "Das alte neue Testament," in A. Ruge, ed., *Anekdota*, Bd. II, 192.

67. B. Bauer, *I. Synoptiker*, 127. Compare B. Bauer, *II. Synoptiker*, 45–46. On the aesthetic limitations of this literary creation, see also B. Bauer, *III. Synoptiker*, 36. Much of *Hegels Lehre* is also devoted ironically to this theme.

68. B. Bauer, *I. Synoptiker*, xxi.

69. Ibid., xxiii n.

70. Ibid., vii–viii. This formulation is very similar to Marx's characterisation of the relation of philosophy to the world as developed in the notes to his doctoral dissertation (1839–41). See Karl Marx, "Difference Between the Democritean and Epicurean Philosophy of Nature," in Karl Marx, Frederick Engels, *Collected Works*, vol. 1 (New York: International Publishers, 1975), 84–86.

71. B. Bauer, *Kritik der evangelischen Geschichte der Synoptiker.* Zweiter Band (Leipzig: Otto Wigand, 1841), 1–172.

72. Ibid., 155.

73. Ibid., 157.
74. On the person of Christ as a product of religious representation (*Vorstellung*), see B. Bauer, *III. Synoptiker*, 12, 14, 247.
75. B. Bauer, *II. Synoptiker*, 158.
76. Ibid., 159–60.
77. B. Bauer, *Hegels Lehre*, 61.
78. B. Bauer, *II. Synoptiker*, 46; cf. 108–09.
79. Ibid., 310. See also 312.
80. B. Bauer, *III Synoptiker*, 98–99, referring to Matthew 19.30 to 20.16. Note also ibid., 125 on "rendering to Caesar."
81. B. Bauer, *Religion des alten Testaments*, 160–61.
82. B. Bauer, *III. Synoptiker*, 236.
83. Ibid., 307–22.
84. Ibid., 310.

4. "Revolution and the Republic": The State and Self-Consciousness

1. For conflicting assessments of these reforms, see J. Droz, *Le romantisme allemand et l'État* (Paris: Payot, 1966), 229; and E. Schremmer, "Die Auswirkung der Bauernbefreiung hinsichtlich der bäuerlichen Verschuldung, der Gantfälle und des Besitzwechsels von Grund und Boden," in K. W. Born, ed., *Moderne deutsche Wirtschaftsgeschichte* (Berlin: Neue wissenschaftliche Bibliothek, 1966), 83. Schremmer argues that it was the agricultural crisis of the early nineteenth century, from 1809 to 1827, which prevented the peasantry from paying off its debts, so that the reforms were unable to attain their goal of a free peasantry. Droz, however, contends that the reforms were designed not to create an independent small peasantry, but to clear the land in the interests of large-scale property. The impossibly high compensation demanded by the former feudal landlords and enacted in the laws of 1809–17 and the unviable size of the resulting peasant holdings are offered as proof that the measures were intended to create a class of landless agricultural labourers through the expropriation of the peasantry.
2. Carla de Pascale, "Archäologie des Rechtsstaates," in Manfred Buhr (ed.), *Das geistige Erbe Europas* (Naples: Vivarium, 1994), 489–505.
3. In the eight Prussian provincial *Landtage*, only proprietorship of taxable landed property of ten years' duration qualified a person of non-noble birth for suffrage. See Erich Jordan, *Die Entstehung der konservativen Partei und die preußischen Agrarverhältnisse vor 1848* (München: Duncker und Humblot, 1914), 29, 144. Bruno Bauer's *Herr Dr. Hengstenberg* initiates the critique of particularism and egoism that underlies his 1841 account of self-consciousness.
4. Critique of the current institutional forms is also undertaken from the right, by elements of the traditional social order who wish to rescind all compromise with the revolutionary tendencies of modernity. They advocate a return to real or imaginary past forms, such as patriarchal monarchy (e.g. Karl von Haller, *Restauration der Staatswissenschaft*, 1816–20, the object of Hegel's visceral polemic in the *Philosophy of Right*, §258). In the *Rheinische Merkur*, Joseph von Görres proposed a modified form of the romantic theory of estates,

espoused by von Haller. He differentiated a *Lehr-*, *Wehr-*, and *Nährstand*, the first consisting of priests and educators, the second of hereditary nobility that would leave the court and return to the direct exploitation of the land, and the third of peasants, artisans, and merchants. He insisted on distinguishing his system, reflecting the predominant Catholicism of the Rhenish provinces of Prussia, from that of Adam Müller and the Schlegels (J. Droz, *Romantisme*, 200). Müller argued for a patriarchal society of decentralised feudal rule, contending that free competition led directly to the community of goods (ibid., 235). See Hans Mommsen, *Grosse und Versagen des deutschen Bürgertums. Ein Beitrag zur politischen Bewegung des neunzehnten Jahrhunderts* (Stuttgart: Deutsche Verlagsanstalt, 1949); and E. Jordan, *Enstehung der konservativen Partei*, 140.

5. Edgar Bauer, letter 22, in B. Bauer, ed., *Briefwechsel zwischen Bruno Bauer und Edgar Bauer während den Jahren 1839–1842 aus Bonn und Berlin* (Charlottenburg: Verlag von Egbert Bauer, 1844).

6. B. Bauer, *Briefwechsel*, letter 8 (February 4, 1840), 36–37.

7. The link between conservative circles in Berlin and Munich is ridiculed in Heinrich Heine's poem "Lobgesange auf König Ludwig," *Deutsch-französische Jahrbücher* (Paris: 1844), 129. On economic and social policy, see J. Gillis, "Aristocracy and Bureaucracy in Nineteenth Century Prussia," *Past and Present* 41 (1968), 105–29.

8. Gustav Meyer, "Die Anfänge des politischen Radikalismus im vormärzlichen Preußen," *Zeitschrift für Politik*, 1913, 1–113, especially 3–16.

9. For contemporary assessments of the struggle between progressive and conservative tendencies in Prussia, see also Arnold Ruge, *Preußen und die Reaktion*, 1838; "Karl Streckfuß und das Preußentum," *Hallische Jahrbücher*, November 1839; "Freiherr von Florencourt und die Kategorien der politischen Praxis," *Hallische Jahrbücher*, November 1840. For a discussion of these texts, see Enrico Rambaldi, *Le origini della sinistra hegeliana* (Florence: Nuova Italia, 1966), 33–34.

10. The official report of the University to the Ministry of Education is reproduced in Barnikol, *Bruno Bauer: Studien und Materialien*, 505–06.

11. B. Bauer, *Briefwechsel*, letter 46 (December 9, 1841), 163.

12. E. Barnikol, *Bruno Bauer: Studien und Materialien*, 504–08. Bauer's case was still being considered in correspondence between the king and minister von Arnim in December 1842 (Barnikol, *Bruno Bauer: Studien und Materialien*, 507–08), in response to Bauer's request to take up residence again in Berlin after his expulsion from Bonn.

13. Instruction of October 14, 1841, to Staats-Minister von Rochow, reproduced in E. Barnikol, *Bruno Bauer: Studien und Materialien*, 504–05.

14. Barnikol ms., Bd. VIII, #101.

15. E. Barnikol, *Bruno Bauer: Studien und Materialien*, 151, 191. On the indecisive results of the pronouncements of the various faculties, ibid., 157–92. The documents themselves are reproduced here, 482–96. Bauer's own characterisation of the *Gutachten* is contained in *Die gute Sache der Freiheit und meine eigene Angelegenheit* (Zürich und Winterthur: Verlag des literarischen Comptoirs, 1842), 225–35.

16. He was also closely linked with Schleiermacher. On Eichhorn, see Barnikol ms. Bd. VIII, no. IV, #13, #31. In his apologetic work, *Zur Beurteilung des Ministeriums Eichhorn von einem Mitglied desselben* (Berlin, 1849), Gerd Eilers attempted to deny the influence of a reactionary mediaeval party on the king and Eichhorn (p. 140). He admitted that Eichhorn considered dangerous "the popularisation of the Hegelian philosophy of God and humanity and its application to the practical field of life" (p. 135); he affirms that the Left Hegelians were correct to see Eichhorn as their principal opponent in the state. Eilers's book appeared on March 10, 1849, at the moment of consolidation of the conservative forces in Prussia against the popular revolution. Cited in Barnikol ms. Bd. VIII, no. II, #60.

17. Zvi Rosen, *Bruno Bauer and Karl Marx* (The Hague: Nijhoff, 1977), 109ff; also by the same author, "The Radicalism of a Young Hegelian," *Review of Politics* 33 (1971), 377–404, esp. 402n, 403, 404. In contrast, L. Stepelevich, "Translator's Introduction," in Bruno Bauer, *The Trumpet of the Last Judgement against Hegel the Atheist and Antichrist. An Ultimatum*, trans. L. Stepelevich (Lewiston, N.Y.: E. Mellen Press, 1989), 26–27, correctly stresses the sense of impending political crisis that informs Bruno Bauer's political reflections in 1840, and the link between the Reformation, the Enlightenment, and the French revolution that Bauer is already seeking to establish. In "The Radicalism of a Young Hegelian," 377–404, Rosen claims (a) that only *after* Bauer's discharge from the University of Bonn does he come to regard the state as opposed to liberating self-consciousness (403); (b) that Bauer sees only the religious aspect of the autocratic Prussian state (404); (c) that Bauer's toast to Welcker, a directly provocative attack on both liberal reformist constitutionalism and the autocratic state, which is the direct occasion for his dismissal from the University, expresses Bauer's view that the Prussian state is still advancing on the road to reform (403), although it is subsequent to Bauer's writing of the *Posaune*. Finally, the author comments on p. 402n.:

> Not political difficulties alone, but in a far greater measure the hope that the Prussian state would become liberal was what caused the Young Hegelians, and first of all their leader, Bauer, not only to refrain from attacking the institutions of the state and their policy, but on the contrary to launch an emotional appeal to the state to try to achieve co-operation with it to the end of introducing freedom of conscience, reducing the influence of the Church, abolishing censorship, etc.

While this characterisation may apply to Ruge and his circle in the period 1838–40, nowhere does Bauer hold such a position. Even in the *Landeskirche*, despite his praise for the Hohenzollern, he carefully advances the view that the state is in the grip of religious reaction and that science must begin the struggle against both church and state.

18. H. Mah, *The End of Philosophy and the Origin of Ideology. Karl Marx and the Crisis of the Young Hegelians* (Berkeley: University of California Press, 1987), 65–71. On p. 70, Mah incorrectly dates Bauer's public critique of Welcker and south German liberalism as occurring in September 1842, rather than September 1841.

19. R. Nola, "The Young Hegelians, Feuerbach, and Marx," in R. C. Solomon and K. M. Higgins, eds., *The Age of German Idealism. Routledge History of Philosophy*, Vol. VI (London: Routledge, 1993), 294–95.

20. H.-M. Sass characterises the *Landeskirche* as a defence of the principle of the modern state, namely, its elevation above particularistic interests and its support of the universal principle of freedom and progress. He defines the course of Bauer's development as initially conditioned more by his theological reflections than by political and social critique. H.-M. Sass, ed., *Feldzüge der reinen Kritik* (Frankfurt a. M.: Suhrkamp, 1968), "Nachwort," 227–28.

21. G.W.F. Hegel, *Science of Logic*, trans. A. V. Miller (London: Allen and Unwin, 1969), inter alia 618–19.

22. G.W.F. Hegel, *Science of Logic*, 227ff.

23. The adequacy of this reading of Hegel is not in question here. For a review of literature on this subject, see Gerhard Göhler, "Neuere Arbeiten zu Hegels Rechtsphilosophie und zur Dialektik bei Hegel und Marx," *Hegel-Studien* 17–18 (1982–83), 355–83; K. Westphal, "The Basic Context and Structure of Hegel's *Philosophy of Right*," in F. C. Beiser (ed.), *The Cambridge Companion to Hegel* (Cambridge: Cambridge University Press, 1993), 234–69.

24. Karl-Heinz Ilting has shown that earlier drafts of the 1820–21 manuscript of Hegel's *Philosophy of Right* admitted the possibility of popular sovereignty, which is absent from the published text. See G.W.F. Hegel, *Vorlesungen über Rechtsphilosophie 1818–1831*, ed. K.-H. Ilting, vols. I–IV (Stuttgart: Fromann-Holzboog, 1973–74).

25. Arnold Ruge, "Zur Kritik des gegenwärtigen Staats- und Völkerrechts" (1840), and "Die Hegelsche Rechtsphilosophie und die Politik unsrer Zeit" (1842), in G.W.F. Hegel, *Philosophie des Rechts*, ed. H. Reichelt (Frankfurt a. M.: Ullstein, 1972), 598–623, 624–49. Ruge's argument offers a parallel to that of Klaus Hartmann, "Towards a New Systematic Reading of Hegel's *Philosophy of Right*," in Z. A. Pelczynski, ed., *The State and Civil Society* (Cambridge: Cambridge University Press, 1984), 114–36.

26. Ludwig Siep, "Recht und Anerkennung," in Helmut Girndt, ed., *Selbstbehauptung und Anerkennung* (Sankt Augustin: Academia Verlag, 1990), 161–76; Michael Theunissen, "The Repressed Intersubjectivity in Hegel's *Philosophy of Right*," in Drucilla Cornell et al., eds., *Hegel and Legal Theory* (London: Routledge, 1991), 3–63.

27. This criticism touches on the complex issue of Hegel's relation to Rousseau, which cannot be addressed here. See Frederick Neuhouser, *Foundations of Hegel's Social Theory. Actualizing Freedom* (Cambridge: Harvard University Press, 2000).

28. M. C. Massey, *Christ Unmasked. The Meaning of the Life of Jesus in German Politics* (Chapel Hill: University of North Carolina Press, 1983).

29. L. Feuerbach, *Das Wesen des Christentums* (Leipzig, 1841); *The Essence of Christianity*, trans. G. Eliot (New York: Harper & Row, 1957); W. Schuffenhauer, *Feuerbach und der junge Marx* (Berlin: Deutscher Verlag der Wissenschaften, 1972); Larry Johnston, *Between Transcendence and Nihilism. Species-Ontology in the Philosophy of Ludwig Feuerbach* (New York: Peter Lang, 1995). Warren Breckman, "Ludwig Feuerbach and the Political Theology of Restoration,"

History of Political Thought, 13/3, 1992, 437–62, offers a discussion of Stahl (438–42), and of Feuerbach's critique of the Restoration use of religion (445–50). Breckman also stresses the importance of Hegel's *Philosophy of Right* for Feuerbach (454, 460). Feuerbach conceives a political economy based on the satisfaction of need, rather than capital accumulation, and a new conception of community based on solidarity, rather than competition. Finding a "principle of social union within civil society" (460) itself, Feuerbach can then dispense with what Breckman calls Hegel's disciplinary state.

30. W. Schuffenhauer, *Feuerbach und der junge Marx*, 88–131.

31. Karl Marx, "On the Jewish Question," and "Economic and Philosophical Manuscripts of 1844," in Karl Marx, Frederick Engels, *Collected Works*, vol. 3 (New York: International Publishers, 1975), 146–74, 270–82.

32. The split between republicanism and socialism is the political basis of Marx's polemics against Bauer in 1844–45. See Karl Marx and Frederick Engels, "The Holy Family, or Critique of Critical Criticism," *Collected Works*, vol. 4 (New York: International Publishers, 1975), 78–154; and Chapter 8 of the present work.

33. Bruno Bauer, "'Einleitung in die Dogmengeschichte,' von Theodor Kliefoth," in A. Ruge, ed., *Anekdota zur neuesten deutschen Philosophie und Publizistik*, vol. II (Zürich und Winterthur: Verlag des literarischen Comptoirs, 1843), 150.

34. On Bauer's republican rigorism, see Chapter 7.

35. The *Posaune* was composed in August 1841 and published in October of that year. H.-A. Baatsch, "Introduction," in B. Bauer, *La trompette du dernier jugement contre Hegel, L'Athée et l'Antéchrist. Un ultimatum* (Paris: Aubier-Montaigne, 1972), 16, mistakenly places Bauer's expulsion from the University of Bonn (March 1842) in the period of composition of this text.

36. Bauer's biblical criticism produces converging results; but the political dimension of this criticism has not received sufficient attention. See J. E. Toews, *Hegelianism. The Path toward Dialectical Humanism* (Cambridge: Cambridge University Press, 1980), 288–326; and by the same author, "Transformations of Hegelianism," in Beiser (ed.), *The Cambridge Companion to Hegel*, 391–403. Toews demonstrates that Bauer's stress on the dialectical synthesis of singularity (or personality, as Toews refers to it) emerges in his critique of D. F. Strauss's tradition hypothesis; and he illustrates Bauer's development of the idea of egoism from 1838 onwards.

37. See B. Bauer, *Briefwechsel*, letters 19 and 26 (May 8, 1840, and July 3, 1840), 74–75, 98–99. Bauer published *Die Landeskirche* anonymously through Otto Wigand in Leipzig in 1840; the second edition bore Bauer's name. On December 15, 1841, its dissemination in Prussia was forbidden (Barnikol ms., Bd. III, No. 47, pp. 12–14).

38. B. Bauer, *Briefwechsel*, letter 26 (July 3, 1840), 97.

39. K. F. Köppen, *Friedrich der Grosse und seine Widersacher* (Leipzig: 1840). See also Rambaldi, *Origini*, 55–56.

40. B. Bauer, *Landeskirche*, 104.

41. B. Bauer, *Briefwechsel*, letter 8 (February 4, 1840), 36–37 (also cited in Barnikol, *Bruno Bauer, Studien und Materialien*, 39n). This letter calls into

question some aspects of Stepelevich's reading of the *Landeskirche*. Though he identifies its progressive political message and its critical thrust against the regime of Friedrich Wilhelm IV, he contends that Bauer still sees the alliance of church and state as based upon a deception rather than a fundamental unity of interests. This formulation might imply that Bauer believes that the existing state is capable of reforming itself. See L. Stepelevich, "Translator's Introduction," 26.

42. Perry Anderson, *Lineages of the Absolutist State* (London: New Left Books, 1974), 236, 247–52; and Geoffrey Barraclough, *The Origins of Modern Germany* (New York: Capricorn, 1963), 387–96, 406–14. Both stress the distinction between the classical form of mediaeval feudal monarchy, characterised by decentralisation of power and rents, and the absolutist form of the seventeenth to nineteenth centuries, based on the subjection of the peasantry to a consolidated political centre, the reduction in autonomy of the towns, and the centralisation of rents in the form of taxes. At the same time, for fiscal and military reasons, these states must co-operate with new productive ventures of a capitalist type. On the bureaucratic-military ideology and practice accompanying this transition, see Hans Rosenberg, *Bureaucracy, Aristocracy and Autocracy: The Prussian Experience* (Boston: Beacon, 1958), 27–45, 202–28. J. Gillis, "Aristocracy and Bureaucracy in Nineteenth-Century Prussia," *Past and Present* 41 (1968), 105–29, on the aristocratic reaction and the state as a supplementary source of Junker incomes.

43. Cf. K.-H. Ilting, "Die 'Rechtsphilosophie' von 1820 und Hegels Vorlesungen über Rechtsphilosophie," in G.W.F. Hegel, *Vorlesungen über Rechtsphilosophie 1818–1831*, ed. K.-H. Ilting, vol. I, 25–126.

44. "Bekenntnisse einer schwachen Seele" is an anonymous article appearing in *Deutsche Jahrbücher*, June 23–24, 1842; reprinted in H.-M. Sass, ed., *Feldzüge der reinen Kritik*, 71–90, p. 86. The latter collection, titled by the editor, contains articles published by Bauer in the *Hallische* and *Deutsche Jahrbücher* and *Allgemeine Literatur-Zeitung* between June 1841 and April 1844. The Ruge correspondence (Barnikol ms., Quellenteil, No. 14. 18, letter of April 24, 1842) establishes Bauer's authorship of "Bekenntnisse."

45. B. Bauer, *Landeskirche*, 30, 54–55.

46. Ibid., 55.

47. B. Bauer, *Das entdeckte Christentum*, 161.

48. B. Bauer, *Landeskirche*, 66. Bauer's language echoes St. Paul's First Letter to the Corinthians, ch. 13, v. 4–7.

49. B. Bauer, *Landeskirche*, 107–08.

50. Ibid., 107–08.

51. Ibid., 99.

52. P. Landau, "Hegels Begründung des Vertragsrechts," in Manfred Riedel, ed., *Materialien zu Hegels Rechtsphilosophie*, Bd. II (Frankfurt/M.: Suhrkamp Verlag, 1975), 179.

53. G.W.F. Hegel, *Philosophie des Rechts*, §1–79.

54. B. Bauer, *Landeskirche*, 104–05, 136.

55. Ibid., 50.

56. For example, Bruno Bauer, *Die Judenfrage* (Braunschweig: Fr. Otto, 1843), 8.

57. Stahl, with Leo and Savigny, was the principal proponent of the Historical School of Law. He was called to the University of Berlin by Friedrich Wilhelm IV; his inaugural address on November 26, 1840, sparked hostile student demonstrations. See H.-M. Sass, "Nachwort," 235.

58. B. Bauer, "Der christliche Staat und unsere Zeit," in *Feldzüge der reinen Kritik*, 19. See also the discussion of this text in H.-M. Sass, "Nachwort," 228–31.

59. B. Bauer, "Der christliche Staat," 20.

60. On the former usage, see C. de Pascale, "Archäologie"; on the latter, "Staat und Souveranität," in O. Brunner, W. Conze, R. Koselleck, eds., *Geschichtliche Grundbegriffe* (Stuttgart: Klett, 1990), Bd. VI, 76–77.

61. O. Brunner et al., "Staat und Souveranität," 60.

62. Cf. B. Bauer, *Die gute Sache der Freiheit und meine eigene Angelegenheit* (Zürich und Winterthur: Verlag des literarischen Comptoirs, 1842), 199.

63. B. Bauer, *Posaune*, 56–58, 117–27.

64. In a letter to Marx dated June 3, 1841, K. F. Köppen suggests that Bauer had borrowed from Marx the idea that the Byzantine state is the genuine Christian political form. (K. Marx, F. Engels, *Historisch-kritische Gesamtausgabe*, ed. D. Ryazanov [Berlin: Marx-Engels Verlag, 1929] I, 1, 2, pp. 255, 257.) The Barnikol ms., Bd. IV , No. 42, pp. 12–13, notes that Bauer was invited by Arnold Ruge to write the review in December 1840, after Bauer's two-month sojourn in Berlin (September–November), where he was frequently in Marx's company. Bauer then wrote the review in Bonn in April 1841, but his intervening correspondence with Marx contains no substantive discussion of the question. Barnikol suggests the possibility that Marx's own report of his conversations with Bauer might be at the root of Köppen's supposition. In Bd. IV, No. 47, p. 16, Barnikol observes, "On the whole, Bruno Bauer's Bonn letters prove his complete intellectual independence from Karl Marx."

65. B. Bauer, "Der christliche Staat," 9–14. On pp. 9–10 of this article (p. 538 in the original) Bauer describes the opium-like influence [*opiumartigen Einfluß*] of theology. In 1842, in *Die Gute Sache*, 212–13, he generalises this effect to all religious experience. Marx adopts the phrase in "Contribution to the Critique of Hegel's Philosophy of Law: Introduction" (1843), in K. Marx, F. Engels, *Collected Works*, vol. 3, 175.

66. B. Bauer, "Der christliche Staat," 41.

67. Ibid., 26.

68. Ibid., 23–24.

69. Ibid., 23.

70. Ibid., 26.

71. Ibid., 33.

5. "Only the Ought Is True": Hegel, Self-Consciousness, and Revolution

1. Bruno Bauer (anon.), *Die Posaune des jüngsten Gerichts über Hegel, den Atheisten und, Antichristen. Ein Ultimatum* (Leipzig: Otto Wigand, 1841).

2. H. M. Sass, "Bruno Bauer's Critical Theory," 99, 106.

3. B. Bauer, *Posaune*, 35–36.

4. Notable among these critics were Ernst Hengstenberg, whom Bauer had already attacked in 1839. Bauer now ironically assumes Hengstenberg's posture that Hegel's teachings were atheistic and disruptive of social tranquillity.

5. Heinrich Leo, *Die Hegelingen. Actenstücke und Belege zu der sogenannten Denunciation der ewigen Wahrheit* (Halle, 1838; second edition, 1839).

6. G.W.F. Hegel, *Werke*, Bd. 11: *Vorlesungen über die Philosophie der Religion*, Bd. 1 (Berlin, 1840). Bauer mentions in his correspondence of March 15, 1840, that the volume "can scarcely have appeared" (*Briefwechsel zwischen Bruno Bauer und Edgar Bauer während der Jahre 1839–1842 aus Bonn und Berlin* [Charlottenburg: Verlag von Egbert Bauer, 1844], letter 12, 48–49). He indicates that he resumed work on Hegel's text in October 1839, as he was preparing his *Johanneskritik* (*Briefwechsel*, letter No. 1 [October 21, 1839]) and experiencing his transition to atheism. These letters are also cited in E. Barnikol, *Bruno Bauer: Studien und Materialien*, ed. P. Reimer and H. M. Sass (Assen: Van Gorcum, 1972), 193. Bauer edited this text in collaboration with Philipp Marheineke, who had published the first edition of Hegel's *Philosophy of Religion* in 1832. Barnikol suggests (*Bruno Bauer*, 195) that discrepancies between Bauer's citations of Hegel's *Philosophy of Religion* and the text of the second edition might be attributable to Marheineke's editorial revision of the latter. Marheineke is described as a leader of university protest against the theoretical reaction after 1840 (Karl Obermann, *Deutschland von 1815 bis 1849* [Berlin: DVW, 1967], 131ff). He defended Bauer during the latter's dismissal from the University of Bonn in 1842. In *Die gute Sache der Freiheit und meine eigene Angelegenheit* (Zürich und Winterthur: Verlag des literarischen Comptoirs, 1842), 92, however, Bauer attacks Marheineke's tendency to vacillation and compromise.

7. Zvi Rosen, *Bruno Bauer and Karl Marx* (The Hague: Nijhoff, 1978), 63, cites some of this literature. There appears to be an error in his footnote 7 on the same page. The text refers to an article appearing in "Hengstenberg's Church Journal," which would be the *Evangelische Kirchenzeitung*, while in the note in question Rosen cites instead an article from the Left-Hegelian journal *Deutsche Jahrbücher* 136–38 (1842), 543, edited by Arnold Ruge. Bauer's first mention of the text occurs in a letter to his brother Edgar on August 16, 1841 (*Briefwechsel*, letter 44, 155), where he states, "Until my departure [end of August] I am preparing a great denunciation of Hegel; it is something of a trumpet blast [*posaunenmässig*] and should bring him only advantage." Ruedi Waser, *Autonomie des Selbstbewußtseins. Eine Untersuchung zum Verhältnis von Bruno Bauer und Karl Marx (1835–1843)* (Tübingen: Francke Verlag, 1994), cites this passage in two places. The first reference (p. 27) omits the important second clause. The second reference occurs twice on page 29, once omitting the first clause, and interpreting "him" as a reference to Wigand, and not to Hegel, as is manifest from the context; and once in full, but without comment. The advantage of the book to Wigand, Waser asserts (p. 29–30), can refer only to his sales figures. Waser wishes to dismiss the *Posaune* as evidence for Bauer's interpretation of Hegel, but he presents no compelling argument for this position.

8. Z. Rosen, *Bauer and Marx*, 63, thinks that Ruge too was deceived by the pietist veneer of the text. The first mention of the *Posaune* in the Bauer/Ruge correspondence occurs in Bauer's letter of December 6, 1841 (Ernst Barnikol, *Bruno Bauer*, Manuscript, International Institute for Social History, Amsterdam, "Brief an Arnold Ruge," #14, 11; also reproduced in *Marx-Engels Gesamtausgabe* 1, 1/2, 263–64). Another letter followed on December 24 (Barnikol ms., #14, 12; *MEGA* 1, 1/2, 265); both of these are some two months subsequent to the publication of the text. However, in a letter of August 17, 1841, to Ruge (Barnikol ms., #14, 9), Bauer informs Ruge of his plan to visit him in Dresden in the second half of September, where he has much to relate to him. That the plans for the *Posaune* were discussed at that time or at least prior to the publication of the text is suggested by Ruge's enthusiastic correspondence with Stahr, Prutz, Michelet, Werner, and Ludwig Feuerbach (Barnikol ms., *Quellenteil*, 13. 2. 9 [f] [g] [h] [i] [j], November 1841), where no doubt is expressed over the political tendency of the *Posaune*. On December 17, 1841, Ruge wrote to Fleischer in Cleves, "You will read the *Posaune* with pleasure and guess the author easily, since you have him very close by [Bauer was then resident in Bonn. DM]. For it is totally impossible to mystify anyone at all with this form. A real pietist could never in his life get so much out of Hegel" (Barnikol ms., *Quellenteil*, 23, 2, 9 [k]; also in P. Nerrlich, *Arnold Ruges Briefwechsel und Tagebuchblätter aus den Jahren 1825–1880*, Bd. 1 [Berlin, 1886], 154–55). Rosen cites 247 of Nerrlich's text (63, note #8), but seems to miss these crucial references and their implications. There is no explicit mention of the text in Ruge's correspondence in the month of October, but a letter to Fleischer dated October 16, 1841, explains the central doctrine of the *Posaune*, the derivation of religious consciousness from self-consciousness (Barnikol ms., *Quellenteil*, 13. 2. 9 [d]), implying close familiarity with Bauer's theoretical development. It is noteworthy that Ludwig Feuerbach, on the other hand, seems unaware of the identity of the author of the *Posaune*, but not of its political and theoretical tendency, in a letter to the *Augsburger Allgemeine Zeitung*, December 1841, where he insists on a difference between his own approach and that of the anonymous author: The latter is not directed *against* Hegel (therefore Feuerbach is not of the opinion that the text is pietistic), whereas his own method is directly opposed because it is based on the "simple truth of nature" against all forms of idealism, including that of the *Posaune* (Barnikol ms., *Quellenteil* 23, 2, 23 [a]; also reproduced in Karl Grün, *Ludwig Feuerbachs Philosophische Charakerentwicklung. Sein Briefwechsel und Nachlass 1820–1850* [Berlin, 1874], 340). Finally, Barnikol's remarks on postal censorship (*Bruno Bauer*, 48, 63) help to explain why references to Bauer's authorship of the *Posaune* are not more explicit.

9. See the announcement of the publication of the *Posaune* in *Deutsche Jahrbücher für Wissenschaft und Kunst*, No. 120, November 18, 1841. Wigand had just issued the first two volumes of Bauer's *Critique of the Synoptics*.

10. B. Bauer, *Die Gute Sache*, 92. The *Posaune* was banned and confiscated in Prussia on December 15, 1841 (Barnikol ms., Bd. 1, #47).

11. B. Bauer, *Posaune*, 163.

12. W. Schuffenhauer, *Feuerbach und der junge Marx* (Berlin: DVW, 1972), 53. F. Engels, "Ludwig Feuerbach and the End of Classical German Philosophy," in K. Marx and F. Engels, *Selected Works* (New York: International, 1968), 602.

13. Rosen, *Bauer and Marx*, 74–75, 83, 170, 216, suggests misinterpretation through error or negligence, although he also mentions certain "pragmatic considerations" (76: elimination of religion, development of freedom, etc.) that condition the Bauerian approach. He sees Bauer deviating from his atheistic interpretation of Hegel in 1845 (101).

14. *Briefwechsel*, letter 12 (March 15, 1840, 50), also cited in Barnikol, *Bruno Bauer*, 195.

15. Ibid., citing *Briefwechsel*, 50. Bauer gives a clear account of his critical procedure in *Kritik der evangelischen Geschichte der Synoptiker*, vol. 1 (Leipzig: O. Wigand, 1841), xxi; and in "Rezension: Bremisches Magazin für evangelische Wahrheit gegenüber dem modernen Pietismus," in A. Ruge, ed., *Anekdota zur neuesten deutschen Philosophie und Publizistik*, vol. 2 (Zürich und Winterthur: Verlag des literarischen Comptoirs, 1843), 131.

16. For a more sober recent assessment of Hegel's rejection of liberalism and conservatism from a politically progressive perspective, see Domenico Losurdo, *Hegel et les libéraux* (Paris: PUF, 1992).

17. See Introduction to the present work.

18. B. Bauer, *Die Posaune*, 6.

19. Ibid., 74.

20. On fideism, see B. Bauer, "Theologische Schamlosigkeiten," *Deutsche Jahrbücher far Wissenschaft und Kunst*, 117–20 (November 15–18, 1841), 465–79.

21. On theological rationalism, see B. Bauer, "Rezension: *Einleitung in die Dogmengeschichte*, von Theodor Kliefoth," *Anekdota*, vol. 2, 140, 154.

22. B. Bauer, *Die Posaune*, 44.

23. This passage is also translated in L. S. Stepelevich, ed., *The Young Hegelians: An Anthology* (Cambridge: Cambridge University Press, 1983), 177. Stepelevich translates *Wälschen* as "wild men," rather than as French, foreigners, or indeed Gauls, all of which are lexically more correct. Luther's usage of *Wälschen* as the French, with derogatory connotation, is established in *Grimm's Deutsches Wörterbuch*, vol. 13 (Leipzig, 1922), 1332, 1338. Compare Bauer's use of the term in "Die deutschen Nationalen" (1842), reproduced in Pepperle, *Die Hegelsche Linke*, 411.

24. B. Bauer, *Die Posaune*, 43.

25. Ibid., 52–54, 57.

26. Ibid., 42.

27. Ibid., 47, 48.

28. Ibid., 45 and *passim*. In this respect Bauer's argument resembles that of Hegel's first writings. See George Lukacs, *The Young Hegel* (London: Merlin, 1975), 74–145.

29. B. Bauer, *Die Posaune*, 137.

30. Ibid., 57–59, 63–64, 137–49.

31. Ibid., 139.

32. Ibid., 140.

33. Ibid., 142–43. This question is treated in greater detail in Bauer's anonymous continuation of the *Posaune, Hegels Lehre von der Religion und Kunst von dem Standpuncte des Glaubens aus beurtheilt* (Leipzig: Otto Wigand, 1842), 138–57, 222–27.

34. B. Bauer, *Die Posaune*, 95–105.

35. Ibid., 146.

36. Bruno Bauer, *Das entdeckte Christenthum* (Zürich und Winterthur: Verlag des literarischen Comptoirs, 1843), 37.

37. B. Bauer, *Die Posaune*, 142.

38. Ibid., 68.

39. Ibid., 45, 81.

40. Ibid., 5–13, 43–45, 79–96, 117–27.

41. Ibid., 80, 81. Cf. Claudio Cesa, *Studi sulla Sinistra hegeliana* (Urbino: Argalia, 1972), 303–05, 319.

42. B. Bauer, *Die Posaune*, 82.

43. B. Bauer, "Die christliche Glaubenslehre, von D. F. Strauss. Rezension," *Deutsche Jahrbucher*, no. 21–24, January 25–28, 1843, pp. 81–95.

44. Ibid., 82–83.

45. Ibid., 85.

46. Ibid., 85.

47. Bruno Bauer, "Charakteristik Ludwig Feuerbachs," *Wigands Vierteljahrschrift* III (1845), 86–88.

48. See Epilogue in the present work.

49. B. Bauer, *Prinzipien*, 107b.

50. B. Bauer, *Die Posaune*, 68, 70, 80–85, 120–22, 163–68.

51. B. Bauer, *Das entdeckte Christenthum*, 108ff.

52. B. Bauer, *Religion des Alten Testaments* (Berlin, 1838), discussed by H. M. Sass, "Bruno Bauer's Critical Theory," 93.

53. G.W.F. Hegel, *Lectures on the Philosophy of World History. Introduction: Reason in History*, translated by H. B. Nisbet (Cambridge: Cambridge University Press, 1975), 147.

54. Notably in Bauer's contributions to the *Anekdota*, vol. 2. See Chapter 6.

55. D. Koigen, *Zur Vorgeschichte des modernen philosophischen Sozialismus in Deutschland* (Bern, 1901), 48. Rosen, *Bauer and Marx*, 84, correctly argues that Fichte is not decisive for Bauer's reading of Hegel. Cesa, *Sinistra hegeliana*, 306n., also denies a direct Fichtean influence: It is not Fichte's philosophy, but the Fichtean element in Hegel that Bauer develops. This position is consistent with Bauer's own argumentation in "Charackteristik Ludwig Feuerbachs," 86–88.

56. B. Bauer (anon.), *Die evangelische Landeskirche Preussens und die Wissenschaft* (Leipzig: O. Wigand, 1840). This text was banned at the same time as the *Posaune*.

57. Private economic interest and religious particularity have an identical theoretical, logical structure but a different systematic place in the historical dialectic, the former being the modern form of particularity. Rosen, *Bauer and Marx*, proposes a more constrictive interpretation of egoism as primarily the religious consciousness, thereby minimising Bauer's critique of possessive

individualism, which is central to his conception of revolution and of modern mass society.

58. B. Bauer, *Die Posaune*, 99, 100. See also B. Bauer "Leiden und Freuden des theologischen Bewußtseins" in *Anekdota*, vol. 2, 89–112.

59. Here the basis of Bauer's differences with Stirner is apparent. Bauer takes as a symptom of the modern crisis what Stirner sees as its solution, the unbridled assertion of particular interest.

60. L. Baronovitch, "Two Appendices to a Doctoral Dissertation: Some New Light on the Origin of Karl Marx's Dissociation from Bruno Bauer and the Young Hegelians," *Philosophical Review* 8 (1978), 234.

61. B. Bauer, *I. Synoptiker*, vi. Rosen makes a similar point, *Bauer and Marx*, 73–84, without, however, stressing the complex and subtle dialectical process by which Bauer develops his concept of universal self-consciousness.

62. Cf. B. Bauer, "Die Fähigkeit der heutigen Juden und Christen, frei zu werden," in G. Herwegh, ed., *Einundzwanzig Bogen aus der Schweiz* (Zürich und Winterthur: Verlag des literarischen Comptoirs, 1843), 56–71; B. Bauer, *I. Synoptiker*, vii–viii.

63. Manfred Buhr, *Revolution und Philosophie* (Berlin: DVW, 1965), 51–53.

64. B. Bauer, *Johannes*, 178–79.

65. B. Bauer, *Prinzipien*, 111a.

66. B. Bauer, *I. Synoptiker*, 69.

67. Ibid., 69; cf. Hegel, *Die Phänomenologie des Geistes*, 330. Rosen, *Bauer and Marx*, 57, cites this passage from *I. Synoptiker* as a simple contradiction with Bauer's general outlook on the universality of self-consciousness.

68. Cf. B. Bauer, *I. Synoptiker*, xxiii n.: "The true positive can only be born when the negation has been serious and universal"; and B. Bauer, *Herr Dr. Hengstenberg*, 6: "Everything positive is as such posited in opposition, is in itself negative."

69. B. Bauer, *Die Posaune*, 82.

70. Ibid., 56–58, 117–27, where the problem of reformism is already clearly posed.

71. This characterisation persists from *Die gute Sache* (1842), to *Vollständige Geschichte der Parteikämpfe in Deutschland* (1846).

72. Bauer's articles of the summer of 1842 are particularly devoted to this problem. See Chapter 6.

73. B. Bauer, *Die Posaune*, 167.

74. Ibid., 166.

75. Ibid., 164, textually the "Verdachtssystem der Jakobiner."

76. B. Bauer, "Bekenntnisse," 86.

6. "To the People Belongs the Future": Universal Right and History

1. Bruno Bauer [anon.], *Hegels Lehre von der Religion und Kunst von dem Standpuncte des Glaubens aus beurtheilt* (Leipzig: Otto Wigand, 1842).

2. Bauer to Ruge, December 6 and December 24, 1841, Barnikol ms., Quellenteil, #14, 11; #14, 12.

3. B. Bauer, *Posaune*, 163n.

4. B. Bauer, *Hegels Lehre*, 69–70.

5. Claudio Cesa, *Studi sulla Sinistra hegeliana* (Urbino: Argalia, 1972), suggests the possible influence of Feuerbach's *Wesen des Christentums* on *Hegels Lehre*, where he finds a tension between materialist and idealist elements, and of *Das entdeckte Christenthum*, where, in contrast to Feuerbach, Bauer attempts to synthesise nature and society as moments of the higher unity of self-consciousness (311ff). Cesa's case that prior to the completion of the *Posaune* Bauer was unfamiliar with Feuerbach's book (311 and note) is weakened slightly by an inaccurate dating of the latter publication; Cesa places it in August 1841, whereas it appeared in June of that year. See W. Mönke, *Die Heilige Familie. Zur ersten Gemeinschaftsarbeit von Karl Marx und Friedrich Engels* (Glashütten im Taunus: Akademie Verlag 1972), 58 and note 175. If we take Bauer to defend a Hegelian unity of thought and being, the tension Cesa observes between (subjective) idealism and materialism disappears.

6. B. Bauer, *Hegels Lehre*, 61.

7. Ibid., 48–49.

8. This text was published in Zürich and Winterthur by Verlag des literarischen Comptoirs, 1842. Marx observed of this text that Bauer had never written better. *Marx-Engels Gesamtausgabe* 1, 2, 308.

9. B. Bauer, *Gute Sache*, 185.

10. Ibid., 23.

11. For the following, Ibid., 113–18.

12. Z. Rosen, *Bruno Bauer and Karl Marx*, 72, argues that Bauer wants to sever the link that Hegel establishes between subject and object. Similarly, David Koigen, *Zur Vorgeschichte des modernen philosophischen Sozialismus in Deutschland* (Bern: Stürzenegger, 1901), 42:

> Bauer's philosophy is nothing but the Hegelian concept, which here exists for itself. Basically it represents an ideal form of our activity of understanding, which is cut off from all substance, that unconditioned component of our knowledge. From our standpoint, this concept is thereby transformed into a capricious abstraction.

13. Attempts such as those of Löwith to link Bauer and Nietzsche must take account of Bauer's rebuttal of the role of genius in history. For Bauer, the particular consciousness that elevates itself to universality through its creative endeavours is not motivated by a drive for power or self-assertion; it is not egoism in another form. He asserts:

> The cult of genius is the last attempt to stain free human relationships with a religious tincture. It is the last effort of religion, once it has been cast out of its chimerical world, to retain itself in the real world. It is the reversal of human freedom within its inner world, its reversal ... into transcendence and estrangement (B. Bauer, *Die gute Sache*, 120).

14. Cf. the depiction of Protestantism in *Landeskirche*, Chapter 4.

15. B. Bauer, *Gute Sache*, 13.

16. Ibid., 92, for Bauer's admission of his authorship of the *Posaune*.

17. Ibid., 203. Religion is characterised as "*Opium-rausch*," 213.

18. Ibid., 217. Cf. Z. Rosen, *Bruno Bauer and Karl Marx*, 85ff, 162ff.

19. B. Bauer, *Gute Sache*, 218–19.

20. Ibid., 13.

21. Ibid., 15, 27.

22. Ibid., 33.

23. Ibid., 202, 206.

24. Ibid., 203–04.

25. Ibid., 220.

26. Ibid., 204–05.

27. Ibid., 220.

28. Ibid., 199.

29. In contrast, Z. Rosen, *Bruno Bauer and Karl Marx*, 80, contends that egoism for Bauer is above all religious. While Bauer believes the consequences of religious alienation and its overcoming to be far-reaching, he also shows it to be a species of private interest, linked to other types of particularism.

30. B. Bauer, *Gute Sache*, 199, 224. In passages like this Marx finds evidence of a hypostasis of history in Bauer. See "The Holy Family," in Karl Marx, Frederick Engels, *Collected Works*, vol. 4 (New York: International Publishers, 1975), 93. I take the description of history as being beyond purposive calculation to be not a repudiation of Bauer's historical idealism but simply a reference to the unforeseeable consequences of ethical action.

31. See, for example, B. Bauer, *Gute Sache*, 20.

32. Ibid., 221–22. Cf. Kant, "An Answer to the Question: 'What Is Enlightenment'" in H. Reiss (ed.), *Kant's Political Writings* (Cambridge: Cambridge University Press, 1970), 54–60.

33. B. Bauer, *Gute Sache*, 223–24.

34. Ibid., 33.

35. Ibid., 119.

36. Barnikol ms. #127, p. 2.

37. Dieter Hertz-Eichenrode, *Der Junghegelianer Bruno Bauer im Vormärz*. Inauguraldissertation (Berlin: Freie Universität, 1959), 86–87. See also H.-M. Sass, "Bruno Bauers Idee der *Rheinischen Zeitung*," *Zeitschrift für Religions- und Geistesgeschichte* 19 (1967), 221–76.

38. B. Bauer, "Die deutschen Sympathien für Frankreich," *Rheinische Zeitung*, Beiblatt, no. 37, February 6, 1842 (dated Paris, January 23).

39. B. Bauer, "Über die neuesten Erscheinungen in der englischen Kirche," *Rheinische Zeitung*, Beiblatt, no. 20, Jan. 20, 1842 (dated London, January 8).

40. B. Bauer, "Lebensbilder aus den Befreiungskriege," *Rheinische Zeitung*, Beiblatt, no. 60, March 1, 1842.

41. B. Bauer, "Lebensbilder aus den Befreiungskriege," *Rheinische Zeitung*, Beiblatt, no. 65, 72, 90, March 6, 13, 31, 1842. See also B. Bauer, "Joseph II und die belgische Revolution," *Rheinische Zeitung*, Beiblatt, no. 72, March 13, 1842.

42. B. Bauer, "Kirche und Staats-Gouvernement," *Rheinische Zeitung*, Beiblatt, no. 88, March 29, 1842.

43. B. Bauer, "*Preussen, seine Verfassung, seine Verwaltung, sein Verhältnis zu Deutschland*. von Bülow-Cummerow. Berlin 1842," *Rheinische Zeitung*, Beiblatt, no. 97, April 7, 1842.

44. B. Bauer, "Die deutschen 'Nationalen,' " *Rheinische Zeitung*, Beiblatt, no. 69, March 10, 1842. He adds that *German* is not an ethnic but a cultural term. It is thus not exclusive or racialist.

45. B. Bauer, "Eine der Tendenzen der Augsburger Allgemeinen Zeitung," *Rheinische Zeitung*, Beiblatt, no. 86, March 27, 1842; "Die Kollisionen in den konstitutionellen Staaten," *Rheinische Zeitung*, Beiblatt, no. 86, March 27, 1842.

46. B. Bauer, "Die deutschen Sympathien fur Frankreich."

47. See, for example, Mario Rossi, *Da Hegel a Marx III: La Scuola hegeliana. Il giovane Marx*, 2nd edition (Milan: Feltrinelli, 1974), 115-16, 120.

48. David McLellan, *The Young Hegelians and Karl Marx* (Toronto: Macmillan, 1969), 74-75.

49. On Ruge, see W. Neher, *Arnold Ruge als Politiker und politischer Schriftsteller* (Heidelberg, 1933).

50. B. Bauer, *Die gute Sache*, 1.

51. B. Bauer, "Kliefoth," 140.

52. B. Bauer, "von Ammon," 162.

53. In *Geschichte der Politik, Kultur und Aufklärung des achtzehnten Jahrhunderts. Fortsetzung: Deutschland während der Zeit der französischen Revolution*. Erste Abteilung (Charlottenburg: Egbert Bauer, 1844), 78, Bauer gives the following characterisation of the counterrevolutionary conservatism of Burke and his German followers, such as Gentz, from which the historical school of law originated: "According to this conception, man is nothing for history. He has no right over his creations – naturally, since he cannot create. What arises stems from a power alien to him, and if it is ever to expire, should only die of old age."

54. B. Bauer, *Die gute Sache*, 2.

55. Ibid., 3.

56. B. Bauer, "Theologische Schamlosigkeiten," *Deutsche Jahrbücher*, November 15-18, 1841, No. 117-20, pp. 465-79. B. Bauer, *Gute Sache*, 183, characterises as shameless the violent opposition in which the theological consciousness stands to philosophical science. The text was written in October 1841. See B. Bauer to A. Ruge, Barnikol ms., #14, 10, letter of October 19, 1841. The article is reproduced in Sass (ed.), *Feldzüge*, 44-69. Page references in the succeeding notes are to the Sass edition.

57. B. Bauer, "Schamlosigkeiten," 55-56.

58. Ibid., 44-53.

59. Ibid., 54-57.

60. Ibid., 56-62.

61. Ibid., 62-65. Further on Schleiermacher, see B. Bauer, "*Einleitung in die Dogmengeschichte*, von Theodor Kliefoth," in A. Ruge, ed., *Anekdota zur neuesten deutschen Philosophie und Publizistik* (Zürich und Winterthur: Verlag des literarischen Comtoirs, 1843), Bd. II, 157.

62. B. Bauer, "Schamlosigkeiten," 65-69.

63. Hegel, *Philosophy of Right*, §258, pp. 278-81.

64. B. Bauer, "Schamlosigkeiten," 54-56.

65. Ruge correspondence, Barnikol ms., No. 14, 13, letter of January 9, 1842. The article was first published in Arnold Ruge, ed., *Anekdota*, Bd. II, 89-112.

The text is structured as a commentary on chapter IV, §212–30 of Hegel's *Phenomenology* (Miller translation).

66. B. Bauer, "Leiden und Freuden," 89.
67. Ibid., 91.
68. Ibid., 89.
69. Ibid., 91.
70. Ibid., 94.
71. Ibid., 92.
72. Ibid., 111.
73. Ibid., 111.
74. No reference to this text could be found in the Ruge correspondence, Barnikol ms. It occupies pp. 113–34 of *Anekdota*, volume II.
75. B. Bauer, "Bremisches Magazin," 131.
76. Ibid., 132.
77. Again, the Ruge correspondence is silent on the date of composition. The text appears in *Anekdota*, volume II, 135–59.
78. B. Bauer, "Kliefoth," 150.
79. Ibid., 150.
80. Cf. Edgar Bauer, *Die liberalen Bestrebungen*, 29–47, 54–55.
81. B. Bauer, "Kliefoth," 150.
82. Ibid., 140.
83. An anonymous article appearing in *Deutsche Jahrbücher*, June 23–24, 1842, No. 148–49, pp. 589–96; reprinted in Sass (ed.), *Feldzüge*, 71–90. The Ruge correspondence (Barnikol ms., no. 14, 18, letter of April 24, 1842) establishes Bauer's authorship. Pagination in the succeeding footnotes is from Sass.
84. Cf. the observations in P.-L. Assoun and G. Raulet, *Marxisme et théorie critique* (Paris: Payot, 1978), 40, 50, 53, on the early Marx, who adopts a similar stance.
85. B. Bauer, "Bekenntnisse," 81–82.
86. Ibid., 85–86. Note that the pseudo-reformers whom Bauer is here criticising anticipate the denunciations of the Hegelian Left by Haym after the defeat of the Revolutions of 1848. See Rudolf Haym, *Hegel und seine Zeit* (Berlin: Gaertner, 1857).
87. B. Bauer, "Bekenntnisse," 86.
88. Ibid., 71.
89. "Die Geschichte des Lebens Jesu mit steter Rücksicht auf die vorhandenen Quellen, dargestellt von Dr. von Ammon. Erster Band. Leipzig 1842. Vogel. Rec. von B. Bauer," *Anekdota*, volume II, 160–85.
90. B. Bauer, "von Ammon," 163.
91. Ibid., 185.

7. "The Fire of Criticism": Revolutionary Dynamics, 1843–1848

1. Ernst Barnikol, *Das entdeckte Christentum im Vormärz. Bruno Bauers Kampf gegen Religion und Christentum und Erstausgabe seiner Kampfschrift* (Jena: Eugen Diederichs, 1927).

2. G.W.F. Hegel, *Phänomenologie des Geistes*, ed. Johannes Hoffmeister (Hamburg: Meiner, 1955), 142–43. See also H. S. Harris, *Hegel's Ladder*, vol. 1, *The Pilgrimage of Reason* (Indianapolis: Hackett, 1997), 356–62.

3. G.W.F. Hegel, *Elements of the Philosophy of Right*, edited by Allen W. Wood, translated by H. B. Nisbet (Cambridge: Cambridge University Press, 1991), §321–40, pp. 359–71.

4. Bruno Bauer, "Neueste Schriften über die Judenfrage," *Allgemeine Literatur Zeitung* I, December 1843, 9. Here he asserts (p. 7) that he has answered the Jewish question "in the interests of progress." See also "Neueste Schriften über die Judenfrage" (continuation), *Allg. Lit.-Ztg.* IV, March 1844, 16.

5. Bruno Bauer, *Das entdeckte Christenthum. Eine Erinnerung an das 18. Jahrhundert und ein Beitrag zur Krisis des 19.* (Zürich und Winterthur: Verlag des literarischen Comptoirs, 1843), 89.

6. Ibid., 89.

7. Warren Breckmann, *Marx, The Young Hegelians, and the Origins of Radical Social Theory. Dethroning the Self* (Cambridge: Cambridge University Press, 1999), 90–130.

8. B. Bauer, *Das entdeckte Christenthum*, 94–95.

9. Karl Marx, "Critique of Hegel's Philosophy of Law: Introduction," in Karl Marx, Frederick Engels, *Collected Works*, vol. 3 (New York: International Publishers, 1975), 173–87.

10. B. Bauer, *Das entdeckte Christenthum*, 94.

11. Ibid., 160–61.

12. Ibid., 161.

13. Bruno Bauer, "Rezension: *Die christliche Glaubenslehre in ihrer geschichtlichen Entwicklung und im Kampf mit der modernen Wissenschaft. von D. F. Strauss. 2 Bde. 1840–1841.*" *Deutsche Jahrbücher*, January 25–28, 1843, nos. 21–24, 85.

14. C. B. Macpherson, *The Political Theory of Possessive Individualism, Hobbes to Locke* (London: Oxford University Press, 1962). For recent accounts, see, Quentin Skinner, *Liberty Before Liberalism* (Cambridge: Cambridge University Press, 1998); and "Two Concepts of Citizenship," *Tijdschrift voor Filosofie* 55/3 (1993), 403–19.

15. G.W.F. Hegel, *Philosophy of Right*, §258, pp. 275–79. For a reading stressing the proximity of Hegel and Rousseau, see Frederick Neuhouser, *Foundations of Hegel's Social Theory. Actualizing Freedom* (Cambridge: Harvard University Press, 2000), 55–81.

16. B. Bauer, *Das entdeckte Christenthum*, 89. Impartiality means lack of particular positive interest, and dedication to the universal. The term recalls the aesthetic judgement of Bauer's 1829 manuscript.

17. Bruno Bauer, *Die Judenfrage* (Braunschweig: Fr. Otto, 1843).

18. Bruno Bauer, "Die Fähigkeit der heutigen Juden und Christen, frei zu werden," *Einundzwanzig Bogen aus der Schweiz*, ed. G. Herwegh (Zürich und Winterthur, Verlag des literarischen Comptoirs, 1843); reprinted in H. M. Sass (ed.), *Feldzüge*, 175–95 (whence pagination).

19. See B. Bauer, *Judenfrage*, 72, 101, and *passim*; on the relation of the French and German Enlightenment, see "Fähigkeiten," p. 184; on hierarchy and political immaturity, see *Judenfrage*, 38.

20. On Hegel's support of Jewish emancipation, see *Philosophy of Right*, §270, pp. 295–96.

21. Karl Marx, "On the Jewish Question," in K. Marx, F. Engels, *Collected Works*, vol. 3, 146–74. David McLellan, *The Young Hegelians and Karl Marx* (Toronto: Macmillan, 1969) sees a strong and pervasive influence of Bauer on Marx until the fall of 1843. He takes as the first evidence of a rift between them not Marx's break with the Freien in November–December 1842 but *The Jewish Question* (74–75). Conversely, he notes a negligible influence on the part of Feuerbach until the spring of 1843, with the writing of the *Critique of Hegel's Philosophy of Right* – that is, after the publication of the "Preliminary Theses" and the *Philosophy of the Future* (96ff).

22. See Chapter 8.

23. See especially David Leopold, "The Hegelian Antisemitism of Bruno Bauer," *History of European Ideas* 25 (1999), 179–206. Another commentary is Yoav Peled, "From Theology to Sociology: Bruno Bauer and Karl Marx on the Question of Jewish Emancipation," *History of Political Thought* 13/3 (1992), 463–85. Peled suggests (467) that besides Hegel, a possible source for Bauer's conception of Judaism might be Moses Mendelssohn's *Jerusalem* (1783). Mendelssohn describes Judaism as a system of revealed law, in consonance with Bauer's view; in contrast, however, Mendelssohn argues for the compatibility of this law with modernity, because the law covers external actions, but not beliefs. See also Julius Carlebach, *Karl Marx and the Radical Critique of Judaism* (London: Routledge and Kegan Paul, 1978). Carlebach summarises contemporary responses to Bauer in the German and Jewish press (138–47), as well as Marx's criticisms from 1844 to 1846 (164–84). He identifies the originality of Bauer's second text on this issue, "Die Fähigkeit," as the rejection of the new claim made by opposition spokesmen that emancipation is to occur *in spite of* adherence to any particular religion (136). The theoretical analysis is relatively weak, however. The author claims that "unlike Feuerbach, Bauer has no substantive theory on which he could build an argument" (128). His schematic distinction (133) of four models in Bauer's account depends on a simple thesis-antithesis-synthesis reading of Hegel; the author finds inconsistencies in Bauer's usage of this model. He misses, further, the continuity of Bauer's account with *Das entdeckte Christenthum* and *Religion des Alten Testaments*, which are not mentioned here.

24. B. Bauer, *Die Judenfrage*, p. 19ff, 62ff.

25. Ibid., 16, 21.

26. Ibid., 94, 96, 97.

27. Ibid., 47.

28. Ibid., 1–5.

29. B. Bauer, "Fähigkeit," 195.

30. B. Bauer, *Die Religion des alten Testaments*, Band II, 140–41; 347ff.

31. Norberto de Sousa, "Ciceronian Republicanism and the History of Civil Society," unpublished ms., 1999. The reference is to Marcus Tullius Cicero, *De Officiis*, trans. Walter Miller (Cambridge: Harvard University Press, 1913).

32. See, for example, Douglas Moggach, "Reciprocity, Elicitation, Recognition: The Thematics of Intersubjectivity in the Early Fichte," *Dialogue, The Canadian Philosophical Review*, 38/2 (Spring 1999), 271–96.

33. B. Bauer, *Die Judenfrage*, 101.

34. Ibid., 102.

35. G.W.F. Hegel, *Frühe politische Systeme*, ed. G. Göhler (Frankfurt/M: Ullstein, 1974), 201–90, for the 1805–06 Jena *Realphilosophie*.

36. G.W.F. Hegel, *Philosophy of Right*, §241–48, pp. 265–69; H. S. Harris, "The Social Ideal of Hegel's Economic Theory," in L. S. Stepelevich and D. Lamb, eds., *Hegel's Philosophy of Action* (Atlantic Highlands: Humanities Press, 1983), 49–74; Jay Lampert, "Locke, Fichte, and Hegel on the Right to Property," in Michael Baur and John Russon, eds., *Hegel and the Tradition. Essays in Honour of H. S. Harris* (Toronto: University of Toronto Press, 1997), 40–73.

37. B. Bauer, *Die Judenfrage*, 8.

38. B. Bauer, *Gute Sache*, 216.

39. J. Droz, *Le romantisme allemand*, 225–38.

40. B. Bauer, *Die Judenfrage*, 8.

41. B. Bauer, "Rezension: 'Einleitung in die Dogmengeschichte' von Theodor Kliefoth," *Anekdota* II, 150.

42. Ibid., 150.

43. Edgar Bauer, *Die liberalen Bestrebungen in Deutschland*, 2 Hefte (Zürich und Winterthur: Verlag des literarischen Comptoirs, 1843).

44. B. Bauer, "Neueste Schriften über die Judenfrage" (continuation), 16; "Die deutschen 'Nationalen,' " *Rheinische Zeitung*, March 10, no. 69, Beiblatt, 1842.

45. B. Bauer et al., *Denkwürdigkeiten zur Geschichte der neueren Zeit seit der Französischen Revolution. Nach den Quellen und Original – Memoiren bearbeitet und herausgegeben von Bruno Bauer und Edgar Bauer and Ernst Jungnitz.* (Charlottenburg: Verlag von Egbert Bauer, 1844). These texts are dismissed by Barnikol as merely derivative compilations, but it is important to see them as continuing and developing Bauer's critical perspective. Some parts of the following are reproduced, with modifications, from Douglas Moggach, "*Nation, Volk, Masse*: Left-Hegelian Perspectives on the Rise of Nationalism," *History of European Ideas*, 15/1–3 (1992), 339–45, with permission from Elsevier Science.

46. Robespierre is described as a dogmatic rationalist, inspired by Rousseau's illusion of an innocent original nature. Bruno Bauer, *Die Septembertage 1792 und die ersten Kämpfe der Parteien der Republik in Frankreich*, part II, *Denkwürdigkeiten zur Geschichte der neueren Zeit seit der französischen Revolution* (1844), 72. See also Bruno Bauer, *Der Process Ludwig XVI und der 21. Januar 1793*, *Denkwürdigkeiten* (1844), 34.

47. Bruno Bauer, *Der 20. Juni und der 10. August 1792 oder der letzte Kampf des Königtums in Frankreich mit der Volkspartei*, *Denkwürdigkeiten* (1843), 59.

48. Bruno Bauer, *Geschichte der Politik, Kultur und Aufklärung des achtzehnten Jahrhunderts. III: Zweite Abteilung: Die Politik der Revolution bis zum Frieden von Basel* (Charlottenburg, Verlag von Egbert Bauer, 1845), 233. [Hereafter *Geschichte der Politik*, III.]

49. Bruno Bauer, *20. Juni*, 59.

50. Bruno Bauer, *Process*, 78; *Geschichte der Politik*, III, 10, 56.

51. Bruno Bauer, *Geschichte der Politik*, III, 267ff.

52. B. Bauer, *Septembertage*, part II, 6, 26.

53. B. Bauer, *Septembertage*, part I, 5. See also *20. Juni*, 6.

54. B. Bauer, *Geschichte der Politik*, III, 256.

55. Bruno Bauer, *Septembertage*, part I, 6.

56. Ibid., 86.

57. On the impossibility of reform or a reforming monarchy, see Bruno Bauer, *Bouille und die Flucht Ludwig XVI, Denkwürdigkeiten*, Charlottenburg 1843; second edition Leipzig 1847, 50; and Bruno Bauer, *Geschichte der Politik, Kultur und Aufklärung des achtzehnten Jahrhunderts, Erster Band: Deutschland während der ersten vierzig Jahre des achtzehnten Jahrhunderts* (Charlottenburg: Verlag von Egbert Bauer, 1843), vi. [Hereafter *Geschichte der Politik*, I.]

58. Bruno Bauer, *Geschichte der Politik*, I, vii.

59. Ibid., vii; cf. *Geschichte der Politik, Kultur und Aufklärung des achtzehnten Jahrhunderts. Fortsetzung: Deutschland und die französiche Revolution. Dritte Abteilung. Die Politik der Revolution von Baseler Frieden bis zum Rastadter Kongress* (Charlottenburg: Verlag von Egbert Bauer, 1845), 194ff. [Hereafter *Geschichte der Politik*, IV.]

60. Bruno Bauer, *Geschichte Deutschlands und der französischen Revolution unter der Herrschaft Napoleons.* Erster Band (Charlottenburg: Verlag von Egbert Bauer, 1846), 88. [Hereafter *Geschichte Deutschlands und der französischen Revolution*, I.]

61. Bruno Bauer, *G. der Pol.* IV, 228.

62. Bruno Bauer, *Geschichte Deutschlands und der französischen Revolution* I, 273.

63. Ibid., 6–9. Note the bitter complaint made by a German supporter of the French Revolution, F. Buchholz, in the *Europäische Annalen* of 1806: "[England] has made use of this commercial monopoly to increase the price of raw materials and to enslave economically the entire continent; she has not tolerated in other countries any other activity than agriculture" (cited in J. Droz, *Le romantisme allemand et l'État*, 97). See also Geoffrey Barraclough, *The Origins of Modern Germany* (New York: Capricorn, 1963), who describes the petty German feudal states as conduits for English capital.

64. B. Bauer, *Geschichte Deutschlands und der französischen Revolution*, 9–10.

65. B. Bauer, *Geschichte der Politik*, I, 1–105; *Geschichte der Politik*, III, 12.

66. B. Bauer, *Geschichte der Politik*, I, 105ff.

67. B. Bauer, *Geschichte der Politik*, III, 19–20. Bauer approves of the Jacobin subordination of property to the common interest not as a socialist measure, but as an attack on possessive individualism and on the absolute validity of private interest. See Chapter 8.

68. B. Bauer, *Geschichte der Politik*, I, 314.

69. B. Bauer, *Geschichte der Politik, Kultur und Aufklärung des achtzehnten Jahrhunderts. Fortsetzung: Deutschland während der Zeit der französischen Revolution. Erste Abteilung.* (Charlottenburg: Verlag von Egbert Bauer, 1844), 59.

70. Ibid., 5–6, 8–9.

71. Bruno Bauer, *Geschichte Deutschlands und der französischen Revolution unter der Herrschaft Napoleons. Zweiter Band. Drei Jahre Kontrerevolution* (Charlottenburg: Verlag von Egbert Bauer, 1846), 230.

72. B. Bauer, *Der Fall und Untergang der neuesten Revolutionen* (Berlin: Verlag von Gustav Hempel, 1850), II. *Der Aufstand und Fall des deutschen Radikalismus vom Jahre 1842.* Erster Band, 96.

73. Cf. J. Jacoby (anon.) *Vier Fragen beantwortet von einem Ost-Preussen* (Leipzig, 1841), and the critique of it in E. Bauer, *Die liberalen Bestrebungen*, 3–7.

74. B. Bauer, *Fall und Untergang*, 154.

75. Ibid., 98.

76. Ibid., 107.

77. Bruno Bauer, *Vollständige Geschichte der Parteikämpfe in Deutschland während der Jahre 1842–1846* (Charlottenburg: Egbert Bauer, 1847).

78. Ibid., 169ff.

79. Marx, *MEGA* I, 1 (2), 277, 280ff. See also D. McLellan, *Marx Before Marxism*, 90–94.

80. B. Bauer, *Parteikämpfe*, 188–189.

81. Ibid., 203ff.

82. Edgar Bauer, ed., *Pressprozess Edgar Bauers über sein Werk: Der Streit der Kritik mit Kirche und Staat. Acktenstücke* (Bern: Jenni, Sohn, 1844); cf. Bruno Bauer, ed., *Acktenstücke zu den Verhandlungen über die Beschlagnahme der "Geschichte der Politik, Kultur und Aufklärung des achtzehnten Jahrhunderts," von Bruno Bauer.* Teil I (Christiania: Verlag von C.C. Werner, 1844).

83. B. Bauer, *Parteikämpfe*, 220.

84. Ibid., 220.

85. Ibid., 161.

8. "The Republic of Self-Consciousness": Revolutionary Politics in 1848

1. Wilhelm Blos, *Die deutsche Revolution. Geschichte der deutschen Bewegung von 1848 und 1849* (Stuttgart: Dietz Verlag, 1893), 4.

2. For a review of the German case, see Walter Schmidt, "Die 1848er Forschung in der DDR," *Zeitschrift für Geschichtswissenshaft*, Vol. 42 (1994), 21–38; and Dieter Langewiesche, "Republik, konstitutionelle Monarchie und 'soziale Frage': Grundprobleme der deutschen Revolution von 1848/49," *Historische Zeitschrift*, Vol. 230, no. 3 (1980), 529–47.

3. See, for example, Helmut Bleiber, Walter Schmidt, and Rolf Weber (eds.), *Männer der Revolution von 1848*, Band II (Berlin: Akademie Verlag, 1987), 24–25; Jonathan Sperber, *The Democratic Movement and the Revolution of 1848–1849* (Princeton: Princeton University Press, 1991), 490.

4. Karl Marx, Frederick Engels, "The Holy Family, or Critique of Critical Criticism. Against Bruno Bauer and Company," *Collected Works*, vol. 4 (New York: International Publishers, 1975), 5–211. Ruge, himself involved in polemics with Marx after the failure of their collaborative effort, the *Deutsch-französische Jahrbücher*, considered *The Holy Family* a lamentable compendium, unworthy of former friends. See Barnikol Ms., Quellenteil, Ruge to Fleischer (May 27, 1845), 23, II.9.cc).

5. Lorenz von Stein, *Der Socialismus und Communismus des heutigen Frankreichs* (Leipzig, 1842).

6. Bruno Bauer, "Hinrichs politische Vorlesungen. Band I," *Allgemeine Literatur Zeitung [ALZ]* I, December 1843, 30. H.F.W. Hinrichs, a member of the Hegelian centre, is described by Ruge in 1841 as politically liberal. Ruge to Rosenkranz, February 25, 1841, in Heinz und Ingrid Pepperle, *Die Hegelsche Linke. Dokumente zu Philosophie und Politik im deutschen Vormärz* (Frankfurt am Main: Röderberg, 1986), 808.

7. Bruno Bauer, "Correspondenz aus der Provinz," *ALZ*, VI (May 1844), 34.

8. Bruno Bauer, "Erste Wahlrede von 1848," in Barnikol, *Bruno Bauer*, 526–29.

9. Bruno Bauer, "Was ist jetzt der Gegenstand der Kritik?", *ALZ*, VIII, June 1844, 18–26.

10. Bruno Bauer (pseudonym A. Fränkel), "Die religiöse Bewegung. Erster Artikel. Die Masse," *Norddeutsche Blätter*, VIII, January 1845, 63.

11. Robert Nola, "The Young Hegelians, Feuerbach, and Marx," in R. C. Solomon and K. M. Higgins (eds.), *The Age of German Idealism. Routledge History of Philosophy*, vol. VI (London, Routledge, 1993), 298–99.

12. See, for example, Bruno Bauer, *Geschichte Deutschlands und der französischen Revolution unter der Herrschaft Napoleons. Zweiter Band. Drei Jahre Kontrerevolution* (Charlottenburg: Verlag von Egbert Bauer, 1846), 230.

13. Istvan Hont and Michael Ignatieff (eds.), *Wealth and Virtue. The Shaping of Political Economy in the Scottish Enlightenment* (Cambridge: Cambridge University Press, 1983).

14. As observed in Chapter 7, Bauer's political position has never been the subject of sustained investigation. Dieter Hertz-Eichenrode, *Der Junghegelianer Bruno Bauer im Vormärz*, Inauguraldissertation (Berlin: Frei Universität, 1959) hardly mentions any texts written after 1842.

15. Bruno Bauer (ed.), *Allgemeine Literatur-Zeitung. Monatschrift.* 12 issues Dec. 1843 – Oct. 1844. Second edition under the title *Streit der Kritik mit den modernen Gegensätzen*. Mit Beiträgen von Bruno Bauer, Edgar Bauer, Ernst Jungnitz, Szeliga und Anderen (Charlottenburg: Egbert Bauer, 1847).

16. Bruno Bauer (ed.), *Norddeutsche Blätter. Eine Monatschrift für Kritik, Literatur und Unterhaltung*, 10 issues July 1844 – April 1845.

17. B. Bauer, "Was ist jetzt der Gegenstand der Kritik," 20–25.

18. Ernst Barnikol, "Bruno Bauer, der radikalste Religionskritiker und konservativste Junghegelianer," *Das Altertum*, Band 7, Heft 1 (Berlin: Akademie Verlag, 1961), 41–49.

19. Edgar Bauer, *Der Streit der Kritik mit Kirche und Staat* (Bern: Jenni, Sohn, 1844), 257. See also his article "1842" in *ALZ*, VIII, July 1844, 1–8.

20. E. Bauer, *Streit*, 285–86.

21. Ibid., 289 (also cited in Wolfgang Eßbach, *Die Junghegelianer. Soziologie einer Intellektuellengruppe* (München: Wilhelm Fink Verlag, 1988), 242 n. 253).

22. Edgar Bauer, *Die Parteien, Politische Revue*, 2es und 3es Heft (Hamburg 1849), 4, 20–28.

23. Edgar Bauer, *Die Parteien, Politische Revue*, 1es Heft (Hamburg 1849), 9.

24. Szeliga [Franz Zychlin von Zychlinski], *Die Organisation der Arbeit der Menschheit und die Kunst der Geschichtsschreibung Schlossers, Gervinus, Dahlmanns und Bruno Bauers* (Charlottenburg, 1846), 32, 42, 44.

25. B. Bauer, "Die Gattung und die Masse," *ALZ*, X, September 1844, 42–48; reprinted in H. M. Sass, *Feldzüge der reinen Kritik*, 213–20.

26. For example, the imposition of a maximum of wages as well as prices generated vigorous opposition by the Parisian workers, whom the Terror did not spare. The execution of Hébert resulted from Robespierre's split with a more leftist or populist faction, though one of dubious and adventurist credentials, especially on the question of military mobilisation. The orchestration of Thermidor took place with the collusion of those Jacobins most closely associated with the Parisian popular forces, notably Billaud-Varenne and Collot d'Herbois. On these issues, see Marc Bouloiseau, *Le comité de salut publique (1793–1795)*, 2nd edition (Paris: Presses universitaires de France, 1968), 68; Georges Lefebvre, *The French Revolution from 1793 to 1799* (London: Routledge and Kegan Paul, 1964), 39–138. On Thermidor, see Jacques Godechot, *The Counter-Revolution, Doctrine and Action 1789–1804* (Princeton: Princeton University Press, 1971), 246; and the materials in Richard T. Bienvenu (ed.), *The Ninth of Thermidor: The Fall of Robespierre* (London: Oxford University Press, 1968), 182–91, 204–06.

27. Bruno Bauer, "Verteidigungsrede vor den Wahlmännern des vierten Wahlbezirkes am 22. 2. 1849," in Ernst Barnikol, *Bruno Bauer: Studien und Materialien*, 522.

28. Karl Marx, "On the Jewish Question," *Collected Works*, vol. 3 (1975), 146–74.

29. B. Bauer, *Die Judenfrage* (Braunschweig: Fr. Otto, 1843), 8.

30. Bruno Bauer, "Der christliche Staat und unsere Zeit," in H.-M. Sass (ed.), *Feldzüge der reinen Kritik* (Frankfurt am Main: Suhrkamp, 1968), 33.

31. Bruno Bauer, *Die gute Sache der Freiheit und meine eigene Angelegenheit* (Zürich und Winterthur: Verlag des literarischen Comptoirs, 1842), 33.

32. On the *Freien*, see W. Eßbach, *Die Junghegelianer*, 215–19.

33. For an analysis, see Joachim Höppner, "Einleitung," in Arnold Ruge and Karl Marx (eds.), *Deutsch-französische Jahrbücher* [1844] (Leipzig: Reclam, 1973), 5–83.

34. Marx, *Holy Family*, 78–143; Karl Marx, Frederick Engels, "The German Ideology," *Collected Works*, vol. 5 (New York: International Publishers, 1976), 19–539; on Bauer, esp. 97–116. In the latter text, particularly in the critique of Feuerbach (27–93), Marx produces his first sketch of a materialist theory of history, the sequence of forms of organisation of labour, involving a variable relation among three terms: the material instruments and objects of the labour process, labour itself as active teleology, and the product of labour, which is differentially distributed among social classes as a consequence of their access to the conditions of labour. Despite its antispeculative intentions, the *German Ideology* (74–83) echoes Hegelian logic in the opposing dialectical syllogisms of class formation that the bourgeoisie and proletariat experience (respectively the many ones, and the many coalesced as one). Cf. G.W.F. Hegel, *Science of Logic*, 163–78.

35. Karl Marx, "On the Jewish Question," 164–68.

36. Karl Marx, "The Bourgeoisie and the Counter-Revolution," in Karl Marx, Frederick Engels, *Collected Works*, vol. 8 (New York: International Publishers, 1977), 154–69.

37. Karl Marx, "Contribution to the Critique of Hegel's Philosophy of Law. Introduction," in Karl Marx, Frederick Engels, *Collected Works*, vol. 3 (New York: International Publishers, 1975), 175–87.

38. Karl Marx, "Theses on Feuerbach," in Karl Marx, Frederick Engels, *Collected Works*, vol. 5 (New York: International Publishers, 1976), 3–5; cf. 6–8.

39. See, for example, Axel Honneth, "Work and Instrumental Action," *New German Critique* (Spring–Summer 1982), 31–54.

40. B. Bauer, *Gute Sache*, 215.

41. Bruno Bauer, "Organisation der Arbeit," *Norddeutsche Blätter*, V, 1844, 76–85.

42. Ibid., 84–85.

43. William James Booth, "The Limits of Autonomy: Karl Marx's Kant Critique," in Ronald Beiner and William James Booth, *Kant and Political Philosophy. The Contemporary Legacy* (New Haven: Yale University Press, 1993), 245–75, argues for the superiority of Marx's view of the relational character of labour, here primarily the engagement of subjective teleological and objective causal processes, over the dualism typical of the Kantian tradition. We might extend this criticism to encompass the restrictive intersubjectivity of Bauer's account of labour.

44. Bruno Bauer, *Kritik der evangelischen Geschichte der Synoptiker.* Zweiter Band (Leipzig: Wigand, 1841), 159–60.

45. G.W.F. Hegel, *Introductory Lectures on Aesthetics*, trans. Bernard Bosanquet, edited by Michael Inwood (Harmondsworth: Penguin, 1993), 14–15.

46. Bruno Bauer, "Die Gattung und die Masse," *ALZ*, X, 1844, 42–48; reprinted in H. M. Sass, *Feldzüge*, 213–20.

47. Bruno Bauer, "Was ist jetzt der Gegenstand der Kritik?", 18–26.

48. All these criticisms are registered in B. Bauer, "Die Gattung und die Masse," *ALZ*, X, 1844, 42–48; reprinted in H. M. Sass, *Feldzüge*, 213–20.

49. Cf. John Stuart Mill, *On Liberty*, chapter 4. Unlike Mill's utilitarianism, however, Bauer argues that social progress comes about not by the accretion of accidental discoveries, but by rational insight into the requirements of the historical moment. Bauer's universal is not a mere summation of particulars, as is Mill's. His critical theory retains the form of the apodeictic judgement against Mill's version of the universal (not the Enlightenment-infinite) judgement.

50. Marx, "German Ideology," 453–539.

51. B. Bauer, *Parteikämpfe*, vol. II, 76–84, vol. III, 13–29, 150ff.

52. See, for example, Julius Faucher, "Berlins Armenwesen," *ALZ*, XI–XII, October 1844, 52–60.

53. See Karl Marx, "Speech on the Question of Free Trade," in Karl Marx, Frederick Engels, *Collected Works*, vol. 6 (New York: International Publishers, 1976), 450–65.

54. J. G. Fichte, *Der geschloßne Handelsstaat, Gesamtausgabe*, Bd. I/7 (Stuttgart: Fromann, 1988), 37–141. For Fichte, the right to work is constitutive of personhood. Its status is categorical, not hypothetical: It cannot be

overridden by appeals to the efficiency of the free market, even if such claims could be empirically sustained. In order to assure that the exercise of this right is undisturbed by the fluctuations of external markets or the vagaries of an international division of labour, the state is to be a bulwark against the intrusions of world commerce.

55. Heinrich Best, "La bourgeoisie allemande a-t-elle trahi la révolution de 1848? Bilan d'une analyse sérielle," *Histoire et mesure*, Vol. 3, no. 4 (1988), 427–40: *Interessenpolitik und nationale Integration. Handelspolitische Konflikte im frühindustriellen Deutschland* (Göttingen: Vandenhoeck und Ruprecht, 1980), 81–279; and "Struktur und Wandel kollektiven politischen Handelns: Die handelspolitische Petitionsbewegung 1848/49," in Heinrich Volkmann and Jürgen Bergmann (eds.), *Sozialer Protest. Studien zu traditioneller Resistenz und kollektiver Gewalt in Deutschland vom Vormärz bis zur Reichsgründung* (Opladen: Westdeutscher Verlag, 1984), 169–97.

56. Aldo Zanardo, "Bruno Bauer hegeliano e giovane hegeliano," *Rivista Critica di Storia della Filosofia*, 1965, 1–57.

57. (anon.) "Das Wohl der arbeitenden Klassen," *Norddeutsche Blätter* IX, March 1845, 52–66. Compare Bruno Bauer, "Die Gattung und Masse," in H. M. Sass, *Feldzüge*, 221; Ruge to Nauwerck (December 23, 1844), observes wryly that even the Bauers are apostles of the absolute economy – that is, of socialism. Barnikol ms., 23. II.9.2 z.

58. E. Bauer, *Streit*, 285. The text on free trade cannot be by Marx or Engels, as it is simultaneous with the publication of *The Holy Family* (for dating of this book, see Ruge to Fleischer [May 27, 1845], Barnikol ms., Quellenteil, 23, II.9.cc); and we cannot imagine Bauer's journal to have had a long production time.

59. (anon.), "Das Wohl der arbeitenden Klassen," 57.

60. Ibid., 57–58.

61. Ibid., 59.

62. Ibid., 58.

63. Ibid., 59.

64. Ibid., 59.

65. Ibid., 58.

66. Bruno Bauer, *Die bürgerliche Revolution in Deutschland seit dem Anfange der deutsch-katholischen Bewegung big zur Gegenwart* (Berlin: Hempel, 1849), 193–94.

67. Karl Marx, "The Bourgeoisie and the Counter-Revolution," *Collected Works*, vol. 8 (1977), 154–69.

68. B. Bauer, "Erste Wahlrede von 1848," and "Verteidigungsrede vor den Wahlmännern des vierten Walhbezirkes am 22. 2 1849," in E. Barnikol, *Bruno Bauer: Studien und Materialien*, 525–31, 518–25.

69. Eric Gamby, *Edgar Bauer, Junghegelianer, Publizist und Polizeiagent* (Trier: Karl-Marx-Haus, 1985), 23–29. Edgar Bauer's activities as police agent are subsequent to 1848–49.

70. B. Bauer, "Verteidigungsrede," 519, 521.

71. Ibid., 521.

72. Ibid., 522.

73. Ibid., 520.
74. Ibid., 521.
75. Bruno Bauer, "Erste Wahlrede von 1848," in Barnikol, *Bruno Bauer: Studien und Materialien*, 525.
76. Ibid., 526–29.
77. Ibid., 531.
78. Ibid., 530.
79. Ibid., 530.
80. It has not been possible to determine Bauer's assessment of the call for war against Russia and Denmark, raised by some republican and socialist circles, and defended especially by the *Neue Rheinische Zeitung*. Such a war, it was argued, would consolidate the scattered German revolutionary forces, and would undercut compromise with the Junkers, who looked to Russia as their saviour. Unfortunately, none of Bauer's correspondence from 1848–49, which might provide evidence for his position on this and other revolutionary issues such as free trade, has been located. His views on Russia after 1848 are outlined in the Epilogue.
81. B. Bauer, "Erste Wahlrede," 526.
82. Ibid., 528.
83. Edgar Bauer, *Die Parteien. Politische Revue.* 1es Heft (Hamburg, 1849), 39–41, advocates as another concrete task of the revolution the universal arming of the people. He links the possession of weapons with the ability to represent oneself as a citizen, and to possess the means to resist tutelage and domination by others. This traditional republican theme, also to be found in Marx's *Manifesto* and in the pages of his *Neue Rheinische Zeitung* in 1848–49, is here interpreted in the language of Bruno Bauer. The principle of the citizen-soldier shows that "from now on, the free personality should be the highest, and, for all social creation, the only element" (p. 40).
84. B. Bauer, *Verteidigungsrede*, 523.
85. Rob Beamish, "The Making of the Manifesto," *Socialist Register* (1998): 218–39.
86. Bruno Bauer, "Die Gattung und die Masse," in H. M. Sass, *Feldzüge*, 213–20.
87. B. Bauer, "Erste Wahlrede," 529.
88. Ibid., 531.
89. Ibid., 529.
90. Ibid., 529–30.
91. Ibid., 530.
92. B. Bauer, "Verteidigungsrede," 519.
93. Cf. Rudolf Haym, *Hegel und seine Zeit* (Berlin: 1857); Ernst Barnikol, "Bruno Bauers Kampf gegen Religion und Christentum und die Spaltung der vormärzlichen preussischen Opposition," *Zeitschrift für Kirchen-Geschichte* XLVI (1928), 1–34.
94. Cf. Julius Carlebach, *Karl Marx and the Radical Critique of Judaism* (London: Routledge and Kegan Paul, 1978).
95. Cf. Sydney Hook, *From Hegel to Marx* (Ann Arbor: University of Michigan Press, 1962).
96. B. Bauer, "Verteidigungsrede," 518.

97. Ibid., 524.
98. Ibid., 520.
99. Ibid., 521.
100. B. Bauer, *De pulchri principiis*, 68a.
101. Ibid., 91a-b.
102. Ibid., 106a.

Epilogue: After the Revolution: The Conclusion of the Christian-Germanic Age

1. For reasons stated in the Introduction, this Epilogue makes no claims to comprehensiveness. It is rather an attempt to trace the major theoretical consequences of Bauer's renunciation of republicanism after 1848. The manuscripts of van den Bergh van Eysinga and, especially, of Barnikol, as well as the latter's published work, have proven immensely useful guides through the profuse writings of Bauer's later period. Aside from these sources, no relevant secondary literature on the texts of this period could be identified, with the exception of Albert Schweitzer, *The Quest of the Historical Jesus. A Critical Study of its Progress from Reimarus to Wrede* (Baltimore: Johns Hopkins University Press, 1998). van den Bergh van Eysinga distinguishes Bauer's negligible political reflections after 1848 from his important theological conclusions, while Barnikol disputes Bauer's claim of Christianity's late origin in the second century, finding it to be implausible and unsupported by other historical research. Barnikol also stresses the late Bauer's anti-Hegelianism.
2. Eduard Schläger, "Bruno Bauer und seine Werke," *Schmeitzner's Internationale Monatsschrift*, vol. 1 (1882), 393–94.
3. Ernst Barnikol, *Bruno Bauer, Studien und Materialien*, ed. P. Riemer und H.-M. Sass (Assen: van Gorcum, 1972), 312.
4. Bruno Bauer, *Die russische Kirche. Schlussheft* (Charlottenburg: Egbert Bauer, 1855), Vorwort. Bauer does, at least, refer earlier to the exhaustion of European nations in "Neue kritische Zeitschriften," *Norddeutsche Blätter* I, July 1844, 12–13.
5. Brudney's claims about Bauer's anti-historical attitude thus appear valid for the late but not the early works. See Daniel Brudney, *Marx's Attempt to Leave Philosophy* (Cambridge: Harvard University Press, 1998), 129–30.
6. E. Barnikol, *Bruno Bauer, Studien und Materialien*, 350–53.
7. Karl Marx, "Contribution to the Critique of Hegel's Philosophy of Law. Introduction," in Karl Marx, Frederick Engels, *Collected Works*, Vol. 3 (New York: International Publishers, 1975), 180–81, where the end of philosophy as alienated thought is at the same time the realisation of its emancipatory demands.
8. Bruno Bauer, "The Present Position of the Jews," *New York Daily Tribune*, June 7, 1852. This seminal article is contained in the van den Bergh van Eysinga archive. Barnikol does not mention this text, but in another context names Charles B. Dana as translator of several of Bauer's journalistic pieces in the United States. E. Barnikol, *Bruno Bauer. Studien und Materialien*, 313.

9. Bruno Bauer, *Über die Prinzipien des Schönen. De pulchri principiis. Eine Preisschrift*, hrsg. Douglas Moggach und Winfried Schultze (Berlin: Akademie Verlag, 1996), 95b.

10. Bruno Bauer, *Russland und das Germanenthum*, Heft I (Charlottenburg: Egbert Bauer, 1853), 40–49.

11. Bruno Bauer, *Theologische Erklärung der Evangelien* (Berlin: Hempel, 1852), 1.

12. Bruno Bauer, *Russland und das Germanenthum*, Heft I, 49–54. Cf. his "Bekenntnisse einer schwachen Seele," *Deutsche Jahrbücher*, 23–24 June, 1842, nos. 148–49, pp. 589–96.

13. For variants on the frequent postmodern allegation that classical rationalism denies otherness, see Kenneth Baynes, James Bohman, and Thomas McCarthy, eds., *After Philosophy. End or Transformation?* (Cambridge: MIT Press, 1987), 21–158. This agreement is not surprising, as many postmoderns claim Nietzsche as their progenitor, and in the late Bauer the path to Nietzsche is being cleared.

14. Bruno Bauer, "Vorwort," *Schmeitzner's Internationale Monatsschrift*, vol. 1 (1882), 4, cited in E. Barnikol, *Bruno Bauer. Studien und Materialien*, 434.

15. B. Bauer, *Über die Prinzipien des Schönen*, 109a.

16. Bruno Bauer, *Einfluss des englischen Quäkerthums auf die deutsche Cultur und auf das englisch-russische Project einer Weltkirche* (Berlin: Eugen Grosser, 1878), 236.

17. Cf. Bruno Bauer, "Rezension: Die Geschichte des Lebens Jesu von Dr. von Ammon. Erster Band." in A. Ruge (ed.), *Anekdota zur neuesten deutschen Philosophie und Publizistik*, vol. II (Zürich und Winterthur: Verlag des literarischen Comptoirs, 1843), 185.

18. B. Bauer, *Russland und das Germanenthum.* Heft I, 1–2.

19. B. Bauer, *Deutschland und das Russenthum* (Charlottenburg: Egbert Bauer, 1854), 3–12.

20. This is Bakunin's thesis in a massive unfinished work, translated as Michel Bakounine, *L'empire knouto-germanique et la révolution sociale 1870–71*, ed. Arthur Lehning (Leiden: Brill, 1981). The idea of a native Russian anti-statism also underlies his polemic against Marx's state socialism. See Michael Bakunin, *Marxism, Freedom and the State*, trans. K. J. Kenafick (London: Freedom Press, 1950).

21. B. Bauer, *Einfluss des englischen Quäkerthums*, 8–27; Bruno Bauer, *Disraelis romantischer und Bismarcks socialistischer Imperialismus* (Chemnitz: Ernst Schmeitzner, 1882), 146–47.

22. B. Bauer, *Disraelis romantischer Imperialismus*, 23.

23. Bauer's major texts on Russia were written between February 1853 and December 1854. Barnikol describes reactions to these texts: Bauer was taken to be a Russian apologist, and perhaps a paid agent, accusations he vehemently denied. He financed these publications by his journalistic earnings, and the sale of parts of his library. See the favourable verdict on Bauer of K. A. Varnhagen von Ense, reported in E. Barnikol, *Bruno Bauer. Studien und Materialien*, 312–13.

24. B. Bauer, *Die russische Kirche*, 3–20.

25. J. G. Fichte, *Grundlage des Naturrechts*, Gesamtausgabe der Bayerischen Akademie der Wissenschaften, ed. R. Lauth et al., Bd. I/3, (Stuttgart:

Fromann, 1966), §1–4. For a comparison of this text with Fichte's *Reden an die deutsche Nation, Werke,* Bd. VII (Berlin: de Gruyter, 1971), 263–499, see Douglas Moggach, "Nationhood and Freedom in Fichte's Political Thought," in Frank Brinkhuis and Sascha Talmor (eds.), *Memory, History, and Critique. European Identity at the Millennium* (Utrecht: University for Humanist Studies, 1998) (CD-ROM), 5 pp.

26. B. Bauer, *Russland und das Germanenthum.* Heft I, 1–2; B. Bauer, *Die russische Kirche,* 11–12; Karl Löwith, *From Hegel to Nietzsche. The Revolution in Nineteenth Century Thought,* trans. David E. Green (New York: Holt, Rinehart and Winston, 1964).

27. Karl Kautsky, *Nationalstaat, imperialistischer Staat und Staatenbund* (Nürnberg: Fränkische Verlagsanstalt, 1915). See also Kautsky's article "Ultraimperialism," *New Left Review,* No. 59, January 1970.

28. The anticipation of this position in Bauer's earlier writings has been alluded to in the Introduction. See, for example, Bruno Bauer, *Die evangelische Landeskirche Preußens und die Wissenschaft* (Leipzig: Otto Wigand, 1840), 19–33.

29. B. Bauer, *Disraelis romantischer Imperialismus,* 17 (cited in E. Barnikol, *Bruno Bauer, Studien und Materialien,* 401).

30. Bruno Bauer, "Vorwort," *Schmeitzner's Internationale Monatsschrift,* 3 (cited in E. Barnikol, *Bruno Bauer. Studien und Materialien,* 434).

31. Bruno Bauer, *Kritik der paulinischen Briefe* (Berlin: Hempel, 1850–51); *Kritik der Evangelien und Geschichte ihres Ursprungs,* 3 vol. (Berlin: Hempel, 1850–51); 4th vol. *Die theologische Erklärung der Evangelien* (Berlin, 1852). Bauer returns to the theme of the Greco-Roman origins of Christianity in *Philo, Strauss und Renan und das Urchristenthum* (Berlin: Hempel, 1874); and in *Christus und die Cäsaren* (Berlin, 1879). Some of this material is discussed in A. Schweitzer, *The Quest of the Historical Jesus,* 157–60. The real existence form of the Pauline *soma christou,* or body of Christ, is described as the Roman Empire (160). Schweitzer compares the late Bauer very unfavourably with his early period (137–57).

32. B. Bauer, *Disraelis romantischer Imperialismus,* 202–03.

33. Friedrich Engels, "Bruno Bauer und das Urchristentum," *Sozialdemokrat* (May 4 and 11, 1882).

34. Karl Kautsky, *Der Ursprung des Christentums. Eine historische Untersuchung* (Stuttgart: Dietz, 1908).

35. Unlike the position he defended in *Das entdeckte Christenthum* of 1843, Bauer, in *Einfluss des englischen Quäkerthums,* 42–95, no longer views German Enlightenment figures like Edelmann as atheists, but as pantheistic disciples of Spinoza. See E. Barnikol, *Bruno Bauer. Studien und Materialien,* 360–61. Bauer attributes to Edelmann the view that God is so fully present in the world that any particular divine incarnation would be pleonastic. For a modern assessment, see Annegret Schapper, *Ein langer Abschied vom Christentum. Johann Christian Edelmann (1698–1767) und die deutsche Frühaufklärung* (Marburg: Tectum-Verlag, 1996). For Bauer's late views on the Enlightenment, see also his *Freimaurer, Jesuiten und Illuminaten in ihrem geschichtlichen Zusammenhange* (Berlin: F. Heinicke, 1863).

36. B. Bauer, *Einfluss des englischen Quäkerthums,* 159–61.

37. Cf. Bruno Bauer, "Theologische Schamlosigkeiten," *Deutsche Jahrbücher für Wissenschaft und Kunst,* 15–18 November 1841, no. 117–20, pp. 465–79.
38. E. Barnikol, *Bruno Bauer, Studien und Materialien,* 363, 370–71.
39. E. Barnikol, *Bruno Bauer, Studien und Materialien,* 393, citing editorial remarks in Karl Marx, Friedrich Engels, *Werke,* Bd. I (Berlin: Dietz, 1957), 635.
40. E. Barnikol, *Bruno Bauer. Studien und Materialien,* 291, 342.
41. E. Barnikol, *Bruno Bauer. Studien und Materialien,* 387–88, on the link with Nietzsche.
42. E. Barnikol, *Bruno Bauer, Studien und Materialien,* 432–33.
43. For example, Bruno Bauer, *Das Judenthum in der Fremde. Separat-Abdruck aus dem Wagener'schen Staats- und Gesellschaftslexikon* (Berlin, 1863), as well as the 1852 article "The Present Position of the Jews."
44. B. Bauer, *Zur Orientierung über die Bismarck'sche Ära* (Chemnitz: Ernst Schmeitzner, 1880), 315–17.
45. B. Bauer, *Disraelis romantischer Imperialismus,* 21 (cited in E. Barnikol, *Bruno Bauer, Studien und Materialien,* 402).
46. B. Bauer, *Disraelis romantischer Imperialismus,* 17 (cited in E. Barnikol, *Bruno Bauer, Studien und Materialien,* 401).
47. B. Bauer, *Disraelis romantischer Imperialismus,* 17 (cited in E. Barnikol, *Bruno Bauer, Studien und Materialien,* 401).
48. The value of Karl Löwith's study, *From Hegel to Nietzsche,* is to identify this transition; but it does so with no recognition of Bauer's early republicanism.
49. I owe this formulation to Quentin Skinner, who expressed it in discussion of an unrelated thinker.

Appendix: Bruno Bauer, "On the Principles of the Beautiful"

1. Cf. Schiller, final line of the Prologue to *Wallenstein* (1798): "Life is serious, art is serene." Friedrich Schiller, *Wallenstein. Ein dramatisches Gedicht* (Reinbek bei Hamburg: Rowohlt, 1961), Erster Teil, *Wallensteins Lager.* Prolog. [The Bauer manuscript lacks all references. Citations provided by me. D.M.] The motto was used by the adjudication committee to identify the manuscripts submitted anonymously for the Prussian royal prize. Page numbers follow the manuscript; [a] and [b] have been added to distinguish facing pages.
2. G.W.F. Hegel, *Enzyklopädie der philosophischen Wissenschaften im Grundrisse* (1827), *Gesammelte Werke,* Bd. 19 (Hamburg: Meiner, 1989), §1; *Glauben und Wissen* (1802), *Gesammelte Werke,* Bd. 4, 1968, 323.
3. "Being is," and "being is thinking."
4. G.W.F. Hegel, *Vorlesungen über die Ästhetik* [1835] Erster Band, *Sämtliche Werke. Jubiläumsausgabe,* ed. H. Glockner, Bd. XII (Stuttgart: Fromann-Holzboog, 1964), 87.
5. G.W.F. Hegel, *Enzyklopädie* (1827), §§37–§41, §60; *Vorlesungen über die Geschichte der Philosophie,* III, *Werke,* Bd. 20 (Frankfurt/M: Suhrkamp, 1971), 332–33.
6. Kant, *Kritik der Urteilskraft, Kants gesammelte Schriften,* Bd. 5, Königlich Preußische Akademie der Wissenschaften (Berlin, de Gruyter, 1908), 175–76, 195.

7. Kant, *Kritik der Urteilskraft*, 177–78; cf. Hegel, *Glauben und Wissen*, 339.

8. Kant, *Kritik der Urteilskraft*, 178.

9. Ibid., 179.

10. Ibid., 179–80.

11. Ibid., 180, 187.

12. Ibid., 187.

13. Ibid., 189, 192.

14. Ibid., 190.

15. Hegel, *Enzyklopädie* (1827), §55; *Glauben und Wissen*, 327, 341; *Vorlesungen über die Ästhetik*, I, 91; *Vorlesungen über die Geschichte der Philosophie*, III, 380.

16. Kant, *Kritik der Urteilskraft*, 197.

17. Hegel, *Enzyklopädie* (1827), §41; cf. I. Kant, *Kritik der reinen Vernunft*, ed. R. Schmidt (Hamburg: Meiner, 1930), A70 = B95.

18. Hegel, *Enzyklopädie* (1827), §56.

19. Kant, *Kritik der Urteilskraft*, §1–§5, 203–11; cf. Hegel, *Vorlesungen über die Ästhetik*, I, 92–93. See also Hegel, *Vorlesungen über die Geschichte der Philosophie*, III, 372–82.

20. Kant, *Kritik der Urteilskraft*, §3–§4, 205–09; 345–46.

21. Hegel, *Vorlesungen über die Ästhetik*, I, 93.

22. Ibid., 93.

23. Kant, *Kritik der Urteilskraft*, 210.

24. Hegel, *Vorlesungen über die Ästhetik*, I, 93.

25. Kant, *Kritik der Urteilskraft*, §6–§9, 211–19; cf. Hegel, *Vorlesungen über die Ästhetik*, I, 93–94.

26. Kant, *Kritik der Urteilskraft*, 211.

27. Ibid., 211, 347.

28. Ibid., 212, 214.

29. Ibid., 217–18.

30. Ibid., 219.

31. Ibid, §10–§17, 219–36; cf. Hegel, *Vorlesungen über die Ästhetik*, I, 94.

32. Kant, *Kritik der Urteilskraft*, 220.

33. Ibid., 220.

34. Ibid., 221.

35. Ibid., 228.

36. Ibid., 231.

37. Ibid., 231.

38. Ibid., 231.

39. The text has "nudam (*bloße*)." D.M.

40. Ibid., 232.

41. Ibid., 232.

42. Ibid., 235.

43. Ibid., §18–§22, 236–40; cf. Hegel, *Vorlesungen über die Ästhetik*, I, 94–95.

44. Kant, *Kritik der Urteilskraft*, 240.

45. Hegel, *Vorlesungen über die Ästhetik*, I, 59–60n.

46. Ibid., 57–58.

47. Cf. G.W.F. Hegel, *Enzyklopädie der philosophischen Wissenschaften im Grundrisse* (1830), *Erster Teil. Die Wissenschaft der Logik*, mit den mündlichen Zusätzen (Frankfurt/M: Suhrkamp, 1970), §45Z.

48. "idea" inserted. D.M.
49. Hegel, *Enzyklopädie* (1827), §42–§45.
50. Ibid., §94.
51. Hegel, *Vorlesungen über die Ästhetik*, I, 69.
52. Ibid., 28–29.
53. Kant, *Kritik der Urteilskraft*, 232.
54. Cf. Hegel, *Vorlesungen über die Geschichte der Philosophie*, III, 371, 384.
55. Hegel, *Enzyklopädie* (1827), §147–§149.
56. Ibid., §60.
57. Hegel, *Glauben und Wissen*, 339.
58. Ibid., 340.
59. Ibid., 343; Hegel, *Enzyklopädie* (1827), §60.
60. Kant, *Kritik der Urteilskraft*, §55–§57, 337–46.
61. Ibid., 344.
62. Ibid., 345.
63. Ibid., 281–85.
64. Ibid., 338.
65. Ibid., 338.
66. Ibid., 338.
67. Ibid., 338–39.
68. Hegel, *Glauben und Wissen*, 340.
69. Cf. Hegel, *Vorlesungen über die Ästhetik*, I, 27.
70. Hegel, *Enzyklopädie* (1827), §556–§60.
71. Hegel, *Glauben und Wissen*, 340.
72. Ibid., 343.
73. Ibid., 343.

BIBLIOGRAPHY

Works by Bruno Bauer, 1829–82

A. 1829–49

De pulchri principiis. Prussian royal prize manuscript, 1829. First published as *Über die Prinzipien des Schönen. De pulchri principiis. Eine Preisschrift,* hrsg. Douglas Moggach und Winfried Schultze, mit einem Vorwort von Volker Gerhardt (Berlin: Akademie Verlag, 1996).

"Rezension: *Das Leben Jesu, kritisch bearbeitet* von David Friedrich Strauss. Erster Band," *Jahrbücher für wissenschaftliche Kritik,* Dec. 1835, no. 109, 879–80; nos. 111, 891; no. 113, 905–12.

"Rezension: *Das Leben Jesu, kritisch bearbeitet* von David Friedrich Strauss. Zweiter Band," *Jahrbücher für wissenschaftliche Kritik,* May 1836, no. 86, 681–88; no. 88, 697–704.

Review of writings on Strauss by Baader, Sack, Lange and others: *Jahrbücher für wissenschaftliche Kritik,* March 1837, no. 41, 321–28; no. 43, 337–43.

"Rezension: *Streitschriften zur Vertheidigung meiner Schrift über das Leben Jesu und zur Charakteristik der gegenwärtigen Theologie* von Dr. D. F. Strauss," *Jahrbücher für wissenschaftliche Kritik,* November 1837, no. 101, 837; no. 103, 838.

Kritik der Geschichte der Offenbarung. Die Religion des alten Testaments in der gechichtlichen Entwicklung ihrer Prinzipien dargestellt, Bd. I and II (Berlin: Ferdinand Dümmler, 1838).

Herr Dr. Hengstenberg. Ein Beitrag zur Kritik des religiösen Bewußtseins. Kritische Briefe über den Gegensatz des Gesetzes und des Evangeliums (Berlin: Ferdinand Dümmler, 1839).

(anon., 1st ed.) *Die evangelische Landeskirche Preußens und die Wissenschaft* (Leipzig: Otto Wigand, 1840); second edition, with author indicated, 1840.

Kritik der evangelischen Geschichte des Johannes (Bremen: Carl Schünemann, 1840).

"Der christliche Staat und unsere Zeit," *Hallische Jahrbücher für deutsche Wissenschaft und Kunst,* 7–12 June 1841, nos. 135–40, pp. 537–58.

Kritik der evangelischen Geschichte der Synoptiker. Erster Band (Leipzig: Otto Wigand, 1841).

Kritik der evangelischen Geschichte der Synoptiker. Zweiter Band (Leipzig: Otto Wigand, 1841).

(anon.) *Die Posaune des jüngsten Gerichts über Hegel den Atheisten und Antichristen. Ein Ultimatum* (Leipzig: Otto Wigand, 1841); *The Trumpet of the Last Judgement against Hegel the Atheist and Antichrist. An Ultimatum*, trans. L. Stepelevich (Lewiston, N.Y.: E. Mellen Press, 1989).

"Theologische Schamlosigkeiten," *Deutsche Jahrbücher für Wissenschaft und Kunst*, 15–18 November 1841, nos. 117–20, pp. 465–79.

"Über die neuesten Erscheinungen in der englischen Kirche," *Rheinische Zeitung für Politik, Handel und Gewerbe* (dated London, Jan. 8), Jan. 20, 1842, no. 20, Beiblatt.

"Die Parteien im jetzigen Frankreich," *Rheinische Zeitung* (dated Paris, Jan. 15), Jan. 23, 1842, no. 23, Beiblatt.

"Die Rheingrenze," *Rheinische Zeitung*, Jan. 30, no. 30, Beiblatt.

"Die deutschen Sympathien für Frankreich," *Rheinische Zeitung*, Feb. 6, 1842, no. 37, Beiblatt.

"Die Zersplitterung der Parteien in Frankreich," *Rheinische Zeitung*, Feb. 10, 1842, no. 41, Beiblatt.

"Das Köllner Quartett," *Rheinische Zeitung*, March 1, 1842, no. 60, Feuilleton.

"Rezension: Lebensbilder aus den Befreiungskriegen," *Rheinische Zeitung*, March 1, 6, 13, 31, nos. 60, 65, 72, 90, Beiblatt.

"Die deutschen 'Nationalen,'" *Rheinische Zeitung*, March 10, no. 69, Beiblatt.

"Joseph II. und die Belgische Revolution," *Rheinische Zeitung*, March 13, 1842, no. 72, Beiblatt.

Kritik der evangelischen Geschichte der Synoptiker und des Johannes, Dritter und letzter Band (Braunschweig: Fr. Otto, 1842).

"Eine von den Tendenzen der 'Augsburger Allgemeinen Zeitung,'" *Rheinische Zeitung*, March 27, 1842, no. 86, Beiblatt.

"Die Kollisionen in den konstitutionellen Staaten," *Rheinische Zeitung*, March 27, 1842, no. 86, Beiblatt.

"Kirche und Staats-Gouvernement" (dated Munich, March 10), *Rheinische Zeitung*, March 29, 1842, no. 88, Beiblatt.

"Wie Lüttich dem deutschen Reiche verloren ging," *Rheinische Zeitung*, April 3, 1842, no. 93, Beiblatt.

"Rezension: Preußen, seine Verfassung, seine Verwaltung, sein Verhältnis zu Deutschland. von Bülow-Cummerow. Berlin 1842," *Rheinische Zeitung*, April 7, 1842, no. 97, Beiblatt.

"Was ist Lehrfreiheit?" *Rheinische Zeitung*, April 12, 1842, no. 102, Beiblatt.

"Der Terrorismus der 'Augsburger Allgemeinen Zeitung,'" *Rheinische Zeitung*, April 24, 1842, no. 114, Beiblatt.

"Die deutschen Artikel der 'Augsburger Zeitung,'" *Rheinische Zeitung*, May 1, 1842, no. 121, Beiblatt.

"Etwas über die Presse in der Schweiz," *Rheinische Zeitung*, May 3, 1842, no. 123, Beiblatt.

(anonymous) *Hegels Lehre von der Religion und Kunst von dem Standpuncte des Glaubens aus beurtheilt.* (Leipzig: Otto Wigand, 1842); new edition Aalen: Scientia Verlag, 1967.

"Rezension: *Deutschlands Beruf in der Gegenwart und Zukunft.* von Th. Rohmer. Zürich und Winterthur 1841," *Rheinische Zeitung*, June 7, 1842, no. 158, Beiblatt.

"Louis Philippe und die Juli-Regierung," *Rheinische Zeitung*, June 19, 21, 23, 1842, nos. 170, 172, 174, Beiblatt.

(anonymous) "Bekenntnisse einer schwachen Seele," *Deutsche Jahrbücher*, 23–24 June, 1842, nos. 148–49, pp. 589–96.

Die gute Sache der Freiheit und meine eigene Angelegenheit (Zürich und Winterthur: Verlag des literarischen Comptoirs, 1842).

"Rezension: *Das Leben Jesu, kritisch bearbeitet*, von D. F. Strauss. 2 Bde. Tübingen 1840." *Deutsche Jahrbücher*, July 10–14, 1842, nos. 165–68, pp. 660–71.

"Die Judenfrage," *Deutsche Jahrbücher*, Oct. 27–Nov. 4, 1842, nos. 274–82, pp. 1093–126.

"Johann Christian Edelmann oder Spinoza unter den Theologen," *Deutsche Jahrbücher*, Nov. 24–25, 1842, nos. 302–03, pp. 205–12.

"Rezension: *Die christliche Glaubenslehre in ihrer geschichtlichen Entwicklung und im Kampf mit der modernen Wissenschaft*. von D. F. Strauss. 2 Bde. 1840–1841." *Deutsche Jahrbücher*, Jan. 25–28, 1843, nos. 21–24, pp. 81–95.

Die Judenfrage (Braunschweig: Fr. Otto, 1843).

"Leiden und Freuden des theologischen Bewußtseins," in A. Ruge (ed.), *Anekdota zur neuesten deutschen Philosophie und Publizistik*, vol. 2 (Zürich und Winterthur: Verlag des literarischen Comptoirs, 1843), 89–112.

"Rezension: *'Bremisches Magazin für evangelische Wahrheit gegenüber dem modernen Pietismus. Erstes Heft.'* Auch unter dem Titel: *'Die verschiedenen theologischen Richtungen in der protestantischen Kirche unserer Zeit'* von Paniel. Bremen. bei Schünemann 1841." *Anekdota* II, 113–34.

"Rezension: *'Einleitung in die Dogmengeschichte'* von Theodor Kliefoth." *Anekdota* II, 135–59.

"Rezension: *Die Geschichte des Lebens Jesu mit steter Rücksicht auf die vorhandenen Quellen dargestellt* von Dr. von Ammon. Leipzig, 1842." *Anekdota* II, 160–85.

"Das alte neue Testament," *Anekdota* II, 186–93.

Das entdeckte Christenthum. Eine Erinnerung an das 18. Jahrhundert und ein Beitrag zur Krisis des 19. (Zürich und Winterthur: Verlag des literarischen Comptoirs, 1843).

"Die Fähigkeit der heutigen Juden und Christen, frei zu werden," in G. Herwegh (ed.), *Einundzwanzig Bogen aus der Schweiz* (Zürich und Winterthur: Verlag des literarischen Comptoirs, 1843), 56–71.

Geschichte der Politik, Kultur und Aufklärung des achtzehnten Jahrhunderts, Erster Band: Deutschland während der ersten vierzig Jahre des achtzehnten Jahrhunderts (Charlottenburg: Verlag von Egbert Bauer, 1843).

Denkwürdigkeiten zur Geschichte der neueren Zeit seit der Französischen Revolution. Nach den Quellen und Original Memoiren bearbeitet und herausgegeben von Bruno Bauer und Edgar Bauer (Charlottenburg: Verlag von Egbert Bauer, 1843–1844). Contains the following pamphlets by Bruno Bauer: (a) "Bouillé und die Flucht Ludwig XVI," 1843. (b) "Der 20 Juni und der 10 August, 1792 oder der letzte Kampf des Königtums in Frankreich mit der Volkspartei," 1843. (c) "Die Septembertage 1792 und die ersten Kämpfe der Parteien der Republik in Frankreich." 2. Abteilungen, 1844. (d) "Der Prozess Ludwig XVI und der 21. Januar 1793," 1844.

"Neueste Schriften über die Judenfrage," *Allgemeine Literatur Zeitung* I, December 1843, 1–17.

"Rezension: Hinrichs, 'Politische Vorlesungen.' Band 1," *Allg. Lit.-Ztg.* I, December 1843, 29–31.

"Neueste Schriften über die Judenfrage" (continuation), *Allg. Lit.-Ztg.* IV, March 1844, 10–19.

"Rezension: Hinrichs, 'Politische Vorlesungen,' Band II." *Allg. Lit.-Ztg.* V, April 1844, 23–25.

Briefwechsel zwischen Bruno Bauer und Edgar Bauer während der Jahre 1839–1842 aus Bonn und Berlin (Charlottenburg: Verlag von Egbert Bauer, 1844).

"Korrespondenz aus der Provinz," *Allg. Lit.-Ztg.* VI, May 1844, 20–38.

"Erkenntnis des Oberzensursgericht in betreff der zwei ersten Bogen des Briefwechsels zwischen Bruno Bauer und Edgar Bauer," *Allg. Lit.-Ztg.* VI, May 1844, 38–41.

"Was ist jetzt der Gegenstand der Kritik?" *Allg. Lit-Ztg.* VIII, July 1844, 18–26.

"Briefe aus Berlin I," *Norddeutsche Blätter für Kritik, Literatur und Unterhaltung* II, August 1844, 20–27.

"Wilhelm Weitling," *Norddeutsche Blätter* II, August 1844, 43–48.

"Die Gattung und die Masse," *Allg. Lit.-Ztg.* X, September 1844, 42–48.

Geschichte der Politik, Kultur und Aufklärung des achtzehnten Jahrhunderts. Fortsetzung: Deutschland während der Zeit der französischen Revolution. Erste Abteilung (Charlottenburg: Verlag von Egbert Bauer, 1844).

"Briefe aus Berlin II," *Norddeutsche Blätter* III, September 1844, 1–12.

"Ludwig Feuerbach," *Norddeutsche Blätter* IV, October 1844, 1–13.

"Innere Geschichte des Illuminaten-Ordens," *Allg. Lit.-Ztg.*, XI-XII, November–December 1844, 1–25.

"Der Sturz des Illuminaten-Ordens," *Norddeutsche Blätter* V, November 1844, 35–49.

"Die Lichtfreunde in Kothen," *Norddeutsche Blätter* V, November 1844, 50–75.

"Die Organisation der Arbeit," *Norddeutsche Blätter* V, November 1844, 76–87.

Acktenstücke zu den Verhandlungen über die Beschlagnahme der "Geschichte der Politik, Kultur und Aufklärung des achtzehnten Jahrhunderts," von Bruno Bauer. Teil I herausgegeben von Bruno Bauer (Christiania: Verlag von C.C. Werner, 1844).

"Marat und Charlotte Corday," *Norddeutsche Blätter* VI, December 1844, 14–27.

"Die zweite Versammlung des Berlin Lokalvereins für das Wohl der arbeitenden Klassen," *Norddeutsche Blätter* VI, December 1844, 39–52.

"Die protestantischen Freunde und ihre Gegner," *Norddeutsche Blätter* VII, January 1845, 20–42.

"Die religiöse Bewegung. Erster Artikel. Die Masse," *Norddeutsche Blätter* VII, January 1845, 60–71.

"Briefe aus Berlin III," *Norddeutsche Blätter* VIII, February 1845, 57–65.

Geschichte der Politik, Kultur und Aufklärung des achtzehnten Jahrhunderts. Fortsetzung. Deutschland und die französische Revolution. Zweite Abteilung: Die Politik der Revolution bis zum Frieden von Basel (Charlottenburg: Verlag von Egbert Bauer, 1845).

Geschichte der Politik, Kultur und Aufklärung des achtzehnten Jahrhunderts. Fortsetzung: Deutschland und die französiche Revolution. Dritte Abteilung. Die Politik der Revolution von Baseler Frieden bis zum Rastadter Kongress (Charlottenburg: Verlag von Egbert Bauer, 1845).

"Charakteristik Ludwig Feuerbachs," *Wigands Vierteljahrschrift* III, 1845, 86–146.

*Geschichte Deutschlands und der französischen Revolution unter der Herrschaft Napoleons.
Erster Band. Bis zum Frieden von Luneville* (Charlottenburg: Verlag von Egbert
Bauer, 1846).

*Geschichte Deutschlands und der französischen Revolution unter der Herrschaft Napoleons.
Zweiter Band. Drei Jahre Kontrerevolution* (Charlottenburg: Verlag von Egbert
Bauer, 1846).

Geschichte der Französischen Revolution bis zur Stiftung der Republik, von Bruno Bauer,
Edgar Bauer und Ernst Jungnitz. Erster Band: *Die ersten Kämpfe der konstitutionellen Prinzips mit dem Königtum und der Volkspartei*. Zweiter Band: *Der Sturz
des Königtums und die ersten Kämpfe der Republik* (Leipzig: Voigt und Fernans
Separat-Conto, 1847) (a reprint of *Denkwürdigkeiten*).

Vollständige Geschichte der Parteikämpfe in Deutschland während der Jahre 1842–1846
(Charlottenburg: Verlag von Egbert Bauer, 1847).

"Erste Wahlrede von 1848," in E. Barnikol, *Bruno Bauer: Studien und Materialien*,
525–31.

"Verteidigungsrede Bruno Bauers vor den Wahlmännern des Vierten
Wahlbezirkes am 22.2. 1849," in E. Barnikol, *Bruno Bauer: Studien und Materialien*, 518–25.

Untergang des Frankfurter Parlaments (Charlottenburg: Verlag von Egbert Bauer,
1849).

*Die bürgerliche Revolution in Deutschland seit dem Anfange der deutschkatholischen Be-
wegung bis zur Gegenwart* (Berlin: Hempel, 1849).

*Der Fall und Untergang der neuesten Revolutionen. I. Der Sturz der französischen Republik
und des deutschen Reiches durch Napoleon Bonaparte. II. Der Aufstand und Fall
des deutschen Radikalismus vom Jahre 1842* (reprints respectively of *Geschichte
Deutschlands und der französischen Revolution*, and of *Vollständige Geschichte der
Parteikämpfe*).

B. 1850–82 (Cited works only)

Kritik der paulinischen Briefe (Berlin: Gustav Hempel, 1850–51).

Kritik der Evangelien und Geschichte ihres Ursprungs, 3 vols. (Berlin: Gustav Hempel,
1850–51); 4th vol. under the title *Die theologische Erklärung der Evangelien*
(Berlin, 1852).

"The Present Position of the Jews," *New York Daily Tribune*, June 7, 1852.

Russland und das Germanenthum, 2 vols. (Charlottenburg: Egbert Bauer,1853).

De la dictature occidentale (Charlottenburg: Egbert Bauer, 1854).

Deutschland und das Russenthum (Charlottenburg: Egbert Bauer, 1854).

Die russische Kirche. Schlussheft (Charlottenburg: Egbert Bauer, 1855).

*Das Judenthum in der Fremde. Separat-Abdruck aus dem Wagener'schen Staats- und
Gesellschaftslexikon* (Berlin, 1863).

Freimaurer, Jesuiten und Illuminaten in ihrem geschichtlichen Zusammenhange (Berlin:
F. Heinicke, 1863).

Philo, Strauss und Renan und das Urchristenthum (Berlin: Hempel, 1874).

*Einfluss des englischen Quäkerthums auf die deutsche Cultur und auf das englisch-
russische Project einer Weltkirche* (Berlin: Eugen Grosser, 1878).

*Christus und die Cäsaren. Der Ursprung des Christenthums aus dem römischen Griechen-
thum* (Berlin: Eugen Grosser, 1879).

Zur Orientierung über die Bismarck'sche Ära (Chemnitz: Ernst Schmeitzner, 1880).
Disraelis romantischer und Bismarcks socialistischer Imperialismus (Chemnitz: Ernst Schmeitzner, 1882).

C. Archives

Barnikol, Ernst, *Bruno Bauer. Darstellung und Quellen,* ca. 1965, unpublished manuscript, International Institute for Social History, Amsterdam.

van der Bergh van Eysinga, Gustaaf Adolf, *Bruno Bauer. Sein Leben und seine theologische Bedeutung,* unpublished manuscript, International Institute for Social History, Amsterdam.

D. Journals edited by Bruno Bauer

(a) *Zeitschrift für spekulative Theologie* in Gemeinschaft mit einem Verein von Gelehrten herausgegeben von Lic. Bruno Bauer, Privat-Docenten an der Universität zu Berlin. Berlin, bei Ferdinand Dümmler (1836–38). Three volumes appeared between 1836 and 1838, including a number of texts by Bauer. Among these are: "Der mosaische Ursprung der Gesetzgebung des Pentateuch," vertheidigt vom Lic. B. Bauer, 1836, vol. I, no. 1, 140–81; "Die Prinzipien der mosaischen Rechts- und Religions-Verfassung nach ihrem innern Zusammenhange," entwickelt von Lic. B. Bauer. 1837, vol. II, no. 2, 297–353; "Die Authentie des Pentateuch, erwiesen von Dr. E. W. Hengstenberg. Erster Band. Berlin, bei Ludwig Oehmigke 1836," von B. Bauer, Lic. 1837, vol. II, no. 11, pp. 439–66.

(b) *Allgemeine Literatur-Zeitung.* Monatschrift. Charlottenburg, 12 issues December 1843–October 1844. Second edition under the title: *Streit der Kritik mit den modernen Gegensätzen.* Mit Beiträgen von Bruno Bauer, Edgar Bauer, Ernst Jungnitz, Szeliga und Anderen (Charlottenburg: Verlag von Egbert Bauer, 1847).

(c) *Norddeutsche Blätter. Eine Monatschrift für Kritik, Literatur und Unterhaltung.* Charlottenburg. 10 issues July 1844–April 1845. Second edition under the title: *Beiträge zum Feldzuge der Kritik. Norddeutsche Blätter für 1844 und 1845.* Mit Beiträgen von Bruno und Edgar Bauer, A. Fränkel, L. Köppen, Szeliga u.s. (Berlin, 1846).

(d) collaboration with Friedrich Wilhelm Hermann Wagener as editor of *Neues Conversations-Lexikon. Staats- und Gesellschafts-Lexikon,* 23 vols. (Berlin, 1859–67).

E. Theses

Licentiate, 1834: "Theses Theologicae quas summe reverendi Theologorum Ordinis in Universitate Literaria Frederica-Guilelma auctoritate pro Gradu Licentiati in Sacro-Sancta Theologia rite obtinendo publice defendet die XV M. Martii A. MDCCCXXXIV Hora XI Bruno Bauer Carolotopolitanus," reproduced in Barnikol and in van den Bergh van Eysinga manuscripts, IISH, Amsterdam.

Works by Other Left Hegelians

Anonymous and unidentified, "Das Wohl der arbeitenden Klassen," *Norddeutsche Blätter* IX, March 1845, 52–66.

Bauer, Edgar, *Bruno Bauer und seine Gegner* (Berlin: Jonasverlag, 1842).

Die liberalen Bestrebungen in Deutschland, 2 Hefte (Zürich und Winterthur: Verlag des literarischen Comptoirs, 1843).

Staat, Religion und Partei (Leipzig: Otto Wigand, 1843).

Der Streit der Kritik mit Kirche und Staat (Bern: Jenni, Sohn, 1844).

Pressprozess Edgar Bauers über sein Werk: Der Streit der Kritik mit Kirche und Staat. Acktenstücke (Bern: Jenni, Sohn, 1844).

Die Parteien. Politische Revue Heft 1–3 (Hamburg, 1849).

Engels, Friedrich, "Bruno Bauer und das Urchristentum," *Sozialdemokrat* (May 4 and 11, 1882).

"Ludwig Feuerbach and the End of Classical German Philosophy," in K. Marx and F. Engels, *Selected Works* (New York: International Publishers, 1968), 594–632.

Faucher, J., "Berlins Armenwesen," *Allg. Lit.-Ztg.* XI–XII, October 1844, 52–60.

Feuerbach, Ludwig, "Zur Kritik der Hegelschen Philosophie" [1839], in W. Bolin and F. Jodl (eds.), *Sämmtliche Werke* II (Stuttgart: Fromann, 1904).

Das Wesen des Christentums (1841), hrsg. Werner Schuffenhauer und Wolfgang Harich (Berlin: Akademie Verlag, 1973); *The Essence of Christianity* (New York: Harper & Row, 1957).

"Vorläufige Thesen zur Reformation der Philosophie," *Anekdota* II, 1843, 62 ff; reprinted in W. Schuffenhauer, ed., *Feuerbachs Kleinere Schriften* II (Berlin: Akademie Verlag, 1970).

"Notwendigkeit einer Veränderung" [1842–43], in Karl Löwith, ed., *Die Hegelsche Linke* (Stuttgart: Fromann, 1962).

Grundsätze der Philosophie der Zukunft (Zürich und Winterthur: Verlag des literarischen Comptoirs, 1843); *Principles of the Philosophy of the Future*, trans. M. Vogel (Indianapolis: Bobbs-Merrill, 1966).

"Über 'Das Wesen des Christentums' im Bezug auf dem 'Einzigen und sein Eigenthum'" *Wigands Vierteljahrschrift* II, 1845, 193–205.

Ausgewählte Briefe von und an Ludwig Feuerbach, Zweiter Band, ed. W. Bolin (Leipzig: O. Wigand, 1904).

Ludwig Feuerbach in seinem Briefwechsel und Nachlass, Bd. I, 1820–1850, hrsg. Karl Grün (Leipzig: C. F. Winter, 1874).

Köppen, K. F., *Friedrich der Grosse und seine Widersacher* (Leipzig: 1840).

Marx, Karl, "Difference Between the Democritean and Epicurean Philosophy of Nature," in Karl Marx, Frederick Engels, *Collected Works*, vol. 1 (New York: International Publishers, 1975), 25–105.

"The Philosophical Manifesto of the Historical School of Law," *Collected Works*, vol. 1 (New York: International Publishers, 1975), 203–10.

"Contribution to the Critique of Hegel's Philosophy of Law. Introduction," *Collected Works*, vol. 3 (New York: International Publishers, 1975), 5–129.

"On the Jewish Question," *Collected Works*, vol. 3 (New York: International Publishers, 1975), 146–74.

"Economic and Philosophical Manuscripts of 1844," *Collected Works*, vol. 3 (New York: International Publishers, 1975), 270–82.

"Theses on Feuerbach," *Collected Works*, vol. 5 (New York: International Publishers, 1976), 3–8.

"Speech on the Question of Free Trade," *Collected Works*, vol. 6 (New York: International Publishers, 1976), 450–65.

"The Bourgeoisie and the Counter-Revolution," *Collected Works*, vol. 8 (1977), 154–69.

Marx, Karl, Friedrich Engels, *Historich-kritische Gesamtausgabe (MEGA)*, hrsg. D. Ryazanov. Dritte Abteilung, Band I: Marx–Engels Briefwechsel 1844–1853 (Berlin: Marx–Engels Verlag, 1929).

"The Holy Family, or Critique of Critical Criticism," *Collected Works*, vol. 4 (New York: International Publishers, 1975), 5–211.

"The German Ideology," *Collected Works*, vol. 5 (New York: International Publishers, 1976), 19–539.

"Manifesto of the Communist Party," *Collected Works*, vol. 6 (New York: International Publishers, 1976), 477–519.

Marx and Engels on Religion (Moscow: Progress, 1957).

Pepperle, Heinz and Ingrid, eds., *Die Hegelsche Linke. Dokumente zu Philosophie und Politik im deutschen Vormärz* (Frankfurt am Main: Röderberg, 1986).

Ruge, Arnold (editor, with Theodor Echtermeyer), *Hallische Jahrbücher für deutsche Wissenschaft und Kunst*, Leipzig (edited in Halle), Jan. 1. 1838–June 30, 1841.

Preußen und die Reaction. Zur Geschichte unserer Zeit (Leipzig: O. Wigand, 1838).

"Karl Streckfuß und das Preußentum," *Hallische Jahrbücher*, November 1839.

"Freiherr von Florencourt und die Kategorien der politischen Praxis," *Hallische Jahrbücher*, November 1840.

"Zur Kritik des gegenwärtigen Staats- und Völkerrechts" (1840), in G.W.F. Hegel, *Philosophie des Rechts*, hrsg. H. Reichelt (Frankfurt a. M.: Ullstein, 1972), 598–623.

"Die Hegelsche Rechtsphilosophie und die Politik unsrer Zeit" (1842), in G.W.F. Hegel, *Philosophie des Rechts*, hrsg. H. Reichelt, 624–49.

(editor), *Deutsche Jahrbücher für Wissenschaft und Kunst*, Leipzig (edited in Dresden), July 2, 1841–January 7, 1843.

(editor), *Anekdota zur neuesten deutschen Philosophie und Publizistik*, 2 vol. (Zürich und Winterthur: Verlag des literarischen Comptoirs, 1843).

(editor, with Karl Marx), *Deutsch–französische Jahrbücher*, 1ste und 2te Lieferung (Paris, 1844; new edition Leipzig: Verlag Philipp Reclam, 1973).

Zwei Jahre in Paris. Studien und Erinnerungen (Leipzig: W. Jurany, 1846).

Briefwechsel und Tagebuchblätter aus den Jahren, 1825–1880, hrsg. P. Nerrlich (Berlin: Weidmann, 1886).

Stirner, Max (Johann Caspar Schmidt), "Rezension: Rosenkranz, 'Königsberger Skizzen,'" *Leipziger Allgemeine Zeitung*, July 20, 1842; *Rheinische Zeitung*, July 26, 1842.

Der Einzige und sein Eigentum (Leipzig: O. Wigand, 1845).

(anon.), "Bruno Bauer," *Wigands Konversations-Lexikon* (Leipzig: O. Wigand, 1846), 78–80.

Strauss, David Friedrich, *Das Leben Jesu, kritisch bearbeitet*, 2 vols. (Tübingen: C. F. Osiander, 1835; second edition 1836, third 1838, fourth 1840).

Streitschriften zur Vertheidigung meiner Schrift über das Leben Jesu und zur Charakteristik der gegenwärtigen Theologie, 3. vol. (Tübingen: C. F. Osiander, 1837).

Szeliga (Franz Zychlin von Zychlinski), *Die Organisation der Arbeit der Menschheit und die Kunst der Geschichtsschreibung Schlossers, Gervinus, Dahlmanns und Bruno Bauers* (Charlottenburg: Egbert Bauer, 1846).

Other Primary Sources

Aristotle, *The Metaphysics*, 2 vols., trans. H. Tredennick (London: Heinemann, 1956–58).
The Nichomachean Ethics, trans. M. Ostwald (Indianapolis: Bobbs-Merrill, 1962)
The Politics, trans. E. Barker (London: Oxford University Press, 1958).
Cicero, Marcus Tullius, *De Officiis*, trans. Walter Miller (Cambridge: Harvard University Press, 1913).
Descartes, R., *Discourse on Method and Mediations*, trans. F. E. Sutcliffe (Toronto: Penguin, 1968).
d'Holbach, Paul-Henry Thiry, *Le christianisme dévoilé, ou Examen des principes et des effets de la religion chrétienne* (London, 1756), *Oeuvres philosophiques*, tome 1, Préface de Jean Claude Bourdin (Paris: Editions Alive, 1998), 1–120.
Epictetus, *The Discourse and Manual*, trans. P. E. Matheson (London: Oxford University Press, 1916).
Fichte, J. G., *Der geschloßne Handelsstaat*, Gesamtausgabe, Bd. I/7 (Stuttgart: Fromann, 1988), 37–141.
Grundlage der gesammten Wissenschaftslehre, Gesamtausgabe, Bd. I/2, (Stuttgart: Fromann, 1965); *Wissenschaftslehre*, ed. and trans. P. Heath and J. Lachs (New York: Appleton-Century-Crofts, 1970).
Grundlage des Naturrechts, Gesamtausgabe der Bayerischen Akademie der Wissenschaften, ed. R. Lauth et al., Bd. I/3 and I/4 (Stuttgart: Fromann, 1966 and 1970).
Reden an die deutsche Nation, Werke VII (Berlin: de Gruyter, 1971), 263–499.
Versuch einer Kritik aller Offenbarung, in *Fichtes Werke* V (Berlin: de Gruyter, 1971), 9–174 [first ed. 1792, second 1793].
Hegel, G.W.F., *Briefe von und an Hegel*, Bd. 3, ed. J. Hoffmeister (Hamburg: Meiner, 1961).
Difference Between the Fichtean and Schellingian Systems of Philosophy, trans. and intro. J. P. Surber (Reseda, Cal.: Ridgeview, 1978).
Early Theological Writings, trans. T. M. Knox (Philadelphia: University of Pennsylvania Press, 1971).
Enzyklopädie der philosophischen Wissenschaften im Grundrisse (1827), *Gesammelte Werke*, Bd. 19 (Hamburg: Meiner, 1989).
Enzyklopädie der philosophischen Wissenschaften im Grundrisse (1830), hrsg. Friedhelm Nicolin und Otto Pöggeler (Hamburg: Meiner, 1969).
Frühe politische Systeme, ed. Gerhard Göhler (Frankfurt/M: Ullstein, 1974).
Glauben und Wissen, Gesammelte Werke, Bd. 4 (Hamburg: Meiner, 1968).
Grundlinien der Philosophie des Rechts, ed. Helmut Reichelt (Frankfurt am Main: Ullstein, 1972); *Elements of the Philosophy of Right*, ed. Allen W. Wood, trans. H. B. Nisbet (Cambridge: Cambridge University Press, 1991).

Introductory Lectures on Aesthetics, trans. Bernard Bosanquet, edited by Michael Inwood (Harmondsworth: Penguin, 1993).

Lectures on Natural Right and Political Science. The First Philosophy of Right (Berkeley: University of California Press, 1995).

Lectures on the History of Philosophy, 3 vols., trans. E. S. Haldane (London: Kegan Paul, 1892–95).

Lectures on the Philosophy of World History. Introduction: Reason in History, trans. H. B. Nisbet (Cambridge: Cambridge University Press, 1975).

Natural Law. The Scientific Ways of Treating Natural Law, Its Place in Moral Philosophy, and Its Relation to the Positive Sciences of Law, trans. T. M. Knox (Philadelphia: University of Pennsylvania Press, 1975).

Phänomenologie des Geistes, ed. J. Hoffmeister (Hamburg: Meiner, 1955); *Phenomenology of Mind*, trans. J. B. Baillie (New York: Harper & Row, 1967); *Phenomenology of Spirit*, trans. A. V. Miller (Oxford: Oxford University Press, 1977).

Philosophy of History, trans. J. Sibree (New York: Dover, 1956).

Philosophy of Religion, trans. E. B. Speirs and J. B. Sanderson (London: Kegan Paul, 1895).

Political Writings, trans. T. M. Knox (Oxford: Clarendon Press, 1964).

Vorlesungen über die Ästhetik, I, Sämtliche Werke. Jubiläumsausgabe, ed. H. Glockner, Band 12 (Stuttgart: Fromann-Holzboog, 1964).

Vorlesungen über die Geschichte der Philosophie, III, Werke, Bd. 20 (Frankfurt am Main: Suhrkamp, 1971).

Vorlesungen über die Philosophie der Religion, Erster Band, 2nd ed., *Werke*, Bd. 11 (Berlin, 1840).

Vorlesungen über Rechtsphilosophie 1818–1831, ed. K.-H. Ilting, vols. I–IV (Stuttgart: Fromann-Holzboog, 1973–74).

Wissenschaft der Logik, Sämtliche Werke, Bd. 5–6 (Stuttgart: Fromann, 1964); *Science of Logic*, trans. A. V. Miller (London: Allen and Unwin, 1969).

Jacoby, J. (anon.), *Vier Fragen beantwortet von einem Ost-Preussen* (Leipzig, 1841).

Kant, Immanuel, *Grundlegung zur Metaphysik der Sitten, Werke*, Bd. 4, ed. A. Buchenau and E. Cassirer (Hildesheim: Gerstenberg, 1973); *Groundwork of the Metaphysics of Morals*, trans. H. J. Paton (New York: Harper & Row, 1964).

Kritik der praktischen Venunft, Werke, Bd. 5 (Hildesheim: Gerstenberg, 1973): *Critique of Practical Reason*, trans. L. W. Beck (New York: Macmillan, 1956).

Kritik der reinen Vernunft, ed. R. Schmidt (Hamburg: Meiner, 1930); *Critique of Pure Reason*, trans. N. K. Smith (New York: St. Martin's Press, 1929).

Kritik der Urteilskraft, Kants gesammelte Schriften, vol. 5, Königlich Preußische Akademie der Wissenschaften (Berlin: de Gruyter, 1908); *Critique of Judgment*, trans. and ed. Werner Pluhar (Indianapolis: Hackett, 1987).

On History, ed. and trans. L. W. Beck (Indianapolis: Bobbs-Merrill, 1963).

Kant's Political Writings, ed. H. Reiss (Cambridge: Cambridge University Press, 1970).

Leo, Heinrich, *Die Hegelingen. Actenstücke und Belege zu der sogenannten Denunciation der ewigen Wahrheit* (Halle: E. Anton, 1838; second edition, 1839).

Luther, M., *Martin Luther: Selections from his writings*, ed. J. Dillenberger (Garden City: Doubleday, 1961).

Machiavelli, N., *The Prince and Discourses* (New York: Modern Library, 1950).

Marcus Aurelius, *Mediations*, 2 vols., trans. A.S.L. Farquharson (Oxford: Clarendon Press, 1964).

Plato, *The Collected Dialogues*, ed. E. Hamilton and H. Cairns (Princeton: Princeton University Press, 1961).

Schiller, Friedrich, *Wallenstein. Ein dramatisches Gedicht* (Reinbek bei Hamburg: Rowohlt, 1961).

Spinoza, B., *Works*, 3 vols., trans. R. H. Elwes (New York: Dover, 1951–55).

Secondary Sources

Anderson, Perry, *Lineages of the Absolutist State* (London: New Left Books, 1974).

Assoun, P.-L., and G. Raulet, *Marxisme et théorie critique* (Paris: Payot, 1978).

Avineri, Shlomo, *Hegel's Theory of the Modern State* (Cambridge: Cambridge University Press, 1972).

Baatsch, H.-A., "Introduction," in B. Bauer, *La trompette du dernier jugement contre Hegel, L'Athée et l'Antéchrist. Un ultimatum* (Paris: Aubier-Montaigne, 1972).

Bakunin, Michael, *Marxism, Freedom and the State*, trans. K. J. Kenafick (London: Freedom Press, 1950).

[Bakounine, Michel], *L'empire knouto-germanique et la révolution sociale 1870–71*, ed. Arthur Lehning (Leiden: Brill, 1981).

Barnikol, Ernst, *Bruno Bauer, Studien und Materialien*, aus dem Nachlass ausgewählt und zusammengestellt von P. Riemer und H.-M. Sass (Assen: van Gorcum, 1972).

"Bruno Bauer, der radikalste Religionskritiker und konservativste Junghegelianer," *Das Altertum*, Band 7, Heft 1 (Berlin: Akademie Verlag, 1961), 41–49.

"Bruno Bauers Kampf gegen Religion und Christentum und die Spaltung der vormärzlichen preussischen Opposition," *Zeitschrift für Kirchen-Geschichte* XLVI (1928) 1–34.

Das entdeckte Christentum im Vormärz. Bruno Bauers Kampf gegen Religion und Christentum und Erstausgabe seiner Kampfschrift (Jena: Eugen Diederichs, 1927).

Barraclough, Geoffrey, *The Origins of Modern Germany* (New York: Capricorn, 1963).

Baynes, Kenneth, James Bohman, and Thomas McCarthy, eds., *After Philosophy. End or Transformation?* (Cambridge: MIT Press, 1987).

Beamish, Rob, "The Making of the Manifesto," *Socialist Register* (1998), 218–39.

Beiser, F. C. (ed.), *The Cambridge Companion to Hegel* (Cambridge: Cambridge University Press, 1993).

Best, Heinrich, "La bourgeoisie allemande a-t-elle trahi la révolution de 1848? Bilan d'une analyse sérielle," *Histoire et mesure*, vol. 3, no. 4 (1988), 427–40.

Interessenpolitik und nationale Integration. Handelspolitische Konflikte im frühindustriellen Deutschland (Göttingen: Vandenhoeck und Ruprecht, 1980), 81–279.

"Struktur und Wandel kollektiven politischen Handelns: Die handelspolitische Petitionsbewegung 1848/49," in Heinrich Volkmann and Jürgen Bergmann, eds., *Sozialer Protest. Studien zu traditioneller Resistenz und kollektiver Gewalt in Deutschland vom Vormärz bis zur Reichsgründung* (Opladen: Westdeutscher Verlag, 1984), 169–97.

Bienvenu, Richard T. (ed.), *The Ninth of Thermidor: The Fall of Robespierre* (London: Oxford University Press, 1968).

Bleiber, Helmut, Walter Schmidt, and Rolf Weber, eds., *Männer der Revolution von 1848*, Band II (Berlin: Akademie Verlag, 1987).

Blos, Wilhelm, *Die deutsche Revolution. Geschichte der deutschen Bewegung von 1848 und 1849* (Stuttgart: Dietz Verlag, 1893).

Böhme, H., *Prolegomena zu einer Sozial- und Wirtschaftsgeschichte Deutschlands im 19. und 20. Jahrhundert* (Frankfurt am Main: Suhrkamp, 1968).

Booth, William James, "The Limits of Autonomy: Karl Marx's Kant Critique," in Ronald Beiner and William James Booth, *Kant and Political Philosophy. The Contemporary Legacy* (New Haven: Yale University Press, 1993), 245–75.

Born, K. W., ed., *Moderne deutsche Wirtschaftsgeschichte* (Berlin: Neue wissenschaftliche Bibliothek, 1966).

Bouloiseau, Marc, *Le comité de salut publique (1793–1795)*, 2nd edition (Paris: Presses universitaires de France, 1968).

Bourgeois, Bernard, *Etudes hégéliennes* (Paris: Presses universitaires de France, 1992).

Bradl, Beate, *Die Rationalität des Schönen bei Kant und Hegel* (München: Fink, 1998).

Brazill, W. J., *The Young Hegelians* (New Haven: Yale University Press, 1970).

Breckman, Warren, "Ludwig Feuerbach and the Political Theology of Restoration," *History of Political Thought*, 13/3, 1992, 437–62.

   Marx, The Young Hegelians, and the Origins of Radical Social Theory. Dethroning the Self (Cambridge: Cambridge University Press, 1999).

Brudner, Alan, "Hegel and the Crisis in Private Law," in Drucilla Cornell et al., eds., *Hegel and Legal Theory* (London: Routledge, 1991), 127–73.

Brudney, Daniel, *Marx's Attempt to Leave Philosophy* (Cambridge: Harvard University Press, 1998).

Brunner, Otto, Werner Conze, and Reinhard Koselleck, eds., *Geschichtliche Grundbegriffe*, Bd. VI (Stuttgart: Klett, 1990).

Buhr, Manfred, *Revolution und Philosophie* (Berlin: DVW, 1965).

Carlebach, Julius, *Karl Marx and the Radical Critique of Judaism* (London: Routledge & Kegan Paul, 1978).

Cassirer, Ernst, *The Philosophy of the Enlightenment* (Boston: Beacon Press, 1951).

Cesa, Claudio, "Diritto naturale e filosofia classica tedesca," in Luca Fonnesu and Barbara Henry, eds., *Diritto naturale e filosofia classica tedesca* (Pisa: Paccini, 2000), 9–38.

   "Figure e problemi della storiografia filosofica della sinistra hegeliana, 1831–1848," *Annali dell' Instituto G.G. Feltrinelli* VI (1963), 62–104.

   ed., *Guida a Hegel* (Rome: Laterza, 1997).

   Studi sulla Sinistra hegeliana (Urbino: Argalia, 1972).

Chitty, Andrew, "Recognition and Social Relations of Production," *Historical Materialism*, no. 2 (Summer 1998), 57–97.

Claudín, Fernando, *Marx, Engels y la revolución de 1848* (Madrid: Siglo veintiuno de España, 1975).

Cohen, G. A., *History, Labour, and Freedom. Themes from Marx* (Oxford: Clarendon Press, 1988).

Conze, Werner (ed.), *Staat und Gesellschaft im deutschen Vormärz* (Stuttgart: Ernst Klett Verlag, 1962).

Cornu, Auguste, *Karl Marx et Friedrich Engels*, vols. I–IV (Paris: Presses universitaires de France, 1955).

Moses Hess et la Gauche hégélienne (Paris: Alcan, 1934).

The Origins of Marxian Thought (Springfield: C.C. Thomas, 1957).

de Pascale, Carla, "Archäologie des Rechtsstaates," in Manfred Buhr (ed.), *Das geistige Erbe Europas* (Naples: Vivarium, 1994), 489–505.

de Sousa, Norberto, "Ciceronian Republicanism and the History of Civil Society," unpublished ms., 1999.

Desmond, William, ed., *Hegel and His Critics. Philosophy in the Aftermath of Hegel* (Albany: State University of New York Press, 1989).

Droz, Jacques, *Europe Between Revolutions 1815–1848* (London: Fontana, 1967).

Les révolutions allemandes de 1848 (Paris: Presses universitaires de France, 1957).

Le romantisme allemand et l'État: Résistance et collaboration dans l'Allemagne napoléonienne (Paris: Payot, 1966).

Eichholtz, Dieter, *Junker und Bourgeoisie vor 1848 in der preussischen Eisenbahn-geschichte* (Berlin: Akademie Verlag, 1962).

Eßbach, Wolfgang, *Die Junghegelianer. Soziologie einer Intellektuellengruppe* (München: Wilhelm Fink Verlag, 1988).

Förster, Eckart, ed., *Kant's Transcendental Deductions* (Stanford: Stanford University Press, 1989).

Fulda, H.-F., and R.-P. Horstmann, eds., *Hegel und die "Kritik der Urteilskraft"* (Stuttgart: Klett-Cotta, 1990).

Furet, François, *Marx et la Révolution française* (Paris: Flammarion, 1986).

Gamby, Eric, *Edgar Bauer, Junghegelianer, Publizist und Polizeiagent* (Trier: Karl-Marx-Haus), 1985.

Gebhardt, Jürgen, "Karl Marx und Bruno Bauer," in *Politische Ordnung und men-schliche Existenz: Festgabe für Eric Voegelin:* (München: Beck 1962), 202–42.

Geraets, Theo, "Hegel: l'Esprit absolu comme ouverture du système," *Laval théologique et philosophique* 42/1 (1986), 3–13.

"Les trois lectures philosophiques de *l'Encyclopédie* ou la réalisation du concept de la philosophie chez Hegel," *Hegel-Studien*, 10 (1975), 231–54.

Gethmann-Siefert, Anne-Marie, "Ästhetik oder Philosophie der Kunst," *Hegel-Studien*, 26 (1991), 92–110.

Die Funktion der Kunst in der Geschichte, Untersuchungen zu Hegels Ästhetik (Bonn: Bouvier, 1984).

"Die Rolle der Kunst im Staat," *Hegel-Studien*, Beiheft 27 (1986), 69–74.

ed., *Phänomen versus System. Zum Verhältnis von philosophischer Systematik und Kunsturteil in Hegels Berliner Vorlesungen über Ästhetik oder Philosophie der Kunst* (Bonn: Bouvier, 1992).

Gethmann-Siefert, Anne-Marie, and Otto Pöggeler, eds., *Welt und Wirkung von Hegels Ästhetik* (Bonn: Bouvier, 1986).

Gilbert, Alan, *Marx's Politics* (New Brunswick: Rutgers University Press, 1981).

Gillis, J., "Aristocracy and Bureaucracy in Nineteenth-Century Prussia," *Past and Present* no. 41 (1968), 105–29.

Godechot, Jacques, *The Counter-Revolution, Doctrine and Action 1789–1804* (Princeton: Princeton University Press, 1971).

Göhler, Gerhard, "Neuere Arbeiten zu Hegels Rechtsphilosophie und zur Dialek-tik bei Hegel und Marx," *Hegel-Studien* 17–18 (1982–83), 355–83.

Grimm's Deutsches Worterbuch, Bd. 13 (Leipzig, 1922).

Guyer, Paul, ed., *The Cambridge Companion to Kant* (Cambridge: Cambridge University Press, 1992).

Habermas, Jürgen, "Labour and Interaction: Remarks on Hegel's Jena Philosophy of Mind," in *Theory and Practice*, trans. J. Viertel (London: Heinemann, 1974).

Hamerow, J. S., *Restoration, Revolution, Reaction: Economics and Politics in Germany 1815–1871* (Princeton: Princeton University Press, 1966).

Harris, H. S., *Hegel's Development*, vol. I: *Towards the Sunlight* (Oxford: Clarendon Press, 1972).

Hegel's Ladder, vol. 1, *The Pilgrimage of Reason*; vol. 2, *The Odyssey of Spirit* (Indianapolis: Hackett, 1997).

"The Social Ideal of Hegel's Economic Theory," in L. S. Stepelevich and D. Lamb, eds., *Hegel's Philosophy of Action* (Atlantic Highlands, N.J.: Humanities Press, 1983), 49–74.

Hartmann, Klaus, "Towards a New Systematic Reading of Hegel's Philosophy of Right," in Z. A. Pelczynski, ed., *The State and Civil Society* (Cambridge: Cambridge University Press, 1984), 114–36.

Haym, Rudolf, *Hegel und seine Zeit* (Berlin: Gaertner, 1857).

Henderson, W. O., *The State and the Industrial Revolution in Prussia 1740–1870* (Liverpool: Liverpool University Press, 1958).

Henrich, Dieter, "Logische Form und reale Totalität. Über die Begriffsform von Hegels eigentlichem Staatsbegriff," in D. Henrich and R.-P. Horstmann, eds., *Hegels Philosophie des Rechts* (Stuttgart: Klett-Cotta, 1982), 428–50.

"Zur Aktualität von Hegels Ästhetik," *Hegel-Studien*, Beiheft 11 (1974), 295–301.

Hertz-Eichenrode, Dieter, *Der Junghegeliander Bruno Bauer im Vormärz*. Inauguraldissertation (Berlin: Freie Universität, 1959).

Hobsbawm, Eric, *The Age of Revolution, 1789–1848* (New York: Mentor, 1972).

Hoffheimer, Michael H., *Eduard Gans and the Hegelian Philosophy of Law* (Dordrecht: Kluwer, 1995).

Hofstadter, A., "Die Kunst: Tod und Verklärung," *Hegel-Studien*, Beiheft 11 (1974), 271–85.

Honneth, Axel, "Work and Instrumental Action," *New German Critique*, Spring–Summer (1982), 31–54.

Hont, Istvan, and Michael Ignatieff, eds., *Wealth and Virtue. The Shaping of Political Economy in the Scottish Enlightenment* (Cambridge: Cambridge University Press, 1983).

Hook, Sydney, *From Hegel to Marx* (Ann Arbor: University of Michigan Press, 1962).

Höppner, Joachim, "Einleitung," in Arnold Ruge and Karl Marx, eds., *Deutsch-französische Jahrbücher* [1844] (Leipzig: Reclam, 1973), 5–83.

Houlgate, Stephen, "Substance, Causality, and the Question of Method in Hegel's Science of Logic," in Sally Sedgwick, ed., *The Reception of Kant's Critical Philosophy* (Cambridge: Cambridge University Press, 2000), 232–52.

Hyppolite, Jean, *Studies on Marx and Hegel*, trans. John O'Neill (New York: Basic Books, 1969).

Genesis and Structure of Hegel's Phenomenology of Spirit (Evanston: Northwestern University Press, 1974).

Ilting, K.-H., "Die 'Rechtsphilosophie' von 1820 und Hegels Vorlesungen über Rechtsphilosophie," in G.W.F. Hegel, *Vorlesungen über Rechtsphilosophie 1818–1831*, hrsg. K.-H. Ilting, vol. I (Stuttgart: Fromann-Holzboog, 1973), 25–126.

"Hegel's Concept of the State and Marx's Early Critique," in Z. A. Pelczynski, ed., *The State and Civil Society*, 93–113.

"The Dialectic of Civil Society," in Z. A. Pelczynski, ed., *The State and Civil Society*, 211–26.

Jaeck, Hans-Peter, *Die französische bürgerliche Revolution von 1789 im Frühwerk von Karl Marx (1843–1846). Geschichtsmethodologische Studien* (Vaduz: Topos Verlag, 1979).

Johnston, Larry, *Between Transcendence and Nihilism. Species-Ontology in the Philosophy of Ludwig Feuerbach* (New York: Peter Lang, 1995).

Jordan, Erich, *Die Entstehung der konservativen Partei und die preussischen Agrarverhältnisse vor 1848* (München: Duncker und Humblot, 1914).

Kamenka, Eugene, *The Philosophy of Ludwig Feuerbach* (New York: Praeger, 1970).

Kautsky, Karl, *Der Ursprung des Christentums. Eine historische Untersuchung* (Stuttgart: Dietz, 1908).

Nationalstaat, imperialistischer Staat und Staatenbund (Nürnberg: Fränkische Verlagsanstalt, 1915).

"Ultraimperialism," *New Left Review* No. 59, Jan. 1970.

Kegel, Martin, *Bruno Bauers Übergang von der Hegelschen Rechten zum Radikalismus.* Inauguraldissertation (Leipzig: Quelle und Meyer, 1908).

Koch, Lothar, *Humanistischer Atheismus und gesellschaftliches Engagement. Bruno Bauers "Kritische Kritik"* (Stuttgart: Kohlhammer, 1971).

Koigen, David, *Zur Vorgeschichte des modernen philosophischen Sozialismus in Deutschland* (Bern: Stürzenegger, 1901).

Kojève, Alexandre, *Introduction to the Reading of Hegel* (New York: Basic Books, 1969).

Kolb, David, ed., *New Perspectives on Hegel's Philosophy of Religion* (Albany: State University of New York Press, 1992).

"The Particular Logic of Modernity," *Bulletin of the Hegel Society of Great Britain*, 41/42 (2000), 31–42.

Krieger, Leonard, *The German Idea of Freedom* (Boston: Beacon Press, 1958).

Kuhn, H., "Die Gegenwärtigkeit der Kunst nach Hegels Vorlesungen über Ästhetik," *Hegel-Studien*, Beiheft 11 (1974), 251–69.

Lampert, Jay, "Locke, Fichte, and Hegel on the Right to Property," in Michael Baur and John Russon, eds., *Hegel and the Tradition. Essays in Honour of H. S. Harris* (Toronto: University of Toronto Press, 1997), 40–73.

Lange, Erhard, et al., eds., *Die Promotion von Karl Marx. Jena 1841. Eine Quellenedition* (Berlin: Dietz, 1983).

Langer, William, *Political and Social Upheaval, 1832–1852* (New York: Harper & Row, 1969).

Langewiesche, Dieter, "Republik, konstitutionelle Monarchie und 'soziale Frage': Grundprobleme der deutschen Revolution von 1848/49," *Historische Zeitschrift*, vol. 230, no. 3 (1980), 529–47.

Lefebvre, Georges, *The French Revolution*, 2 vols. (London: Routledge & Kegan Paul, 1962).

Leopold, David, "The Hegelian Antisemitism of Bruno Bauer," *History of European Ideas* 25 (1999), 179–206.

Losurdo, Domenico, *Hegel et les libéraux* (Paris: Presses universitaires de France, 1992).

Löwith, Karl, *From Hegel to Nietzsche. The Revolution in Nineteenth Century Thought.* (Garden City, N.Y.: Doubleday, 1967).

Löwy, Michael, "'The Poetry of the Past': Marx and the French Revolution," *New Left Review*, 177 (1989), 111–24.

Lukacs, Georg, *Der junge Hegel. Über Beziehungen von Dialektik und Ökonomie, Werke,* Bd. 8 (Berlin: Luchterhand, 1967); *The Young Hegel* (London: Merlin Press, 1975).

"Moses Hess and the Problems of the Idealist Dialectic," *Telos,* 10 (1971), 3–34.

Lütge, Friedrich, *Deutsche Sozial- und Wirtschaftsgeschichte* (Berlin: Springer, 1966).

Macpherson, C. B., *The Political Theory of Possessive Individualism, Hobbes to Locke* (London: Oxford University Press, 1962).

Mah, Harold, *The End of Philosophy and the Origin of Ideology. Karl Marx and the Crisis of the Young Hegelians* (Berkeley: University of California Press, 1987).

Marcuse, Herbert, *Reason and Revolution. Hegel and the Rise of Social Theory* (Boston: Beacon Press, 1960).

Massey, M. C., *Christ Unmasked: The Meaning of the Life of Jesus in German Politics* (Chapel Hill: University of North Carolina Press, 1983).

Mayer, Gustav, "Die Anfänge des politischen Radikalismus im vormärzlichen Preußen," *Zeitschrift für Politik* (1913), Heft 1, Sonderdruck, 1–113.

McCarney, Joseph, *Hegel on History* (London: Routledge, 2000).

McLellan, David, *Marx Before Marxism* (Toronto: Macmillan, 1970).

The Young Hegelians and Karl Marx (Toronto: Macmillan, 1969).

Mehlhausen, Joachim, *Dialektik, Selbstbewußtsein und Offenbarung. Die Grundlagen der spekulativen Orthodoxie Bruno Bauers in ihrem Zusammenhang mit der Geschichte der theologischen Hegelschule dargestellt* (Bonn: Friedrich-Wilhelms-Universität, 1965).

Mehring, Franz, *Philosophische Aufsätze. Gesammelte Schriften,* Band 13, 1961.

Moggach, Douglas, "Absolute Spirit and Universal Self-Consciousness: Bruno Bauer's Revolutionary Subjectivism," *Dialogue, The Canadian Philosophical Review* 38, 2 (1989), 235–56.

"Bruno Bauer's Political Critique, 1840–1841," *Owl of Minerva,* vol. 27, no. 2 (1996), 137–54.

"*Nation, Volk, Masse:* Left-Hegelian Perspectives on the Rise of Nationalism," *History of European Ideas,* 15/1–3 (1992), 339–45.

"Nationhood and Freedom in Fichte's Political Thought," in Frank Brinkhuis and Sascha Talmor (eds.), *Memory, History, and Critique. European Identity at the Millennium* (Utrecht: University for Humanist Studies, 1998) (CD-ROM).

"New Goals and New Ways: Republicanism and Socialism in 1848," in Douglas Moggach and Paul Leduc Browne (eds.), *The Social Question and the Democratic Revolution: Marx and the Legacy of 1848* (Ottawa: University of Ottawa Press, 2000), 49–69.

"Reciprocity, Elicitation, Recognition: The Thematics of Intersubjectivity in the Early Fichte," *Dialogue, The Canadian Philosophical Review,* 38/2 (Spring 1999), 271–96.

Mommsen, Hans, *Grosse und Versagen des deutschen Bürgertums. Ein Beitrag zur politischen Bewegung des neunzehnten Jahrhunderts* (Stuttgart: Deutsche Verlagsanstalt, 1949).

Mönke, Wolfgang, *Die Heilige Familie. Zur ersten Gemeinschaftsarbeit von Karl Marx und Friedrich Engels* (Glashütten im Taunus: Akademie Verlag, 1972).

Mottek, Hans (ed.), *Studien zur Geschichte der industriellen Revolution in Deutschland* (Berlin: Akademie Verlag, 1970).

Wirtschaftsgeschichte Deutschlands, Ein Grundriss, I (Berlin: DVW, 1964).

Negt, Oskar, *Lebendige Arbeit, enteignete Zeit,* 2nd ed. (Frankfurt/M.: Campus Verlag, 1985).

Neher, Walter, *Arnold Ruge als Politiker und politischer Schriftsteller* (Heidelberg: C. Winter, 1933).

Neuhouser, Frederick, *Foundations of Hegel's Social Theory. Actualizing Freedom* (Cambridge: Harvard University Press, 2000).

Noyes, P. H., *Organization and Revolution, Working Class Association in the German Revolution of 1848–1849* (Princeton: Princeton University Press, 1966).

O'Neill, John, ed., *Hegel's Dialectic of Desire and Recognition* (Albany: State University of New York Press, 1996).

Obermann, Karl, *Die deutschen Arbeiter in der Revolution von 1848* (Berlin: Dietz, 1953).

Deutschland von 1815 bis 1849 (Berlin: DVW, 1967).

Patten, Alan, *Hegel's Idea of Freedom* (Oxford: Oxford University Press, 1999).

Pelczynski, Z. A., ed., *Hegel's Political Philosophy. Problems and Perspectives* (Cambridge: Cambridge University Press, 1971).

"Hegel's Relevance Today: Culture, Community, and Political Power," *Europa,* vol. 2, no. 2 (1979), 7–20.

ed., *The State and Civil Society* (Cambridge: Cambridge University Press, 1984).

Peled, Yoav, "From Theology to Sociology: Bruno Bauer and Karl Marx on the Question of Jewish Emancipation," *History of Political Thought,* 13/3 (1992), 463–85.

Pepperle, Ingrid, *Junghegelianische Geschichtsphilosophie und Kunsttheorie* (Berlin: Akademie Verlag, 1978).

Pinkard, Terry, *Hegel. A Biography* (Cambridge: Cambridge University Press, 2000).

Pinson, J.-C., *Hegel, le droit et le libéralisme* (Paris: Presses Universitaires de France, 1989).

Pippin, Robert, "Hegel, Freedom, the Will," in Ludwig Siep, ed., *Grundlinien der Philosophie des Rechts* (Berlin: Akademie Verlag, 1997), 31–53.

Hegel's Idealism. The Satisfactions of Self-Consciousness (Cambridge: Cambridge University Press, 1989).

Idealism as Modernism. Hegelian Variations (Cambridge: Cambridge University Press, 1997).

Plant, Raymond, *Hegel* (London: Allen and Unwin, 1973).

Pöggeler, Otto, et al., eds., *Hegel in Berlin, Preußische Kulturpolitik und idealistische Ästhetik* (Berlin: Staatsbibliothek Preußischer Kulturbesitz, 1981).

Pöggeler, Otto, and A. Gethmann-Siefert, eds., *Kunsterfahrung und Kulturpolitik im Berlin Hegels* (Bonn: Bouvier, 1983).

Rambaldi, E., *Le origini della sinistra hegeliana* (Florence: Nuova Italia, 1966).

Rawls, John, "Themes in Kant's Moral Philosophy," in Eckart Förster, ed., *Kant's Transcendental Deductions* (Stanford: Stanford University Press, 1989), 81–113.

Riedel, Manfred, ed., *Materialien zu Hegels Rechtsphilosophie*, Bd. II (Frankfurt am Main: Suhrkamp, 1975).

Zwischen Tradition und Revolution, Studien zu Hegels Rechtsphilosophie (Stuttgart: Klett, 1982).

Rihs, Charles, *L'école des jeunes-Hegeliens et les penseurs socialistes français* (Paris: Anthropos, 1978).

Rosen, Stanley, *G.W.F. Hegel, An Introduction to the Science of Wisdom* (New Haven: Yale University Press, 1974).

Rosen, Zvi, *Bruno Bauer and Karl Marx* (The Hague: Nijhoff, 1978).

"The Influence of Bruno Bauer on Marx's Concept of Alienation," *Social Theory and Practice* 1 (1970), 50–65.

"The Radicalism of a Young Hegelian: Bruno Bauer," *Review of Politics*, vol. 33 (1971), 377–404.

Rosenberg, Hans, *Bureaucracy, Aristocracy and Autocracy. The Prussian Experience, 1600–1815* (Boston: Beacon Press, 1958).

Politische Denkströmungen im deutschen Vormärz (Göttingen: Vandenhoeck und Ruprecht, 1972).

Rossi, Mario, *Da Hegel a Marx III: La Scuola hegeliana. Il giovane Marx*, 2nd edition (Milan: Feltrinelli, 1974).

Rotenstreich, Nathan, *Basic Problems in Marx's Philosophy* (Indianapolis: Bobbs-Merrill, 1965).

From Substance to Subject: Studies in Hegel (The Hague: Nijhoff, 1974).

Rotta, Graziella, *Applicazione del punto di vista kantiano e sviluppi originali nel "Saggio di una critica di ogni rivelazione" di J.G. Fichte*, Tesi di Laurea, Università degli Studi di Pisa, 1987–88.

L'Idea Dio. Il pensiero religioso di Fichte fino allo Atheismusstreit, Tesi di Dottorato, Università di Torino, 1992–93.

Sass, H.-M., "Bruno Bauer's Critical Theory," *Philosophical Forum* 8 (1978), 93–103.

"Bruno Bauers Idee der *Rheinischen Zeitung*," *Zeitschrift für Religions- und Geistesgeschichte* 19 (1967), 221–76.

"Nachwort," in Bruno Bauer, *Feldzüge der reinen Kritik*, ed. H.-M. Sass (Frankfurt am Main: Suhrkamp, 1968), 227–28.

Schapper, Annegret, *Ein langer Abschied vom Christentum. Johann Christian Edelmann (1698–1767) und die deutsche Frühaufklärung* (Marburg: Tectum-Verlag, 1996).

Schmidt, Walter, "Die 1848er Forschung in der DDR," *Zeitschrift für Geschichtswissenshaft*, vol. 42 (1994), 21–38.

Schnädelbach, Herbert, "Zum Verhältnis von Logik und Gesellschaftstheorie bei Hegel," in Oskar Negt (ed.), *Aktualität und Folgen der Philosophie Hegels* (Frankfurt am Main: Suhrkamp, 1971), 58–80.

Schuffenhauer, Werner, *Feuerbach und der junge Marx* (Berlin: DVW, 1972).

Schweitzer, Albert, *The Quest of the Historical Jesus. A Critical Study of Its Progress from Reimarus to Wrede* (Baltimore: Johns Hopkins University Press, 1998).

Sedgwick, Sally, ed., *The Reception of Kant's Critical Philosophy. Fichte, Schelling, and Hegel* (Cambridge: Cambridge University Press, 2000).

Sens, Walter, *Karl Marx: Seine irreligiöse Entwicklung und antichristliche Einstellung. Christentum und Sozialismus* (Halle: E. Klinz, 1935).

Skinner, Quentin, *The Foundations of Modern Political Thought*, vol. 1, *The Renaissance* (Cambridge: Cambridge University Press, 1978).

Liberty Before Liberalism (Cambridge: Cambridge University Press, 1998).

"Two Concepts of Citizenship," *Tijdschrift voor Filosofie* 55/3 (1993), 403–19.

Schläger, Eduard, "Bruno Bauer und seine Werke," *Schmeitzner's Internationale Monatsschrift, Zeitschrift für allgemeine und nationale Kultur und deren Literatur,* vol. 1 (1882), 377–400.

Siep, Ludwig, *Anerkennung als Prinzip der praktischen Philosophie* (Freiburg und München: Karl Alber, 1979).

"Recht und Anerkennung," in Helmut Girndt, ed., *Selbstbehauptung und Anerkennung* (Sankt Augustin: Academia Verlag, 1990), 161–76.

Solomon, R. C., and K. M. Higgins, eds., *The Age of German Idealism. Routledge History of Philosophy*, vol. VI (London: Routledge, 1993).

Sperber, Jonathan, *The Democratic Movement and the Revolution of 1848–1849* (Princeton: Princeton University Press, 1991).

Steinkraus, W. E., and K. I. Schmitz, eds., *Art and Logic in Hegel's Philosophy* (Brighton: Harvester Press, 1980).

Stepelevich, L. S., ed., *The Young Hegelians. An Anthology* (Cambridge: Cambridge University Press, 1983).

Stuke, Horst, *Philosophie der Tat, Studien zur 'Verwirklichung der Philosophie' bie den Junghegelianern und den Wahren Sozialisten* (Stuttgart: Klett, 1963).

Taylor, Charles, *Hegel* (Cambridge: Cambridge University Press, 1975).

Was ist Liberalismus? Hegelpreis 1997 (Frankfurt: Suhrkamp, 1997).

Theunissen, Michael, "The Repressed Intersubjectivity in Hegel's Philosophy of Right," in Drucilla Cornell et al., eds., *Hegel and Legal Theory* (London: Routledge, 1991), 3–63.

Toews, J. E., *Hegelianism. The Path toward Dialectical Humanism* (Cambridge: Cambridge University Press, 1980).

"Transformations of Hegelianism," in F. C. Beiser (ed.), *The Cambridge Companion to Hegel* (Cambridge: Cambridge University Press, 1993), 391–403.

Tucker, Robert, *Philosophy and Myth in Karl Marx* (Cambridge: Cambridge University Press, 1961).

van den Bergh van Eysinga, G. A., "Aus einer unveröffentlichten Biographie von Bruno Bauer. Bruno Bauer in Bonn 1839–1842," *Annali Feltrinelli* (1963), 329–86.

Verweyen, Hansjürgen, "Offenbarung und autonome Vernunft nach J. G. Fichte," in K. Hammacher and A. Mues, eds., *Erneuerung der Transzendentalphilosophie* (Stuttgart: Klett, 1979), 436–55.

Recht und Sittlichkeit in J. G. Fichtes Gesellschaftslehre (Freiburg/München: Alber, 1975).

von Stein, Lorenz, *Der Socialismus und Communismus des heutigen Frankreichs* (Leipzig, 1842).

History of the Social Movement in France, trans. K. Mengelberg (Totowa, N.J.: Bedminster, 1964).

Waser, Ruedi, *Autonomie des Selbstbewußtseins. Eine Untersuchung zum Verhältnis von Bruno Bauer und Karl Marx (1835–1843)* (Tübingen: Francke Verlag, 1994).

Williams, R. R., *Hegel's Ethics of Recognition* (Berkeley: University of California Press, 1997).

Winfield, R. D., "Rethinking the Particular Forms of Art: Prolegomena to a Rational Reconstruction of Hegel's Theory of the Artforms," *Owl of Minerva*, 24/2 (1993), 131–44.

Zanardo, Aldo, "Bruno Bauer hegeliano e giovane hegeliano," *Rivista Critica di Storia della Filosofia*, 1965, 1–57.

INDEX

absolute, the, 10, 30, 43, 59, 68, 102, 103,
106, 107, 110, 114, 203–04, 208, 211
Absolute Spirit
in Bauer, 35, 37, 59, 69, 71, 106, 111
in Hegel, 10, 29, 44, 111, 114, 119, 122
absolutism, absolutist state, 10, 16, 32, 50,
53, 71, 77, 78, 79, 90, 93, 94–95,
114, 126, 132, 134–35, 154, 180–81,
182–83
abstract right 7, 8, 14, 91
actuality (*Wirklichkeit*), 5–6, 22, 23–24, 113
aesthetics
in Bauer 11, 13, 14, 16, 21, 33, 35–37,
121, 156, 180
in Hegel 29–30
see also art; beauty; judgement, aesthetic;
sublime, the
alienation, 2, 10, 11, 12, 33, 36, 37, 48–49,
51, 59–60, 64–65, 79, 99, 106–07,
114, 119, 120, 122, 124, 129, 132,
139–42, 144, 146, 150
Altenstein, Karl von, 63, 81
antinomy, 5, 13, 22, 49, 62, 78, 90, 107,
139, 171
of aesthetic judgement, 208–10
of critical judgement, 109–10
antiquity, 6, 61, 65, 72–73, 114, 116
anti-Semitism, 17, 181, 186
Aristotle, 5, 121, 151, 188
Arnim, Bettina von, 229 n.25
art, 10, 21, 22, 29–30, 35, 37–38, 76, 88,
105–06, 107, 120, 121, 122, 124, 188,
194–95, 204–05, 210–11
autonomy, 8, 10, 11, 12, 31, 32, 33, 51–52,
53, 73, 78, 91, 99, 101, 116, 132, 133,
134–35, 151, 152, 159
in Hegel, 41

Bakunin, Michael, 183
Barnikol, Ernst, 17, 126, 139, 161, 181, 186,
218 n.1, 228 n.10

Bauer, Bruno
Allgemeine Literatur Zeitung, 96, 157,
161–62
Anekdota, 132–35, 136
"Der christliche Staat," 71, 75, 77, 93–96,
130, 134
Denkwürdigkeiten, 150–54, 156
electoral addresses, 1848–49, 173–78
Endeckte Christenthum, 48, 73, 79, 89, 106,
107, 120, 135, 139–44, 145, 146,
148, 185
Gute Sache, 100, 120–25, 127, 144
Hegels Lehre, 3, 36–38, 66, 76–77, 106,
119–20, 121, 128, 132, 160
Herr Dr. Hengstenberg, 60, 62, 63–65, 107,
121, 184
Johannes, 3, 66–71, 74, 104, 107, 116,
117
Judenfrage, 145–49, 155, 164
Landeskirche, 3, 66, 86–93, 94, 113, 114,
123, 144, 161, 166, 182, 185
Norddeutsche Blätter, 96, 161, 169–71
Posaune, 3, 35, 66, 68, 70, 73, 74, 81, 85,
90, 94, 96, 99–118, 119, 128, 131,
133, 134, 135, 156, 157, 160, 185
Prinzipien des Schönen, 5, 15, 21–35, 45,
55, 59, 60, 101, 104, 108, 116, 121,
154, 178–79, 182
Religion des Alten Testaments, 49, 59–60,
69, 120
Rheinische Zeitung, 38–39, 126–28, 149,
158
"Schamlosigkeiten," 130–32
Synoptiker, 65, 68, 71–79, 81, 116, 129, 142
see also aesthetics; critique; ethics;
infinite self-consciousness;
judgement; republicanism)
Bauer, Edgar, 1, 62, 65, 80, 156, 162–63,
169, 170, 173
beauty, beautiful, 10, 21–26, 34–35, 53,
113, 149, 178, 192–212

Beethoven, Ludwig van, 38–39
being, unity of thought and
    in Bauer, 5, 9–10, 15, 17, 21, 22, 23–24,
        25, 31, 32–37, 38, 39, 40, 46, 59, 67,
        70, 74, 90, 104, 108, 109–10, 112,
        118, 121, 123, 179, 180
    in Hegel, 5–6, 111–12
Bergh van Eysinga, G.A. van den, 4, 17, 42
Bismarck, Otto von, 175, 185
Brudney, Daniel, 4
Buchholz, F., 251 n.63
Buonarroti, Philippe, 157
Burke, Edmund, 246 n.53

Calvinism (Reformed church), 69, 81,
    86–89, 92
capital, capitalism, 150, 157, 164, 170–71,
    176
Catholicism, 86, 87, 122, 185
censorship, 3, 86, 100, 121, 139
Christianity, 30, 59–61, 63–64, 66–67, 134,
    147
    and absolutism, 77, 107
    and critique, 70, 79
    and feudalism, 77–78
    and modernity, 120
    and Roman Empire, 184–85, 186
Cicero, Marcus Tullius, 149
civil society, 2, 8, 9, 13, 55, 92, 94, 110, 158,
    166, 175
community, 7, 32, 40, 45, 55, 61, 63, 73, 74,
    114, 121
    religious, 67, 72, 111, 154
    republican, 84, 124, 149, 151, 152, 163,
        167
conservatism, 2, 17, 63, 99, 100, 119, 129,
    130–31, 172, 181
constitutional monarchy
    in Hegel, 9, 125, 151
    in Strauss, 62
constitutionalism, 13, 81, 134–35, 149, 151,
    154
contradiction, exacerbation of, 99, 117,
    128–30, 171, 177
corporations, Bauer on, 150
Crimean War, 183
critique: in Bauer, 5, 61, 66, 69, 70, 74–75,
    107, 109, 117, 139, 157, 161, 173,
    177–78, 182

Dana, Charles B., 258 n.8
Descartes, René, 22, 189
Disraeli, Benjamin, 185

Edelmann, Johann Christian, 15, 260 n.35
Eichhorn, J.A.F., 81, 234 n.16
empiricism, 26, 29, 182, 189–90, 193
energeia, 5, 37, 52, 114–15, 121, 160

Engels, Friedrich, 176, 184, 231 n.62
Enlightenment, the, 4, 5, 11, 13, 16, 17, 26,
    44, 48–50, 61, 78, 88–89, 90, 95,
    106, 109, 110, 111, 114, 117, 119,
    132, 139, 141–44, 154, 180, 184
Epicureanism, 7
ethical life (Sittlichkeit), 8, 32, 33, 35, 40,
    44, 46, 51, 52, 53, 60, 74, 79, 91, 99,
    140, 141, 146, 149, 159, 160
ethics: in Bauer, 11, 14, 35, 39, 51–52, 55,
    69, 99, 115, 144, 149, 179, 182

faith, 23, 29, 30, 35, 37, 59, 101, 130, 132,
    134, 142, 189
Faucher, Julius, 169
feudalism, 12, 13, 78–79, 117, 125, 126,
    127, 153, 158, 160, 170, 172, 173,
    174, 176, 178, 186
    Middle Ages, 189
Feuerbach, Ludwig, 9, 35, 44–45, 49, 60,
    62, 84, 129, 141, 166, 177, 217 n.49,
    240 n.8
Fichte, J. G., 7, 14, 46, 78, 107, 108, 113,
    149, 159, 181–82, 183, 184
    and economics, 169, 255–56 n.54
    and religion, 60, 141
fragmentation (diremption: Zerrissenheit),
    5, 16, 23, 29, 76, 160, 189
Frederick the Great (Friedrich II), 80,
    86
free trade, 169–71, 172
freedom, 6–8, 10, 11, 12, 17, 23, 32–34,
    36–37, 44, 48, 68, 77, 111, 112–13,
    131, 143–44, 147, 153, 156, 164,
    173, 174, 177, 182, 191, 194, 203,
    206, 210
    Edgar Bauer on, 162
    religious views of, 61
    see also autonomy
Freien, die (The Free), 165
Friedrich Wilhelm III, 62, 80, 86
Friedrich Wilhelm IV, 71, 80–81, 87, 93

genius, 211
    cult of, 244 n.13
Germany, 126–27, 132, 135–36, 152,
    153–54, 170, 174, 182, 183,
    185–86
Gironde, the, 152
Goethe, J.W. von, 185
Greece, 7, 22, 23, 26, 30, 35, 61, 120, 184,
    186, 188, 194
    beautiful individuality 40–41

Hadrian, emperor 184
Haller, Carl Ludwig von, 131, 232 n.4
Hardenberg, Karl August, 80
Haym, Rudolph, 213 n.5

Hegel, G.W.F.
  Bauer on, 13, 85–86
    in 1840, 89–91
    in 1841, 100–01, 102, 103–06,
      110–12
    in 1841–42, 119, 125, 127, 134, 135
    in 1843–44, 151
    in 1845, 108–09
    after 1848, 181–82, 182–83
  conservatives on, 62, 136
  Hegel's Aesthetics, 27–28, 29–30, 167
  Encyclopaedia, 23, 26, 28
  History of Philosophy, 25, 26, 101
  Phenomenology, 59, 101, 103, 139–40
  Philosophy of History, 5–6, 48, 101
  Philosophy of Religion, 43, 60, 101, 102–03
  Philosophy of Right, 8–9, 32, 41, 46, 82–84,
    116, 140, 150
  Science of Logic, 47
Hellenism, 1, 61, 184
Hengstenberg, Ernst Wilhelm, 61–65, 67,
    72, 130–31, 136, 227–28 n.9
heteronomy, 2, 12, 31–33, 51, 52, 54, 61, 73,
    99, 114, 116, 146, 159–60, 172
Historical School of Law, 130–31
history
  Hegel's concept of, 5–9
  Bauer on, 4, 6, 9–12, 15, 32–34, 36, 39,
    41, 43, 46–48, 50, 51, 61, 65, 68–71,
    76, 88, 104, 107, 112–13, 115,
    116–17, 122, 124–25, 133, 139, 141,
    142–43, 144, 179, 182, 211
Holbach, Paul-Henry Thiry d', 48, 142
Hotho, H. G., 21, 30
Hume, David, 189

idea, 22–26, 28, 33, 34, 42, 108, 182,
    194–95, 202–03, 205–06, 207, 208,
    210–12
idealism, 9, 11, 15, 16, 22, 24, 25, 44, 48,
    189–90
  ethical, in Bauer, 9–12, 14–15, 16, 31–32,
    33, 40, 104, 121. See also ethics
  subjective, 41, 193
imperialism, 174, 179, 180, 182–84,
    186–87
individualism, 13, 16, 96, 114, 124, 127,
    144, 150, 152, 158
infinite, spurious, 6, 14, 34, 53, 95, 178
infinite self-consciousness, 6, 10, 12, 21, 22,
    31, 32, 33–36, 40, 42–43, 47–49, 52,
    71, 73, 76–78, 94–96, 99, 100, 102,
    114–17, 119–20, 124, 134, 146, 154,
    160. See also self-consciousness
interest, 117, 120, 144, 158, 162
  material, 36, 51
  particular, 12, 14, 22, 30, 32–33, 36, 39,
    40, 51, 53, 86, 167

private, 12, 13, 53, 85, 93, 123, 126, 127,
    149, 151, 152, 160, 173
  universal, 12, 149
intersubjectivity, 25, 83, 91, 111, 114, 144,
    167

Jacobi, F. H., 102
Jacobinism, 11, 13, 17, 54, 99, 101, 118,
    151, 152–53, 156, 160, 163–64,
    172
  Marx on, 165
Jewish question, the, 14, 51, 55, 64, 79, 85,
    115, 124, 140, 145–49, 166, 173,
    177, 178, 186
John, St., 65–71, 72, 142
judgement, 68–69, 190–92, 193
  aesthetic, 22, 34, 113, 192–212
  categories of, 195–99
  Bauer's criticism of, 26–29,
    199–206
  apodeictic, 11, 17, 41–42, 45–48, 50, 51,
    53, 99, 104, 106, 112, 116–17, 118,
    127, 141,143, 178
  infinite, 48, 50, 79, 106, 109, 141
  universal, 144

Kamarilla, 62, 63
Kant, Immanuel, 10, 11, 14, 15, 21, 34, 36,
    52, 55, 74, 107, 108, 109, 113, 119,
    142, 148, 159, 181, 182, 184,
    188–212
Karlsbad decrees, 80
Kautsky, Karl, 183, 184, 187
Koigen, David, 52
Köppen, K. F., 86, 238 n.64

labour
  Bauer on, 76, 85, 164, 167, 186
  Edgar Bauer on, 162
  Marx on, 84, 166–67
  and religion, 133
Lassalle, Ferdinand, 175
Leibniz, G. W., 22, 52, 189
Left Hegelians, 1, 31, 32, 40, 62, 64, 81,
    82–83, 91, 100, 136, 151
Leo, Heinrich, 62, 64, 99–100, 130–32,
    228 n.9
liberalism, 7, 50, 53, 78, 159
  Bauer's critique of, 2, 13, 15, 17, 33, 44,
    53–54, 86, 117, 131, 135, 145, 149,
    151, 156, 158–59, 163, 173
  Bauer on, in 1848–49, 175, 178
  German, 80, 81, 127, 145, 148
Locke, John, 22, 189
Löwith, Karl, 17, 183, 214 n.7
Luke, St., 72, 74
Luther, Martin, 99, 241 n.23
Lutheranism, 69, 81, 86–89

Mah, Harold, 82
Marheineke, Philipp 239 n.6
Mark, St. 72, 74
market, 150, 151, 153, 158–59, 163, 179
Marx, Karl, 1, 4, 9, 39, 44, 53, 82, 157, 173,
    176, 216 n.37, 222 n.59, 231 n.70,
    254 n.34
  and critical judgement, 47, 51, 126
  critique of Hegel, 84
  on free trade, 170
  polemics with Bauer on *Rheinische
    Zeitung*, 108, 128
  on political and human emancipation,
    124, 145
  on religion, 141
  on socialism, 164–67, 168, 169
masses, mass society, 3, 8, 13, 54, 63, 65, 77,
    92, 96, 115, 117, 124, 136, 150,
    151–52, 153, 158–59, 161–62, 163,
    178
materialism, 44, 111, 166–67
Matthew, St., 72, 74, 77–78
Mill, John Stuart, 168, 255 n.49
modernity, 7–8, 17, 24, 26, 29, 30, 35, 48,
    86, 94, 120, 159–60
morality, 14, 74, 89

Napoleon, 126, 152, 153, 174
nation, 152, 153, 186
nationalism, 153, 183
Neander, August, 214 n.6
New Testament, the, 72, 184
Nietzsche, Friedrich, 17, 181, 187
Nola, Robert, 82

Objective Spirit, 7–8, 9, 40–41, 43, 88, 89,
    90–91, 111, 114, 122, 151
objectivity, 5–6, 8, 9, 12, 21, 23, 24, 78, 104,
    108, 114, 143, 162, 178, 194,
    203–04, 206, 207, 210–11
Old Testament, the, 31, 59, 64–65
"ought" (*Sollen*), 25, 28, 31, 35, 42, 46,
    48, 111, 112, 113, 162, 191, 206,
    208

Panslavism, 183
pantheism, 44, 103, 260 n.35
Parmenides, 188
particularism, 10, 54, 60, 110, 127, 167
  national, 153
  religious, 67, 73, 94, 103, 124, 133,
    139–40, 145–46
  see also interest: particular
particularity, 7–8, 12, 31, 43, 44, 50, 60, 64,
    91, 158, 159, 183, 191–92
  in syllogisms, 6, 9
Paul, St. (epistles), 184, 231 n.66
pauperism. *See* social question, the

pauperism, political, 184
peasantry, 154, 172
people (*Volk*), 65, 73–74, 136, 151–52, 153,
    160, 162, 163, 174, 182
Pepperle, Ingrid, 4
perfectionism (*Vollkommenheit*), 11, 16, 33,
    52, 85, 99, 113, 147, 160, 168, 178,
    180, 181
personality, 182, 186
  Greek conception of, 65
  Hegel on, 8, 40–41
  Roman conception of, 77
Peter the Great, Czar, 183
Philo, 68, 184
pietism, 31, 59, 62, 81, 99–100, 101, 102,
    130, 134, 185
Plato, 24, 52, 188
popular sovereignty, 55, 83, 160, 174–75
proletariat (workers), 14, 51, 54, 96, 159,
    164, 167–68, 169–70, 172, 175,
    178
property, 54, 158, 159, 160, 162–63, 166,
    171–72, 178
Protestantism, 61, 94, 122, 147. *See also*
    Calvinism; Lutheranism;
    Reformation, the
Proud'hon, Pierre-Joseph, 168
Prussia, 21, 63, 80, 81, 82, 86, 87, 88, 90,
    93, 100, 145, 150, 156, 161, 170,
    173, 174, 175, 185, 186

Quakers, 183, 184

rationalism, 26, 29, 48, 76
  theological, 129, 130–31, 134, 142
Raumer, Friedrich von, 21
reason, 10, 11, 22–23, 34, 37, 39, 42, 55, 66,
    130, 181, 192, 193, 203–04, 205,
    206–07, 208–09, 212
  instrumental, 7
  practical, 13, 24–25, 33, 52, 60, 113, 134,
    144, 159, 184–85, 193
  teleological, 23
Rechtsstaat, 80, 93–94, 95
recognition, 14, 41, 89, 91, 131, 136,
    139–40, 148, 149
reflection, 5, 23, 24, 29, 34, 42, 72, 206
  abstract, 37, 67, 132–33, 208–09,
    212
Reformation, the, 93, 140
religion, 10, 36, 118, 120
  and alienation, 37–38, 48–49, 122,
    139–44
  and philosophy, 21, 35, 59, 106
  and Restoration, 12–13, 15, 16, 32, 50,
    60, 79, 110, 124
  and self-consciousness, 64–79, 114,
    132–33

republicanism
in Bauer, 2, 5, 8, 10–17, 25, 35, 40,
53–55, 60–61, 64, 65, 85–87, 91,
94–96, 99, 117–18, 122–23, 125,
126–28, 131–32, 133, 135–36,
147–49, 150–51, 158, 160–62,
163–64, 167–68, 171–79
abandoned, 55–56, 180, 187
Marx on, 165–66
French, 44, 49–50
German, 9, 83–85, 145, 148, 155, 169
Restoration, the 2, 9, 12, 60, 62–63, 64, 77,
78, 79, 83, 86, 107, 110, 117, 120,
124, 125, 131, 132, 158. *See also* state:
Restoration
Revolution, English, 13, 126, 127, 158
Revolution, French, 2, 3, 13, 17, 36, 44, 50,
55, 95, 99, 102, 110, 111, 113, 114,
118, 119, 126–27, 132, 150–54,
158–59, 160, 162, 180
Revolution of 1848, 1, 13, 16, 17, 55, 109,
156, 157, 161, 172–78, 180, 186
rights, 124, 127, 143, 147, 148, 149, 153,
154, 159, 174
rigorism, 12, 85, 149
Robespierre, Maximilien, 152, 250 n.46,
254 n.26
Romanticism (Romantic), 30, 71, 81
Rome, Roman Empire, 77, 184, 186
Rosen, Zvi, 59, 82
Rossi, Mario, 4
Rousseau, Jean-Jacques, 144, 171
Ruge, Arnold, 3, 9, 83–84, 100, 108, 128,
130, 155, 165, 240 n.8
Russia, 16, 126, 179, 180–81, 182–83
Rutenberg, Adolph, 81

Sass, Hans-Martin, 4
Schelling, F.W.J. von, 62, 81
Schiller, Friedrich, 261 n.1
Schleiermacher, Friedrich, 59, 63, 102–03,
105, 130, 131, 185
Schultze, Johannes, 63
Schweitzer, Albert, 1, 260 n.31
sectarianism, 14, 61, 139–40
Bauer's, 148, 155, 166, 178
self-consciousness, 4, 24–25, 26, 44, 59,
85–86, 88–89, 93, 110–118, 119,
127, 129, 131–33, 141–42, 147, 154
contradictions within, 132–33
relation to Christianity, 67, 68, 72
and revolution, 135–36
universal, in Hegel, 41
see also infinite self-consciousness;
substance
self-deification, 213–14 n.6
self-transcendence, 12, 60, 133, 147, 160,
165

Siep, Ludwig, 84
social question, the, 14, 17, 96, 152, 156,
157, 162, 164
socialism, 1, 2, 13, 15, 45, 85, 117, 157, 162,
184
Bauer's critique of, 158, 163–65, 166,
167–69, 175–76, 178, 184
see also state: socialist
Spinoza, Benedict, 44–45, 68, 73, 104–05,
108–09, 181–82
spirit (*Geist*), 5–6, 21, 36, 42, 69–70, 76, 88,
95, 111–12, 116, 144, 188. *See also*
Absolute Spirit; objective spirit;
subjective spirit
Stahl, Friedrich Julius, 71, 81, 93, 94, 129,
131
state
Bauer on, 86–96, 113, 134. *See also*
republicanism
Christian, 93–95, 101, 107, 113, 122, 124,
145, 147
Hegel on, 8–9, 13, 32, 83, 85, 125, 175
liberal, 53, 160
republican, 83–85, 123, 164, 177
Restoration, 12, 15, 30, 36, 53, 125, 127,
144, 164
socialist, 165, 168, 176
Stein, Lorenz von, 157, 168
Stirner, Max [Johann Caspar Schmidt], 4,
44, 215 n.27, 224 n.13
Stoicism, 7, 61, 117, 184
Strauss, David Friedrich, 44–45, 60, 62–63,
68, 73–74, 84, 104, 115, 121, 129,
181
subjective spirit, 41, 88, 89
subjectivism, 10, 32, 39, 42, 106, 121
subjectivity, 24–25, 35, 45, 50, 56, 68,
69–70, 73, 90, 112, 113, 121, 144,
194, 195, 204–05, 211
sublime, the, 10, 11, 16, 34–35, 38, 113,
147, 156, 160, 178
substance, 6–7, 41, 44–45, 68, 70, 108, 121,
128, 181–82
as a moment of self-consciousness,
102–05, 114–16
substantiality, 30, 44, 54, 56, 65, 73, 107,
112, 114, 134, 135, 181
supersensible, 24, 191, 192, 205, 207, 210
syllogism, 6, 9, 24, 25, 121
Szeliga [Franz Zychlin von Zychlinski], 163

teleology, 69–70, 76, 112, 115
telos, 35, 37, 48, 78, 111, 114, 160
theology, 36, 67, 120, 122, 132–33, 142
Thermidor, 152–53, 254 n.26
Theunissen, Michael, 84
thing-in-itself, 190, 193
Tholuck, August, 62, 228 n.9

Tölken, Ernst Heinrich, 21
transcendent, 12, 33, 36, 44, 60–61, 64, 76,
    111, 182

understanding, 24, 26, 29, 66, 89, 132,
    191–92, 193, 207, 208
unhappy consciousness, 61, 114
universal, universality, 6, 8, 9, 10, 18, 33,
    39, 40, 53, 63, 64, 68, 85, 88, 91, 93,
    104, 115, 121, 124, 133, 139, 150,
    152, 156, 190, 191–92, 193
    abstract, 31, 32, 73, 121, 133
    immanent, 32, 43, 44, 47, 52, 59, 65,
    104, 134

Varnhagen von Ense, Karl August, 259
    n.23
Vormärz, the, 1, 2, 3, 9, 13, 15, 16, 17, 21, 22,
    32, 34, 40, 50, 53, 56, 82, 113, 157,
    158, 169, 179, 182

Weber, Max, 186
Weisse, Christian Hermann, 230 n.54
Welcker, Karl Theodor, 81, 82, 93, 127
Wigand, Otto, 100
Wilke, Ferdinand Wilhelm, 230 n.54
Wolff, Christian, 26, 193

Zollverein 81